DATE DUE

LABOR AND FARMER PARTIES IN THE UNITED STATES, 1828-1928

LABOR AND FARMER PARTIES
IN THE UNITED STATES
1828--1928

BY NATHAN FINE

NEW YORK
RUSSELL & RUSSELL
1961

COPYRIGHT, 1928, BY THE RAND SCHOOL OF SOCIAL SCIENCE

L. C. CATALOG CARD NO: 61–12124

PRINTED IN THE UNITED STATES OF AMERICA

To
Robert Franklin Hoxie
Pathfinder
in the
Study and Interpretation
of the
American Labor Movement

CONTENTS

CHAPTER   PAGE

   I   THE IRREPRESSIBLE CONFLICT   9

  II   THE UNITED FRONT OF 1886   35

 III   GRANGERS, GREENBACKERS AND POPULISTS .   56

  IV   FOUNDING OF THE SOCIALIST LABOR PARTY   88

   V   KNIGHTS, TRADE UNIONISTS AND SOCIALISTS   118

  VI   DE LEONISM   147

 VII   SOCIALIST UNITY   184

VIII   THE RISING TIDE OF SOCIALISM . . .   214

  IX   THE SOCIALIST PARTY PROGRAM . . .   262

   X   1917   301

  XI   COMMUNIST VERSUS SOCIALIST   324

 XII   NONPARTISAN LEAGUE AND FARMER-LABOR
            PARTY   363

XIII   THE CONFERENCE FOR PROGRESSIVE POLITI-
            CAL ACTION   398

CHAPTER I

THE IRREPRESSIBLE CONFLICT

BEFORE there could be any independent labor politics in the United States the property-less wage earners had to exist in sufficient numbers, they had to possess the ballot, and they had to have the provocation and desire to unite on the political field. The democratic forces which swept Andrew Jackson into the presidency brought the franchise to the white man without property. The change in marketing processes and the introduction of the factory system developed a distinct and growing wage earning class in the cities. Economic abuses and social inequalities drove this class into independent political action.

In July, 1828, after a referendum vote of the membership, in much the same way as the Chicago Federation of Labor organized the Cook County Labor Party ninety years later, the trade unions of Philadelphia launched the first workingman's party in the United States. The movement spread to other cities in Pennsylvania, New York, most of the New England states, and into Delaware, New Jersey, and Ohio. A knowledge of the economic and political conditions which gave birth to it is necessary for a proper understanding of the first labor party in the new republic.

§

The property-less wage earner obtained the suffrage in the United States because on the frontier all men were equal economically and therefore equal politically and socially. When Vermont and Kentucky entered the Union in 1791 and 1792 they provided full manhood suffrage in their constitutions. When the new agricultural states later applied they, too, granted the same right in their fundamental law. The older colonies also had a frontier which helped to drive them forward to democratic policies. Pennsylvania adopted in 1790 the moderate tax-paying qualification that the voter must have paid public taxes. South Carolina adopted a somewhat similar clause the same year. Delaware and New Hampshire decreed full manhood suffrage in 1792. In the industrial states of Massachusetts and New York, however, it was only after a hard fight that property qualifications were wiped out. In Rhode Island there was a small-sized rebellion before the die-hards accepted defeat. By the time of Jackson's election in 1828 it was the exceptional s⁺ate which retained any effective property test for suffrage for white males.

It has been pointed out by others, but it is well to repeat, that the American workers did not have to organize as a class in order to win the right to vote. The British toilers did not directly benefit by the Reform Bill of 1832. Despite the tremendous agitation of the Chartists in the late thirties and forties, the English urban and agricultural workers were not enfranchised until 1867 and 1884. And the German Lassalean socialists sounded the war cry for universal manhood suffrage only at a time when in America the northern states were giving away free land and the prospect of economic independence by the homestead act of 1862. The three-class voting system of Prussia was not abolished and republican institutions were not introduced in Germany until after the revolution of 1918. This was exactly ninety years after the election of Andrew Jackson to the American presidency. Political democracy and the ballot may not be the open sesame to bread and liberty, but they are civilized weapons to obtain both.

Before 1830 railroads had not been developed. But immediately after peace was concluded between the American colonies and the mother country in 1783, transportation projects were energetically pushed by the building of turnpikes—which charged tolls—and canals, and by improving roads and rivers. The steamboat was a familiar sight in the early twenties. The Erie Canal was opened up for its whole distance by 1825. With this improvement in transportation facilities, and the extension of markets which went with it, the labor movement came into being. It was not the unskilled factory hands in the textile mills who first organized on the economic or the political field. It was the skilled workers and mechanics, who still used hand tools, who founded the first trade unions and labor parties.

In the earliest colonial days the skilled worker is an itinerant who visits a farmer or villager with his tools and completes an article on his premises. Later, he may set up a shop. He may employ one or more journeymen. There is no conflict between the master and his workmen because both are free from competition in a restricted local market, circumscribed by inadequate transportation facilities.

With improved roads and faster river movement of goods, the wholesaler and the merchant-capitalist enter the scene. The wholesaler is merely the master-retailer reaching out for orders beyond his village and town. The merchant-capitalist buys raw materials, has them made up, and sells the finished goods to retailers. In order to meet competition and make larger profits the wholesaler and merchant-capitalist feel impelled to reduce wages and the workers' standards to get increased output at decreased labor cost.

It was this pressure of the merchant-capitalist and the wholesaler which, before the factory system was developed in the United States, drove the journeymen to organize into trade unions and enter politics independently, to protect their standard of life, to guard their skill, and to strike at social and economic abuses generally.

Any general march of wage earners for shorter hours, especially against great resistance, is bound to unite them and drive them to class action. It is not surprising that the struggles of the Philadelphia and New York unionists a century ago for the ten-hour day should have directly led to the first united movement of labor on the political field. The awakening of labor was part of the new Jacksonian democracy. The men of toil wanted their place in the sun. Once organized, the workingmen's parties filled their platforms with all their economic and social grievances.

In New York City the unions had won the ten-hour work-day. The building trades of Philadelphia struck in 1827 for the same benefit. These pioneer steps toward shorter hours aroused more opposition than did the movement for eight hours several decades later. People still thought in terms of a hard life on the soil and were dominated by rigorous religious concepts of the moral worth of industrious habits, which also explains the prevailing attitude toward the value of child labor.

The fight for the ten-hour day was the occasion, but back of the launching of the first labor party by the Mechanics' Union of Trade Associations of Philadelphia was a labor philosophy of natural rights and equalitarianism, characteristic of the radical eighteenth century. The preamble of this central body declared:

As freemen and republicans, we feel it a duty incumbent on us to make known our sentiments fearlessly and faithfully on any subject connected with the general welfare; and we are prepared to maintain that all who toil have a natural and unalienable right to reap the fruits of their own industry; and that they who by labor (the only source) are the authors of every comfort, convenience and luxury, are in justice entitled to an equal participation, not only in the meanest and the coarsest, but likewise the richest and the choicest of them all.

The labor party of 1828 in Philadelphia and elsewhere was made up of natives. Between 1790 and 1830 only 400,000 aliens entered the country, which had grown to nearly thirteen millions. The "spirit of 1776" was still fresh in the minds of Americans. The labor party leaders turned to their newly enfranchised citizens:

Your fathers of the Revolution secured to you a form of government which guarantees to you, almost universally, the elective franchise. . . . If you possess the rights of freemen, you have exercised them as the privileges of slaves. . . . Awake, then, from your slumbers; and insult not the memories of the heroes of '76, by exhibiting to the world, that what they risked their lives, their fortunes, and their sacred honor to obtain, you do not think worth preserving.

§

The working people of 1828 demanded, first, "an equal participation" in knowledge. The labor parties of the period everywhere stressed the necessity for a system of free, tax-supported schools. A committee of the Philadelphia labor party put the matter as follows:

The original element of despotism is a monopoly of talent, which consigns the multitude to comparative ignorance, and secures the balance of knowledge on the side of the rich and the rulers. If then the healthy existence of a free government be, as the committee believe, rooted in the will of the American people, it follows as a necessary consequence, of a government based upon that will, that this monopoly should be broken up, and that the means of equal knowledge (the only security for equal liberty), should be rendered, by legal provision, the common property of all classes . . . until the means of equal instruction shall be equally secured to all, liberty is but an unmeaning word, and equality an empty shadow.

The more radical workers of New York added:

Your committee agree with the people's friend and firm advocate, the immortal Jefferson, "that the tax which will be paid for educating the common people, is not more than the thousandth part of what will be paid to kings, nobles and priests, who will rise up among us if we leave the people in ignorance."

In Pennsylvania at this time the entire state, outside of Philadelphia, Lancaster, and Pittsburgh, was destitute of provisions for public instruction. There were private elementary schools, but they were run for profit and the poor could not afford to send their children to them. In the three cities named, charity schools were established for those whose parents were unable to educate them at their own expense. But the workers objected to the taint of pauperism attached to these schools. They protested their meagreness of instruction and their inefficiency. In all of the states the children of the poor were going without schooling by the tens of thousands.

One faction of the labor party in New York City, headed up by Robert Dale Owen, Frances Wright, and George Henry Evans, held that common day schools—however improved, and however well the children attended them—were not enough. They maintained:

. . . . that state schools to be republican, efficient and acceptable to all, must receive the children not for six hours a day, but altogether; must feed them, clothe them, lodge them, must direct not their studies only, but their occupations and amusements; must care for them until their education is completed, and then only abandon them to the world, as useful, intelligent, virtuous citizens.

They wanted the children to receive the same food, to be dressed in the same simple clothing, to be taught the same branches, "in a word, that nothing savoring of inequality, nothing reminding them of the pride of riches, or the contempt of poverty, should be suffered to enter these republican safeguards of a young nation of equals." No one was to be compelled to send his children to these schools, but the tax would be paid by all. The teachers were to be elected by the people. A training school was to be established to provide competent instructors.

While these advanced ideas were limited to a very small group, the foundation of the American free school system is in large measure to be credited to the labor movement.

The workers called for the abolition of imprisonment for debt. The Boston Prison Discipline Society's report of 1829 estimated that about 75,000 debtors were thrown into prison yearly, the majority for sums less than $20. The condition of some of the prisons beggars description.

Other demands of the labor parties included a mechanics' lien law, radical alteration or abolition of the compulsory militia system, abolition of chartered monopolies, softening of the conspiracy law against labor organizations, abolition of prison labor, reform in legal procedure and adequate fees for jurors and witnesses, reductions in the salaries of public officials, abolition of the lottery and auction systems, besides a number of local city and village measures.

The candidates of the workingmen's parties did not always run on an exclusively independent ticket. In Philadelphia many of the nominees were adopted by the existing parties. The labor party there was not able to keep itself free from the activity of the old party politicians, who used force, flattery, patronage, and the slogans of the workers to break up the following behind it. There was fusion on the part of one labor party wing in New York City with the old parties. A New York state convention was held in August, 1830, at which the uncompromising faction of Robert Dale Owen was kept out. This convention nominated two prominent politicians for governor and lieutenant governor. The gubernatorial candidate announced two weeks before the election that he was not the candidate of the workingmen. Forty-two years later, in 1872, another politician left a labor party in the same way, this time for the office of president. The workers have discovered after bitter experience that old party politicians are more concerned about their own political fortunes than in promoting a cause, with an up-hill fight and little prospect of immediate victory.

In the first few elections the labor parties made very good showings. In the city and county of Philadelphia the Working Man's Party obtained the balance of power in 1829, the second year of its existence. But in the election of October, 1830, the democrats secured a decisive majority, and in the following fall the labor party made its last nominations. In New York City the workingmen polled 6,000 out of a total of about 21,000 votes in 1829, the first election they participated in. They elected Ebenezer Ford to the legislature. A movement to unseat Ford was begun—it seems that the Sweets and Stevensons of 1920 had their predecessors—but proved unsuccessful. Outside of Philadelphia and New York, although the labor parties elected a number of public officials, they did not survive the excitement of the presidential election of 1832. The national contest helped to take the workers' interest away from local issues and their local parties.

§

The farmers and workers were at some places united in the independent political movement. In New England there was an Association of Farmers, Mechanics, and Other Workingmen, a sort of industrial union, which in Massachusetts took the plunge into independent politics in 1833 and 1834. The issues of the labor parties were the demands of mechanics, unskilled workers, and farmers who were relatively poor, as against the bankers, the land speculators, the money lenders, the holders of public securities, who were relatively rich. Free, tax-supported schools, ending of imprisonment for debt, abolition of monopolies and banks, these were matters upon which the farmers and the workers could unite.

The early trade unions in this country were not induced to take independent political action—with one exception—because of anti-conspiracy prosecutions directed against them. Before 1828 only a few shoemakers were so attacked. It was not until 1835 that the decision against the Geneva, New York, boot and shoemakers was handed down by the supreme court of the state. The following year twenty tailors were indicted and convicted of conspiracy in New York City. As a result of the decision in this case the workers entered the political arena by uniting with the Equal Rights Party—the anti-monopoly and progressive off-shoot of Tammany Hall.

§

The intellectual played a leading role in the New York City movement. Although Thomas Skidmore was a machinist, he educated himself and became the exponent of a primitive agrarian communism. In those days when a man wrote a book his title expressed his thesis. Skidmore's work was entitled *The Rights of Man to Property! Being a Proposition to Make it Equal among the Adults of the Present Generation: and to Provide for its Equal Transmission to Every Individual of Each Succeeding Generation, on Arriving at the Age of Maturity.* Skidmore was an aggressive and domineering man. He managed to capture the first general meeting of the mechanics of New York, called to protest against an increase of hours. He argued that if property relations were attacked, the employers would readily concede the point as to hours in order to prevent further discussion of the more dangerous topic. A Committee of Fifty was appointed to assist needy mechanics in the ten-hour fight. Under Skidmore's influence this committee turned to independent political action and adopted rather hastily a report which expressed not theirs but Skidmore's views. In the first election the New York labor men were charged with being agrarians or communists, and destroyers of property. After the election they overwhelmingly repudiated Skidmore. He started his own party and paper but they had little influence.

Frances Wright was a rationalist and feminist. Associated with her were George Henry Evans and Robert Dale Owen. Their state guardianship plan of education, their anti-religious and feminist views hurt the political organization with which they were prominently identified. The old party politicians and the ruling classes of that day eagerly stigmatized the labor parties in New York, Phil-

adelphia, and elswhere—movements which rested on programs independent of the personal views of some of their
members in one city alone—as communistic, as breeders
of infidelity, and destroyers of property and the home.
By these epithets they injured the labor parties, exactly as
the Conservative Party of Great Britain defeated the
Labor Party in the 1924 elections by the forged Zinoviev
letter.

§

The first labor parties failed and passed into oblivion.
And so did the first trade unions. In the years immediately preceding the panic of 1837 there was, due to the
rapid increase in prices and the cost of living, an extraordinary growth of labor organization. A New York
City newspaper of 1836 claimed that two-thirds of the
workingmen in the metropolis belonged to trade unions.
The panic of 1837 wiped the unions out. The panics of
1857 and 1873 and the depressions which followed also
played havoc with whatever labor bodies had grown up
in the preceding periods. President Gompers' statement
in his report to the 1893 convention of the American
Federation of Labor is oft quoted: "while in every
previous industrial crisis the trade unions were literally
mowed down and swept out of existence, the unions now
in existence have manifested, not only the powers of resistance, but of stability and permanency." According to
this view of the late president of the federation, it took
over half a century before the unions developed staying
powers. It is not strange, then, that in the United States
as we know it to have been, the independent labor parties
did not gain a permanent national footing until the nineties also. It was not until then that capitalism had matured and there was no longer any escape to the land.

Even in the beginning, when the factory system was
being introduced in the United States, the workers and
reformers were not unaware of its ultimate effects. Already in the thirties the National Trades' Union officially

declared: "This factory system is essentially opposed to the spirit of our institutions, since from its nature, it must throw large bodies of people together, and by degrees render them wholly dependent upon a few employers, and forever crush that spirit of independence which is the only safeguard of freedom." The articulate artisans realized that democracy was impossible without industrial freedom, that political power rested upon economic power.

In 1834 President Comerford of the National Trades' Union pointed out some of the immediate effects of the new methods of production: "We are aware that this country, from a mistaken policy, has become a competitor with England in the manufacturing system . . . her wealth has arisen from these sources; but it is equally true, that the moral degradation of her people may be attributed to her manufacturing system." In the textile centers of America women and children of tender age were being used up in unsanitary factories. When the immigrants began to come in hordes, starting with the forties, the over-crowding and housing conditions in the factory towns and cities were frightful. The factory system left its trail of misery in this as in every other land where it ruthlessly forced its way.

§

Noting the effect of the machine system on human beings, Robert Owen, the philanthropist and utopian socialist, set out to take the workers away from its blighting influences and to subject them to another order, a communistic society where they could flower under the most favorable circumstances. To carry out his ideas on a much larger scale than in England he migrated to America, where land was cheap and men would listen. In 1825 he launched New Harmony in the state of Indiana. There was discord from the start and inside of a few years it disbanded.

In the forties Albert Brisbane and a galaxy of brilliant followers introduced the theories of Charles Fourier in America. The French utopian was opposed to Owen's communism. His whole system was an attempt to protect capital against the rising discontent of the working class by arranging a sort of partnership between them. This in part explains the interest in it of Horace Greeley and a number of others, middle class humanitarians, who sought an escape from the rising factory system in flight to an ideal phalanx, with capital and labor in loving embrace.

These utopian communities had little meaning for the wage earners who remained in the cities, to struggle on with bread and butter problems. The Associationists—or colonizers—regarded the phalanx or ideal community as the only way out. To them the ten-hour movement was "neither more nor less than a demeaning compromise . . . which only modified the condition but does not change the terms of dependence on masters." The failures of the Owenites, the Associationists, and the like did not prevent others from taking up the colonizing idea from time to time. Eugene Victor Debs and the Social Democracy which he founded fondly believed for a short while that the cooperative commonwealth could be ushered into the world by a colonization plan. The hard facts of experience taught the workers that a communistic society could not be set up outside of the gates of capitalism; that they had to be possibilist and work within the system if they were to improve their lot.

§

The land reformers were much closer to reality, but they also minimized the labor movement. For them escape from the evils of the factory system lay in migrating to the West, in settlement upon the public domain. The undisposed land was not accessible because the government set a price upon every acre of it. Speculators also

held large quantities. George Henry Evans, Horace
Greeley, Alvin E. Bovay, and a host of others started an
agitation for a free homestead to be given *bona fide* settlers. They demanded that the homestead be strictly
limited in size so that none might monopolize or inherit
more than he and his family could use. These home-
steads were to be inalienable, that is, they "must never be
subject to any liability to alienate for any consideration
whatever, such as that of sale, debt, tax, mortgage, primo-
geniture, etc." The land reformers also declared—and
this is pivotal—that "property must be owned separately
by individuals and not in communized bodies," thereby
distinguishing themselves from the colonizers.

With their program of freedom of the public lands,
homestead exemption, and land limitation, the land reformers turned to politics. They first tried an independent ticket in Massachusetts in 1846, but made a poor
showing. They then adopted the slogan: "Vote Yourself a Farm." They organized, they dominated the industrial congresses of the period, often to the disgust of
the trade unionists. They put pressure on candidates of
all parties, and they memorialized Congress and the state
legislatures. As John R. Commons pointed out long ago,
the Republican Party "was not an anti-slavery party. It
was a homestead party."

The homestead policy did not prove the solution of
industrial evils as dreamed by the land reformers, no
more than did the public school system fulfill the expectations of its first advocates. Free land undoubtedly
eased the general industrial situation, but it also tended
to speed up the development of the factory system. Free
land helped to keep wages up and make the use of man-
power expensive. This fact, plus the presence of semi-
skilled and unskilled labor from abroad, promoted the
introduction of machinery. This in turn tended to
mechanize industrial processes. The large national market
made it profitable for this mechanization to go farther in
this country than in any other.

Again, the existence of this opportunity of going West and taking up a homestead, with its prospect of independence, drew off the hardiest spirits of the cities, natural leaders, and thereby weakened the organizations of the masses who stayed at home. Furthermore, the labor movement in all countries has received considerable encouragement and intellectual support from middle class elements. In the United States these idealists were for a long time absorbed, first in the demand for free land, with its complement, the abolition of slave labor, and later in an agitation against land monopolists. The working class movement had to wait until free land was a thing of the past, in the nineties, before it could secure the best proletarian and the most idealistic middle class leadership, and take root in fertile econmic soil.

§

In some of the good years of the fifties and sixties the trade unions took on new life. In 1850 the printers organized nationally; the stone cutters got together in 1853; the hat finishers in 1854. In 1859 the molders and machinists—who contributed so many of the outstanding labor leaders of the sixties and seventies—followed suit; the miners in 1861, the locomotive engineers in 1863 and the cigarmakers in 1864. In the latter year there was a phenomenal increase in trade union membership.

This growth prompted the Louisville trades assembly to send out a call for a national convention of labor organizations. A conference was held on September 21, 1864, but no national federation resulted. The number of national unions continued to increase. In 1865 the carpenters and the bricklayers started their careers as national bodies, while in 1868 the most important union of the whole period, the Knights of St. Crispin—shoemakers in work hours—arose. By 1870 there were anywhere from 200,000 to 300,000 in the unions. The Knights of St. Crispin were credited with about 50,000 members;

the miners, molders, printers, bricklayers, and the machinists with memberships each in excess of 10,000.

With increased numbers and a greater sense of power the trade unionists now reached out for the eight-hour day. They demanded it not merely for themselves, but for all workers. As in the forties they first turned to nonpartisan, but unlike the earlier hectic period, they also resorted to independent political action to obtain the shorter workday. The philosopher and organizer of the eight-hour movement was Ira Steward. His chief disciples were George E. McNeill and George Gunton. Their agitation led to the formation of the first important national labor federation in the United States, the National Labor Union.

Steward argued that the new and improved methods of production were increasing the quantity of goods. The reduction of hours would raise the standard of living of the workers because the effect of leisure, according to him, was to stimulate wants. A universal eight-hour law would force even the poorest paid worker to increase his needs and to demand more pay. Not only would the wage earners receive the same pay for eight as for longer hours, but they would, by ever raising their standard of life, force ever higher wages and threaten the profits of the capitalists.

The political eight-hour movement was thus applicable to skilled and unskilled, to organized and unorganized. The workers turned to politics because they wanted shorter hours for all. And as this class demand was tied up with another, that for a greenback currency, the National Labor Union which supported both soon found itself headed toward independent labor politics.

§

William H. Sylvis, Richard F. Trevellick, and Andrew C. Cameron were three of the leading spirits of the National Labor Union. Trevellick was an orator, Cameron an editor and politician, but Sylvis was a labor leader of the first rank, a thinker and man of action. The articles by Sylvis on money which first appeared in the *Workingmen's Advocate,* the official organ of the National Labor Union, help to explain how a trade unionist like the president of the National Labor Union could be carried away by the greenback philosophy.

Sylvis started out by saying that the American republic was founded on the basis of "the equal rights of man, civil equality, and common privileges, and whose end was to be the general prosperity, virtue and happiness of the people." However, said Sylvis, a class of "bankers, brokers, bond-holders, usurers and other plunderers of labor, the moneyed aristocracy is fast sapping the foundations of our government, and destroying the liberties of the people."

He answered those of his day, as radicals do of our own, who point to the relative prosperity of America:

It is true that, compared with the wretched population of despotic Europe and Asia, the people of this country, even under existing unjust relations of man to man, enjoy many things not common to the people of other countries. But comparative superiority may still be a condition fraught with much misery to the human family, and not less repugnant to benevolence than revolting to justice. Even in Europe and Asia this superiority forms the boast of one nation over another, throughout the long-continued chain of comparative wretchedness among the great mass of the population.

In America too, he declared, there is a great deal of misery, although "nature has abundantly supplied the industry of man with the means of universal comfort."

The labor greenbacker noted that all the improved methods of production have availed labor little, for "the increase in production, the improvement in quality, with the increased means of transportation, have but tended to augment the wealth of the few and impoverish the many." He was struck by the fact that interest takes its toll, that it goes to a few, and that it represents "a vast load of debt heaped upon the backs of the toiling millions—the very heart's blood of the workingman is mortgaged from the cradle to the grave."

Sylvis did not claim that all interest was robbery. He declared that annually "the increase in wealth has not been over three per cent, while the rate of interest has averaged fully fifteen per cent." Anything above three per cent was, therefore, "a mortgage upon the productive industry of the country." Because the interest rate was so high, employers of labor and self-employers were unwilling to borrow. Said Sylvis:

A high rate of interest is the mill-stone about the neck of labor; it cripples the energy of the whole people, and retards production . . . reduce the rate of interest to three per cent, and give us a national currency made of paper, and new enterprises will be started, machinery now idle will be put in motion; there will be work for all.

The argument in brief ran as follows: The rate of interest is high because there is a limited amount of money, deliberately kept so because a gold currency is used, which fluctuates not in accordance with need, but as the bankers and lenders who monopolize it under the national banking law, decide. The remedy is plain. The amount of money must be increased and thereby the rate of interest reduced. This must be done by an agency which is supposed to be solely concerned with the welfare of all the people, the government. The power of issuing money, which was given to the national banks during the Civil War, must be taken away from them. Instead, the government must issue paper money, greenbacks. The national debt should be converted into bonds bearing three per cent interest. Any owner of such a bond should be allowed to take it to the government treasury and receive paper money in exchange. When he can make more than three per cent with his money he will employ it in industry; when he cannot, he will reconvert it into these three per cent government bonds. In this way, argued the labor greenbacker, there will be no raising of the interest rate by parasitical bankers and middlemen; there will be no monopoly of money, and the government will be the only banker and money lender.

This plan was an adaptation of the theories of Edward Kellogg expounded many years before the National Labor Union was born. It differed from the program of the later cheap money advocates—greenbackers and populists of the seventies and nineties—in that the latter demanded an increase in the quantity of money in order to raise prices, chiefly of agricultural products, while Sylvis and the National Labor Union emphasized the necessity of getting the wheels of industry going by enabling the manufacturers and self-employers to obtain credit on cheap terms and thus provide employment at high wages to labor. Sylvis placed so much hope in his financial reforms that he could repeatedly say: "We must show them that when a just monetary system has been established there will no longer exist a necessity for trades unions."

§

The convention which organized the National Labor Union met in Baltimore, August 20, 1866. One of its chief decisions was to form a national labor party, "the object of which shall be to secure the enactment of a law making eight hours a legal day's work by the national Congress and the several state legislatures." This party, the convention decided, was not to be immediately launched. An organization campaign was to be instituted, eight-hour leagues established, and in the meantime localities were to be free to take nonpartisan or independent political action as they chose. A Lassallean socialist named Schlaeger was instrumental in putting the convention on record in favor of independent politics. The conservative unionists were placated by the compromise that no party was to be immediately set going.

When the federation of national unions met for its second convention in Chicago on August 19, 1867, the committee on eight hours reported:

Eight-hour laws have been passed by the legislatures of six states, but for all practical intents and purposes they might as well have never been placed on the statute books, and can only be described as frauds on the laboring class.

The same old joker which nullified the ten-hour laws of the forties was embodied in the eight-hour statutes, *viz.*, the provision that the shorter hours would constitute a day's work except "where there is no special contract or agreement to the contrary." The experience of the labor leaders with the wily politicians tended to clinch their determination to cut loose from any connection with them.

In the latter part of 1866 business slowed down considerably. The government had been retiring the greenbacks issued during the Civil War. The labor greenbackers now came forward in the convention of the National Labor Union of 1867 with their pet financial program. Cameron expressed the prevailing view:

That an antagonism between labor and capital should or must necessarily exist, we do not believe; that under our iniquitous monetary and financial system—the result of legislation—it does exist, is a self-evident proposition.

To get rid of the legislation and the class antagonism it was argued that the workers must organize their own party, supported by all who suffered from the acts of the old party legislators who put the legislation on the statute books and who would not change it. The National Labor Union gladly admitted, therefore, the representatives of the farmers' anti-monopoly associations and the land and labor leagues in the 1867 convention. The federation had already opened its doors in 1866 to the eight-hour leagues. All of these associations included some who were not wage earners.

From 1867 on the National Labor Union began more and more to stress monetary reforms and the necessity of independent political action to put them on the law books. When the presidential election of 1868 rolled around a conference was held in New York City on July 2.

The labor leaders agreed that the movement was as yet too weak to put up a national ticket. In the following year the first and important test came in Massachusetts.

§

During the sixties a revolution took place in the boot and shoe industry, the center of which was in Massachusetts. The skilled shoemaker was faced with the competition of "green hands" by the rapid spread of new machinery. The meteoric rise of the Knights of St. Crispin was the workers' answer. The labor movement in Massachusetts had been militant in the forties, it subsided in the fifties, and it came to life again the following decade. The champions in the eight-hour and ten-hour fights hailed from this commonwealth. The independent labor party movement of the sixties was born in the home of Daniel Webster and Wendell Phillips. Webster represented the protected manufacturers, Phillips the unprotected toilers.

The Massachusetts eight-hour enthusiasts, however, were opposed to laying much if any stress on financial reform, and before the leaders of the Knights and the National Labor Union could have things their own way they had to overcome the opposition of Steward, McNeill, and their followers. The Boston Eight-Hour League, of which McNeill was the leading spirit, adopted the following resolution, expressing the antagonism between the financial reformers and the eight-hour men:

Financial reform, so-called, is interesting and important chiefly to that small per cent of our fellow citizens who belong to the capitalist classes; who regard themselves as a permanent class in society, and believe that upon their financial successes must depend all who work with their hands . . . who . . . are able through their wealth to fix public attention upon questions of taxation, railroad and banking management, currency and interest, protection and free-trade, franking, mileage, salary, civil service, and economical humbugs, the settlement of which the best way, still leaves the laborer a laborer, and the capitalist a capitalist, between whom there is an irrepressible conflict which must continue until all are laborers and all are capitalists.

The Massachusetts labor men, without the eight-hour vanguard, went ahead and nominated a ticket and adopted a platform in September, 1869, calling for payment of the national debt in greenbacks and demanding taxation of government bonds. They also added planks for an eight-hour day for state and city employees, a ten-hour day for all women workers and minors, no coolie immigration, a national department of labor, and the equalization of bounties for soldiers and sailors. The result of the election was, as is often the case with labor parties in their first campaigns, very encouraging. Edwin M. Chamberlin, the candidate for governor, received 13,567 votes, as against about 125,000 for both other candidates. The labor reformers elected twenty-one members out of eighty to the lower house of the legislature, and one to the upper.

The Prohibition Party as well as the laborites nominated Wendell Phillips for governor in 1870. The revised platform demanded that the public lands should be held for settlers only and not given away to railroads or speculators; and that the law allowing banks to issue money be repealed. In this campaign the still-young Republican Party took note of the existence of the labor party in its platform:

The Republican Party, which, in the ten years of its history, has accomplished more for the elevation of the laborers of America than had been accomplished before since the government was framed, hears with surprise and indignation the claim of any other organization to arrogate to itself the title of "labor party"; that in our judgment the intellectual and social advancement of the laborers of the country, their improvement in wealth, comfort and happiness, the security of their personal and political rights, are not only important objects of public care and regard, but are the very purpose for which the state was created, and are the end and object of all political effort.

Phillips received 21,946 votes on both tickets. The labor reformers retained their one member of the senate but only elected eleven to the house. In 1871 the Labor Reform Party rewrote its platform. With decreased numbers and greater determination to survive, the crusaders became militant—in words:

> We declare war with the wages system . . . war with the present system of finance . . . war with the lavish grants of the public lands to speculation companies . . . war with the system of enriching capitalists by the creation and increase of public interest bearing debts.

But unfortunately, the party did not have an army to go to war with, and Chamberlin received in that year only 6,848 votes, half of what he got in 1869. The heart was taken out of his followers. The National Labor Union by this time was also crumbling. Prior to this time it had been given hope and political courage by the results in Massachusetts.

§

The third and fourth conventions of the National Labor Union were well attended. No further steps were taken looking to independent political action until the fifth congress in Cincinnati, August 15, 1870. The Labor Reform Party of Massachusetts had in the previous year made its first splendid showing. It was Samuel P. Cummings of the Crispins and president of the Massachusetts party who proposed that a committee consisting of the head of the federation and one delegate from each state perfect the organization of a national labor party, to be launched by a special convention for that purpose. His suggestion was adopted. Trevellick, a strong greenbacker and independent party man, called the committee together as president. The political labor convention was supposed to be held in October, 1871, at Columbus. But it was decided to postpone it until February 21, 1872.

John Siney, an outstanding leader of the miners, was temporary and Chamberlin permanent chairman of the nominating convention. The platform adopted included the financial reforms of the greenbackers besides a number of the demands of the workers of that period. When it came to the picking of candidates the delegates from the fourteen states faced the problem that every labor and farmer party must face in the United States: the selection of a popular and appealing figure to head the ticket. They tried to meet the difficulty by turning to a so-called liberal in the Republican Party.

After the Civil War serious limitations had been placed on the political rights of southerners. Under the leadership of Carl Schurz and B. Gratz Brown a movement was started to liberalize the Republican Party generally and wipe out the political disabilities. In 1870 the liberals held a separate state convention in Missouri and adopted a platform demanding civil service extension, the abolition of political disqualifications, and some other measures of reformers of those days. After electing their candidate for governor they joined hands with men in other states and issued a call for a national convention in 1872. Among the contenders for the nomination of president was Justice David Davis of Illinois, of the United States Supreme Court. The convention picked Horace Greeley, whom the democrats subsequently endorsed.

The nominating convention of the laborites and currency reformers took place in February, 1872, before the gathering of the Liberal Republican Party. The three candidates spoken of were Judge Davis, Governor John W. Geary of Pennsylvania, and Wendell Phillips. The last-named was the only one identified with the labor or reform movement in any sense. The delegates went ahead and nominated Davis. After the Liberal Republican Party nominated Greeley, Davis wrote to the labor men that "having regarded that movement as the initiation of a policy and purpose to unite the various political elements in a compact opposition and [having] consented to the use of my name before the Cincinnati convention," where Greeley was chosen, he was compelled to decline.

He did not want to lead a cause, he wanted to run for president with a chance to win. A few days after Davis notified the laborites and reformers that they had no old-party Moses to save them the trouble of building up a political organization of their own and developing their own leaders, their candidate for vice-president, Joe! Parker, informed them that he had "always been a member of the Democratic Party," and presumably intended to remain one.

The activity in Massachusetts, the concentration on financial reforms and the shift in control to the green-backers inside the federation, all helped to make the National Labor Union less of a trade union than a political organization. The fiasco of 1872 put the finishing touches on the little political life the body had. The panic of 1873 and the long depression now put the trade unions on the defensive and compelled them to fight for their lives. Some went underground in this period. The Knights of Labor started as a secret organization and remained so for a decade. The Molly Maguires dominated the anthracite coal fields of Pennsylvania, until uncovered and wiped out in 1875.

§

The long depression, which lasted until 1879, brought great hardship to the working people. On December 22, 1873 a committee, followed by about twenty thousand marchers, wound up at the City Hall of Chicago and begged in vain for relief. Samuel Gompers records in his autobiography that free soup kitchens were opened in New York. The workers selected a Committee of Safety in the metropolis to assist the unemployed. On January 13, 1874, an out-door mass meeting was scheduled to be held in Tompkins Square. When the parading workers reached the square the police swept down upon them, clubbing right and left. Samuel Gompers, who is said to have died with the words "God bless our institutions" on his lips, according to his own account, barely saved his head from a policeman's club on this occasion.

In *Appleton's Annual Cyclopedia* for 1877 there appears for the first time the topic, "Labor-Strikes." This is suggestive. The American people awoke one day, and as usual with a start, to the existence of a labor problem. In this land of the sensational it was a violent upheaval which drew their attention to it. The writer in the encylopedia stated:

> The most grievous conflict between employers and the employed, and the most extensive, if not the most disastrous, riots which the country has witnessed, occurred during the months of July and August, 1877, in consequence of the dissatisfaction of the railroad employees on several of the lines with the reduction of ten per cent in their wages, which had been made generally throughout the country in June and July.

The cuts were to go into effect on June 1 on the Pennsylvania system, July 1 on the New York Central, and July 16, on the Baltimore and Ohio. Efforts were made by the railroad employees—outside of the conservative engineers who adopted a cautious waiting policy, to organize a secret Trainmen's Union to oppose the reduction. They failed to pull off a strike. But the workers resisted and spontaneously walked out.

On July 17 the men on the Baltimore and Ohio refused to allow trains to leave the station at Martinsburg, West Virginia, and on July 19 the workers on the Pennsylvania system went out on strike in and around Pittsburgh. The state militia of Pennsylvania was called out. The militiamen of Pittsburgh fraternized with the strikers. The Philadelphia militia, however, showed fight. They killed twenty-six persons in one battle, after which they took refuge in a roundhouse, from which point they kept up a running fire with a crowd intent on their destruction. In Martinsburg and Reading federal troops were called out. There were disturbances, with a number killed and wounded, in many of the railroad centers of Maryland, Pennsylvania, and West Virginia, and con-

siderable excitement in some of the railroad points in
Illinois, Indiana, Missouri, New Jersey, New York, Ohio,
and elsewhere.

A number of sympathetic turn-outs occurred on the
part of the workers outside of the railroad employees
directly affected. The switchmen on the Michigan Central struck in Chicago on July 23. For three days the
strikers and a constantly growing army of recruits went
about the city closing railroad yards, factories, and stockyards, until stopped in a deadly battle by federal and
state troops and police. Leading members of the Socialist
Labor Party in Chicago were arrested, including Albert R.
Parsons and the national secretary, Philip Van Patten.
The socialists called immense mass meetings and secured
the election of delegates from each factory—in soviet
fashion—to a special committee to manage the general
strike situation. The committee demanded the eight-hour
day and an increase in pay of not less than twenty-five
per cent. In St. Louis also there was a general strike, and
an executive committee of the workers was set up which
ran the city for a week.

The long years of hard times served as fertile ground
for the development of bitterness and the revolt which
began with the strikes of the railroad workers. The
pitched battles between the militia and soldiers and the
strikers and their sympathizers awakened and added fuel
to the smouldering fire. A tremendous wave of independent labor politics followed. The workers either independently or in coalition with the greenbackers rolled
up extraordinary polls in 1877 and 1878. The political
movement was, however, predominantly agrarian and
middle class.

CHAPTER II

THE UNITED FRONT OF 1886

THE trade union and labor political movement of any country at any given time reflects the stage of its economic development. In the United States, in the late twenties, when the merchant-capitalist began putting pressure upon the petty employer to sweat his journeymen, the workmen organized trade unions and central bodies and after the ballot was placed in their hands, took the plunge into independent politics. The movement was necessarily local in character and the efforts of the workers were largely directed against social abuses. The market area was limited, economic stratification had only begun, and a permanent workingmen's party was impossible. The trade unions were also mushroom affairs and passed out of existence after the panic of 1837. In the sixties and seventies national trade unions arose and the first attempt at a national trade union federation was made. State labor parties now took the field, and a national labor reform party appeared. The extension of the railroad and the development of machine production had created a national market, the workers in one locality were subject to competition by journeymen from the outside and by the machine, and they were growing weaker in bargaining power as against the corporation. The trade unionists, therefore, had to unite nationally. But the individualistic tradition of the American people, the presence of free land, and the long business depressions, turned the attention of the wage earners to financial reforms which they hoped would result in starting the wheels of industry, to a demand for an eight-hour law in order to give them the benefits of mass production, and to a law providing assistance to producers' cooperatives with the opportunity of self-employment.

The mighty industrial forces which had been gathering momentum for a century got their real stride in the United States in the eighties. It was now possible, therefore, to add 600,000 members to the Knights of Labor in one year, between 1885 and 1886. The leaders of the Knights could not hold these workers because they were steeped in the individualistic philosophy of financial and land reform, plus cooperation, which had characterized the labor movement of the two previous decades, while the economic developments called for a radically different approach. The American Federation of Labor arose in 1881 to answer the need of the hour with a pure and simple trade union. In contrast to the federation's philosophy, the Socialist Labor Party came forward with a program of working class solidarity on the economic and political fields. The Knights of Labor was beaten into nothingness by both of these organizations.

A determining factor in making the American Federation of Labor decide to hold fast to its pure and simple trade unionism and eschew independent political action, and the Socialist Labor Party to adopt its uncompromising position of going it alone, was the results of the campaigns of 1886. The most important of these political struggles were waged in New York and Chicago, although a host of minor ones were fought throughout the country. The political was but one phase of a mighty upheaval of labor in the eighties, of skilled and unskilled, with general strikes for eight hours, an avalanche of strikes and boycotts, the Haymarket affair, and a sharpening everywhere of the contest between the employing class and the workers.

§

The most spectacular, but not most typical, political contest took place in New York. Unfortunately, it centered around one man, Henry George. The conditions under which it was launched made for a meteoric and temporary movement. About a week before five workers were sentenced to prison for participating in the boycott of the beer garden of George Theiss, the immediate cause of the Henry George campaign, John Swinton, a strong advocate of independent political action, wrote in his weekly of June 27, 1886:

> The experience of "labor candidates" in New York would make good stuffing for a comic paper. We recall about a score of them in the past dozen years. One horny-handed candidate for governor did not get votes enough to make the "scattering" column look decent. One candidate for mayor of this city, who was nominated with terrific enthusiasm, and who woke the echoes with his speeches, had the satisfaction of rallying nearly one hundred voters to his horny standard on election day. . . . Even when a "labor candidate" has got the endorsement of one or other of the old parties, his "labor record" has nearly in every case insured his burial at the polls, under the tears of his mourning friends. Queer isn't it?

Swinton quoted Thomas A. Armstrong, the editor of the Pittsburgh *Labor Tribune,* who had run for governor in 1884 on a labor ticket: "As candidate for governor he gave the labor vote every opportunity to show itself. . . . The result is well known. Labor was enthusiastic until election day." Samuel Gompers, as might be expected, was skeptical. In his trade union paper, the *Picket*—they all had their own organs—Gompers wrote: "Our friends, John Swinton and Tom Armstrong, and a few others we could name, might give our friends who are anxious for workingmen to rush into politics some reminiscences."

J. T. McKechnie, writing a history of the New York Central Labor Union in Swinton's paper of February 28, 1886, coolly and confidently declared that "the land question and the greenback question no longer offer themes for discussion, while 'independent politics,' although still advocated and believed in by many, are relegated to a future time." This was only a few months before labor took the initiative in the Henry George campaign. In 1882 and 1883 the Central Labor Union, in cooperation with the socialists, had nominated in several assembly and aldermanic districts, but by 1886 had given up the policy.

District Assembly 49 of the Knights of Labor, the largest district body of the order, and which alone had over 60,000 members by July 1, 1886, was under the constitution forbidden to take any political action. As a matter of fact, the local labor leaders in the Central Labor Union and District Assembly 49 were then, as the New York labor leaders are today, active and conspicuous in the politics of the two old parties, mostly in Tammany Hall, because it has power. In other cities they are in the Republican Party. There were elements in the two central bodies of New York, however, which forced the step and which swept aside the opposition to labor entering politics independently, when the occasion played into their hands.

In the first place there were the socialistic unions, made up largely of Germans, with the New York *Volkszeitung* and the Socialist Labor Party as their guides. The socialists were a well organized nucleus inside the Central Labor Union at this time. Supporting them were some Irish nationalists, and those who favored independent political action, such as the greenbackers, single taxers, and anti-monopolists, and the politically minded, of whom John Swinton was an outstanding example. The general labor awakening of the eighties swept into the unions and the local assemblies of the Knights of Labor thousands of newcomers, made up of the semi-skilled and unskilled. They joined on the crest of a wave for an eight-hour day and general labor improvement. An independent political movement received a ready response from these workers, for their class feeling was just being stirred. Above all, when the Central Labor Union and District Assembly 49 were growing by leaps and bounds, it was human that they should rise in their might and hit back at the politicians and judges who had gone so far as to jail workers for participating in an ordinary union struggle. The local labor leaders, with their sympathies for the old parties, were helpless before the socialists, the newcomers, the action of the courts, and the sense of power which the New York labor movement felt. They were also not so well entrenched as today. Once the new party was started, Henry George and his close associates took charge; after the campaign they pushed the socialists out of it. The warmed-up workers, however, left George's party as they did the unions. Then George fell out with his allies, and he quit. Of the remaining leaders, one group wound up in a miserable national fiasco, the other "sold out" to the highest bidder.

§

"The great weapon of the boycott has been popularized by the Central Labor Union." Thus wrote J. T. McKechnie, in his history of that body. The trades assembly claimed over 100 affiliated unions and clubs, with an estimated membership of about 40,000. District Assembly 49 of the Knights of Labor had about 60,000, with some overlapping between the two. With this membership, and the spirit of class feeling abroad, the boycott was a powerful club in the hands of the wage earners. It was high time, therefore, for the courts to step in. In 1836 when the unions were making rapid strides to meet the rising cost of living the courts decided that they were conspiracies. In 1886, fifty years later, they did not go so far, but they declared boycotters guilty of crime.

Of twenty-six jurors called to try the boycotters of Theiss' place, John Swinton charged that "every one was either an active employer or a retired employer." The five men convicted and sentenced to prison were not leaders, but just "five honest, sober, industrious workingmen, of character wholly beyond reproach." Be that as it may, the reaction was quick and decisive. There was to be an election for mayor in the fall. The Central Labor Union decided to take independent political action. A conference was called for August 5, to which all *bona fide* unions inside or outside the central body were invited to send delegates.

The meeting was held, with over 400 delegates. The sentiment of the conference was expressed by the following statement of John Swinton: "Henry George is to be the candidate for mayor, if he will accept the nomination. . . . He embodies the aspirations of the masses. He is a worker, a printer, a unionist, a Knight of Labor, a man of business experience. . . the most renowned living American author." But the conference took no action, for the leader of the single tax doctrine did not show great haste in accepting the nomination. Finally, he yielded, but stipulated that the laborites secure the signatures of 30,000 voters pledged to support his candidacy. In his letter of acceptance he wrote: "The party that shall do for the question of industrial slavery what the Republican Party did for the question of chattel slavery, must, by whatever name it shall be known, be a workingman's party. . . . . In its broad political sense, the term 'workingman' does not refer to particular occupations but divides those who have to work that others may enjoy, from those who can appropriate the produce of others' work." All of which read well, but it meant one thing to the single taxers and quite another to the socialists. George also pointed out that he thought it wise to begin in the cities "where we may address ourselves to what lies nearest at hand, and avoid dissensions that, until the process of economic education has gone further, might divide us on national issues." This was a fond hope, to be smashed to smithereens.

On September 23, 1886, Henry George was officially nominated, and it was announced that 39,000 signatures had been secured. Five weeks were left to run a campaign. The Central Labor Union, the Knights of Labor, the Socialist Labor Party, the greenbackers, the antimonopolists, the single taxers, and a host of intellectuals and professional men and women endorsed him. Once nominated, Henry George dominated the movement. He ran on his own platform. He gave it from the start a single tax twist. His platform declared that the corruption of government and the impoverishment of labor flowed from a system "which compels men to pay their fellow creatures for the use of God's gifts to all [land], and permits monopolizers to deprive labor of natural opportunities for employment." He made it clear that he wanted "the maintenance of that sacred right of property which gives to every one opportunity to employ his labor." In accordance with his doctri..e he demanded no taxes on buildings and improvements, but a single tax on land. To placate the socialists and laborites he added the following planks: government ownership of the railroads and telegraphs, home rule, abolition of property qualifications for jurors, abolition of the system of drawing grand juries from one class, simplification of court procedure to give the poor equality before the law, opposition to officious meddling of police with peaceful meetings, building laws to be enforced, direct employment in public works, and municipal ownership of transit lines.

§

The platform was a single tax document, the candidate for mayor was the outstanding advocate of the single tax theory, but the Henry George campaign was not a single tax campaign. The election was a municipal affair in New York, Chicago, and in dozens of other cities, but the issues at stake were not local matters. The political battles throughout the country in 1886 were of the same cloth as the general strikes for eight-hours. The success or failure of one or the other were significant for the entire labor movement and to the whole nation. They aroused the bitterest class feeling in all quarters.

The New York democracy was divided—like ancient Gaul—into three parts: the city organization, the county democracy, and Irvington Hall. Tammany Hall, the city body, in view of the crisis went outside of its own ranks and chose ex-Congressman Abram S. Hewitt, a member of the county democracy, for mayor. He was a large employer and therefore able to fill the campaign chest. He was chairman of the National Democratic Committee and a leading figure behind whom Tammany Hall could wage a successful fight. The republicans picked Theodore Roosevelt, whom Swinton characterized as of "blue-blooded ancestry and inherited fortune." The real fight was, however, between Henry George and Hewitt. Gompers expressed the opinion that "word was sent out from republican quarters that . . . republican voters ought to cast their ballots for Mr. Hewitt."

The Irish workers were behind the Henry George campaign in large part. Their nationalism had been stirred. The theory of single tax aimed a body blow at land monopoly which cursed Ireland, and Henry George had travelled and lectured in their home land. Besides, they had been caught up by the labor upheaval of the period. The *Irish World* and its editor, Patrick Ford, as well as a priest, Edward McGlynn, joined Henry George and took a prominent part in the campaign. It was not a pleasant sight for Tammany Hall to see Irish workmen inside an independent labor party. The chairman of its committee on resolutions, therefore, wrote Thomas S. Preston, vicar-general of the Catholic church, and inquired as to the position of the Catholic clergy toward Henry George. The answer came that they were opposed to his views. Samuel Gompers states in his autobiography that "the Catholic church was fundamentally opposed to the Henry George movement." The politicians of Tammany Hall used the religious issue to the utmost to divide the ranks of the Irish workers. Tolerant Tammany Hall apparently does not hesitate to use the religious question when it serves its purposes.

§

Not even Samuel Gompers could stay out of this fight, for, as he said many years later, while "political action had no appeal for me . . . I appreciated the movement as a demonstration of protest." As a matter of fact he was thicker in independent politics than he cared to admit forty years afterward. As secretary of the committee which was in charge of the torchlight demonstration and parade on the Saturday night before election, he appealed to the workers to support "the new party of equal rights, social reform, true republicanism and universal democracy." He said the workers and the common people would be benefitted because they would have suburban homes, freedom from the landlord, cheaper prices for fuel and for all articles of consumption. Even Terrence V. Powderly, the head of the Knights of Labor when it was in its zenith and who later "sold out" to Mark Hanna in 1896, came to New York to get on the "band wagon." Not a few labor leaders deserted in the heat of the battle.

The unions contributed generously, and the rank and file assessed itself. Hundreds of street meetings were held, and a daily paper called the *Leader* was started, largely through the aid of the German trade unionists and socialists. A newspaper debate between Hewitt and George was one feature of the campaign. On election day there was intense excitement, and the old party politicians and their henchmen left nothing undone to beat George. Gompers, who knew a lot about Tammany and told only a bit, wrote: "In those halcyon days of the big Fourteenth Street organization, there were methods that effectively secured for preferred candidates necessary votes," a polite way of saying that they stopped at nothing to win an election. Hewitt was given 90,456, Roosevelt 60,474 and George 67,930.

John Swinton, immediately after the election, declared the result a great victory:

The New Political Forces, largely made up of raw recruits, struck a blow truly astounding, under the circumstances. They were confronted by the huge machines of both old parties—by the monopolies that shadow the city—by Wall Street and all that the term implies, by the press that enters into every mind, by the City, State and National governments, with all their retainers, by hundreds of hostile pulpits, by the criminal classes, by the garrison of police who play a strong hand in politics, by the gangs of "heelers" who vote for money, and by the organized army of liquor dealers and their hired hands.

Only he who has been up against some of these influences can fully realize that Swinton was not far wrong. The Henry George campaign "was by all odds the most formidable demonstration yet made by the forces of organized labor in the United States."

But it was only a demonstration. The movement did not contain elements of cohesion and growth. The component parts were mechanically, not organically, united. After the election these separate and centrifugal groups made themselves felt, and tore the United Labor Party to pieces. The first battle took place between the single taxers and the socialists. The latter were organized in the Socialist Labor Party, had a German daily and weekly newspaper, and were an important factor in the Central Labor Union. The former had Henry George, the standard bearer of the party with all his prestige, Louis F. Post, an able organizer and a confirmed single taxer, in control of the *Leader,* Father McGlynn with his Irish following, many of the intellectuals, and the support of the non-German trade unionists—the majority.

§

When Henry George stipulated that he required at least 30,000 signatures before he would accept the nomination, the socialists through their national organ, *Der Sozialist,* complained that "we are creating a Henry George party and that is not a labor party." A little later, they said: "We cannot warm up to a Henry George party without a platform." But as the campaign went on and revealed its class character, the paper wrote: "Henry George is no socialist. His program is not socialistic. But Henry George stands for socialistic demands and if his program were carried out, it would be an advantage for the workers and a heavy blow for capitalism." In the issue of October 23, 1886, it went so far as to say that the campaign emphasized the class struggle in the greatest city of the nation, and that while George was only demanding the abolition of private property in land, "he will be driven to demand the abolition of the wage system." On October 30 the party editor could not contain himself with joy that he and his comrades were actually witnessing the beginning of The Day:

A born American, Henry George, takes up our standard. . . . We are living through a period of revolution in New York City.

In the same number which declared the campaign "a period of revolution," the English daily, the *Leader,* was credited with a circulation of 100,000. It was printed by the New York *Volkszeitung,* although owned by an independent Leader Publishing Association. The hint was given that inasmuch as stock of the association sold for $5 to individuals and $100 to labor organizations, it would be wise for members of the Socialist Labor Party to enter their subscriptions. Editorially the *Leader* represented Henry George's land theory. The socialist organ felt that "its narrow limits must obviously broaden out after the election." And in January the *Leader* fell under socialist control. In place of Louis F. Post, the socialists made Sergius E. Schevitsch, one of the outstanding figures of the New York socialist movement, editor. Henry George countered this move by establishing his own weekly, *The Standard,* devoted to the principles of single tax and later to free trade.

On November 6, 1886, in the first issue after the election, *Der Sozialist* carried a leading article on "the difference between Karl Marx and Henry George." The fight was on. It first took a theoretical turn. But young men like Hugo Vogt, while they enjoyed theory not a little, wanted to see some action too. At a meeting of Section New York of the party on April 24, Vogt moved to have an agitation committee organized in each assembly district to push socialistic principles.

On May 5, 1887, the New York County Committee of the United Labor Party met and read the call for the state convention to be held on August 17 in Syracuse, to nominate a state ticket and adopt a platform. The leading socialists attacked the wording of the call; to them it embodied nothing but Henry George's pet land theory. It did not attack the capitalist. The call put labor and capital together as needing relief from taxation. John McMackin, chairman of the party, accused the socialists of sowing the seed of discord with their abstract theories; he did not seemingly see that he and his party had endorsed another abstract theory, that of single tax. At this meeting Schevitsch just barely secured a vote of confidence in the *Leader,* after McMackin and others assailed it for its opposition to George's theories.

On May 21, 1887, all the sections of the Socialist Labor Party gathered at a special meeting to discuss the relations of the party to the United Labor Party. Alexander Jonas, editor of the *Volkszeitung,* was one of the chief speakers. The meeting resolved to bring forward the socialist position of class struggle and push it with might and main in the United Labor Party, and to prevent any state platform from being adopted which was not in accordance with socialist tenets. Vogt soon afterwards followed this up by getting the tenth assembly district organization of the United Labor Party to adopt a resolution condemning the watering down of the call for the state convention and demanding that emphasis be put on the class struggle. This branch sent the resolution to other district organizations of the United Labor Party for endorsement.

Election of delegates to the Syracuse convention was now under way. In the storm center, the tenth district, August Mayer, chairman of the meeting of July 13, ruled that members of the Socialist Labor Party could not belong to the United Labor Party and therefore could

not be elected delegates to the state convention. The
question raised—a staggering blow to the socialists who
had so far been on the inside throughout the history of
the United Labor Party—was taken to the New York
County Committee meeting of August 4, and McMackin
decided that Mayer was right, and the committee sustained
him. The constitution of the United Labor Party read
that no person "shall be eligible to membership . . . unless . . . he has severed all connections with all other
political parties, organizations, and clubs." And so, although members of the Socialist Labor Party had
cooperated in drafting this constitution, and no one had
dreamed that it would be used against them, it became the
technical ground on which they were ousted. There followed active manoeuvring for control of the Syracuse
state convention. But the socialists were beaten from the
start. The majority of those behind the labor party
movement were under the influence of George, McGlynn,
and the more conservative unionists. The best the socialists could do was to send twenty-six delegates, among
them the contested delegations from three assembly districts.

§

   At the Syracuse convention the line-up was shown by
the vote for chairman. Louis F. Post, the right hand
man of George, was elected by 91 against 61 votes. His
opponent was Frank J. Farrell, the colored machinist
whom the New York delegates to the Richmond convention of the Knights of Labor nobly backed up to the hilt
against southern prejudice. Schevitsch made the principal
speech against expulsion of the socialists. He argued
that it was the socialist workingmen who had started the
ball rolling for independent political action. It was true,
he said, that "there were socialistic writers who criticised
Mr. George's theories, but the very life of a great idea
is discussion and criticism." He pleaded with the delegates not to give way to prejudice against foreigners in

the labor movement. They were devoted to the cause. The convention upheld, as expected, the New York committee's ruling, and refused to seat the contesting socialist delegates. The vote was 94 to 54.

The socialists returned to New York and called together the radical unions and proceeded at once to organize a dual political organization which they called the Progressive Labor Party. They wrote a socialistic platform and nominated candidates for state office. They admitted later that they launched it in a spirit of revenge, and that it was from the beginning but a duplicate of the already existing Socialist Labor Party. They discarded it after the election. George threw them a little bouquet in *The Standard* :

> It is a pity that they have laid aside their true name, the Socialist Labor Party, and have decided to call themselves the Progressive Labor Party. It is doubtful if by any other name they will smell more sweet. . . . They have also greatly crippled freedom of speech among themselves by determining to conduct their discussions in the English language.

After the socialists were expelled the Syracuse convention adopted a platform along the lines of Henry George's theory and nominated the author of it for the leading office, secretary of state. The declaration of principles expressed the single taxers' position. Its preamble read as follows :

> We do not aim at securing any forced equality in the distribution of wealth. We do not propose that the state shall attempt to control production, conduct distribution, or any wise interfere with the freedom of the individual to use his labor or capital in any way that may seem proper to him. . . . Nor do we propose that the state shall take possession of land and either work it or rent it out. . . . What we propose is not the disturbing of any man in his holding or title, but by abolishing all taxes on industry or its products, to leave to the producer the full fruit of his exertion and by the taxation of land values, exclusive of improvements, to devote to the common use and benefit those values, which arising not from the exertion of the individual, but from the growth of society, belong justly to the community as a whole. This increased taxation of land, not according to its

area, but according to its value, must, while relieving the working farmer and small homestead owner of the undue burdens now imposed upon them, make it unprofitable to hold land for speculation, and thus throw abundant opportunities for the employment of labor and the building of homes.

The platform included planks for municipal ownership of water works, lighting and heating plants; that the government alone issue money; government ownership of railroads and postal telegraphs; reduction of the hours of labor; no child labor; no convict labor in competition with free labor; sanitary inspection of buildings, factories, and mines; abolition of conspiracy laws; and the Australian ballot.

The delegates as usual were enthusiastic. They made claims freely that the state vote would run up to 250,000, of which 100,000 would come from New York City. They did not appreciate to the full the actual situation. In the first place, the labor upheaval had subsided considerably between 1886 and 1887. The unions were weaker and the Central Labor Union had been split wide open after the formation of the Progressive Labor Party. Immediately after the launching of the latter on Sept. 8, the Central Labor Union meeting on the 11th voted, amid a riotous scene, to repudiate it and to support the United Labor Party. The Knights of Labor was also losing its appeal. As a result, labor was on the decline and divided. When the socialists were put out, the labor party lost one of its most energetic, devoted, and honest groups. They meant far more than the 3,000 votes the Progressive Labor Party polled in the city or the 5,000 in the state.

On the eve of the state election Patrick Ford, in his paper the *Irish World*, attacked the George party, which he had so warmly supported a year before. The Irish voters were drifting back to Tammany Hall. Edward McGlynn, the Catholic leader, who was chairman and treasurer of the state executive committee and the head of the Anti-Poverty Society, was now an ex-communi-

cated priest. His fight with the church augured no good
for the party. According to Archbishop Corrigan, as
early as 1882 and 1883 McGlynn had been called to account by the cardinal prefect of propaganda for speeches
reported in the *Irish World*. On August 23, 1886, "Doc-
tor McGlynn was gently reminded after having resumed
the practice of speaking in political gatherings. . . . Dr.
McGlynn never withdrew the main statement that private
ownership of land is unjust." On December 4, 1886, he
was ordered to Rome. He refused to go. In July, 1887,
he was ex-communicated. The Irish workers held meetings of protest and after McGlynn was expelled from
the pastorate of St. Stephen's, they organized the Anti-
Poverty Society on March 26, 1887. A monster parade
was held to protest the action of the church, and the
society acted as a medium through which McGlynn
preached single tax to thousands.

§

The presidential election of 1888 and the divisions it
raised among the remaining adherents of the United
Labor Party gave the finishing blow to the movement. At
a private conference of some of the leaders, George,
McGlynn, Post, W. T. Creasdale, McMackin, J. W. Sulli-
van, and Gaybert Barnes, held immediately after the state
election in November, 1887, a discussion of the presidential situation took place. One group wanted to go ahead
and call a national convention and put up a vigorous campaign on the principles of the Syracuse platform. Gaybert Barnes was national secretary and had, since January, 1887, organized and cooperated with local groups and
labor parties throughout the country. But the decline in
the vote in the election of November, 1887, and the divisions among the farmers, laborites, and reformers in the
nation, were not encouraging signs. Henry George himself
was veering over to the Democratic Party and Cleveland's
candidacy. He wanted to take part in the campaign as a
free trader and show the absurdity of all tariffs. Gaybert

Barnes, on the other hand, secured the adoption of a resolution by the New York county committee which put the organization on record as "not to be diverted by an issue of tariff tinkering, from exclusive and unswerving support of the fundamental reforms set forth in the Syracuse platform." Brooklyn went further and repudiated Henry George. The latter replied that a national movement would "land the United Labor Party in the same ignominious death trap into which Butler led the Greenback-Labor Party." He accused McGlynn, Barnes, and the rest as wanting "a party on any terms and at any cost, because their connection with it, even if it be a little, wee bit of a party, may give them position and influence that they would not have without it."

The result of this division was that the Anti-Poverty Society was disrupted and destroyed. A majority of the executive committee of the society were against McGlynn and for George. But inasmuch as McGlynn, under the constitution, had sole power of appointing the members of the executive, he dismissed those who were opposed to him and selected others obedient to his will. In February, 1888, George announced his withdrawal from the United Labor Party and the Anti-Poverty Society, and with him went the original single tax element. The McGlynn group, however, also espoused the single tax theory. George claimed that McGlynn was dominated by a spirit of revenge "towards the 'ecclesiastical machine,' which he seems to think is identified in our cities with the Democratic Party."

A national convention was accordingly held in May, 1888, at Cincinnati, at the same time when another and larger group of farmers and laborites was also meeting to launch a national party. There were eighty-six delegates present at the McGlynn-Barnes convention, forty-one from New York, twenty-five from Ohio, five each from Kentucky and Michigan, and a scattering smaller number from seven other states. The name United Labor Party was adopted and the platform called for absolute free trade and a single tax on land values. McGlynn acted as go-between in negotiations with the group which later named itself the Union Labor Party, but arrived at no agreement. The single tax doctrine and McGlynn's dogmatic manner were largely responsible. The United Labor Party nominated Robert H. Cowdrey of Illinois for president, and W. H. T. Wakefield of Kansas for vice-president. Cowdrey received the enormous total of 1,721 votes in New York and Brooklyn.

Meanwhile, another faction in the metropolis used the name of the United Labor Party to float the candidacy of James J. Coogan for mayor of New York City on a sea of good greenbacks. Coogan was friendly to labor, was a leading merchant, and naively figured or was sold the idea that he could get George's vote of 1886, plus the additional number needed for election, if he spent enough money in a political world where all things were purchasable. The *News* of New York under date of November 7, after noting that Coogan had gotten less than 9,000 votes, remarked: "In the eighth election district of the seventh assembly district, although Colonel Coogan had five men to work around the polls, he didn't get a single vote." Gompers added: "I was fairly reliably informed that Coogan spent over two hundred thousand dollars in that campaign." The republicans won the national contest in 1888 and McMackin was given a job in the Custom House. Some years afterward, James P. Archibald was appointed turnkey at the Ludlow Street jail. He was secretary of the United Labor Party at one stage of its career. McGlynn afterwards rejoined the Catholic church.

The campaigns of 1886, 1887, and the wind up in 1888 in New York City have been dealt with in such great detail because they illustrate the difficulties involved in independent labor politics. A campaign in the metropolis may be expected to have this complex character and its own peculiar quality. But New York City is not the United States. Chicago in 1886 was more representative of the big cities of the country as a whole. There were significant campaigns of labor in the Windy City in 1886 and 1887, characteristic of the movement outside of New York.

§

Contrary to the oft-expressed easy generalization that the Haymarket bomb destroyed the Chicago labor movement, the fact is that despite police repression, newspaper incitement to hysteria, and organization of the possessing classes, which followed the throwing of the bomb on May 4, the Chicago wage earners only united their forces and stiffened their resistance. The conservative and radical central bodies—there were two of the trade unions and two also of the Knights of Labor—the socialists and the anarchists, the single taxers and the reformers, the native born and English-speaking workers and the foreign born Germans, Bohemians, and Scandinavians, all got together for the first time on the political field in the summer following the Haymarket affair. Chicago was the banner city of the general strike for eight-hours in May, 1886, with over 80,000 on the streets in the first four days. Thereafter the Knights of Labor doubled its membership, reaching 40,000 in the fall of 1886. On Labor Day the number of Chicago workers in parade led the country. Moreover, in this city the leaders of the labor movement were not intellectuals as in New York, but members of trade unions and labor assemblies.

The labor party in 1886 was one answer—as it always has been—of an awakened and powerful trade union movement, led by militant men. In 1918 and 1919, after the Chicago Federation of Labor went ahead and organized packing-house and steel workers at home to make this country safe for democracy, the federation took the next step and launched the Cook County Labor Party. The same men who backed up the union organization campaigns, John Fitzpatrick and Edward Nockels, president and secretary of the city central body, were responsible for the labor party. And William Z. Foster, who was enabled to use his brains because he closely cooperated with these men at that time, wore a delegate's badge in the labor party convention. Then we had, as in 1886, a *bona fide* and a real united front, on the economic and political fields.

The Chicago labor party of 1886 was constituted in the same way as the Cook County Labor Party of 1919. Both were made up of delegates from the trade unions. The first conference met on August 21, 1886, but had to adjourn to the 23rd, to get rid of the influence of labor leaders wedded to the old parties. On September 27 the United Labor Party nominated a state and county ticket, with Frank Stauber, a socialist and ex-alderman, for county treasurer. The preamble to the platform pointed to the "power of aggregated wealth" over the old parties, and declared that the "time has come to drive the political go-between from our ranks. . . . It is impossible for a trade unionist or a Knight of Labor to be an active political worker in the Republican or Democratic Parties and remain an honest man in the ranks of labor." A national, state, and local platform was adopted. Demands were made for an eight-hour day for all government employees and for the employees of corporations given special privileges, government ownership of all means of communication, an anti-contract labor law, a national monetary system, tax reform, forfeiture of all unearned land grants, restrictions upon the ownership of land, the reservation of all public lands to actual settlers, abolition of private police, weekly payment of wages, an employers' liability law, state insurance, and the abolition of contract convict labor.

The result of the first campaign bore out John Swinton's statement that "the labor vote has been the heaviest in those cities where the despotism of judges, politicians, and the police was the severest." Stauber received 24,845 votes out of a total of 92,493. The labor party elected one state senator and sent six to the lower house, but

failed to elect a congressman by only 64 votes. Five of
the six judges—running on old party tickets—whom the
laborites endorsed, in part because they did not have
trained men to fill those positions and in part because the
life of the labor movement was at stake, were also elected.

Preparations followed for the spring election. The old
parties put up only one candidate for mayor. They were
genuinely concerned. The United Labor Party nominated
Robert Nelson, a molder by trade and master workman
of District Assembly 24 of the Knights of Labor. In this
election the opposition was determined to beat the "red-
flag communists." Police superintendent Ebersold personally instructed the police to vote against the labor party
candidates. Despite this kind of attack Nelson rolled up
25,410 votes against 51,491 for the democratic-republican
candidate. This marked the high-water point of the party.
William Gleason, a member of the executive committee,
bought off by a clerkship in the election commissioners'
office, in collusion with the democrats started a party
which he called the United Labor Party, and incorporated
it, too! In the fall of 1887 his party, popularly known
as the Free Lunch Party, endorsed the democratic candidates. The Radical Labor Party—the name adopted because of Gleason's act—received about 7,000 votes in November, 1887. In the national election of 1888 the
Chicago movement supported the Union Labor Party
candidate for president and gave him 2,180 votes. The
trade unions and local assemblies were now on the decline; the workers had shown that they could make a
powerful protest, but that they were not yet able to build
a permanent and growing independent political movement.

In Milwaukee, where the eight-hour strike in May,
1886, led to bloodshed, the labor party elected a congressman and carried the city in 1886 and 1887. Of the cities
where labor tickets were put up from coast to coast in
the spring of 1887, Cincinnati was lost by only a few
hundred votes, while about twenty smaller communities
were won.

CHAPTER III

GRANGERS, GREENBACKERS, AND POPULISTS

DURING and immediately after the Civil War the farmers of the North enjoyed unusually prosperous times; indeed, those were their halcyon days. There were also some prosperous periods for them interspersed during the seventies, eighties, and nineties, but the western tillers of the soil knew what adversity meant in those decades. The agriculturists of the South were bankrupt after the war. They did not recover rapidly. They suffered far worse than even the western farmers. The granger, greenback, and populist movements represented the efforts of the agricultural producers of the West and the South to find a solution for their ills.

§

When one of the leading grangers, James Dabney McCabe, wrote his *History of the Grange Movement,* he described it as the farmers' war against monopolies: being a full and authentic account of the struggle of the American farmers against the extortions of the railroad companies. Before the Civil War the farmers demanded the building of railroads. Illinois was the center of the granger uprising. It was this state which first secured from Congress on September 20, 1850, a grant of six sections of land per mile of track to be given to the Illinois Central Railroad. The farmers not only petitioned Congress to give away land, but they themselves subscribed for stock, mortgaging their farms to do so. The municipalities, counties, and states also subscribed and raised money by issuing bonds. The deflation after the war and the methods of the Frankenstein which they had in part created, however, turned the farmers from friends into bitter foes of the transportation companies.

At a time when prices were going down the farmers wanted lower freight rates. McCabe claimed: "The farmers find that to get the product of one acre of corn to market they must pay the railroad the product of three acres; the cost of transportation to the East eats up about one-half of the value of the wheat." The railroads could not or would not meet their demands. The farmers took the matter into the state legislatures. Solon J. Buck, who made a thorough study of the granger movement, remarked: "The contest between the railroads and the farmers was intense while it lasted. The farmers had votes; the railroads had money; and the legislators were sometimes between the devil and the deep blue sea in the fear of offending one side or the other."

The railroad corporations were among the first very powerful aggregations of wealth in this country. They were accused of debauching and demoralizing courts and legislatures. The New York *Herald*—at a time when the Union Pacific was looted and the bribery of congressmen by the Credit Mobilier came to light—editorialized:

The corruptions which have grown up in the national government, from the general demoralizations of our late Civil War, are fearful to contemplate. One hundred millions a year lost to the Treasury from the spoliations of the whiskey rings "beats out of sight" anything in the line of whiskey frauds under any other government on the face of the globe; but on a corresponding scale with their field of operations, the Indian rings, the Post Office and Interior Department rings. . . . The latest developments, however, show, that in the grandeur and number of their schemes of spoils and plunder, the congressional rings of railroad jobbers throw into the shade all the other rings.

The farmers had seen their railroad stock decreased or wiped out in value. And they had to pay taxes to meet the bonds which their communities had issued to help the roadroads. They observed that the public lands—a veritable empire—which the railroads had received, were held for speculative purposes. They felt that as they and the government had helped to pay for the railroads, the latter ought to be run in part at least for their benefit. They demanded, therefore, that the governments of the states step in, fix fair rates, and correct the abuses.

§

The granger movement, as an independent political force, developed in California, Illinois, Indiana, Iowa, Kansas, Michigan, Minnesota, Missouri, Nebraska, Oregon, and Wisconsin. The Illinois farmers embodied the leading demand of the granger parties in their platform:

We will agree to no truce and will submit to no compromise short of the complete vindication and reestablishment of the supremacy of the state government in its rights, through its legislature, to supervise and control the railroads of the state, in such manner as the public interest shall demand.

The Illinois state constitution, adopted in 1870, declared that the "General Assembly shall, from time to time, pass laws establishing reasonable maximum rates of charges for the transportation of passengers and freight on the different railroads in this state." The legislature accordingly passed a law in 1871 which provided for the appointment by the governor of a Board of Warehouse and Railroad Commissioners to fix maximum fares and freight rates. The board set a passenger rate of three cents a mile. The Illinois Central Railroad refused to abide by this ruling and instructed its conductors to put off passengers by force if need be if they insisted on paying on the basis of the three-cent rate. Three-cent clubs were, therefore, organized and their members travelled en masse to prevent intimidation. There were some lively encounters.

In 1873 Chief Justice Lawrence of the state supreme court declared the act of 1871 unconstitutional. He held that this law prevented all discriminations, not merely unjust ones. The legislature passed a new law to go into effect July 1, 1873, the same year. Meanwhile, the June judicial elections were drawing near, and Judge Lawrence was up for reelection. The farmers of Illinois took to the political arena, and nominated independent candidates in the counties. They succeeded in defeating the chief justice. In sixty-six counties where they did not unite or fuse with either of the two old parties they received 94,188 votes out of a total of 176,263.

The Illinois State Farmers' Association held its first annual convention at Decatur on December 17, 1873, with delegates from every county of the state except three. The organization adopted a platform which expressed the demands of the grangers in Illinois and elsewhere. It included the following planks:

Unconditional repeal of the salary-grab law by which the Illinois legislators had increased their own salaries; opposition to the tariff on clothing, lumber, salt, iron and steel; no more grants of public lands or loans of public credit, or national, state or local subscriptions, in aid of corporations; a legal tender currency to be issued direct from the Treasury and interchangeable for government bonds bearing the lowest possible rate of interest; patent laws serving monopolists to be revised and restricted; railroad legislation of the state to be enforced until tested in the courts, with no congressional interference with the control of the railroads by the states; no free passes to be given any public official; all public expenditures and taxes to be reduced; improvement of the navigation of lakes and rivers; and manufacturers of plows to be boycotted until they consent to sell direct at wholesale rates.

The platform of the Indiana grangers declared war on the following classes of monopolies:

1. Banking and moneyed monopolies, by which, through ruinous rates of interest, the products of human labor are concentrated in the hands of non-producers. This is the great central source of these wrongs, in and through which all other monopolies exist and operate.

2. Consolidated railroads and other transit monopolies, whereby all industries are taxed to the last mill they will bear, for the benefit of the stockholders and stock-jobbers.

3. Manufacturing monopolies, whereby all small operators are crushed out, and the price of labor and its products are determined with mathematical certainty in the interest of the capitalists.

4. Land monopolies, by which the public domain is absorbed by a few corporations and speculators.

5. Commercial and grain monopolies, speculating and enriching the bloated corporations on human necessities.

A northwestern farmers' convention was held in Chicago, October 22, 1873, with delegates mainly from Illinois, Indiana, Iowa, Michigan, New York, and Wisconsin. This conference adopted a program embodying the national demands of the grangers:

1. Congress should pass a law fixing maximum freight and passenger rates between the states, and should grant no subsidies to any private corporation.
2. The government should build railroad lines to compete with and effectively regulate the private railroad companies.
3. Home manufactures should be promoted in order to lessen the necessity for and to cut the costs of transportation.
4. "Debt should ever be held as one of our greatest enemies."
5. One industry should not be protected at the expense of the other.

§

The states where the grangers were most active were predominantly republican, with the exception of Missouri. The Democratic Party had suffered in prestige after the war, it was regarded as anti-Union and pro-slavery. Not in all but in a number of the states—where they were weak—the democrats were glad to fuse with the independents. In Missouri the republicans got together with the farmers.

The new parties were called Anti-Monopoly, Reform, Independent, and Independent Reform. They scored some signal successes in 1873 and 1874 and were responsible for the selection of independents as United States Senators by three state legislatures. In Wisconsin the Reform Party elected the governor and captured the lower house in 1873, and sent three congressmen to Washington in 1874. The Illinois Independent Reform Party also secured three members of Congress in the latter year. The Minnesota Anti-Monopoly Party elected a state treasurer in 1873. The Iowa party, in fusion with the democrats, carried a congressional district the following year. In several of the state legislatures the farmers' parties held the balance of power, or in fusion with the democrats, controlled them. In California, where the railroad interests dominated the politics of the state, the anti-monopolists in 1873 elected forty-one members to the lower house.

Despite these successes, however, the granger movement did not get very far. The railroad companies discouraged the farmers by making a dead letter of the state legislation against them. According to Solon J. Buck, "in all the states but Illinois the granger laws were repealed before they had been given a fair trial." In Wisconsin, where the independent political party was the strongest, the railroads gave poorer service and broke up popular support behind the Potter law. They intimidated shippers and farmers and compelled them to seek the repeal of their own legislation.

The grangers drew to their support the workers in the smaller towns. The Anti-Monopoly Party in Iowa was also known as the Farmers' and Laboring Men's Party. The preamble of the Illinois Independent Reform Party read that "the farmers, mechanics and other citizens of Illinois" had decided to take independent action "in behalf of the producing, industrial and other business classes and in opposition to corporate monopolies." The platform of the Minnesota Anti-Monopoly Party expressed opposition to a monopoly of wood and coal by rings in great cities and demanded reasonable limitation of hours in shops and factories. McCabe appealed to the workers of the East to "join hands with the farmers of the West in their courageous war upon monopolies of all kinds." He declared that the anthracite coal beds of Pennsylvania were monopolized by the railroad companies and he suggested a government railroad from Chicago to New York to bring bituminous coal at a reduced price to the eastern consumer. The financial planks of the grangers also fitted in with the greenback philosophy of the labor leaders who had led and survived the death of the National

Labor Union. The greenbackers, anti-monopolists, grangers, and opposition elements generally were now ripe for a national organization in preparation for the presidential campaign of 1876.

§

A national independent party was accordingly formed at a conference in November, 1874, with James Buchanan of Indiana, an aspirant for the presidential nomination, in the chair. A national committee chosen at this Indianapolis meeting included Robert Schilling of Milwaukee, R. F. Trevellick of Detroit, and Andrew C. Cameron of Chicago, all greenback-labor men. A second convention was held in March, 1875, at Cleveland. Some anti-monopolists organized their own conference in Philadelphia and still other greenbackers got together in Detroit. The upshot of all the meetings and negotiations between the groups was that on May 17, 1876 a nominating convention was held with about 240 delegates from eighteen states. Ignatius Donnelly and Thomas J. Durant were temporary and permanent chairmen. Peter Cooper, the New York philanthropist, was nominated for president, and Newton Booth of California for vice-president. When the latter declined, the national committee put Samuel F. Cary in his place.

About two weeks after he was nominated the presidential candidate declared that "there is a bare possibility that the sorely needed relief from the blighting effects of unwise legislation relative to finance . . . may yet be had through either the Republican or Democratic Party." He was a very old man, and could not make an aggressive campaign. Ex-Congressman Cary was the author of the "Ohio Idea," to pay the national debt in greenbacks. He was highly regarded by trade unionists because of his favorable labor record.

The platform on which these two men ran ascribed the economic depression to a "serious mismanagement of the national finances." It called for the "immediate and unconditional repeal of the specie resumption act of January 14, 1875;" that "United States notes be issued by the government, and convertible on demand into United States obligations, bearing a low rate of interest not exceeding one cent a day on each one hundred dollars, and re-exchangeable for United States notes at par." It protested "any further issue of gold bonds for sale in foreign markets," and "the sale of government bonds for the purpose of purchasing silver." The national executive selected Marcus M. Pomeroy, familiarly known as "Brick" Pomeroy, as chairman of the special committee to organize greenback clubs. In two years he is said to have chartered about 4,000 of them.

The presidential contest of 1876 was a close race. The democrats secured a larger popular vote, but the republican Hayes was declared elected by a political manoeuvre in which the partisanship of so-called impartial judges played a decisive role. And as is usual in American politics, the presidential battle between the giants swallowed up all interest, to the detriment of minority parties and their candidates. The farmers had not yet been won over to the program of the financial reformers. Their fight with the railroads had largely subsided. Cooper's candidacy did not take hold at all in the industrial states. He polled 81,737 votes over against 8,317,560 for the republican and democratic candidates. What support he got came from the agricultural states in the Middle West, the heart of the anti-railroad and anti-monopoly fight:

Arkansas	289	Minnesota	2,311
California	44	Missouri	3,498
Connecticut	774	Nebraska	2,320
Illinois	17,233	New Hampshire	76
Indiana	9,533	New Jersey	712
Iowa	9,001	New York	1,987
Kansas	7,776	Ohio	3,057
Kentucky	1,944	Oregon	510
Maine	663	Pennsylvania	7,187
Maryland	33	Rhode Island	68
Massachusetts	779	West Virginia	1,373
Michigan	9,060	Wisconsin	1,509

The granger movement had come and gone, Peter Cooper's campaign gave little hope for the future, and the country was absorbed in the aftermath of the Hayes-Tilden contest. But economic forces, like subterranean rivers, continued their unseen, silent, and uninterrupted course. The depression, instead of giving way to a revival, lasted until 1879, with unemployment and cuts in wages for the workers and falling prices for the farmers. It precipitated the railroad strikes and general labor revolt of 1877. The greenbackers, who were a disorganized political group after the election of 1876, found themselves two years later with over 1,000,000 votes and fourteen congressmen. They now had the hearty support of the workers and the farmers. The laborers demanded a plentiful supply of paper money in order to reduce the rate of interest and set the wheels of industry going. The farmers demanded more money to raise the prices of farm products and to enable them to pay back their obligations with less goods. The greenbackers wanted the government to issue paper money, greenbacks, in abundance. The populists who came later, in the nineties, demanded an increase in the monetary supply through the free coinage of silver.

In the off-year of 1877 the greenbackers and laborites nominated in about a dozen states. They received the following vote in the nine where they made any kind of a showing:

Connecticut	4,000	New York	20,282
Iowa	34,228	Ohio	29,401
Kansas	9,880		
Maine	5,266	Pennsylvania	52,854
New Jersey	5,058	Wisconsin	26,216

The labor reformers of New York met in convention in Troy on October 9, 1877, and nominated a leading cigar maker, John J. Junio, for secretary of state. The greenbackers reached no agreement with the trade unionists and nominated separately. They received 997 votes against 20,282 for Junio. In Pennsylvania the United Labor Party combined with the Greenback Party and the joint ticket ran up 52,854 votes out of a total of about 550,000. In Ohio the workers split, one faction going along with the greenbackers, the other acting independently. In these industrial states, as well as in the others where the independents polled a good vote, the recent labor disturbances were a determining factor and the localities where they took place contributed heavily to its size. The New Jersey platform declared that the cause of the railroad strikes could "be removed by the inauguration of a financial policy which will give money to productive industry, and full employment, at good wages, to labor, instead of an increase of the army." In the agricultural states of Iowa, Kansas, and Wisconsin the platforms were out-and-out greenbackers' documents.

The crest of the greenback-labor wave came in 1878. Now for the first time did any independent party make a dent in the southern states, to be repeated on a much larger scale by the populists. The industrial and agricultural areas contributed equally to a national sweep. The central executive committee of the National Party claimed 1,260,000 votes but *Appleton's Annual Cyclopedia* lists only about a million:

Alabama	6,675	Mississippi	1,500
Arkansas	4,416	Missouri	70,000
California	39,000	Nebraska	21,100
Colorado	1,200	New Hampshire	6,385
Connecticut	9,059	New Jersey	22,000
Delaware	3,208	New York	80,000
Florida	590	North Carolina	2,500
Georgia	15,181	Ohio	33,332
Illinois	45,000	Oregon	2,100
Indiana	39,415	Pennsylvania	96,659
Iowa	123,517	Rhode Island	990
Kansas	28,000	South Carolina	650
Kentucky	2,500	Tennessee	6,000
Louisiana	7,000	Texas	15,000
Maine	43,200	Vermont	7,983
Maryland	8,883	Virginia	12,250
Massachusetts	110,000	West Virginia	11,312
Michigan	73,000	Wisconsin	30,000
Minnesota	22,600		

Knights of Labor men were especially active in Pennsylvania, where they were fairly well organized. In the spring of 1878 they elected Terrence V. Powderly mayor of Scranton. The heavy vote in Maine, about one-third of that cast, swept Thompson Murch, secretary of the granite cutters' union, into Congress. Fusion with the democrats sent James B. Weaver to Washington from Iowa, where the greenbackers polled their highest vote in the country in 1878. The same combination failed, however, to elect Benjamin F. Butler governor of Massachusetts, although it gave him 110,000 votes.

The extraordinary unemployment, the presence of the Chinese, land monopoly, unequal taxation, and the agitation of Dennis Kearney were responsible for the good showing in California. Kearney, from his forum on the vacant sand lots in front of the City Hall in San Francisco, crystallized the unrest of the workers around an attack on Chinese labor. He stirred up enough interest to compel the state legislature to pass a special law, in an attempt to gag him or "any person who, in the presence or hearing of twenty-five or more persons, shall utter any language with intent either to incite a riot . . . or who shall suggest . . . any act or acts of criminal violence." He so frightened the powers that be that the militia was prepared on several occasions to go into action, and a committee of safety was organized. His harangues, parades, and demonstrations kept the city in turmoil and on edge.

The Workingmen's Party which Kearney helped to organize held a secret state convention on January 19, 1878, and adopted a platform with a few unique proposals. One of these was that malfeasance in office was to be punished by imprisonment for life, without the possibility of pardon. The party demanded the abolition of Chinese labor, the restriction of land holdings to 640 acres, no prison contract labor, day labor only on public works at current rates of pay and on an eight-hour basis, and equal taxation. In August, 1882, Congress passed a law prohibiting Chinese immigration for ten years. However flighty and irresponsible Kearney may have been, he helped to center attention on the Chinese problem, he stood for national unity with the greenback-labor men, and he emphasized the grievances of the workers and farmers against the railroads and land speculators in his state.

A number of the platforms of the state greenback-labor parties of 1878 included a paragraph which indicated opposition to the Socialist Labor Party, which also nominated independently in some of the industrial cities. The Indiana platform, for example, declared: "We denounce the red flag communism imported from Europe, which asks for an equal division of property, and we denounce the communism of the national banks, of the bond syndicates, and of the consolidated railroad corporations."

§

Over 800 delegates attended the spirited convention which launched the National Party in Toledo, February 22, 1878. Independent party men generally choose Washington's or Lincoln's birthdays or Independence Day as an appropriate time to emphasize their Americanism and their loyalty to the fathers. The labor men had no difficulty in obtaining the adoption of their demands: reduction of hours, government bureaus of labor, no contract prison labor, and the suppression of Chinese immigration. The platform adopted, however, was a greenbacker's bible. It accounted for the business depression as due to "legislation in the interests of, and dictated by money-lenders, bankers and bondholders, the limiting of the legal-tender quality of greenbacks, the changing of currency bonds into coin bonds, the demonetization of the silver dollar, the exempting of bonds from taxation, the contraction of the circulating medium, proposed forced resumption of specie payments, and the prodigal waste of the public lands." It offered the following six proposals:

1. It is the exclusive function of the general government to coin and create money and regulate its value. All bank issues designed to circulate as money should be suppressed. The circulating medium, whether of metal or paper, shall be issued by the government and made a full legal tender for all debts and taxes in the United States at its stamped value.

2. There shall be no privileged class of creditors. Official salaries, pensions, bonds and all other debts and obligations, public and private, shall be discharged in the legal tender money of the United States, strictly according to the stipulations of the laws under which they were contracted.

3. The coinage of silver shall be placed on the same footing as that of gold.

4. Congress shall provide said money adequate to the full employment of labor, the equitable distribution of its products, and the requirements of business, fixing a minimum amount per capita of the population as near as may be, and otherwise regulating its value by wise and equitable provisions of law, so that the rate of interest will secure to labor its just reward.

5. It is inconsistent with the genius of popular government that any species of private property should be exempt from bearing its just share of the public burdens. Government bonds and money should be taxed precisely as other property, and a graduated income tax should be levied for the support of the government and the payment of its debts.

6. The public lands should be reserved for actual settlers only and granted in limited quantities.

§

According to Orin G. Libby, the majority of the supporters of the Greenback Party among the farmers

. . . came from what may be termed the inland regions of the states, districts lacking in natural communication with the rest of the state, and but for the railroads, commercially isolated from the outside world. The counties in these regions . . . display certain well defined characteristics, which distinguish them from all others. Predominantly agricultural in occupation and having a comparative simple life, they were also poorer than the average county of their state and more heavily burdened with debt.

Clyde O. Ruggles has contrasted the economic basis of the greenback movement in Iowa and in Wisconsin, showing that in the former state the farmers raised corn and wheat almost exclusively, while in Wisconsin diversification was more pronounced. Less wheat was raised in Wisconsin in 1880 than in 1870. The Iowa producers who developed the dairy did not become greenbackers. The year of the poorest wheat yield in Iowa, 1876, saw the organization of the Greenback Party in that state, while "the years of the lowest prices and the greatest agricultural depression were also the years of the greatest strength of the Greenback Party." There was also more manufacturing in Wisconsin than in Iowa.

To sum up, the greenback counties in Iowa and Wisconsin and elsewhere represented more frontier-like conditions, the farms were more heavily mortgaged, and there was "marked concentration upon grain farming." In the agricultural regions of the older states of the East neither the greenback nor the populist movements made much headway. Here frontier conditions had been succeeded by more favorable circumstances for the declining farming population which did not specialize on a few staples.

The congressional election of 1878 occurred after the railroad labor revolt, and at a time when the prices for the farmers' products were low, in a word, when the producers were common sufferers. But when prosperity returned in 1879 and provided work for the unemployed and better prices for the farmers there was a recession from politics. In the eighties the wage earners began to join the trade unions and the local assemblies of the Knights of Labor. The farmers also started their own economic organizations. The presidential elections of 1880, 1884, and 1888, therefore, marked the decline and end of the greenback-labor agitation. As against a million votes in 1878 the independent parties polled 308,578 in 1880, 175,370 in 1884, and only 144,836 in 1888. The most marked losses occurred in the industrial areas. The vote by states for the three elections was:

State	1880	1884	1888
Alabama	4,642	873	....
Arkansas	4,079	1,847	10,613
California	3,392	2,017	....
Colorado	1,435	1,958	1,266
Connecticut	868	1,688	240
Delaware	120	....	....
Georgia	969	145	....
Illinois	26,358	10,910	7,134
Indiana	12,986	8,293	2,694
Iowa	32,701	....	9,105
Kansas	19,851	16,341	37,788
Kentucky	11,499	1,691	....
Louisiana	439	....	....
Maine	4,408	3,953	1,345
Maryland	818	531	....
Massachusetts	4,548	42,243	....
Michigan	34,895	....	4,555
Minnesota	3,267	3,583	1,097
Mississippi	5,797	....	222
Missouri	35,135	....	18,589
Nebraska	3,950	....	4,226
New Hampshire	528	552	42
New Jersey	2,617	3,496	....
New York	12,373	16,994	626
North Carolina	1,126	....	....
Ohio	6,456	5,179	3,496
Oregon	249	1,726	363
Pennsylvania	20,668	16,992	3,877
Rhode Island	236	422	....
South Carolina	566	....	....
Tennessee	5,917	3,321	....
Texas	27,405	....	29,459
Vermont	1,215	785	....
West Virginia	9,079	810	1,508
Wisconsin	7,986	4,598	8,552

§

The greenbackers held their nominating convention of
1880 in Chicago on June 9, with about 800 delegates.
They invited in forty-four delegates of the Socialist
Labor Party, who welcomed the excitement of the larger
conclave. Old Richard Trevellick was permanent chair-

man and Dennis Kearney chief sergeant at arms. Congressman and General James Baird Weaver was nominated for president. He was a splendid campaigner. He invaded the South. The democrats fought back and circulated a forged letter in an effort to prove that he was in the pay of the republicans. Despite Weaver's fighting qualities and the impetus of the vote of 1878 the returns showed that he had received only a third or less of the poll of that year. And the bulk of it came from the agricultural states. The National Party elected eight members to Congress and proved it was still a factor in some states, if a dying one.

Four years later, in 1884, the greenbackers had only about half as many delegates at their convention as in the gathering of 1880. After a hot fight they selected Benjamin F. Butler over Jesse Harper, chairman of the national committee, as candidate for president. Butler had finally been elected governor of Massachusetts in 1882. He had aspirations to become president. Despite the fact that he already was the candidate of the greenbackers and the anti-monopolists—the latter had nominated him also—he went as a delegate to the Democratic Party convention. The leaders of the latter rode rough shod cver him. Thereupon he announced, two months or more after his selection, his acceptance of the nomination. He threw himself into the campaign in earnest, however, and worked energeticaly in the industrial states. He did not increase the vote in these areas and received only half of Weaver's vote throughout the country. The party fused in a number of the states and there was considerable friction over local and state deals. The late start, Butler's politics, and the improvement in economic conditions sounded the death knell of the greenback movement.

But hope springs eternal in the third party man's breast. When labor turned to independent politics in 1886, the land, money, and transportation reformers took courage and called a conference for September 1, 1886, at Indianapolis. There was little response from the industrial centers. They called again, and they succeeded in holding a convention in Cincinnati on February 22, 1887. An unfriendly correspondent in *Der Sozialist,* the organ of the Socialist Labor Party, described the 450 delegates as members of the following groups:

(1) Greenback Party (Greenback-Democrats, Greenback-Labor); (2) Farmer Alliance; (3) Grangers; (4) Wheelers of Kansas and Arkansas; (5) Oklahoma Boomers; (6) Grand Army of the Republic; (7) Knights of Labor; (8) United Labor Party; (9) Anti-Monopoly Party; (10) Trade Unions; (11) Socialist Labor Party, national, and of Oregon; (12) Red International; (13) Industrial Union; (14) Equal Rights Party; (15) Women suffragists; (16) Temperance Union; (17) Cranks; (18) A dozen editors; (19) About fifty workers.

"Old timers" were everywhere in evidence. A. J. Streeter was chairman and Robert Schilling on the committee on resolutions. This convention adopted the name of National Union Labor Party. The remnant of the Greenback Labor Party was officially dissolved then and there. The new name hurt A. J. Streeter, the candidate for president, in the very agricultural states where he received almost all his votes, however few they were. The labor parties had gone up like skyrockets, and were now no more. The grangers, the greenbackers, the anti-monopolists, the third-party men, all were now without a home. The People's Party that soon arose was to them like a shelter sent from heaven.

§

The People's Party was born out of the economic tribulations suffered by the southern and western farmers. In his study of the populist movement in Georgia, Alexander M. Arnett describes the lien system which caught in its meshes between eighty and ninety per cent of the cotton growers, proprietors and tenants, white and black alike. Under this scheme the producer was practically dependent on the merchant. He quotes from M. B. Hammond's *The Cotton Industry*:

> When one of these mortgages has been recorded against the southern farmer, he has passed into a state of hopeless peonage to the merchant who has become his creditor. . . . He is subject to the constant oversight and direction of the merchant. Every mouthful of food that he purchases, every implement that he requires on the farm, his mules, cattle, the clothing for himself and family, the fertilizers for his land, must all be bought of the merchant who holds the crop lien.

The merchant charged from twenty to fifty per cent above cash price for what was purchased in this way. While the farmer was thus obligated to the merchant-mortgagee, the price of cotton which had been one dollar at the close of the Civil War, averaged about twelve cents in the seventies, nine cents in the eighties, and seven cents in the nineties. Loans were made by northern capitalists at a nominal rate of eight per cent but a fat commission was first deducted.

The farmer of the South and West alike suffered from a high protective tariff, which was a form of indirect taxation, raising prices for them as consumers at a time when their own produts were falling in price. The tariff also tended to curtail foreign sales of agricultural produce.

The western farmer had his special grievances. In the years 1888-1891, the farm price of wheat was 82 cents a bushel; for 1892-1895 it had declined thirty-three per cent and was 55 cents a bushel. The average aggregate farm value of wheat crops in the two periods showed a decline of thirty-one per cent: from 393 million to 249 million dollars. There had also been crop failures in many counties of the Dakotas, Kansas, Nebraska, and Texas. Between 1890 and 1895 the population of Kansas had gone down by a hundred thousand. Farm labor was slightly cheaper, but railroad rates eastward had not declined appreciably, and taxes had been maintained at the old rates or had increased. There was no income tax. Personal property was not bearing its fair share of the burden. Stocks and bonds were seldom returned. Railroads and corporations also escaped in large part. "Land bore the chief burden. If it were mortgaged, its owner received no consideration . . . he and not the creditor must pay the tax on the mortgage." There were also striking differences between the prices the farmers received for their products and the prices at which they sold in the cities.

The farmers and workers also had cause to be bitter against the railroad corporations. They observed the practices which enabled the private owners and managers of the common carriers to augment their wealth and power: rebates and discriminatory rates; interlocking directorates; excessive salaries to officials, fraud by insiders, and bankruptcies for gain; secret agreements; bribery. The laborers resented the high-handed methods of railroad officials toward them and their unions in the seventies, eighties, and nineties.

As summarized by C. F. Emerick at the time, the fall in agricultural prices

. . . made more difficult the payment of interest charges and mortgage debts, increased the number of mortgage foreclosures, prolonged the period required for tenants to rise to land ownership, caused the expense for hired labor to be a greater drain upon the resources of the farm, made the inequitable burden imposed upon the farmer by the general property tax more difficult to carry, increased the strain of maintaining a higher standard of living and rendered less endurable the tyranny of railway discriminations and the exactions of trusts. Furthermore, since the great mass of farmers, after starting in life with no other resources than an abundance of energy and a willingness to work, have attained only very modest incomes, any losses to which they have been subjected have been more keenly felt than if they had been possessed of more abundant means.

Because all prices fell steadily the debtor class had to pay with more goods the interest and principal of their mortgages and obligations which were fixed in amount. In terms of the purchasing power of the dollar, there was obviously a steady appreciation, to the decided advantage of the creditors, the holders of the obligations. The eastern and English bond holders were naturally content to let matters take their course, when "sound money" was so sound for them, in terms of providing them with ever-increasing wealth, prestige and power on both sides of the Atlantic. In fact, all the holders of stocks and bonds and their intellectual propagandists were for "sound money," because it so obviously was to their advantage.

The creditors cried "confiscation" when the debtors tried to inflate the currency so as to increase prices and cause a depreciation of the dollar, and thus pay their debts back with less goods. These same "sound" elements were perfectly willing, however, to receive between 1865 and 1896 more goods than they had loaned, in terms of an appreciating dollar. They were quite willing to see the steady fall in prices and the contraction of currency and "loss to those who were least able to lose, and gain to those who held the places of advantage for a generation." It is Arnett's opinion after a careful study of populism that "if the gold-hungry world had not soon been relieved by the discovery of new supplies of the precious metal, some kind of radical change in our currency system might have been forced upon us."

§

The People's Party rested upon the economic organizations of the tillers of the soil and the sons of toil. On February 22, 1892, there gathered in St. Louis 860 representatives from farmers' and workers' associations to give the new two-year old party a proper base. At this notable convention there were delegates from the following:

Organization	No. of Delegates
National Farmers' Alliance and Industrial Union	246
Colored Farmers' Alliance and Citizens' Union	97
Knights of Labor	82
Patrons of Industry	75
Farmers' Mutual Benefit Association	53
National Farmers' Alliance	49
National Citizens' Alliance	25

Organization	No. of Delegates
National Citizens' Industrial Alliance	25
Patrons of Husbandry	25
National Reform Press Association	25
Michigan Union Conference	25
Ancient Order of Anti-Monopolists	25
International Wire Workers	25
United Mine Workers of Ohio	25
National Alliance and Independent Union	10
Alliance Assemblies of the Industrial Union	6
Knights of Agriculture	3
Nebraska State Assembly, Knights of Labor	3
Central Labor Exchange	2
Central Labor Union of St. Louis	2
National Farmers' League of Missouri	1
District Alliance of Washington	1
Union Reform Committee	1
Citizens' Alliance, Wyoming, Minnesota	1
Trades and Labor Union, Kansas City	1
Central Labor Union of Springfield, Missouri	1
Central National Club	1

The National Farmers' Alliance and Industrial Union took an official census of its membership in July, 1890, and claimed 1,062,000 in the southern and 202,000 in the western states. This was popularly known as the southern alliance, and in contrast to some of the western farmers' organizations was at first opposed to independent political action. The other farmers' bodies claimed hundreds of thousands of members. These associations were started to purchase or to sell cooperatively, promote diversification of crops, and secure legislation by nonpartisan or independent political action, in the interest of the farmers. Their main demand became known as the sub-treasury plan. Under this scheme the government would warehouse non-perishable farm products and advance legal tender money up to eighty per cent of their market value, at one or two per cent interest. The farmers believed that through this sub-treasury plan the volume of money would become adequate and elastic enough at harvest time and the rate of interest low enough to permit of their moving their crops at a good profit.

The congressional elections of 1890 showed the political strength of these alliances, associations, and unions of the farmers. In the South three governors, one United States Senator, forty-four congressmen, and five legislatures were won; in the West, two United States Senators, eight congressmen and two legislatures. South of the Mason and Dixon line candidates of the Democratic Party were pledged to the program of the farmers, but in Kansas, Michigan, South Dakota and other parts of the North, independent parties were organized.

Spurred on by these successes the People's Party men made preparations for the national contest of 1892. The Industrial Congress at St. Louis on Washington's birthday welded the economic organizations together and paved the way for the nominating convention in Omaha on July 4, 1892. The delegates to this great gathering of populists fell back on the war horse of the 1880 campaign, James Baird Weaver, to be their standard bearer. After they adopted their platform, the document formulated at St. Louis, with some minor changes, they gave vent to their pent-up enthusiasm in typical American convention style:

> Cheers and yells . . . rose like a tornado from four thousand throats and raged without cessation for thirty-four minutes, during which women shrieked and wept, men embraced and kissed their neighbors, locked arms, marched back and forth, and leaped upon tables and chairs in the ecstacy of their delirium.

§

The platform which occasioned such rejoicing and which was the populist's declaration of faith, read as follows:

> We declare, First, That the union of the labor forces of the United States this day consummated shall be permanent and perpetual; may its spirit enter into all hearts for the salvation of the republic and the uplifting of mankind.
>
> Second. Wealth belongs to him who creates it, and every dollar taken from industry without an equivalent is robbery.

"If any will not work, neither shall he eat." The interests of rural and civil labor are the same; their enemies are identical.

Third. We believe that the time has come when the railroad corporations will either own the people or the people must own the railroads, and should the government enter upon the work of owning and managing the railroads, we favor an amendment to the Constitution by which all persons engaged in the government service shall be placed under a civil service regulation of the most rigid character, so as to prevent the increase of the power of the national administration by the use of such additional government employees.

Finance. We demand a national currency, safe, sound and flexible, issued by the general government only, a full legal tender for all debts, public and private, and that without the use of banking corporations, a just, equitable and efficient means of distribution direct to the people, at a tax not to exceed two per cent per annum, to be provided as set forth by the sub-treasury plan of the Farmers' Alliance, or a better system; also by payments in discharge of its obligations for public improvements.

1. We demand free and unlimited coinage of silver and gold at the present legal ratio of 16 to 1.

2. We demand that the amount of circulating medium be speedily increased to not less than $50 per capita.

3. We demand a graduated income tax.

4. We believe that the money of the country should be kept as much as possible in the hands of the people, and hence we demand that all state and national revenue shall be limited to the necessary expenses of the government, economically and honestly administered.

We demand that postal savings banks be established by the government for the safe deposit of the earnings of the people and to facilitate exchanges.

Transportation. Transportation being a means of exchange and a public necessity, the government should own and operate the railroads in the interest of the people. The telegraph and telephone, like the post office system, being a necessity for the transmission of news, should be owned and operated by the government in the interest of the people.

Land. The land, including all the natural sources of wealth, is the heritage of the people, and should not be monopolized for speculative purposes, and alien ownership of land should be prohibited. All land now held by railroads and other corporations in excess of their actual needs, and all lands now owned by aliens, should be reclaimed by the government and held for actual settlers only.

The Omaha convention adopted a number of resolutions of specific import to labor: more effective laws against contract labor; further restriction of undesirable immigration; shorter hours; abolition of the "army of mercenaries, known as the Pinkerton system," and endorsement of a label of the Knights of Labor. The populist legislature of Kansas of 1893 adopted several labor bills, one calling for check-weighmen for miners and payment of wages weekly in cash. In Minnesota the populists extended their hand of fellowship to the oppressed workers at Homestead. In Colorado the People's Party demanded a child labor and an eight-hour law, as well as an employers' liability measure. In Idaho the party condemned the state and federal authorities and expressed its sympathy with the battling miners' union.

But outside of the Northwest the People's Party did not receive much support from the wage earners in 1892. General Weaver met with determined opposition from the southern democrats who voted disfranchised Negroes right and left, particularly in Alabama and Georgia, and counted out the candidates of the People's Party, wherever they ran in opposition on local and state tickets. Despite these and other tactics the populists rolled up about a million votes in 1892, against Cleveland's 5,554,414 and Harrison's 5,190,802. The Democratic Party did not have a presidential ticket in Colorado, Idaho, Kansas, North Dakota, or Wyoming. Weaver carried the first three of these states, as well as Nevada, and received one electoral vote each in North Dakota and Oregon, a total of twenty-two in the Electoral College. He failed to win Nebraska by less than a hundred votes. His vote came mostly from the agricultural states:

State	Vote	State	Vote
Alabama	85,181	Georgia	42,937
Arkansas	11,831	Idaho	10,520
California	25,311	Illinois	22,207
Colorado	53,584	Indiana	22,218
Connecticut	809	Iowa	20,595
Florida	4,843	Kansas	163,111

State	Vote	State	Vote
Kentucky	23,500	North Dakota	17,700
Maine	2,405	Ohio	14,852
Maryland	796	Oregon	26,965
Massachusetts	3,348	Pennsylvania	8,714
Michigan	19,931	Rhode Island	228
Minnesota	29,313	South Carolina	2,410
Mississippi	10,102	South Dakota	26,544
Missouri	41,213	Tennessee	23,730
Montana	7,334	Texas	99,418
Nebraska	83,134	Vermont	44
Nevada	7,264	Virginia	12,275
New Hampshire	293	Washington	19,105
New Jersey	969	West Virginia	4,166
New York	16,436	Wisconsin	9,909
North Carolina	44,732	Wyoming	7,722

§

In the congressional elections of 1894 the populists added another half million votes to their total. There was almost a tidal wave in the South. It frightened the Democratic Party and forced it to adopt the slogan of the independent movement, the free coinage of silver at a ratio of 16 to 1. In the West and Northwest the democrats were practically wiped out. It was the populists, therefore, who determined the course the Democratic Party was to take in the presidential election of 1896.

The panic of 1893 had descended upon the country. The prices of farm products dropped to their lowest point, and there was a currency famine everywhere. Gold had been exported in 1892 and 1893 and the bankers were draining the Treasury as well. President Cleveland, a monometallist and gold man, favored the repeal of the law which required the government to purchase a limited quantity of silver. He was accused of playing hand-in-glove with the eastern bankers. He brought down upon himself the wrath of the organized workers by sending federal troops to Illinois over the protest of Governor Altgeld during the Pullman strike. The issuance of injunctions during this labor dispute and the jailing of

Debs augured no good for the administration. The suffering of the unemployed was intense. The time was
ripe for a vehement campaign.

The Democratic Party had already committed itself in
the South and West to expansion of the currency. It
was the delegates from these sections in the convention
of 1896 who rode rough-shod over the supporters of
Cleveland and the conservatives from the East. It was
they who repudiated the "gold bugs" in their own party
with a ruthlessness hardly paralleled in the annals of
old party politics. Declaring that "the money question
is paramount to all others at this time," the convention
came out with a ringing demand for "the free and unlimited coinage of both silver and gold at the present
legal ratio of 16 to 1 without waiting for the aid or consent of any other nation." The battle of the standards
was on.

The democratic platform of 1896 contained something
more than the usual old party buncome. It went further
than the populists to get at the Supreme Court for its
decision declaring the income tax law unconstitutional.
It proposed that Congress use all its constitutional power
to obtain a reversal by a reorganized court, "packed" for
the purpose. The platform denounced "arbitrary interference by the federal authorities in local affairs," referring
to the act of a democratic president. It protested "government by injunction." On the money question the document read:

Recognizing that the money question is paramount to all others
at this time, we invite attention to the fact that the Federal Constitution named silver and gold together as the money metals
of the United States, and that the first coinage law passed by
Congress under the Constitution made the silver dollar the monetary unit and admitted gold to free coinage at a ratio based upon
the silver-dollar unit.

We declare that the Act of 1873 demonetizing silver without
the knowledge or approval of the American people has resulted
in the appreciation of gold and a correspondindg fall in the prices
of commodities produced by the people; a heavy increase in the

burdens of taxation and of all debts, public and private; the enrichment of the money-lending class at home and abroad; the prostration of industry and impoverishment of the people.

We are unalterably opposed to monometallism which has locked fast the prosperity of an industrial people in the paralysis of hard times. Gold monometallism is a British policy, and its adoption has brought other nations into financial servitude to London. It is not only un-American but anti-American, and it can be fastened on the United States only by the stifling of that spirit and love of liberty which proclaimed our political independence in 1776 and won it in the War of the Revolution.

We demand the free and unlimited coinage of both silver and gold at the present legal ratio of 16 to 1, without waiting for the aid or consent of any other nation. We demand that the standard silver dollar shall be a full legal tender, equally with gold, for all debts, public and private, and we favor such legislation as will prevent for the future the demonetization of any kind of legal-tender money by private contract.

We are opposed to the policy and practice of surrendering to the holders of the obligations of the United States the option reserved by law to the government of redeeming such obligations in either silver coin or gold coin.

We are opposed to the issuing of interest-bearing bonds of the United States in time of peace and condemn the trafficking with banking syndicates, which, in exchange of bonds and at an enormous profit to themselves, supply the Federal Treasury with gold to maintain the policy of monometallism.

Congress alone has the power to coin and issue money, and President Jackson declared that this power could not be delegated to corporations or individuals. We therefore denounce the issuance of notes intended to circulate as money by national banks as in derogation of the Constitution, and we demand that all paper which is made a legal tender for public and private debts, or which is receivable for dues to the United States, shall be issued by the government of the United States and shall be redeemable in coin.

In answer to this demand of the democrats and populists for the free coinage of silver at a legal ratio of 16 to 1, the Republican Party platform had the following to say:

The Republican Party is unreservedly for sound money. It caused the enactment of a law providing for the redemption of specie payments in 1879. Since then every dollar has been as good as gold. We are unalterably opposed to every measure calculated to debase our currency or impair the credit of our country. We are therefore opposed to the free coinage of silver, except by international agreement with the leading commercial nations of the earth, which agreement we pledge ourselves to promote, and until such agreement can be obtained the existing gold standard must be maintained. All of our silver and paper currency must be maintained at parity with gold, and we favor all measures designed to maintain inviolable the obligations of the United States, of all our money, whether coin or paper, at the present standard, the standard of most enlightened nations of the earth.

§

The People's Party met in convention about two weeks after the democrats had nominated Bryan and Sewall, July 22-24, in St. Louis. There were two factions, those in favor and those opposed to fusion. The latter won the first victory by securing the nomination of Thomas Watson of Georgia for vice-presiednt, by a vote of 539½ against 257 for Arthur Sewall. "A New England ship builder, a railroad president, and a national banker" was a rather unpalatable dish for even the fusion populists to put over. When it came to the nomination for president, a group of socialists worked up some enthusiasm for Eugene Victor Debs. The "machine" in control turned off the lights and adjourned the meeting when the socialists became too active in their boring from within tactics. Debs was not, however, in the running. He received but eight votes. The contest was between an out-and-out populist, S. F. Norton, and the nominee of the Democratic Party, William Jennings Bryan.

In Bryan's favor was the fact that he hailed from Nebraska, that he was a young, vigorous, and outstanding representative of the West, and that he knew how to utter the shibboleths of the populists. He was the candidate of a major party which had four years previously elected a president. Against Bryan were those who felt that they were signing their death-warrant when they endorsed him. The vote stood 1,042 for Bryan and 321 for Norton.

The platform included the populist demands on money and others of a radical character: public works for the unemployed, government ownership of the railroads and telegraphs, and reclamation of land by the government. The populists accepted the Democratic Party's leader and fused because the People's Party had been built up and developed on the money issue. Once the campaign of 1896 was over, the farmers' independent political movement was through. It had been swallowed up. The increase in prices drew the attention of the farmers away from politics, and the return of prosperity made for unionism and socialism.

Although both the Democratic and Republican Parties were split by the free silver question, and new parties were organized by gold democrats and silver republicans, the presidential contest of 1896 was a struggle between Bryan and McKinley exclusively. Leading democratic newspapers abandoned the silver-tongued orator shortly after he was nominated. "Thousands of business men, merchants, manufacturers, grain dealers, railroad officials, building associations, insurance companies, newspapers and others, published at their own expense brief and pointed documents on the currency question, distributing them through their daily correspondence or by other methods." The Republican Party sent out hundreds of millions of tracts. It spent millions of dollars in a thoroughly organized capitalistic enterprise, engineered and directed throughout by the master hand of Marcus A. Hanna.

Feeling ran high. Edward Lauterback, chairman of the New York Republican Committee, was reported to have stated publicly:

No blood will be shed—at least not yet, but if they attempt to subvert your Supreme Court, if they should succeed, by any chance, in foisting upon you these horrible doctrines—anarchistic, socialistic and communistic—which that platform, adopted by this populistic brood, contain, we will not abide by that decision.

The railroad corporations distributed cards to their employees, reading as follows: "Application by ————— ———————— to the Railway Men's Sound Money Club. I do hereby pledge myself to use my vote and influence for the defeat of the free coinage of silver." Employers discharged workmen for going out to meet the train carrying Bryan on his record speaking tour. Business contracts were made out on the understanding that they were not effective if McKinley was defeated. The republicans warned the people against the panic which they predicted was bound to follow if Bryan was elected. Richmond Mayo-Smith, John Bates Clark, and J. Laurence Laughlin, to mention only a few of the economists, threw their learning into the heat of the fray to "educate" the people in "sound money." Labor men, such as Terrence V. Powderly, once the exalted grand master workman of the Knights of Labor, who wrote on November 1, 1888: "Damn the Republican Party, the party that gave us a perpetuation of the national banks, of the bond system, of the rule of the shylock," who represented the Knights at the conferences with the farmers which hammered out the populist program—Powderly campaigned for McKinley.

The owners of the silver mines matched the contributions of Standard Oil and the bankers to the Republican Party. The Democratic Party selected a conservative easterner for vice-president. Neither in the South nor the West were the hungry office-hunters of the Democratic Party much to grow enthusiastic over. This party became the champion of the farmers, lower middle class elements, and the workers in 1896 because it wanted to survive and win. It was and is no more fitted to represent the producing classes than the tiger to become a household pet, regardless of how much effort the old or the new Tammany spends in trying to convince the American people to the contrary.

The populists nominated separately for local offices in a number of the states, but in the South they generally fused with the republicans; in the West, with the democrats and silver republicans. As an illustration of the confusion and destruction of old party lines, there were thirteen tickets on the ballot in Illinois, namely, the Democrat, Republican, Prohibition, People's, Socialist Labor, National, Middle-of-the-Road, Independent Gold Standard Democrat, Independent, Independent Democratic, Independence Silver, Independent Republican, and National Silver.

The People's Party continued to cooperate with the old parties or their split-offs in 1898. And the poor middle-of-the-road populists, those opposed to any fusion whatever, continued to raise their helpless voices in protest. In California a minority which withdrew from a convention which had drawn up a common ticket with the democrats and silver republicans, put its case thus:

> When fusionists speak of success they can mean nothing except that they may succeed in getting some offices and the emoluments thereof. . . . Fusion simply places the party in the hands of democratic political opponents, and they gain complete control of the fusion organization.

In Iowa the anti-fusion populists entered a strong denial that the democrats had adopted populist principles:

> We deny that the platform of any other leading political party is in harmony with the principles enunciated in the platform of the People's Party adopted at Omaha and St. Louis on the subjects of money, land, transportation, government ownership of public utilities, monopolies, bonded indebtedness and coin, or gold redemption.

They were right, but the people do not read platforms, and they do not grasp more than a few issues at a time. Above all, the populists themselves had endorsed Bryan and the Democratic Party. They had given up their identity because they wanted victory. Rising prices and prosperity played havoc with their appeal and they gave way to the Socialist Party.

When the presidential contest of 1900 loomed, the fusion wing of the People's Party met at Sioux Falls, South Dakota, on May 10, 1900, and nominated Bryan by acclamation. Its candidate for vice-president, Charles A. Towne of Minnesota, withdrew in favor of A. E. Stevenson, whom the democrats selected as Bryan's running mate. The anti-fusion or middle-of-the-road populists convened in Cincinnati, also in May, and picked Wharton Barker of Pennsylvania for president, and the veteran Ignatius Donnelly of Minnesota for vice-president. The platforms of the two wings differed but slightly. The middle-of-the-roaders received 50,373 votes, of which 20,976 came from Texas, and the bulk of the rest from the South. The great national protest of the farmers on the political field, independent of the two old parties, was now a thing of the past. The American farmers did not rise again until A. C. Townley in 1915 and Robert M. La Follette in 1924 rallied them around their standards.

CHAPTER IV

FOUNDING OF THE SOCIALIST LABOR PARTY

"THE beginnings of modern socialism appeared on this continent before the close of the first half of the nineteenth century, but it took another half century before the movement could be said to have become acclimatized on American soil." When Morris Hillquit, one of the foremost American socialists, wrote this sentence in 1903 there was evidence that at last a socialist party had taken hold in the United States. In 1919, however, the American Socialist Party was rent asunder. A national labor party was launched, apart from and independent of the organized socialists. Hillquit has written of the Socialist Labor Party that the endeavor to Americanize the socialist movement was the keynote of its activity throughout its entire career. Up until 1928 the Socialist Party has not fully succeeded where the Socialist Labor Party had largely failed. For, had the Socialist Party been truly acclimatized, neither the war, nor the Russian Revolution, nor America's relative prosperity could have beaten it down.

The mission of the Socialist Labor Party, the Socialist Party, and the Workers' (Communist) Party was and is still fundamentally the same as when they were first founded: to propagate and establish socialism. And this also was the mission of the individual and organized radicals who introduced and promulgated Marxian socialism for twenty years before the Socialist Labor Party was born in 1876. Socialism and the socialist movement are a reflex of particular periods, countries, peoples, and are not the same things at all times and in all places. In the

United States the socialists have always differed and still differ as to the tactics, the methods, and the programs by which that which they call socialism can be advanced. And similarly, bread and butter trade unionists have had and still have their struggles, with their own divisions, over the manner in which that which they call trade unionism can be furthered. The American socialist movement can only be understood, therefore, in terms of the specific conditions which shaped and determined its changing character.

The history of the American socialist movement can conveniently be divided as follows: (1) Beginnings; (2) Socialist Labor Party; (3) Socialist Party; (4) Postwar period.

§

The founder of modern socialism, Karl Marx, was born and raised in Germany. The first socialist party to command attention in the world was the German Social Democratic Party, which polled half a million votes by the seventies and drove Bismarck to pass the exception laws in 1878 in the vain attempt to destroy it. Until 1914 the Germans held a position of prestige and power in the international socialist movement second to none. The theoretical literature of socialism, from the day that the *Communist Manifesto* was written down to the outbreak of the World War, was mainly of German origin. The spirit of a disciplined, intelligent, and aggressive socialist army was typified by the organized working class movement of Germany. The leaders of this mighty force were deeply respected at home and abroad. It was men trained in such a movement who tried to build up a duplicate in the United States.

The Teutons migrated to America in large numbers. In every ten-year period from 1851-1860 to 1891-1900 the immigrants from Germany exceeded those from any other country, while in the two decades, 1831-1840 and 1841-1850, they were outnumbered only by the Irish.

Period	Total Number of Immigrants	From Germany	From Ireland
1831-1840	 599,125	152,454	207,381
1841-1850	1,713,251	434,626	780,719
1851-1860	2,598,214	951,667	914,119
1861-1870	2,314,824	787,968	435,778
1871-1880	2,812,191	718,182	436,871
1881-1890	5,246,613	1,452,970	655,482
1891-1900	3,687,564	505,152	388,416

The intelligent and educated German worker and the idealistic intellectual brought their socialism with them to America. Immediately upon landing they set themselves the task of organizing their fellow-countrymen and then reaching out for the native and English-speaking workers. The socialist and free-thinking German immigrant was handicapped by a foreign tongue, however, and was up against an individualistic Anglo-Saxon tradition, a religious people, and relative prosperity and economic opportunity. It was not until capitalism had matured at the end of the nineteenth century and a native socialist movement began to develop that the Germans slipped into the background.

It was the German worker also—and here he had greater immediate success—who laid the foundations for the trade union movement in the United States. The Germans were good organization men, they helped to teach Samuel Gompers and Adolph Strasser and the other leaders of the American Federation of Labor their first lessons in the philosophy and tactics of trade unionism. That socialism did not make greater strides in the leading capitalist country of the world is no fault of the tireless and conscientious German-American wage earners, the pioneers of Marxism in America.

§

Among the earliest interpreters of modern socialism in America the names of Joseph Weydemeyer and F. A. Sorge stand out most prominently. Wilhelm Weitling cannot be included, for he was far closer to Proudhon than to Marx. He was not concerned with the development of a working class movement. For him the bank of exchange was the "soul of all reforms." He wanted to give the small, independent self-employer the full product of his toil. Although he kept up a lively agitation in 1850 and 1851, no exchange banks were established, the colony which his followers launched in Iowa ended in failure, and the wage earners abandoned him and his ideas. Joseph Weydemeyer came to the United States in 1851, a man of 33, and Sorge arrived a year later. Both had come into close personal contact with Karl Marx and Frederick Engels, and were convinced socialists. They devoted themselves for a good many years in an able and effective way to directing the organized socialist movement in this country.

Largely through Weydemeyer's efforts the New York German trade unionists established the American Workingmen's Alliance on March 21, 1853. Its object was to build up an independent labor party and support the trade unions. It organized German branches in New Jersey, Ohio, and Pennsylvania, and an English local in Washington. Its platform, as given in Hermann Schlueter's *Die Anfaenge der deutschen Arbeiterbewegung in Amerika,* was as follows:

Immediate naturalization; congressional instead of state legislation; equal and cheap justice; elimination of antiquated statutes; abolition of blue laws; priority of workers' wages and claims; a ten-hour work day; no child labor under 15 and compulsory education; free higher education; civil service; and retention of the public lands, with large scale cultivation by the state in the interests of the people.

Weydemeyer's paper, *Die Reform,* which had been started on March 5, 1853, ended its career in less than a year, and his organization exerted an influence for only a few years in New York.

A group of Marxians, including F. A. Sorge, Conrad Carl, and Sigfried Meyer, launched the Communist Club on October 25, 1857, in the eastern metropolis. It kept in touch with the European socialist movement and in 1867 became a section of the International Workingmen's Association. The General German Workingmen's Union, which was started by a group of Lassallean socialists in New York in October, 1865, united with the Communist Club in December, 1867, to nominate a local ticket the following year under the name of Social Party. Its platform was akin to that of the National Labor Union. It made a very poor showing and disappeared a few months after election.

§

In the souvenir program commemorating the sixtieth anniversary of the First International, issued by the Labor and Socialist International in 1924, Karl Kautsky wrote that the British Labor Party had "become the most powerful element in the international, and so, in a certain sense we come back to the point from which the First International started." For it was the conservative and skilled British workers who paved the way for the organization of the International Workingmen's Association in 1864. Their real wages over the better part of the two previous decades had risen. They had the best organized labor movement in the world. It was to protect their rising standard of life and their trade unions, and to promote the organization of a labor movement on the continent, that the English wage earners set in motion the forces which led to the birth of the first international of labor. They hoped that it would help to prevent the importation of strike-breakers, provide mutual assistance, and generally unite the workers against economic and political reaction. Since 1850 Karl Marx had been in England and, in the words of Kautsky, he

. . . had studied this state which was the most progressive in the world from the capitalist point of view, and which was pointing the way to other states in their economic development. He had recognized and extolled the workers of England at that time as the champions of the working classes of the world, and had held them up to the workers of all countries as a pattern in their fight for a legal working day.

The International was launched on September 28, 1864, at a meeting in St. Martin's Hall, London, attended by English, French, German, Italian, and Polish workers and intellectuals. Marx was made a member of the organizing committee. He opposed the plan of a follower of Mazzini, Major L. Wolff, which would have turned the International into a federation of secret republican societies. He presented his own inaugural address and set of rules, which were unanimously adopted by the committee.

The preamble to the rules declared that the International had been formed:

Considering:
That the emancipation of the working classes must be conquered by the working classes themselves; that the struggle for the emancipation of the working classes means, not a struggle for class privileges and monopolies, but for equal rights and duties and abolition of all class-rule;
That the economical subjection of the man of labor to the monopolizer of the means of labor, that is, the sources of life, lies at the bottom of servitude in all its forms, of all social misery, mental degradation, and political dependence;
That the economical emancipation of the working classes is therefore the great end to which every political movement ought to be subordinate as a means;
That all efforts aiming at that great end have hitherto failed from the want of solidarity between the manifold divisions of labor in each country, and from the absence of a fraternal bond of union between the working classes of different countries;
That the emancipation of labor is neither a local, nor a national, but a social problem, embracing all countries in which modern society exists, and depending for its solution on the concurrence, practical and theoretical, of the most advanced countries;
That the present revival of the working classes in the most industrious countries of Europe, while it raises a new hope, gives solemn warning against a relapse into the old errors, and calls for the immediate combination of the still disconnected movements.

Marx stressed the trade union movement as basic. He pointed to the passage of the ten-hours bill as a victory of a principle: "It was the first time that in broad daylight the political economy of the middle classes succumbed to the political economy of the working class." He held that it was the "great duty of the working classes to conquer political power and to make use of the machinery of the state to promote their interests." In view of the machinations of governments which played upon national and racial hatreds in order to spill the blood of the workers in dynastic and imperialistic wars, Marx urged the toilers "to master the mysteries of international politics, to watch the diplomatic acts of their respective governments, to counteract them, if necessary, by all means in their power, and, when unable to prevent, to assemble in simultaneous demonstrations and to vindicate the simple laws of morality and justice, which ought to govern the relations of private individuals, as well as the intercourse of nations. To fight for such a foreign policy forms a part of the general struggle for emancipation of the working classes. Workingmen of all countries, unite!"

The First International had two types of members: those belonging to affiliated trade unions and those individuals who were part of a section or branch. The predominance of the trade union affiliations tended to make the International conservative, while the influence of the political sections tended toward revolution. Outside of Great Britain the trade union movement was very weak. The continental workers were still lost in the woods, looking for guidance from the Belgian and French mutualists, Proudhon and Colins, and later from the Russian anarchist, Bakunin. The labor party of Ferdinand Lassalle had just been started in Germany.

In its short existence of less than ten years the First International stimulated the organization of trade unions and provoked strikes for which it helped to raise funds. It made the fight for the franchise its own. It put a healthy fear into the reactionary governments which greatly magnified its power and finances. The First International broke up and disappeared because of internal differences between trade unionists and socialists, between socialists and mutualists, and between socialists and anarchists, and because there was no labor movement on the continent. The outbreak and the defeat of the Paris Commune in 1871, with the repression which followed, made its presence in Europe impossible.

§

The American labor and socialist movement participated in the work of the First International through the National Labor Union and the separate sections which were at first independent and later formed the North American Federation of the International Workingmen's Association. The Philadelphia convention of the National Labor Union, held in 1869, elected A. C. Cameron, the greenbacker and individualist, as delegate to the Basle congress of the International. The following year the National Labor Union declared its adherence to the principles of the International Workingmen's Association, but never joined formally. The New York Communist Club became a section in October, 1867. Two years later the General German Workingmen's Union became Section 1. This body sent Sorge to the 1870 convention of the National Labor Union which declared in favor of the principles of the International. The Chicago Lassallean Schlaeger and the New York Marxians promulgated the ideas of socialism inside the National Labor Union and received encouragement from William H. Sylvis and William J. Jessup, leader of the New York State Workingmen's Assembly. In 1868 German sections of the International were started in San Francisco, and in 1869 in Chicago; a Bohemian and French section in New York in 1870. By December of that year a provisional central committee was established, with F. A. Sorge as corresponding secretary. There were over 30 sections in 1871, with several thousand members. Two sections, known as 9 and 12, composed of native Americans, which were admitted about the middle of 1871, now began to threaten the unity of the movement.

Victoria Woodhull and Tennessee Claflin, two sisters, dominated Section 12, which in turn influenced all the English-speaking sections of New York. As natives they tended to oppose themselves to the foreign-born, and as advocates of feminism and a broad humanitarianism, to belittle the economic philosophy of the Marxians. The inevitable split took place on November 20, 1871, when the central committee was dissolved, and a provisional federal council was established by the foreign-speaking sections. In March of 1872 the General Council of the International expelled Section 12. The supporters of the latter held a convention in 1872, the call of which was addressed to all male and female beings of America, and they nominated a woman, Victoria Woodhull, as candidate for president. The Marxian socialists held their convention in July, 1872, and elected Sorge and Deveure as delegates to the Hague Congress of the International, although the former alone was able to attend. By this time, however, the First International was ready to give up the ghost. The congress of 1872 transferred the seat of the governing body, the General Council, from London to New York, with Sorge as general secretary and receiver.

Removal of the headquarters to America did not stem the tide of dissension. First there was conflict between Section 1 of New York, the oldest and controlling body, and the local council of the city, made up of one delegate from each of the five sections. The local council refused to dissolve after a referendum was carried on October 9, 1873, to that effect. The sections which opposed dissolution of the local council were suspended, and Section 1 completely dominated the national convention held on April 11, 1874, in Philadelphia. The opposition and some other elements thereupon organized the Social Democratic

Workingmen's Party of North America, of which Adolph Strasser, later the president of the cigarmakers, was national secretary. The regular organization had been running a weekly, the *Arbeiter-Zeitung,* founded in 1873. In March of 1875 this paper passed into oblivion as a result of another internal fight. Now it was Section 1 that was arrayed against the General Council. Inasmuch as this section controlled the paper—by force—the General Council appealed to the courts. When it won the decision, however, there was nothing to continue the paper with. The American sections of the International had now about run their course. On July 15, 1876, it was officially announced that the First International was dead in America, as well as in Europe. Four days later the Workingmen's Party of the United States saw the light of day. In 1877 it changed its name to the Socialist Labor Party.

§

While the International occupied the attention of the New York socialists, a movement in which independent political action played a larger role developed in Chicago. A considerable number of German Lassalleans had settled in this fast-growing city. In 1869 the Chicagoans organized the Universal German Workingmen's Association, the same name as that used by the Lassalleans in the home country. They launched a paper, *Der Deutsche Arbeiter,* with Karl Klinge as editor. As with *Die Arbeiter Union* in New York, of which Adolph Douai was editor, the Franco-Prussian war played havoc with the Chicago weekly, which was also opposed to Bismarck's venture. In 1871 the name Socio-Political Workingmen's Association replaced the German importation.

The panic of 1873 and the ineffectual efforts of the Chicago unemployed to obtain relief raised the question of independent political action. The strength of the German socialists in the unions, the organization of the farmers into independent parties, and the presence of

Lassallean leaders settled the matter, and the Labor Party of Illinois was formed in January, 1874. The *Verbote,* a German labor weekly which was to have a long and eventful career, appeared on February 14 of that year as the mouthpiece of the new party. The planks of the platform were ten:

(1) Abolition of monopoly. (2) Public ownership of the means of transportation. (3) Public ownership of banks, with public money in public banks. (4) No contract system on public works. (5) Weekly payments of wages, and speedier legal adjustments for wages due. (6) No contract prison labor. (7) Compulsory public education between seven and fourteen, and no child labor under fourteen. (8) Direct payment of all public officials, no fees. (9) Recall of public officials. (10) Establishment of workingmen's cooperatives, with state aid to workers' undertakings.

This last plank had been a prominent feature of Ferdinand Lassalle's agitation in the Germany of the early sixties. Lassalle had emphasized the importance of the toilers winning the franchise, organizing an independent political party, and then with their votes compelling the state to advance credits to workingmen's cooperatives, as the quickest way out of wage-slavery.

The labor party at first took a friendly attitude toward the grangers, the farmers' independent political movement. The *Verbote* in its first issue wrote: "The union of the farmers with the industrial workers of the cities is necessary, for the latter are the major consumers of the products of the soil and they also suffer from the transportation monopoly. Only through common action will results be achieved." The German socialists made the point that the monopolist and middle men took all the profits. There was no real conflict between the farmer's and the urban consumer's price. The worker could well afford to pay the farmer a fair price if the middle man's slice was wiped out. The farmers were now opposed to monopolies, said the *Verbote,* why not ultimately against the whole system? The task of the socialists was to awaken them to the larger aim. When the Illinois farmers convened in Springfield on June 10, 1874 the labor party sent delegates. Despite the opposition of Cameron and others who called them communists and foreigners, the delegates were admitted. They accomplished little, however, but they were satisfied to have made the contact. The granger movement went its own way without the socialists.

The labor party had its troubles with those who tried to tie it up with the old parties. Two members of one of the English-speaking branches went to the mayor of Chicago early in 1874, asked him to join, and promised him the party's support. After a stormy central committee meeting these gentlemen found that they were in the wrong party. In the fall of the same year, one day before election, a number of the party's candidates went over to their opponents. In this election only 785 votes were officially given the labor party. This highly incensed its supporters. Affidavits were made by voters living in precincts where no votes were recorded, declaring that they had voted for the labor party candidates. The *Verbote* declared that intimidation had been practiced to drive off party workers, that votes had been purchased, that labor party tickets had been refused at the polling places, and every form of thievery practiced to deprive them of their share of the votes cast.

After this election the party devoted itself to fundamental socialist propaganda and changed its platform accordingly. At the annual meeting of 1875 it decided against participating in elections until it was much stronger and in a position to nominate reliable socialists. "The ballot box in its present form," said a party statement, "is a colossal swindle." Meanwhile Conrad Conzett replaced Karl Klinge as editor of the *Verbote*. The decision to emphasize socialism, disappointment with politics, and the advent of Conzett, a strong supporter of trade union action, led to an amalgamation with two surviving sections of the old International in Chicago. The paper took on added life, its circulation went up, and the number of pages increased. It paved the way for unity in the socialist movement.

§

The Social Democratic Workingmen's Party of North America was organized in New York City at a convention on May 17, 1874. Those sections of the International which had lost out in the fight with Section 1, together with groups in Newark and Philadelphia, were responsible for its formation. Its platform stressed the Lassallean demand for cooperative associations to replace the wage system. Its evolution was also similar to that of the Chicago labor party. Gustav Lyser, a Lassallean, was replaced in 1875 as editor of its official organ by one who would stress the greater importance of trade union action. This eastern Lassallean body, with Strasser as secretary, tried to secure local unity, and offered to join hands with the local sections of the International and an English-speaking socialist group which styled itself the United Workers, but did not succeed. A national convention, however, brought all socialist leaders together and paved the way for one organization.

John M. Davis, a prominent Knight of Labor and editor of the *National Labor Tribune,* which the *Verbote* credited with 10,000 readers, and other Knights issued a call for a national convention to organize a new federation as a successor to the dead National Labor Union. The socialist groups sent delegates. The meeting was held on December 28, 1875, but it was not representative enough. A second convention was called for April 17, 1876, in Pittsburgh. The socialists organized their forces to capture it. P. J. McGuire, later the secretary of the carpenters, introduced a resolution calling for government aid to workers' cooperatives. It was carried. The greenbackers woke up. They were in the majority. They turned around, reconsidered and defeated the resolution. They then adopted their own pet greenback proposals.

The socialists would have none of their financial remedies and withdrew in a body. But in thus cutting loose from the Knights and the greenbackers they now found themselves. The socialist leaders were ready for unity and sent out a call for a congress of all factions to be held in Philadelphia, July 19-22, 1876.

§

The delegates to this unity convention spoke for the enormous total of about 3,000 members, and those mostly German-Americans. Strasser, McGuire, and A. Gabriel represented about 1,500 members of the Social Democratic Workingmen's Party. Conzett spoke for the Labor Party of Illinois, with 593 members. Charles Braun came from a Socio-Political Labor-Union of Cincinnati, 250 adherents, while F. A. Sorge and Otto Weydemeyer added 635 members of the North American Federation of the International. The convention adopted the name of Workingmen's Party of the United States and committed it to fundamental socialist principles. In the matter of tactics the united party declared that it would not enter into a political campaign until it was strong enough to exercise a perceptible influence. Consent of the executive was required for any section to take political action, that is, to nominate a ticket. Conzett expressed the prevailing view as follows: "We can only become strong . . . when instead of wasting our time and money at the ballot box, we devote ourselves with all our energy to the demands of the trade unions and bring material advantages to the workers." A political movement, he said, would be developed if trade unions were first organized and their members and leaders educated in socialism. "Every responsible socialist," he wrote, "acquainted with the conditions in this country, admits that only damage will come by participation in the elections." In accordance with socialist practice and the smallness of the party the members in one city, this time Chicago, were empowered to elect the national executive committee, and the members of another, Newark, to choose the board of control which acted as a check on the executive and passed on appeals. Philip Van Patten, a native, and an active member of the Knights of Labor, was chosen national secretary.

The inherent weakness of the party lay not in its numbers nor in its principles, nor in its dominance by German-Americans. In March, 1877, it had eighteen English-speaking sections, thirty-five German, five Scandinavian, six Bohemian and two French, in forty-four cities of nineteen states. The party was, however, a house divided against itself over the old issue which split the North American sections of the First International: trade union action to the exclusion of independent political action.

On September 16, 1876, the New Haven section, dominated by Americans, petitioned the executive for permission to put up a local ticket. The opposition—the trade union socialist faction—claimed that greenbackers were behind this move, but the Chicago executive sanctioned it. The experiment turned out favorably, the socialists receiving 640 votes. Now Chicago, Cincinnati, and Milwaukee demanded the same right to participate in the coming spring elections. They were told to go ahead. In the headquarters of the executive the party nominated Albert R. Parsons in one ward. He made a good showing. In Cincinnati the socialists received 3,491 votes out of a total of about 34,000 cast, and in Milwaukee they elected several candidates to office.

The political faction, to which the national secretary belonged, took on added courage. In the East, where the trade union group had its strength, controversy developed between the national executive and the board of control, located in Newark. It came to a head over the *Labor Standard,* a party paper edited by the trade unionist, P. J. McDonnell. The executive suspended the Newark board of control and called the New Haven members to choose a new board, and sent out a referen-

dum for a new convention. In July, 1877, however, the
railroad strikes broke out. The question of political
action versus trade union action was taken by events out
of the hands of the Socialist Labor Party. An elemental
mass movement of the workers had arisen. The economic
depression precluded direct trade union action. The
socialists could only take advantage of the opportunity to
organize and direct the political uprising into socialist
channels.

§

The fever for politics now gripped the socialists. Between the fall of 1877—the first election after the strike—
and the presidential contest of 1880, spirited political
battles were waged in the important industrial cities of
the country. In almost all these cases the campaigns
were carried on independently, although efforts were
made to get together with the greenbackers in some in-
stances and joint tickets resulted. The socialists tasted
the fruits of office by electing one alderman in Chicago
in the spring of 1878, three state representatives and one
state senator the following fall, three assemblymen and
two aldermen in St. Louis in 1878, and three more aldermen in the Windy City in April, 1879. The results of
the last election disappointed the Chicagoans. They were
out to elect their candidate for mayor, Dr. Ernest
Schmidt. The *National Socialist,* official organ of the
party, claimed that 15,000 illegal votes were cast which
decided the result. Money, intimidation, repeaters, and
all the tricks of the American game of politics, it charged,
were used. The socialists officially received 11,575 votes,
the democrats 25,146, and the republicans 20,118. Despite this remarkable poll, the vote fell to one-quarter as
much in the fall of the same year, and in the presidential
election of 1880 the party was eliminated as a serious contender for public office in Chicago.

In Cincinnati the party received 9,071 votes in the fall
of 1877, but only about 500 the following year, and 420

in the succeeding spring of 1879. The sharp decline in
this city was a hard blow. It is explained by the fact
that in the November, 1878, election there was a bitter fight
between the republicans and democrats which absorbed
the voter's interest, and the democrats took up the greenbackers' demands. There were also dissensions among
the German-Americans, who unlike the Chicago socialists,
had few contacts with the trade unions. The editor of
the *National Socialist* threw out a suggestive comment
on the way American voters act: "Success is wanted now,
and if not possible of accomplishment upon the exact
basis desired, they will take the nearest movement that
partially represents them."

Outside of Chicago, Cincinnati, and St. Louis the
socialists polled 6,000 votes in Buffalo in the spring of
1877, and in alliance with the trade unionists 9,000 out
of a total of about 14,000 in Louisville at the same time.
In Baltimore a labor party which wanted "nothing to do
with the communists" polled 17,000 votes in this election.
The East, outside of New Haven, made a poor showing.
The party received but 1,800 votes in New York and
1,200 in Brooklyn, figures which it only doubled in the
great sweep of November, 1878.

The new-born socialist party had gone through a series
of political battles. It had learned what victory meant and
it had felt the sting of defeat. By its participation in the
election struggles, however, it brought the internal differences within its organization to a climax. The first convention after the unity congress of 1876 was held in
Newark, on December 26, 1877, representing seventy-two
sections with about 7,000 members. Flushed with the
showings made on the political field, the delegates repudiated the trade union faction, with its tactics of caution
and exclusive devotion to the economic arm of the movement. They changed the name of the organization to the
Socialist Labor Party. They adopted a new platform,
with a preamble which stated that, "The industrial emancipation of labor, which must be achieved by the working

classes themselves, independent of all political parties but their own, is . . . the great end to which every political movement should be subordinate as a means." They added a long list of immediate demands for practical use in political campaigns. The convention removed the seat of the national headquarters to Cincinnati and reelected Van Patten as secretary.

The trade union group did not give up the fight, however. The semi-annual report of the national executive, dated August 31, 1878, discussed the differences between the two factions. The majority interpreted the trade union position as follows:

Political efforts are for agitation only . . . leaving the actual work of changing the system to the wage earners themselves, who must through class organization and centralization of trade unions, compel higher wages and shorter hours of labor, thus raising themselves up, and enter into cooperation.

The political actionists, on the other hand, the majority said:

. . . aim at political success in order to encourage the workers; they want legislation controlled by the labor party; want unjust laws repealed, protective laws enforced and justice administered in all offices. They declare that the most necessary measures demanded by the trades unions can only be gained through political action, and that since capitalistic parties cannot take up such demands, the labor party must. They claim that workingmen who will not act politically for their own interest, have no hope and cannot be trusted in trades unions. More than all it is claimed that one-half of our population are farmers who cannot act as wage workers in trades unions, and the other half is so divided by the introduction of machinery, that the few trades unions can accomplish nothing beyond self-protection, even they being surely and inevitably forced down.

The *Verbote,* the organ of the western trade union group, put its side as follows:

The trade-union organization always appears to us as the natural and fundamental organization of the working class, and, being convinced that it should be entitled to all the support we can possibly give it, for its own sake, we cannot utter too strongly our feeling of protest, when here and there the over-zealous but unintelligent followers of the political labor movement desire to use the trade unions as mere auxiliaries for the Social-Democracy and demand that they should become socialistic in the sense in which that word applies to our political party.

§

Chicago was the center of both the political and the trade union factions of the party. As long as the Socialist Labor Party was growing and winning victories in the elections there was peace. There were also intimate relations between the socialists and the conservative trade unionists. Thomas J. Morgan in those days was a militant member of the machinists' union and not yet a lawyer, and Albert R. Parsons, another leading member of the party, was secretary of the trades council. But with the advent of the Educational and Defensive Societies (Lehr und Wehr Vereine), the decline in the vote, the corrupt methods used by the old parties, and the overtures which the national body made to the greenbackers in the 1880 presidential contest, the trade union socialists gained strength and caused the first split in the party which was then less than five years old. In the succeeding years, between 1880 and 1886, the political socialists marked time. The trade union faction developed a considerable anarchist and syndicalist movement which, however, blew up with the Haymarket bomb which exploded on May 4, 1886.

The Lehr und Wehr Vereine were armed bodies which drilled and practiced in military fashion, their object being to compel respect for socialists and their organizations. The first of them was incorporated in the state of Illinois in 1875 by the German socialists of Chicago. The *Verbote* of June 26, 1875, gave the following reason for their existence: "Inasmuch as the bourgeoisie of this place are building up a servile militia with its powers directed against the working man, the workingmen, man for man, should join the above named organization and willingly give the few dollars necessary to arm and uniform themselves. When the workingmen are on their guard, their just demands will not be answered with bullets." The brutality of the police toward the "Dutchmen," foreigners, and workers greatly incensed the latter. As early as 1850 the central committee of the United German Trades of New York adopted a resolution criticising the police for their behavior during a tailors' strike: "We protest with all the power of revolted feelings against the brutality and insolence with which many of our policemen have conducted themselves in the numerous arrests which have been made. We did not expect to find in this free country a Russian police, nor do we believe that the people will sustain these officials in their evident abuse of power."

When the panic of 1873 hit the country the people resorted to protest meetings to make known their sufferings. The "massacre" of peaceful demonstrators by the police at Tompkins Square, in New York, has already been mentioned. In 1877, after five years of industrial depression, the American wage earners revolted actively. There were pitched battles between the police, militia, and Pinkertons, on one hand, and the workers. On July 26 of that memorable year the police invaded a business meeting of the Chicago Furniture Workers' Union. According to Judge McAllister, not a biased authority, "a force of fifteen to twenty policemen came suddenly into the hall, having a policeman's club in one hand and a revolver in the other, and making no pause to determine the actual character of the meeting, they immediately shouted: 'Get out of here you damned ——,' and began beating the people with their clubs and some of them actually firing their revolvers. One young man was shot through the back of the head and killed. . . . When the people hastened to make their escape from the assembly room, they found policemen stationed on either side of the stairway leading from the hall down to the street, who applied their clubs to them as they passed, seemingly with all the violence practicable under the circumstances."

In 1893, when Governor John P. Altgeld of Illinois pardoned the anarchists imprisoned after the Haymarket affair, he decared that no attention had been paid to the decision of Judge McAllister upholding freedom of assemblage, and that peaceable meetings continued to be invaded and broken up, and inoffensive people clubbed. The governor cited the case of the strike at the McCormick reaper works in Chicago in 1885. Some Pinkerton detectives, while on their way there, were hooted at by people on the street. They immediately fired into the crowd and fatally wounded several persons who had taken no part in any disturbance. Although four of the Pinkerton men were indicted for murder, in the end they went scot free.

The attitude of the propertied classes toward tramps—wage earners out of work because of the depression—illustrated their callousness. The labor press quoted leading dailies. The New York *Herald* wrote: "It is very well to relieve real distress wherever it exists, whether in city or country; but the best meal that can be given to a regular tramp is a leaden one, and it should be supplied in sufficient quantity to satisfy the most voracious appetite." The Chicago *Tribune* suggested: "The simplest plan, probably, when one is not a member of the Humane Society, is to put strychnine or arsenic in the meat and other supplies furnished tramps. This produces death in a short time and a warning to other tramps to keep out of the neighborhood." The New York *World* gave the following advice to the free-born and otherwise independent citizens of the great republic: "The American laborer must make up his mind henceforth not to be so much better off than the European laborer. Men must be contented to work for less wages. In this way the workingman will be near to that station in life to which it has pleased God to call him." The unwarranted and brutal use of force by the police and militia, and the indifference of press and public opinion to the outrages committed, and to the lot of the people, were partly responsible for the development of the armed bodies. The theory of anarchism supplied the rest of their *raison d'etre*.

§

In the beginning the members of these Lehr and Wehr Vereine belonged to the Workingmen's Party or the Socialist Labor Party. The English-speaking element and the political socialists did not welcome them. On June 12, 1878, the national executive of the party ordered all members to withdraw from the defense groups, all sections to avoid any official connections with them, and also to prohibit the carrying of arms in processions. On the 20th of the same month the executive dropped the *Verbote* as an official party paper for sanctioning the armed bodies. Van Patten, the secretary of the party, explained: "The question of arming is with us neither a matter of protection nor an assertion of rights, but a matter of policy, as every clear-minded member knows. The capitalistic class is most anxious to force us into the position of an armed mob." In the Allegheny City convention of December, 1879, the opposition on this question was strong enough, however, to compel the adoption of a motion censuring the party officials for demanding the withdrawal of members from the defense organizations.

The presidential election of 1880 threw another bone of contention among the socialists. The trade union faction and the left-wing accused Van Patten and the editor of the *National Socialist,* John McIntosh, of being altogether too friendly toward the paper money reformers and the Californian, Dennis Kearney. They secured control of the party paper, when it was moved to Chicago in September, 1878, and Frank Hirth, a vigorous anti-greenbacker, became editor. The factional fight came to a head after the socialists sent delegates to the greenbackers' nominating convention and obtained nothing but the adoption of a meaningless resolution. In the middle of August a party referendum upheld the compromise made with the greenbackers and drove the opposition to launch a secession movement.

The left wing socialists comprised those who opposed fusion with the financial reformers and those who minimized political action and the use of the ballot. In Chicago, in the spring of 1880, the socialists had reelected Frank A. Stauber alderman; the results were officially announced in the polling place. Two election judges, however, deliberately changed the tally sheet, and it was not until after long and costly litigation that Stauber took his seat. The two old party election workers were tried but acquitted. Such crooked doings gave a talking point to those who were already opposed to stressing or even using parliamentary tactics.

The first get-together of the syndicalists and the anarchists, the former from the West, the latter from the East—took place on October 21, 1881. Two armed groups sent delegates. This convention declared against political action and recommended the formation of defense bodies "to render armed resistance to encroachments upon the rights of workingmen." A form of organization was adopted which permitted five members to start an autonomous group, while ten such groups could call a national congress. There was to be merely a committee of information in the headquarters in Chicago. The name Revolutionary Socialist Party was adopted.

The second convention, which assembled in Pittsburgh on October 18, 1883, was attended by the anarchist Johann Most, who had arrived in America the previous December and had had a triumphal tour through the country. The party's name was changed to that of the anarchist international, the International Working People's Association —not the same as Marx's First International, which was called the International Workingmen's Association. A clear-cut anarchist program was adopted. It was declared that the ballot was useless and the trade unions were merely means for organizing the workers for revolutionary struggles; the ruling class would only listen to one argument: force. This was the spirit of the Pittsburgh manifesto which called for the destruction of the existing system of class rule "by all means, *i.e.,* by energetic, relentless, revolutionary, and international action," with the "establishment of a free society based upon cooperative organization of production," with "free exchange of equivalent products by and between the productive organizations without commerce and profit-mongery."

Soon after this congress was held it was announced that there were fourteen armed clubs. The anarchist movement, which at first was confined to the foreign-born, had spread to the English-speaking workers. An English paper, *The Alarm,* was started in October, 1884, in Chicago. The daily and weekly in German, the *Arbeiter-Zeitung* and the *Verbote,* were already in anarchist hands. The anarchist trade unionists of Chicago organized their own central trade union body and heatedly discussed the question of the use of force and the necessity of armed groups. With their propaganda of anarchism they prepared the way for their own destruction. They played into the hands of the authorities who used the Haymarket bomb to put anarchism on trial, hang and imprison its leaders, and crush it.

§

The McCormick harvester works were seriously affected by the eight-hour general strike of May 1, 1886, which the workers of Chicago took up with great enthusiasm. Thousands of the toilers of this factory laid down their tools. On the afternoon of May 3, August Spies, the editor-in-chief of the *Arbeiter Zeitung,* and a leading anarchist, was addressing an open air meeting of the McCormick strikers, when the bell of the plant sounded. A part of the audience broke away to meet the strikebreakers as they were coming out of the gates. Police arrived and in the ensuing fight six of the workers were killed. Spies hurried to the office of his paper. Incensed by the murder of the work-

ingmen he composed and had printed what has become
known as the "Revenge Circular." It began: "Revenge!
Workingmen, to arms!" It ended: "To Arms! Destruction to the human monsters that call themselves your
masters!" That night arrangements were made for a
protest meeting to be held in Haymarket Square the following evening.

On May 4, several thousand people gathered at the
meeting place. Spies, Albert R. Parsons, and Samuel
Fielden spoke. The meeting was peaceful. Mayor Harrison, who attended, left after he heard Parsons. He instructed Captain Bondfield to send all the police in reserve
to their homes. But after the mayor had left, and when
the crowd had dwindled as a result of a cold wind and
threatened rain, the police suddenly marched in formation upon the meeting. The captain of the squad of 176
policemen ordered the audience to disperse. Fielden, who
was speaking from the wagon, answered that the meeting
was peaceful. Just then a dynamite bomb was thrown into
the ranks of the police. Shooting between the police and
the audience followed. As a result of the bomb and the
shootings about ten were killed and a larger number
wounded on both sides. The outstanding anarchists of
Chicago were indicted and put on trial. They were
charged with having "advised large classes of the people,
not particular individuals . . . to commit murder . . .
that in consequence of that advice . . . somebody not
known did throw the bomb." This was the statement of
Judge Joseph E. Gary, the trial judge, who truly wrote
that "this case is without a precedent: there is no example
in the law books of a case of this sort."

Albert R. Parsons, the editor of *The Alarm,* voluntarily gave himself up. Rudolph Schnaubelt escaped, and
William Seliger supplied the state with evidence. Parsons, Spies, Fielden, Michael Schwab, Adolph Fischer,
George Engel, Oscar W. Neebe, and Louis Lingg were
found guilty. All, with the exception of Neebe, were
sentenced to death. Schwab and Fielden petitioned the

governor for clemency and had their sentences commuted
to life imprisonment. Parsons refused to ask for executive clemency on the ground that he feared that the chances
of the others might be diminished, for he might be saved
while they would be hung. The supreme court of the state
upheld the verdict. Despite hundreds of appeals, Governor Oglesby refused to save the four men, Parsons,
Spies, Fischer, and Engel. They were hung on November
11, 1887. Louis Lingg had committed suicide in prison.
Six years later, on June 26, 1893, Governor Altgeld
pardoned Fielden, Schwab, and Neebe.

In view of the refusal of Governor Alvin A. Fuller of
Massachusetts to save Nicola Sacco and Bartolomeo Vanzetti, Altgeld's reasons for pardoning the Chicago anarchists may have interest. The Illinois governor declared
first that the jury was packed: "The twelve jurors whom
the defendants were finally forced to accept, after the
challenges were exhausted, were of the same general
character as the others, and a number of them stated
candidly that they were so prejudiced that they could not
try the case fairly, but each, when examined by the court,
was finally induced to say that he believed he could try
the case fairly upon the evidence that was produced in
court alone." Henry L. Ryce, the special bailiff who
selected these jurors, was appointed by the prosecuting
state's attorney. He told his friends that he was managing the case, and "that these fellows would hang as
certain as death; that he was calling such men as the
defendants would have to challenge peremptorily and
waste their challenges on, and that when their challenges
were exhausted they would have to take such men as the
prosecution wanted." Governor Altgeld made a blunt
attack in his statement on the captain who ordered the
police to disperse the Haymarket meeting: "Captain
Bondfield is the man who is really responsible for the
death of the police officers." The governor severely
condemned the prejudiced behavior of Judge Gary during
the trial. The judge who tried the case in the court room

was accused as being as unfair as the newspapers and the powers that be that settled it on the outside; seemingly as determined to have the men hung as Judge Webster Thayer is accused of having desired Sacco and Vanzetti executed.

§

According to Edward B. Mittelman's account, in his history of the Chicago labor movement of those days, the Chicago *Herald* of January 4, 1892, revealed the telling fact that after the bomb was thrown about 300 prominent citizens met and subscribed $115,000 to stamp out anarchy and pledged $100,000 annually for such purpose. This money was paid until 1891. Three days after payment of this money was discontinued, the police invaded a meeting of stockholders of the *Arbeiter Zeitung*. An interview with Chief of Police Ebersold of Chicago, published in the Chicago *Daily News* of May 10, 1889, threw some light on the causes of anarchy scares in those days, and may possibly help us to understand also why some people discover "red plots" in our own day. Ebersold declared: "It was my policy to quiet matters down as soon as possible after the 4th of May. The general unsettled state of things was an injury to Chicago. On the other hand, Captain Schaack wanted to keep things stirring. He wanted bombs to be found here, there, all around, everywhere . . . this man Schaack, this little boy who must have glory or his heart would be broken . . . after we got the anarchist societies broken up . . . wanted to send out men to again organize new societies right away. . . . He wanted to keep the thing boiling, keep himself prominent before the public." Was it only that? Who got the $100,000 each year? And who is interested in keeping himself before the public today, and at what cash consideration?

§

The Socialist Labor Party was hard hit after the split with the anarchists. At its second and third conventions, held in New York and Baltimore in December, 1881 and 1883, a membership of only about 1,500 was reported. On April 22, 1883, Van Patten, the national secretary, threw up the sponge and mysteriously disappeared. Many of the leaders at first tried to make peace with the anarchists, but they were told to join as autonomous groups, in other words to crawl in on their knees. On March 4, 1885, the party secretary, V. L. Rosenberg, admitted: "Let us not conceal the truth: the Socialist Labor Party is only a German colony, an adjunct of the German-speaking Social Democracy." The fifth national convention, however, which met in Cincinnati on October 5, 1885, showed a little revival. One of the demands incorporated in the platform called for the abolition of the office of president of the United States. Again, when the party was small, a resolution was carried which said that the party was first of all an educational and propaganda organization. Sections were told not to enter the political arena unless they had a chance to make a good showing or to carry on some effective agitation. There was to be no compromise with any other party or candidates. The last point illustrates how time makes fools of us all. In less than a year after this convention adjourned the American workers launched their independent labor parties, and the Socialist Labor Party everywhere actively participated; and what is more, it fought tooth and nail to stay inside the *bona fide* workingmen's parties.

Two questions had to be disposed of at the party convention which opened in Buffalo on September 17, 1887. The United Labor Party of New York had but a month previously ousted the socialists. Outside of New York the socialists were still holding on, but without much joy, for there was internal friction between the Marxians and the pure and simple trade unionists. A considerable sentiment developed, therefore, for the Socialist Labor Party to go it alone. In view of the approaching elections, however, the convention decided to allow each section to choose its own course, whether to tie up or nominate independently. The other matter which faced the delegates concerned amalgamation with an American anarchist group which styled itself the International Workingmen's Association. In ultimate goal, akin to the anarchists, it stressed education, however, as the means of achieving it. The organization claimed about 6,000 members, located in the far West and Northwest. The socalists insisted that the platform of the party be the basis of any union. The anarchist group, which did not believe in stressing political action, refused, and soon disappeared.

§

The New York *Volkszeitung* had been established in 1878 as a German socialist daily. In 1880 it accepted the compromise with the greenbackers. In the contest between the anarchists and the socialists it unreservedly supported the latter and helped to sustain the party in the dark days when the anarchist tide was rising. In 1886, when the trade unionists of New York were in a mood to listen and strike back at the old parties and a judge who had sent workers to prison in a boycott case, the *Volkszeitung* enthusiastically backed up the independent political move. Alexander Jonas and Sergius E. Schevitsch, its editors, took an active part in the campaign, while the printing plant published the daily *Leader,* the organ of Henry George's United Labor Party. After the split with the laborites and single taxers the *Volkszeitung* continued to maintain close and friendly relations with the German unions. As the Socialist Labor Party was largely a German and New York affair, and as the *Volkszeitung* and its editors dominated the socialist movement in that city, also the headquarters of the national party, it held a commanding position.

Between 1886 and 1889 there developed an ever-increasing hostility between the national executive committee of the party, headed by the secretary, V. L. Rosenberg, and the *Volkszeitung* group. The former was lukewarm toward the labor parties which sprang up in 1886.

It also minimized the importance of trade union action. When the American Federation of Labor announced another general demonstration and strike for the eight-hour day the official party paper, *Der Sozialist,* edited by Rosenberg, declared that the move would get the workers nowhere. Rosenberg contended that the shorter work day could only be obtained by political action and that the workers must support the Socialist Labor Party.

The *Volkszeitung* faction took matters into its own hands. On September 10, 1889, a meeting of the members of the New York sections, which elected the national executive committee, declared the seats of the latter vacant. Schevitsch called Rosenberg and his fellow committee members an inefficient clique; charged them with being too doctrinaire; declared that they were making a sect of the movement and that because of their attitude on the eight-hour day and toward the unions they had cooled the interest of the latter in the party. The secretary and the national executive refused to accept the verdict of the New York membership meeting, run by the *Volkszeitung* crowd. Each side then called a national convention. The *Volkszeitung* faction won the majority of the sections. Its convention in Chicago, October 13-16, 1889, legalized the acts of the New York members who had unseated the old executive, defended the trade unions, and adopted a platform written by Lucien Sanial in the phraseology of the Declaration of Independence. The Rosenberg group continued a meagre existence until 1897 when it united with the Chicago Social Democracy.

CHAPTER V

KNIGHTS, TRADE UNIONISTS, AND SOCIALISTS

THE men who founded and led the Noble Order of the Knights of Labor belonged to an America of the sixties and seventies. There was still an abundance of free land. Capitalism had not yet gotten its full stride. The leaders of the Knights did not, therefore, think in terms of a permanent wage earning class and its needs as such. The first grand master workman, Uriah S. Stephens, considered the object of the order to be "the complete emancipation of the wealth producers from the thraldom and loss of wage slavery; the entire redemption of the world's toilers from the political tyranny of unjust laws, and the annihilation of the great anti-Christ of civilization manifest in the idolatry of wealth, and the consequent degradation and social ostracism of all else not possessing it, and its baneful effects upon heaven ordained labor." This devout American Christian, who organized the first local assembly of the Knights on December 26, 1869, put the universally human, American, and social religious cry for economic opportunity, political and social equality into religious words when he said that the Knights built "upon the immutable basis of the Fatherhood of God, and the logical principle of the Brotherhood of Man." This good man believed in the dignity of labor. His ideal society in America meant the chance for every one to take up enough land for his own use, and the combination of wage earners in the cities into producers' cooperatives, so that they would have no masters. His ideal labor organization to achieve these ends was to be as broad as the

American human family, to include white and black, man and woman, skilled and unskilled, proletarian and intellectual, worker and farmer, all—with the exception of a very few, the banker, the broker, the lawyer, the gambler, and the liquor dealer.

Terrence V. Powderly succeeded Stephens as grand master workman of this secret order and directed it between 1879 and 1893, the years when it was a power to be reckoned with. He was a skilled machinist, but did not believe in elevating the conditions of his craftsmen alone. He wrote: "The rights of the common, everyday laborer were to be considered by the new order, because the members of trades unions had failed to see that they had rights. . . . It was because the trade union failed to recognize the rights of man, and looked only to the rights of the tradesman that the Knights of Labor became a possibility." Powderly thus added a touch of eighteenth century philosophy to the genuine Christianity of Stephens. Among these "rights of man" were first and foremost the right to a share in the country's boundless natural resources. "We undertook to direct the attention of the wage earner to the fact that, though he might call himself the 'natural and proper guardian of his inherent rights,' the unnatural and improper uses to which natural opportunities were put—the contraction of the currency, the monopoly of land, and the placing of the railroad king upon an altar before which millions must worship or become tramps—made it utterly impossible for him to properly guard his 'inherent rights' without associating with other men in an effort to overturn the existing conditions in the industrial world which made of him a serf in a land of liberty and sunshine." To Powderly the questions of land, transportation, and money were paramount. In his day, as in our own, the individualistic American had to be persuaded to combine with his fellows for economic improvement.

In his presidential address to the 1882 convention of the Knights, Powderly stated clearly his economic philos-

ophy: "The eight-hour law, the prohibition of child
labor . . . are all of weighty moment to the toiler. But
high above them all stands the land question. Give me
the land, and you may frame as many eight-hour laws as
you please. . . . Prohibit child labor if you will, but give
me the land, and your children will be my slaves." The
1884 session accordingly adopted a land plank which demanded "that the public lands, the heritage of the people,
be reserved for actual settlers; not another acre for railroads or speculators, and that all lands now held for
speculative purposes be taxed to their full value." The
Knights put this emphasis on the land question not merely
because they hoped it would ease the labor market and
raise wages in the industrial cities. Powderly declared
repeatedly: "We must free the land and give men the
chance to become their own employers. . . . We must
strike a death blow at usury and the credit system . . . by
the issue of an adequate currency." Powderly and the
Knights were deep down in their hearts still yearning
for a refuge from the wages system.

This aim made the grand master workman impatient
with those who wished to turn the Knights of Labor into
a pure labor organization. He could write of the 1883
convention in the following terms: "The records of that
session show that a great deal of valuable time was spent
in legislation upon strikes and lockouts. With these harassing details to attend to, the General Assembly was
worn out before the time arrived when consideration
could be given" to the land question and other general
matters "alluded to in the address of the grand master
workman." This man, the leader of a labor organization, could say that time spent on strikes and lockouts was
wasted, and describe these subjects as "harassing details."
On March 13, 1886, Powderly and the general executive
board issued a secret order to their hundreds of thousands
of members not to participate in the general strike of
May 1 for eight hours. To be sure, there was rivalry
between the chiefs of the Knights of Labor and the

American Federation of Labor, and the organizations as well, but Powderly did not really have much faith in the struggle on the economic field for the shorter work day. He said on a subsequent occasion, in the official journal: "The organization which would shorten the hours of labor, while the efforts to dump thousands of workmen on the spot where hundreds only may be required are not questioned, cannot permanently succeed, and for saying this I suppose certain men will ignore the truth and call me an enemy of the trade union." As early as 1880 Powderly expressed his opinion that "strikes are a failure. Ask any old veteran in the labor movement and he will say the same. I shudder at the thought of a strike, and I have good reason."

The Knights of Labor was launched, then, as an idealistic, all-inclusive labor organization, to educate the workers in human and class solidarity and to develop producers' cooperatives. But as education was an intangible good, and producers' cooperatives required capital and then might not succeed, the leaders of the order reluctantly accepted the more materialistic and immediate objects of the members. In the eighties, tens of thousands of workers, chiefly unskilled, joined it. By July, 1886, the order had grown to close to 6,000 local assemblies with over 700,000 members. These newcomers wanted something here and now. They had a lively expectation of receiving some immediate advantage, such as the eight-hour day, or an increased wage, when they affiliated. The membership of the Knights, therefore, fluctuated tremendously. The workers withdrew in large numbers when they found that they could not obtain their demands at one stroke. Although the leaders were opposed to strikes, except as a last resort, the new members were ever ready to down tools. But as they were unprepared, undisciplined, and in the case of the unskilled, easily replaced, they suffered defeat more frequently than they gained victory.

As a result of losses in membership and repeated failures in labor disputes the editor of the official journal went so far as to argue against strikes altogether. He wrote: "To fight capitalism with strikes is like bringing old fashioned flint-lock muskets into battle against modern artillery. Every new machine invented makes it harder for labor to contend against capitalism." His contention was that the machine increased the number of unemployed who were prepared to take the places of the strikers; and that it also destroyed the difference between skilled and unskilled labor so that the former could be easily replaced. The editor hammered home the lesson of every defeat. He pointed out the "increasing power of resistance of capitalism, consequent upon the policy of combination and alliance among employers," and the inequality of the contest in which the men pitted their empty stomachs against the wealth of the capitalists. The defeats on the economic battlefield reenforced the conviction of the editor "that the policy of fighting employers is out of date, and that the only way . . . is to sweep away every form of monopoly." After the miners in Durham County, England, were beaten, he said: "When the majority of the people of England realize that the coal mines really belong to them and ought to be worked in the national interest instead of to enrich a few wealthy thieves and exploiters, it will not be necessary for coal miners to strike in order to secure living wages."

§

When the Knights of Labor held its first national convention in January, 1878, at Reading, Pa., it adopted a platform and a constitution for a national body. In the eight years which had passed since the handful of garment cutters of Philadelphia had formed a secret society and decided to admit workers outside of their craft as sojourners, the organization had spread to most of the important industrial states east of the Mississippi. Eleven district assemblies were represented at the first congress.

The platform and rules adopted by this gathering stamped the Knights throughout their history.

The preamble declared that "industrial and moral worth, not wealth" was "the true standard of individual and national greatness," and that the order proposed "to bring within the folds of organization every department of productive industry." Specific demands called for bureaus of labor statistics, productive and distributive cooperatives, public lands for actual settlers, "the abrogation of all laws that do not bear equally upon capital and labor," health and safety laws, weekly pay-days and wages in legal currency, a mechanics' lien law, abolition of the contract system on public works, substitution of arbitration for strikes, no child labor, no contract prison labor, equal pay for equal work for both sexes, reduction of hours to eight a day, and a circulating medium issued directly by the government. At subsequent conventions, or sessions as they were called, the national body adopted additional planks for the prohibition by law of the Pinkerton Protective Patrol; abolition of the militia; restriction of immigration; the Australian ballot; the initiative and referendum; immediate possession by the government of the Union Pacific Railroad; and government ownership of the railroads and telegraphs.

The structure of the Knights of Labor corresponded to its aims and objects. At its base were the local and mixed assemblies; the former included the workers of one trade, while the latter contained those of all occupations. Uniting and controlling these local bodies in a city or larger area or in one trade through the country were the district and national trade assemblies. Above and supreme over all was the general assembly or national convention of delegates. Between its sessions the general executive board ruled. The final word in all matters —until a convention was held—thus rested in the national headquarters. The Knights of Labor was a highly centralized body with tremendous power lodged in the hands of its national officers. They could order members out on strike and send them back to work; they could expel a local assembly; they could expel an individual member. This is in marked contrast with the situation in the American Federation of Labor, where the affiliated international unions control and the officers of the federation have only delegated and very limited powers.

The leaders of the Knights were politically minded. Terrence V. Powderly organized the Greenback-Labor Party of Luzerne County, Pennsylvania, and was elected mayor of Scranton in 1878 and 1880. He was offered the nomination for Congress and various state offices on several occasions and was talked of as candidate for the then newly created office of Commissioner of the Bureau of Labor Statistics at Washington in 1884. Uriah S. Stephens was once a greenback candidate for Congress. Ralph Beaumont, chairman of the legislative committee and general worthy foreman, ran for Congress also on the greenback-labor ticket in New York, and was prominently identified with the greenback movement. A. W. Wright, an outstanding national leader of the Knights, was a lecturer for the greenbackers. Charles H. Litchman, grand secretary of the order, was up for office as a greenbacker in Massachusetts and took part in the convention which nominated General James B. Weaver in 1880. The platform of the Greenback-Labor Party contained the demands of the Knights of Labor. After the greenback movement had subsided, and when the producers turned to independent political action again, the Knights joined those behind the labor parties of the eighties. In 1889 the Knights of Labor definitely tied up with the farmers in an alliance which led to the formation of the People's Party. When put to the test, the order was not able to assimilate or hold its membership. It did not come out victorious in labor disputes and bring tangible advantages to the workers; it did not make a success of the numerous producers' cooperatives which it sponsored; and it did not succeed on the political field after it had failed on the economic. Its contribution lay

in being one of the finest educational labor organizations
in the history of the United States.

§

It was three old greenbackers, T. V. Powderly, A. W.
Wright and Ralph Beaumont, who represented the
Knights of Labor and signed the agreement at St. Louis
on December 5, 1889, with the committee of the National
Farmers' Alliance and Industrial Union, to act in concert
in the effort to secure legislation from Congress. The
Knights had as early as 1878 committed themselves to
the program which was then adopted; the abolition of national banks and a sufficient amount of legal tender treasury notes to place the business of the country on a cash
basis; prohibition of alien ownership of land, and the re-
covery of land held by railroads and other corporations
in excess of their needs; and government control and
operation of the means of communication and transportation. The St. Louis agreement added one new demand:
the free and unlimited coinage of silver. In 1889 the
Knights of Labor had already lost a good part of its
membership in the industrial cities. It now had its
strength in the small towns, and it also counted in its
ranks a number of farmers. When the populist movement began to sweep the Middle West the official journal
could report for the November, 1890, election that "every
one of the newly elected state officers of Kansas is a
Knight of Labor." The editor added that "the vast majority of the truest and most trustworthy men of the
Alliance are in deep sympathy with the Knights of Labor
. . . they received their education in reform in many in-
stances in this order."

Accordingly, the general assembly of the Knights of
Labor decided, in its November, 1890, session, in favor of
independent political action. The following year Powderly
sent out a call to the American Federation of Labor, the
railroad brotherhoods, and the independent unions. Few
responded. The Knights went ahead, however, and

cooperated with those farmers' organizations which
founded and supported the People's Party. The order
sent 82 delegates to the Industrial Congress of February
22, 1892, in St. Louis. Again in the national labor conference of April 28, 1894, held in Philadelphia, at which
delegates were present from the American Federation of
Labor, the railroad brotherhoods, independent unions, and
the Knights of Labor, the spokesmen of the latter proposed an endorsement of the People's Party. The conference adopted a common policy to resist wage reductions in view of the depression, to promote industrial legislation, and to harmonize the differences between the
rival organizations, if possible. It did not accept the
proposition of officially approving the third party. In
1896 the Knights of Labor as an organization threw itself
into the free silver campaign.

§

The socialists had kept up a running fight with the pure
and simple trade unionists of the American Federation
of Labor from its formation, and with Samuel Gompers
since the seventies. In 1877, when Gompers sought the
election of Adolph Strasser as president at a convention
of the Cigar Makers' International Union, a socialist
gave him a long drawn out battle before he succeeded in
electing his man. Four years later, in 1881, when the
former president of the federation tried to get the New
York socialist cigarmakers to vote for Edward Grosse,
who was up for reelection on an old party ticket, because of his help in securing the enactment of the first
tenement house bill in the interest of cigarmakers, the
socialists refused to support him. In the following year
there was a split in the Cigar Makers' International
Union as a result of a decision of Strasser, who voided
an election in Local 144 of New York, and pronounced
the man elected by the socialists as not legally qualified
to take his seat. From the very first days to the end of

his life in the American labor movement Gompers fought and was fought by the socialists.

Samuel Gompers came by his philosophy of pure and simple trade unionism in large part, he stated, through the influence of Karl M. F. Laurrell. Laurrell was educated in the First International, the International Workingmen's Association, and met Gompers in 1872. The latter paid the following tribute to his mentor: "The man whom I loved most and for whose brain, heart, and character I have always had boundless admiration was Karl Malcolm Ferdinand Laurrell. . . . Karl . . . had been convinced that the trade union was the fundamental agency to which working people must trust."

In the seventies the First International played a large role in the labor movement of New York and Gompers learned considerable from the German-American Marxians. "I remember asking Laurrell whether in his opinion I ought to keep in touch with the socialist movement," wrote Gompers. "He replied, 'Go to their meetings by all means, listen to what they have to say and understand them, but do not join the party.' I never did." Of Karl Marx, he said: "Marx did not beguile himself into thinking the ballot was all-powerful." According to Gompers, "he grasped the principle that the trade union was the immediate and practical agency which could bring wage earners a better life. . . . Marx was not consistent in all his writings, but his influence contributed to emphasize the necessity for organization of wage earners in trade unions and the development of economic power prior to efforts to establish labor government through political methods." The underlying assumption of the trade union philosophy of Samuel Gompers was, in his own words, "that economic organization and control over economic power were the fulcrum which made possible influence and power in all other fields. Control over the basic things of life gives power that may be used for good in every relationship of life." Gompers never denied that a class struggle existed in modern industrial

society and that it was the *sine qua non* of the trade union
movement. He did maintain, however, "that class consciousness was a mental process shared by all who had
imagination, but that primitive force that had its origin
in experience only was Klassengefuehl (class feeling).
This group feeling is one of the strongest cohesive forces
in the labor movement."

§

Unlike Stephens and Powderly, the leaders of the
Knights of Labor, the founder of the American Federation of Labor believed with all his being in trade unionism. He called himself with joy a trade unionist, pure
and simple. He considered the unions *"the* organizations
of the working class, for the working class, by the working class," in his own way, and as all-sufficient for the
emancipation of the working class. He was a strong believer in strikes and therefore always advocated high dues
and the building up of a war-chest. He believed in militancy. He held that "workers who have intelligence and
manhood enough in their make-up to contend against the
imposition of poorer or to strike for better conditions,
never go down in the economic scale. . . . A strike involving
wages, hours, and other conditions of employment, even if
temporarily defeated in the attainment of the immediate
purpose, has always checked greater invasion on the part
of the employers, or has paved the way for the ultimate
achievement of the object sought by the workmen."

In 1892, after he saw the defeat of the powerfully organized steel workers at Homestead and the bloody struggles at Coeur d'Alene, Idaho, and at Tracy City, Tennessee, Gompers did not take the position of the Knights
of Labor or of the triumvirate of the Socialist Labor
Party, that the day of the strike was over. He declared
that the fact that, "the capitalist class having assumed
the aggressive, and after defeating the toilers in several
contests, the wage workers of our country have maintained their organizations is the best proof of the power,

influence and permanency of the trade unions. They have not been routed, they have merely retreated." Gompers, Strasser, and the pure and simplers strongly advocated the addition of beneficiary features to trade unions. Gompers very early in his career wrote: "As a rule, the most intelligent workingmen can always be relied upon to remain members of their organizations through prosperity or adversity. The interests of the men who have no inclination or ability or time to clearly see the benefits and advantages of organization should be made so inseparable from the union as to make it a direct and decided loss to them to sever their connection with the union. . . . I know of no better means to secure that end than to make our unions beneficial and benevolent, as well as protective." The Cigar Makers' International Union, founded in 1864, and developed along these lines, was one of the largest and most successful organizations —in 1881, when the Federation of Organized Trades and Labor Unions was born. Unfortunately, Samuel Gompers did not learn easily or change much, although he lived long.

Although he voted for Peter Cooper in 1876 and for James B. Weaver in 1880 and 1892, Gompers did not put much stock in the greenback, nor later, in the free silver movement. He had "learned that cheap money was not the answer to labor or financial problems." And he had no hopes of smashing monopolies or trusts. He considered them "simply an evolution from the old-time individual establishments merged into partnerships, into companies and again into corporations, and finally into the company of corporations, the trusts." He was "convinced that the state is not capable of preventing the development or the natural concentration of industry." In 1882, at the second convention of the Federation of Organized Trades and Labor Unions, he put himself on record in reference to the land question. A resolution had been introduced calling for a system of land tenure "that will guarantee to all an equitable share of the

natural resources of the land." Gompers "denied that
land controlled wages, and declared that wages controlled
land and everything else." He added: "It is not the
ownership of land that should be fought, but the doings
of the capitalists we are organized to oppose." Because
of his hatred of socialism and state interference—he was
a believer in *laissez-faire*—he lined up against government ownership of the railroads. He likewise, and here
vehemently, fought any effort to secure from the state
what the trade unions could obtain on the economic field.
He did not believe in independent political action because
to him the trade union came first, nay, it was the end-all,
and everything else was only a means. Samuel Gompers
indelibly stamped his philosophy of pure and simple trade
unionism on the labor organizations of this country. He
was its protagonist; he never wearied expounding, in-
terpreting and defending it. And Samuel Gompers is
partly, if not largely responsible for the difficulties and
perils which the American labor movement faces today,
both on the economic and the political field.

§

The Federation of Organized Trades and Labor
Unions, the predecessor of the American Federation of
Labor, was formed by trade unionists who did not feel
at home in the Knights of Labor. It was intended to be a
labor clearing house and legislative agency along the
lines of the loose British Trades Union Congress. The
first convention, which was held in Pittsburgh in November, 1881, contained besides delegates of trade unions also
a considerable number of representatives from assemblies
of the Knights of Labor, motivated by their fears and
curiosity concerning a possible rival. The first convention adopted a declaration of principles which clearly
enunciated the Marxian concept of class struggle:
"Whereas, a struggle is going on in the nations of the
civilized world between the oppressors and the oppressed
of all countries, a struggle between capital and labor,

which must grow in intensity from year to year and work disastrous results to the toiling millions of all nations if not combined for mutual protection and benefit. . . ." The planks of the platform strikingly pointed to the working class character of the federation. There were no general demands of interest to farmers, to money reformers, to non-proletarian elements. The form of organization, and the method of representation provided for future conventions, gave the national trade unions complete control by allowing them an increasing number of delegates in proportion to their membership. Samuel Gompers was chairman of the constitution committee of this first convention, and when it adjourned was a member of its important legislative committee, whose duties were "to watch legislative measures directly affecting the question of labor."

The conventions which annually followed offered little encouragement, however, to the founders of the federation. At Cleveland in 1882 there were but nineteen delegates. The leading union, the Amalgamated Iron and Steel Workers, and the Knights of Labor, were no longer represented. And in the absence of John Jarrett, president of the steel workers and an advocate of a protective tariff, the delegates wiped out their previous endorsement of it. Frank K. Foster made an effective speech against retaining the protective tariff plank. He argued as follows:

The rate of wages depends upon other causes than the tariff. . . . Subsidies paid to the iron, wool, cotton, and other favored industries of the United States have only served to concentrate wealth in the hands of the few, to the disadvantage of the many. . . . An artificial stimulus causes an excessive amount of capital to be employed, resulting in over-supply, lock-outs, and shut-downs. . . . "Protected" workers are receiving lower wages while the industries are being further protected. . . . Our national congress is turned into a manufacturers' lobby, where the clique that brings the heaviest pressure secures the greatest monopoly. . . . As consumers, wage workers are taxed for the support of monopolies, forced to pay toil to the brigands infesting our commercial highways.

Even as early as this, in 1882, the report of the legislative committee spoke of the election of friends and the defeat of enemies of labor. A mass meeting was held during the convention and two friends of labor, Congressmen M. A. Foran and Thompson Murch, former labor leaders, were the main speakers.

In 1884 Frank K. Foster, secretary of the legislative committee, sent letters to the chairmen of the national committees of the Republican and Democratic Parties, asking their stand on enforcement of the eight-hour law and other planks of the federation's platform. He did not even receive a reply. Notwithstanding the rebuff, he and others appeared before the appropriate committees of the two old parties. In the 1885 convention, when Henry Emrich introduced a resolution calling for the formation of a workingmen's party he received one vote in favor, his own. When this delegate of the furniture workers, however, presented a proposition for effectively carrying out an eight-hour general strike which had been voted in 1884, it was unanimously carried.

§

The Trades and Labor Assembly of Chicago had introduced in the 1882 convention a resolution in favor of the eight-hour day. Inasmuch as it embodied the philosophy of the eight-hour reformers, the resolution has historic interest. It declared:

The eight-hour work day will furnish more work at increased wages. . . . It will permit the possession and enjoyment of more wealth by those who create it. . . . It will lighten the burden (of carrying the useless classes) by providing work for the unemployed. . . . It will diminish the power of the rich over the poor, not by making the rich poorer, but by making the poor richer. It will create the conditions necessary for the education and intellectual advancement of the masses. It will diminish crime and intemperance. It will increase the power of wage-laborers to control the conditions that affect them. It will enlarge the wants, stimulate the ambition, and decrease the idleness of wage laborers. It will stimulate production and increase the consump-

tion of wealth among the masses. It will compel the employment of more and better labor-saving machinery. It will not
disturb, jar, confuse, or throw out of order the present wage-
system of labor. It is (the only) a measure that will permanently
increase wages without at the same time increasing the cost of
the production of wealth. It will decrease the poverty and increase the wealth of all wage laborers. And it will after a few
years gradually merge the wage system of labor into a system of
industrial cooperation in which wages will represent the earnings
and not as now the necessities of the wage laborers.

The resolution was adopted *in toto,* except for the parts
in parentheses.

The American Federation of Labor was not always
opposed to general strikes. In the 1884 session the secretary of the legislative committee proposed that a referendum be taken "as to the feasibility of a universal strike
for a working day of eight (or nine) hours" but by a vote
of twenty-three to two the convention took matters into
its own hands and resolved "that eight hours shall constitute a legal day's labor from and after May 1, 1886,"
and called on the workers to lay down their tools throughout the length and breadth of the land to enforce that
resolution. Despite the fact that the general strike did
not succeed in gaining its immediate objective, the legislative committee's report to the 1886 convention stated
that "the desire for fewer hours led thousands to affiliate
with the organizations existing, besides being the means
of organizing large numbers that had hitherto been indifferent."

This demand for the eight-hour day was a fighting
slogan of the American Federation of Labor for many
years to come. Back of it was a basic principle of the
pure and simple trade unionist, who made his case always
on the demand for more, more, more, now, in terms of
higher wages and shorter hours. It was also an effective
weapon which could be used against the political socialists.
Frank K. Foster presented this side of it when he said
in the 1884 session: "In the world of economic reform

the working classes must depend upon themselves for the enforcement of measures as well as for their conception. A united demand for a shorter working day, backed by thorough organization, will prove vastly more effective than the enactment of a thousand laws depending for enforcement upon the pleasure of aspiring politicians or sycophantic department officials."

In the campaign for the eight-hour day by a general strike the leaders of the American Federation of Labor sought the cooperation of the Knights of Labor. They sent the resolution adopted in the 1885 session to Powderly, but received no reply. They soon learned that in March, 1886, the executive board of the Knights of Labor had issued a secret order against their members participating in the May 1 general strike. The causes of friction between the federation and the order were fundamental. The former represented the point of view of the skilled—those able to help themselves—while the latter spoke for the producing classes, including the unskilled wage earners. The pure and simple trade unionists believed in protecting and improving their own conditions, by direct action against their own employers. The Knights sought to raise the level of all producers by a general attack on the monopolist, financier, and legislator. The leaders of the Knights of Labor belonged to an America that was fast receding into the past, while the trade unionists—foreign-born and native mechanics with less expectation of becoming farmers or employers —fitted into the United States of the nineties and succeeding decade. The center of the battle between the American Federation of Labor and the Knights of Labor was in the cigarmakers' trade. In New York District Assembly 49 supported a seceding organization 'and pushed the white label of the order against the Gompers-Strasser union and the blue label of the federation. Other international unions had also to meet the rival claims of the order which wanted to dominate them or threatened their exclusive jurisdiction.

In 1886 the national trade unions united their forces and presented a set of propositions to the Knights of Labor, which, if the latter had adopted them, would have converted it into merely an educational body. Two conventions of the Knights of Labor, held in this year of its greatest strength, refused to accept them. Accordingly, delegates of the leading unions met in December, 1886, at Columbus, and launched the American Federation of Labor, with a constitution and platform not much different from that of the Federation of Organized Trades and Labor Unions, which merged with it. They elected as president, Samuel Gompers who, with the exception of one year, held the office until his death in 1924.

§

The year which saw the birth of the American Federation of Labor witnessed some remarkable independent political campaigns of labor. These demonstrations had their reflex in the first convention of the federation. The organization went on record in favor of the movement by adopting the following resolution:

Whereas, this subject is one which has in the past been a prolific source of dissension and trouble in the ranks of the workingmen; but, happily, the revolution recently witnessed in the election contests in several states, notably, that remarkable and extraordinary demonstration made by the workingmen of New York, Milwaukee, Chicago, and other places, shows us the time has now arrived when the working people should decide upon the necessity of united action, as citizens at the ballot box; and

Whereas, the necessity of this is apparent from the subjection of the police power to the interest of corporate capital, in enforcing upon their employees conditions repulsive to free labor and liberty; and if the nefarious work of the Pinkerton Detective Agency is to be stopped the workers must secure a greater share of political power; therefore, be it

Resolved, that the convention urge a most generous support to the independent political movement of the workingmen.

In 1887, however, the annual report of President Gompers came out against an independent political party "in view of recent experiences." The labor parties were now split and already on the decline.

In an article by G. A. Hoehn in the *American Federationist* of the nineties, entitled "True Socialism," the St. Louis socialist veteran—then a young man—gave F. A. Sorge's suggestion as to possible cooperation between socialists and pure and simple trade unionists. Hoehn quoted Sorge as follows: "If, from reasons of honesty, a harmonious working together has become impossible— a thing that may happen or may have happened—then a *modus vivendi* must be found to enable a *working side by side* in a peaceable way." Hoehn went on to give Sorge's estimate of the contribution of the American Federation of Labor:

The federation is a *bona fide,* a true labor organization, an organization of wage workers, without clauses and back doors in its statutes, through which middle class and wealthy capitalists, would-be reformers and politicians, might creep in. With all its faults and defects, the American Federation of Labor is the representative of the working class, of the proletariat of this country, and as such, it is to be respected; but it has, also, to fulfill a great task. The federation deserves considerable merit for many a good work done for the working class of these United States. Under strong opposition the federation made an end to the nonsensical fight about high protective tariff and free trade in its own ranks; it has mightily advanced the aspirations for shorter work hours; it has favorably influenced the legislation for the protection of the working people; it has, without interruption, pushed the indispensable organization of the wage workers; it has protected and guarded the right of labor to open, manfully-acting organization, against the secret form, in a long struggle, and has expressed the duty of the wage workers to carry on their struggles with open weapons.

The federation has also shown economic intelligence by considering the formation of trusts, syndicates, etc., as a natural consequence to the industrial development, and by its refusal to join in the chorus of stupid howlers. . . . As a matter of fact, the federation did not permit itself to be made the field of experiments by the American mushroom reformers and sectarians of all sorts. Although its class consciousness is not yet sufficiently developed, it must be declared that the American federation has represented the class position and guarded the class character of its organization. The federation's struggles were class struggles.

It was because the German-Americans of the *Volkszeitung* group, whether in New York or elsewhere, believed what Sorge wrote of the American Federation of Labor that they split the Socialist Labor Party in 1889. The trade union and Marxian socialists—Sorge expressed the position of a well-grounded Marxian on the place of the federation—wanted above all else a rapprochement or at least "a working side by side" with the pure and simple trade unionists. The defeat of V. L. Rosenberg, the national secretary, and the success of the Schevitsch-Jonas faction offered hope for possible cooperation between the trade conscious and class conscious groups. In March, 1890, the federation selected Paul Grottkau, a socialist leader, as one of the lecturers to push the eight-hour fight. But in December of the same year the militants of the Socialist Labor Party made a tragic error. Lucien Sanial, one of the famous triumvirate, bore the brunt of a fight to get representation of the party in the federation.

§

The struggle in the Detroit convention of the American Federation of Labor, in December, 1890, centered around the question whether the Socialist Labor Party could be directly represented in a city central body. The Central Labor Federation of New York had been organized on February 12, 1889, under socialist control, with a charter from the American Federation of Labor. The central body fused with the existing Central Labor Union on December 15, of the same year, but resumed its own separate existence in June, 1890, after having found marriage with the Central Labor Union undesirable. The Central Labor Federation, when it decided to separate from the Central Labor Union, requested a return of its charter from Gompers, with whom the officers had deposited it for safe-keeping. The president of the federation, however, refused to return the charter or grant a new one, on the ground that an American or English-speaking section of the Socialist Labor Party was affiliated wih the central body. The decision of Gompers was then appealed to the convention of the American Federation of Labor, and Lucien Sanial was sent as the delegate of the New York Central Labor Federation to plead its case.

He took the ground that his party "was not a political party as understood by workingmen." He argued that the Socialist Labor Party had organized trade unions and "was a *bona fide* labor organization." He maintained that on the European continent the socialists had established the first trade unions and had kept them free of corruption from the capitalist parties. He also pointed out that the party had already belonged to the central body which was once regularly chartered, but that Gompers raised the question. A committee of five reported on the matter:

We recommend the cordial acceptance of the proferred fraternity of the Socialist Labor Party. . . . The hope and aspiration of the trade unionists is closely akin to that of the socialist. That the burden of toil shall be made lighter, that men shall possess larger liberty, that the days to be shall be better than those that have been, may properly be the ideal of those in all movements of labor reform. . . . We affirm the trade union movement to be the legitimate channel through which wage earners of America are seeking present amelioration and future emancipation. Its methods are well defined, its functions specialized, its work clearly mapped out. . . . We are of the opinion that a political party of whatsoever nature is not entitled to representation in the American Federation of Labor.

No delegates were to be barred, however, because of their radical beliefs. Frank K. Foster, secretary of the committee, said that "the Socialist Labor Party is admittedly an integral part of the labor movement, but we must decline to permit it as a political organization to engraft itself and its methods upon the American Federation of Labor. . . . If a distinction is made in favor of the Socialist Labor Party, every variety of the reform movement, single taxists, anarchists, and greenbackers have a right to be admitted."

In his report to the convention, President Gompers wrote: "I have ever held that trade unions were broad enough . . . to admit of any and all shades of thought upon the economic and social question." He added, however, that "the trade unions pure and simple are the natural organizations of the wage workers to secure their present material and practical improvement and to achieve their final emancipation." On the floor of the convention, with his accustomed fire, Gompers charged that "acrimony was brought into the discussion," and that the Socialist Labor Party had published "scandalous and false statements through the press." He did concede, however, that if the Socialist Labor Party would withdraw now, it might be admitted later, when the trade union movement had grown much stronger. He admitted the good work done by the socialists in organizing the toilers into unions. But he wound up by again noting "the venom that had been interjected by the advocates of the claimants for admission," and declared "that there was a labor movement before the Socialist Labor Party was ever in existence," and that "the methods of the trade unions and the Socialist Labor Party are inherently different."

Thomas J. Morgan, the socialist leader from Chicago, thought the New York men had made one of the greatest mistakes by carrying the fight to the convention. He wanted harmony and regretted to see it destroyed by attacks upon socialists and foreigners. He proposed, therefore, reference back to the organizations for instruction of delegates to the following year's gathering. Gompers replied that a year's discussion would only widen the gap and cause greater bitterness. By a vote of 1,574 against 496—each vote representing approximately 100 members—the committee's report was accepted. The bakers, brewers, and furniture workers, Germans and socialists, voted against the majority. But so did the United Mine

Workers. John McBride, the president of the coal diggers, said that "the American Federation of Labor encouraged home rule," thus evading the real issue, and added tactfully for the benefit of the conservatives that constitutional safeguards prevented the destruction of the organization by central bodies—which had only one vote each at conventions. Of such stuff are presidents of great bodies—including the United States—made.

§

The socialists were thus defeated in their effort to remain on the inside, as a party, with their ablest leaders as spokesmen on the floor of unions, regardless of their membership or influence in the trade union movement. At the same convention of 1890 Thomas Morgan ran for president against Samuel Gompers and polled but 194 to the latter's 1,716 votes. The socialists introduced a resolution calling for "the abolition of the wage system." It was defeated. They also proposed the following: "That the convention recommends to the members of all the organizations affiliated with the American Federation of Labor to join the Socialist Labor Party in its contest against capitalism upon the field of independent political action." This resolution was not acted upon. The socialists received little comfort indeed from the historic Detroit convention.

But they were soon to have their revenge. They had, a year previously, shown Gompers their power. According to his own account, the republicans had nominated Gompers for the New York senate in 1889. He claimed that he was also supported by a faction of the democrats and that his election was assured if the socialists would back him up. He and his friends saw S. E. Schevitsch who told Gompers that the socialists could not vote for him if he ran on an old party ticket. This uncompromising policy greatly incensed Gompers, and he gave up the race.

The panic of 1893 gave the socialists their first real opportunity to strike at Gompers and the pure and simplers. The federation met that year in Chicago, in the old City Hall. Gompers described the setting of the convention as follows:

When the sessions of the convention ended for the day, there were hundreds of homeless, workless men seeking refuge in the corridors. When we held evening sessions, as the elevators did not run at night, we had to walk down the stairs very carefully for we had to pick our way over men who were lying on the steps and on the floor with only newspapers for protection.

In his annual report he stated:

It is no exaggeration to say that more than three million of our fellow toilers throughout the country are without employment.

In the convention call the former president asked "What is wrong?" His answer was:

It requires but little study to come to the conclusion that the ownership and control of the wealth, of the means of production, by private corporations which have no sympathy or apparent responsibility, is the cause of the ills and wrongs borne by the human family. . . . Production, production, production, faster, greater, was the impulse, the thought and motive of the capitalist class. . . . The great store-houses are glutted with the very articles required by the people, without their ability—or rather their opportunity to obtain—consume them. . . . The right to life, liberty and the pursuit of happiness should be a guarantee that employment, remunerative, safe and healthful, is accorded to all.

His remedy was simple:

The only method by which a practical, just and safe equilibrium can be maintained in the industrial world for the fast and ever increasing introduction of machinery, is a commensurate reduction of the hours of labor.

And the trade union was, in his opinion, the only effective instrument to bring this about.

§

The socialists were in agreement, in fact had taught Gompers his theory of over-production as the cause of panics and unemployment. But they sharply differed with him as to the immediate and ultimate remedies. Thomas J. Morgan, elected secretary of the international machinists' union that year, introduced the resolution embodying the socialist viewpoint. The convention adopted it. Morgan's propositions were:

Resolved, That a system of society which denies to the willing man the opportunity to work, then treats him as an outcast, arrests him as a vagrant and punishes him as a felon, is by this convention condemned as inhuman and destructive of the liberties of the human race; and

Resolved, That the right to work is the right to life, that to deny the one is to destroy the other. That when the private employer cannot or will not give work the municipality, state or nation must.

The Chicago socialist leader followed up this success with another. By the overwhelming vote of 2,244 against 67 he got the convention to adopt the following resolution on political action:

Whereas, The trade unionists of Great Britain have, by the light of experience and the logic of progress, adopted the principle of independent labor politics as an auxiliary to their economic action, and

Whereas, Such action has resulted in the most gratifying success, and

Whereas, Such independent labor politics are based upon the following program, to wit:

1. Compulsory education.
2. Direct legislation.
3. A legal eight-hour workday.
4. Sanitary inspection of workshop, mine and home.
5. Liability of employers for injury to health, body or life.
6. The abolition of the contract system in all public works.
7. The abolition of the sweating system.
8. The municipal ownership of street cars, and gas and electric plants for public distribution of light, heat and power.
9. The nationalization of telegraphs, telephones, railroads and mines.
10. The collective ownership by the people of all means of production and distribution.
11. The principle of referendum in all legislation.

Therefore, Resolved, That this convention hereby indorse this political action of our British comrades, and

Resolved, That this program and basis of a political labor movement be and is hereby submitted to the labor organizations of America, with the request that their delegates to the next annual convention of the American Federation of Labor be instructed on this most important subject.

The introducer of the resolution did not entertain any illusions because the vote in favor was so large. Shortly after the convention he expressed his doubts in an article in the *American Federationist*:

The sentiment expressed by the convention in favor of independent political action was in one sense a mere abstraction, a repetition of misleading declarations, as old as the federation itself, voiced and supported by those whose alliances with both the dominant political parties is open, avowed and notorious. But if taken in the sense expressed and implied by those whose attitude and feelings are of the deepest bitterness and antagonism toward the political organizations of the master class, then the sentiment and declarations assume an importance of the most encouraging description. . . . But it is socialism! Why, of course it is, and instead of concealing the fact, we would have your whole attention and thoughts directed to it, so that the vote may be the measure of your understanding and conviction.

To Morgan's demand for a vote on a clear-cut issue Gompers answered in the magazine, of which he was editor:

The thinking world regards the program submitted by the Chicago convention as a step in advance, whether the tenth plank [declaration in favor of socialism] is adopted or not. Does it not seem that the dictates of wisdom as well as policy should prompt all the well wishers of the wage workers to aid in inaugurating a thorough, a clean, and an aggressive working class movement, economically and politically? And we are decidedly of the opinion that the best aid and impetus which can be given to such a movement would be a hearty cooperation to eliminate the divisions in labor's ranks and to tone down the bitterness of personal differences.

Frank K. Foster also pleaded with the socialists. He felt that

. . . . to go before the American people asking them to support
a party which proposes the extreme of state socialism . . . is
to commit hari-kari as often as it is done. If our state socialistic
friends have a particle of desire for a practical unity of the
labor voters of the country, they will show their wisdom by
refraining from insisting upon this extreme plank. . . . The time
is not yet for forced conversion.

The plain truth of the matter was, however, that neither
Gompers nor Foster believed in independent political
action, all their fine words and pleas for unity to the contrary notwithstanding. They were afraid of defeat, and
they wanted a breathing spell until they were strong
enough to beat the socialists to their knees. In fact, when
the 1894 convention rolled around, Gompers and his supporters found that they had enough delegates—despite
instructions from the rank and file—to dispose of the
whole program.

§

There had been a decided move for some time to have
the convention held in a far western city. The 1893
gathering picked Denver, Colorado. Accordingly, the
delegates to the 1894 convention were treated to an unusual written address from a populist governor, Davis
H. Waite, who did not mince words, and who did not
make the ordinary polite speech of greeting. He quoted
the French socialist, Paul Lafargue, and spoke of "the
capitalism which controls our legislation, which dominates
our national conventions, and dictates political platforms
and policies." He attacked the usurpations of constitutional authority by presidents Harrison and Cleveland
and the federal courts. The convention also listened to
John Burns and David Holmes, fraternal delegates from
the British Trades Union Congress. These visitors
proudly pointed to the presence of 100 members of Parliament and holders of local offices among the 400-odd delegates to their own convention across the Atlantic—the
English delegates always have stressed before the con-

ventions of the federation the need for independent political action. Even Gompers made a different-sounding presidential report to this convention. For the first and only time this opportunist used the socialist and the later Industrial Workers of the World salutations, "comrades" and "fellow-workers," and not "brothers" or "fellow-trade unionists."

Although a majority of the membership of the federation, to the extent that the referendum had been taken, had declared in favor of the Morgan resolution of 1893, and despite the specific wording of the resolution which called for an expression of opinion of the rank and file, the pure and simple trade union leaders, headed by Samuel Gompers himself, repudiated the demands of the membership.

The delegates were lined up, those for the program and those against. The former could muster only 861 votes against 1,345 of the latter on the pivotal first motion, endorsement of independent political action. The pure and simplers defeated plank 10, calling for the collective ownership by the people of all means of production and distribution, by a subterfuge, the vote being 1,217 to 913. They adopted plank 3, demanding the nationalization of the telegraphs, telephones, railroads and mines, but at subsequent conventions mutilated it. They were able to "get away with" these acts without a revolt, because the rank and file did not really care enough about the matter, and because it was not and is not easy to unhorse the leadership of a trade union—or of any other organization for that matter. The men in control dig themselves in, and it often takes a volcanic eruption or an avalanche to tear them loose.

The pure and simplers had decisively defeated the socialists. The latter could take what comfort they might from electing McBride in place of Gompers, and removing the headquarters from New York to the Middle West, by a vote of 1,170 to 976. McBride, president of the miners, was opposed to independent political action and socialism and did not possess the devotion to the labor movement that characterized Gompers. He was actively identified with one of the two old parties and when he was defeated in the 1895 convention retired from the labor movement. When Gompers ran again in the convention which turned McGuire down for a second term, not all the socialist delegates voted against the "old man." They had learned that it was wiser to choose the lesser of two evils at that time, as on other occasions, not so long ago in the annals of the American Federation of Labor.

CHAPTER VI

DE LEONISM

THE Knights of Labor also had its experiences with the socialists and anarchists. In a letter of August 19, 1879 Uriah S. Stephens wrote:

You must not allow the socialists to get control of your assembly. They are simply disturbers, and only gain entrance to labor societies that they may be in better position to break them up. You cannot fathom them, for they are crafty, cunning and unscrupulous. I detest the name of socialism on account of the actions of the men who profess to believe in it. They rush to every gathering and attempt to man or officer it. Having done that, and having driven all decent men away, they are supremely happy in the delusion that they have spread their ideals still further. I have had an experience with them that you could not possibly have had, and I warn you against having anything to do with them either individually or as a body. . . . If the socialists ever gain control of the * * * * * [secret sign of the Knights of Labor] they will kill off the work of years. If they were sincere they would build up their own societies.

Powderly also had his opinion "of the kind of socialism that bubbled to the surface from the depths of the beer saloon." He could, however, accept a membership card from a fellow-Knight, the secretary of the Socialist Labor Party, Philip Van Patten, and flash it on occasion. The anarchists and the leaders of the Knights of Labor also fought each other without gloves. After the Haymarket bomb was thrown and the Chicago anarchists were condemned to be hung, Powderly would not even allow an appeal for mercy in their behalf to be voted on at the national convention.

In fundamental aim and program the Knights of Labor was opposed to socialism. The order was not consciously

147

founded on the theory of a class struggle between wage
earners and employers. It did not rest its hopes on the
workers organizing themselves economically and politically
and thereby emancipating themselves. The leaders of the
Knights of Labor thought in terms of an America which
still offered opportunities for self-employment. They,
therefore, stressed the importance of free land, plenty of
money, adequate credit facilities, cheap transportation,
freedom of competition, and the "rights of man." From
Uriah S. Stephens, through Powderly to J. R. Sovereign,
the Knights of Labor began and ended as an organization
of the industrial classes, the workers and farmers, for
economic and political reform, in an America, as they saw
it, where the "money power" and not the employer, where
the legislator and not the capitalist, prevented the producers from reaping the full product of their toil.

§

The leaders of the Knights had easily vanquished the
socialists and the anarchists in the seventies and the
eighties. But in the nineties—when they were declining
—they had a foeman who all but took their organization
away from them. That man was Daniel De Leon. He
was born on December 14, 1852, on the island of Curacoa,
off the coast of Venezuela. He received his early education in Germany, and after coming to the United States
in the early seventies, studied law and won a prize lecture-
ship in international law at Columbia. He had his first
political experience in the Henry George campaign of
1886 in New York City. After the United Labor Party
petered out De Leon joined the nationalists.

Edward Bellamy's novel *Looking Backward,* which appeared in 1887 and reached a sale of anywhere from a
quarter to a half million, helped to make socialist ideas
palatable to Americans. On December 1, 1888, the first
nationalist club was organized in Boston. Its humani-
tarian program declared: "We advocate no sudden or ill-
considered changes; we make no war upon individuals;

we do not censure those who have accumulated fortunes."
The nationalists tried independent political action in California and Rhode Island in 1890 but gave up the attempt
after a very poor showing. They threw their lot in with
the People's Party soon after it was organized.

Daniel De Leon could not belong to such an organization after he discovered the tender-mindedness of its supporters. He joined the Socialist Labor Party in 1890.
He quickly rose to a dominant place in its counsels and
became editor of its official English organ, *The People*,
in 1892. By the foreign-born socialists of New York
and the few natives he was most heartily welcomed. Before De Leon had him brought to the "guillotine"—before
he was expelled from the party—Charles Sotheran in
his book on *Horace Greeley* referred to him as *the* authority, with the right to speak *ex cathedra* on socialism.
He described him as follows:

Here is, although not of American aboriginal stock, a genuine
"old American," who bears the surname of Juan Ponce De Leon,
the discoverer of Florida in the sixteenth century. Professor
De Leon is a native of .... South America, his ancestors
having emigrated from Spain to America in 1562. When this
ardent apostle of socialism—who has stumped for the cause from
the Atlantic to the Pacific—graduated from Columbia College
in 1878 he took both prizes in constitutional and international law.

Through a domineering personality which brooked no
opposition, De Leon maintained a position of unquestioned
authority in his party until the day of his death in 1914.
The Socialist Labor Party to this day worships at his
shrine, and runs regularly in its weekly paper reprints of
editorials that he wrote. De Leon's policies and personality led to repeated splits in the Socialist Labor Party
and the development of extreme bitterness between the
leaders of the trade unions and himself.

§

Daniel De Leon, soon after he obtained power in his
party and became editor of *The People*, began to preach

what he called the new trade unionism. He was supported in this propaganda by two others, Hugo Vogt and
Lucien Sanial. These three constituted the unofficial
triumvirate at the head of the party. De Leon presented
the case for the new trade unionist who

. . . . has his heart aflame and his mind inspired with the loftiest
thoughts and aspirations. No mean groveling "improvements"
or hunger-aggravating crumbs for him. His voice is the clarion's
voice: "You are robbed, wealth producers," he cries to the
proletariat lying prone; "arouse yourselves; strike off the chains
that fetter you as wage slaves; a world of freedom and enjoyment lies ready at your hand; take it . . . leave to your descend-
ants the heritage of the Cooperative Commonwealth and Freedom."

In contrast to the new unionist, there was the old pure
and simple trade unionist, the Gompersite, who, according
to De Leon,

. . . . grants the principle of private ownership in the means
of production; grants the right of the possessors of these means
to keep their profits; talks about fair and legitimate profits; he
is satisfied with wages. In other words, he has no inkling of
the fact that all wealth comes from labor; that wages are only
a part of the workman's own product; that all "profit" pocketed
by the capitalist is illegitimate and a theft; that the capital in
the possession of the capitalist is accumulated profits; or thefts
from the workers; that the system under which wages and profits
exist is one that tends to increase the latter and reduce the
former.

The last bit gives the clue to his attitude toward the
day-by-day struggles of bread and butter, or pure and
simple trade unionists. De Leon did not believe that the
workers of one trade or industry, or as a class, could
raise their real wages or improve their conditions by the
economic weapon, under capitalism.

Lucien Sanial, at a conference on strikes and boycotts in 1894, divided labor organizations into three
classes: (1) Those whose industry had reached the highest degree of capitalist concentration, and which, for this
reason, could no longer use with success the strike and

the boycott; (2) those whose industry was midway between competition and concentration, and in which the
effect of labor's traditional weapons was always more or
less doubtful; (3) those whose industry was still largely
in the competitive stage, and which, under proper conditions, may yet for some time turn the strike and the
boycott to some immediate, though not permanent advantage. Sanial clinched his argument by declaring that
the strike and boycott were fast getting out of date.

In 1896 Hugo Vogt made a survey of the leading
unions in the American Federation of Labor. He declared that the cigarmakers' union was holding its membership solely through sick, death, and out-of-work benefits, that the International Typographical Union was no
longer in a position to conduct an important struggle successfully, and that the miners' union was dying. This
was in the days before the American Federation of Labor
even began to make its first rapid strides. Yet Vogt had
already counted out the miners, for example, an organization which was to have 500,000 members. His conclusion was that "nothing but the growing force of labor,
exhibited by the socialist vote, can give the workers
courage to persist in their organizing work and continue
their unions for those favorable opportunities that sometimes offer for a successful economic contest with capital."

The executive committee of the Socialist Labor Party,
in its report to the party convention of 1893, some years
before the Socialist Trade and Labor Alliance was organized, officially declared that "the implicit faith in the
possibility of guarding their material prosperity by means
of purely economic organization and action, hitherto
exhibited by so many American workingmen, is on the
wane." The wish was father to the thought. Just after
the fight to keep the Socialist Labor Party inside the
central bodies of the American Federation of Labor had
failed, Vogt wrote in 1891: " . . . a close union between the party and the trade union organization was a
necessity . . . the membership would then be raised above

the *paltry routine business of the unions* and brought to understand the broad questions that would inspire them with the requisite revolutionary spirit."

In his lecture on *The Burning Question of Trades Unionism,* delivered on April 21, 1904, De Leon probably stated the maturest view he had on the subject before he joined the I. W. W.:

> The trades union has a supreme mission. That mission is nothing short of organizing by uniting, and uniting by organizing, the whole working class industrially—not merely those for whom there are jobs, accordingly, not only those who can pay dues. That unification of organization is essential in order to save the eventual and possible victory from bankruptcy, by enabling the working class to assume and conduct production the moment the guns of the public powers fall into its hands— or before, if need be, if capitalist political chicanery pollutes the ballot box. The mission is important also in that the industrial organization forecasts the future constituencies of the parliaments of the Socialist Republic.

De Leon always emphasized this ultimate end, this supreme mission of trade unionism. He very reluctantly conceded a minor place to immediate trade union demands, both before and after 1905. If the immediate trade union demand squared with the ultimate aim, he held it to be worth fighting for. If, on the other hand, it was a trap, a sop, or a palliative "that the foes of labor's redemption are ever ready to dangle before the eyes of the working class, and at which, aided by the labor lieutenants of the capitalist class, the unwary are apt to snap—and be hooked" then it was of course not worth while from his point of view to fight for it.

§

The pure and simple union, with its bread-and-butter philosophy and its opportunist cry for more, more, more, now, was dominated, according to De Leon, Sanial, and the rest of their supporters, by the "labor faker." De Leon's greatest virtue was not restraint of language in attacking an opponent. Again and again in *The People* and in his lectures and debates he took occasion to assail the pure and simple labor leader whom he charged with doing "picket duty for capitalism." He accused him of living in the "hope of getting some fat political job."

De Leon's hatred of the "labor faker" was based on the following analysis:

The first thing necessary to convert a man is to get at him. The labor misleaders, so long as they were left alone by us, barred the way: it was not possible, at least it was the most difficult thing to get at the men. . . . Attack is necessary. Wherever capitalism shows its hideous head it must be attacked unsparingly. A labor crook, who assumes to do the dirty work of the capitalist is no better than the capitalist himself. His exposure and overthrow is a necessary preliminary to education: it is in itself the most essential part of education. . . . The capitalist with all his vices at least fills a historic mission; he furnishes object lessons. The labor crook is an unqualified ulcer on the face of the earth.

Typical of De Leon's onslaughts was the following in *The People* of October 8, 1893, which he headed "Kick the rascals out!" "The 'pure and simpler' has been found out. Some are ignorant, others are corrupt, all are unfit for leadership in the labor movement. To civilize and unite them is out of the question. The social revolution must march over the bodies of each and all of them. . . . Clear the way. Kick the rascals out." In *Two Pages from Roman History* De Leon collected from all over the country records to prove his thesis that "the labor leader of today is nothing but a masked battery, from behind which the capitalist class can encompass what it could not without—the work of enslaving and slowly degrading the working class."

§

Previously, while others were carrying on the attack in the American Federation of Labor, De Leon had taken it upon himself to lead the fight inside the Knights of Labor. He was a member of a mixed assembly, as were other intellectuals and noted women, and an elected delegate from the local to the New York District Assembly 49. His plan was to capture District Assembly 49, the most influential in the national body, through it to strike at Powderly, and then dominate the organization throughout the country.

The secretary of the district assembly was Patrick J. Murphy, a genial Irishman and devoted Socialist Labor Party member, elected largely on his personality. He knew how to "make majorities" for De Leon. Partly through his efforts the Jewish tailors were induced to affiliate with the district assembly. With the help of these East Side workers and other socialists De Leon was able to have himself elected in 1893 as one of the delegates to the general assembly or the national convention of the Knights of Labor. The socialist delegates—there were some outside of New York—united with J. R. Sovereign and defeated T. V. Powderly, who had been in office continuously since 1879. They helped to elect Sovereign in his place. The new leader of the Knights and De Leon spoke from the same platform at a meeting in New York the following December. Full of enthusiasm De Leon said that the Knights of Labor "was an industrial or economic organization that well merited the attention of the toilers, seeing that it repudiated the baneful principles of the 'pure and simple trade unions'; it demanded the absolute abolition of the wage system . . . and it called upon the workers to rally under the banner of labor at the polls." Sovereign, who followed De Leon, tactfully omitted to say what he really believed. All apparently was peace and harmony. But only on the surface. Sovereign was a populist, De Leon was a socialist, and they were headed for a merry falling-out.

On May 11, 1894, the general executive board of the Knights of Labor issued a statement in which it urged the membership not to vote for any congressman who did not commit himself to the money plank of the order. Now *The People* had for years been hammering the populists and the money reformers and pointing out that a socialist organization could not accept the main plank of the People's Party. In fact, the Chicago convention of the Socialist Labor Party, held in July, 1893, had adopted the following resolution in reference to the third party:

Whereas, a number of American citizens, who on the one hand, by their individual poverty and personal industry are related to the proletariat, while on the other hand, by their precarious ownership and tenure of land, and their limited employment of wage labor, they are related to the capitalistic and exploiting class, have constituted themselves into a political party, for their own special benefit, and sole advancement, under the misnomer, "People's Party"; and

Whereas, this portion of a great hybrid and transitory class that is doomed to dispossession and disappearance through the action of economic forces evolved by the modern system of production, the other portion consisting of small adventurers in manufactures and commerce, appeals to the wage workers for the support it needs in order to save it from an early fall into the ranks of that very proletariat which it has heretofore exploited and will continue to exploit as long as it is permitted to protract its wretched existence; and

Whereas, among the measures through which this "People's Party" proposes to so use the powers of government as to transfer to the small farmers a considerable portion of the plunder heretofore chiefly levied by the plutocratic class upon the wage working masses, are the following:

1. The depreciation of the currency, so that the debtor farmer may, like the creditor plutocrat, become gratuitously possessed of valuable property, to the exclusion of the said wage working masses.

2. The establishment of official public warehouses and the use of the public credit, so that the necessaries of life may be withheld on speculation, to be sold for the benefit of the small farmer at prices higher than are warranted by the growing application of machinery to land and the resulting decrease in the cost of production; therefore be it

Resolved, that the wage working class cannot possibly support this movement which is fully as antagonistic to the interests and aims of the proletariat as the rule of the plutocracy itself can be, and which is only calculated to retard the final emancipation of all, the small farmers included; and be it further

Resolved, that we call upon the intelligent and honest members of the People's Party to recognize the facts above stated, and, seeing that their own emancipation depends upon the triumph of the principles of the Socialist Labor Party, to join hands with this party in a supreme effort to snatch the reigns of government from the capitalist class and then accomplish their emancipation by abolishing all classes and introducing universal cooperation.

The People, accordingly, ran an editorial on August 5, 1894, in De Leon's direct and inimitable style, headed, "A Word with Grand Master Workman J. R. Soverign," and concluding with these significant words: "It matters not whether this individual or that is laid low." The populist and the socialist, the reformer and the revolutionist, were now preparing for battle. But they had not yet declared war. They held a "disarmament conference" at the national convention of the Knights of Labor, in New Orleans, November 13-23, 1894, to which De Leon was again sent by District Assembly 49. He acted as leader of the socialist delegates and supported Sovereign and the administration—at a price; namely, that the grand master workman was to appoint a socialist, Lucien Sanial, as editor of the official journal of the Knights of Labor. De Leon's plans were thus seemingly on their way to fulfilment.

The following January, after a bitterly contested and adjourned election, William L. Brower, a member of the Socialist Labor Party, was chosen master workman of District Assembly 49, and Patrick Murphy—the "maker of majorities" for De Leon—re-elected secretary. Trouble had been brewing between the socialists and the pure and simple Knights in D. A. 49, and the election showed how deep-seated it was. The national officers now stepped into the situation. Since the convention they had switched from friendly to open foes of the Socialist Labor Party leaders. The editor of the official journal, H. B. Martin, the secretary, John W. Hayes, and J. R. Sovereign were not going to let De Leon take over the national body as he had D. A. 49. They carried the fight to New York by "investigating" two socialist assemblies, to destroy them.

The date of the convention, November 12-22, 1895, drew near and the contest began for delegates. As is usual in such cases the group in office held the whip hand. No administration, where it has had the brains and energy, has failed to use its strategic position. And so the national officers got their majority, although the vote was close, 23 to 21. They controlled the convention and they did what they wished with the assemblies in New York. Instead of capturing the Knights of Labor, Daniel De Leon was driven back to New York to find what comfort he could among his own supporters.

Shortly after the convention, on December 1, 1895, District Assembly 49 met and in the presence of Sovereign and Hayes castigated the administration and charged that the convention had been packed by representatives of bogus assemblies, with their expenses paid by the national officers and their supporters. D. A. 49 declared that it would not belong to such an organization and announced its withdrawal. The leaders of the national body hotly replied in the official journal that "the rats cannot scuttle the ship." The Knights of Labor by this time was a dying organization. When De Leon had started out to capture it the order still claimed a quarter of a million members. The socialists did not credit it with more than 30,000 in good standing at the time D. A. 49 repudiated it, and they claimed that they took 13,000 with them when they seceded.

§

While the New York triumvirate was busy in the campaign to capture the Knights of Labor it did not overlook any opportunity to intensify the running fight with Gompers and the American Federation of Labor. The relations between it and the pure and simplers were of the deadliest hostility. In his autobiography Gompers spoke of his hated foe, De Leon, in these words: "No more sinister force ever appeared among the socialists. . . . He infused vitriol into socialist propaganda. . . . He used his intellectual ability and training to embitter the differences between socialists and trade unionists." In 1895 Gompers referred to De Leon's paper, *The People,* as "that monumental libeler, that assassin of men's characters." A few years later he called its editor "a paid agent . . . an *agent provocateur.*" He described the triumvirate in these words: "These professors, and such as they, have always been barnacles on the body of organized labor, and at the most critical moments in the movement have either flunked or turned traitor—that is, if they were not traitors and paid hirelings all through." In a communication of February 12, 1895, Ernest Bohm, then secretary of the socialist Central Labor Federation, reminded Gompers of his defeat by McBride in the American Federation of Labor in this confident tone: "The Denver convention laid you on the shelf—forever!" The old war horse replied: "I shall meet you and yours in the days to come and then and there when the labor movement is antagonized by your organization." Gompers could not use stronger language in print. He did not quickly forget.

As for Daniel De Leon's choice characterizations of Gompers and the American Federation of Labor—the dearest thing to the pure and simpler's heart—there is room for only a few samples. In *The People* of October 8, 1893, De Leon wrote: "In upholding 'pure and simpledom' he does so in deference to his own wishes; he tells a deliberate falsehood when he claims his conduct is directed by the wishes of the rank and file. . . . Mr. Samuel Gompers, president of the American Federation of Labor, is an entrapped swindler." When Gompers was beaten the following November for delegate to the constitutional convention of New York state, De Leon rubbed acid in the wound: *"The People* of Sunday, April 12, 1891, consoled itself over the then recent decease of the Great American Humbug and king of circus shows, with the reflection: 'Barnum is dead, but Gompers is alive.' That consolation proved short lived. In the light of recent events and the election returns, there is no consolation left: Barnum is dead, and so is Gompers." Two years before the Socialist Trade and Labor Alliance was started, the organ of the party, *The People* of December 24, 1893, printed an editorial on the American Federation of Labor:

> The dry-rot has set in the American Federation of Labor. As an organization the American Federation of Labor is at best a cross between a wind-bag and a rope of sand; it has no cohesion, vitality or vigor worth mentioning. . . . A numerically strong element . . . could find no better candidate around whom to rally than the politician labor leader, John McBride, a fellow who either is already out of a job, having pretty successfully wrecked the miners, or who expects to be soon out of his job, and would like to get a living out of the movement . . . . An organization that is put to such a Hobson's choice as Gompers . . . and John McBride, has no reason for being. In point of fact, it is deader than dead.

At an excursion on June 11, 1893, for the benefit of the paper, the Central Labor Federation carried a large banner with this inscription: "Leave the Poor Old Stranded Wreck (Trade Unionism Pure and Simple) and Pull for the Shore!"

Among the causes for De Leon's abandoning the tactic of boring from within was his defeat in the Knights of Labor, and the fact that he played no role in the effort to capture the American Federation of Labor. He also knew that a decentralized body such as the federation could not be easily manipulated. He had never cooperated with and he had given practically no mention at any time to the militants, such as Morgan, Barnes and others inside the American Federation of Labor. In the back of De Leon's mind, moreover, was the fixed belief that the labor leaders effectively barred the way to converting the existing unions to socialism, and if the socialist unionists chose to remain on the inside, they had to trim their sails and make their peace with these "labor fakers." They could not then carry on their revolutionary propaganda. You either fought the pure and simple labor leader on the inside, he believed, and then you found yourself kicked out, as he had been forced out of the Knights of Labor; or you pretended to fight the "labor faker" with paper resolutions and capitulated completely as the price of remaining. De Leon claimed that you could not "bore from within," because the "machine" would not allow you to continue to bore when you threatened to undermine their foundations, their structure, above all, their control over the rank and file.

§

In less than a week after De Leon printed in *The People* of November 27, 1895, a report of his ouster from the Knights and the appeal to his followers to "reorganize upon that higher plane . . . the plane of economic and political efforts, consolidated, inspired, guided and purified by the class consciousness of the wage slave," District Assembly 49 issued a call to "all Knights of Labor assemblies and all progressive organizations to join with us in establishing a national body on the only natural lines of the labor movement, the lines plainly marked out by the class struggle." It appointed a committee to confer with the executive boards of the Central Labor Federation of New York, the federation in Brooklyn, the United Hebrew Trades, and the Newark Central Labor Federation. On December 13, 1895, a Cooper Union mass meeting adopted the following resolution:

We, the socialists of New York, in mass meeting assembled, urge upon all our fellow workingmen throughout the United States the necessity of joining the Socialist Trade and Labor Alliance.

Thus did Daniel De Leon create, socialist central bodies of New York and vicinity supply the membership, and the socialists bless the new federation. *The People* took the new trade union body to its bosom and declared war to the knife on the American Federation of Labor and the Knights of Labor. On December 22 the paper indulged in the following bit of self-satisfying emotionalism: "If in the past we have been unsparing with these outposts of capitalism—the labor bunco-steerers—we shall in the future smite them more relentlessly; the sledge hammer of facts shall drop henceforth all the more pitilessly upon the numskulls, whose perverse ignorance and ignorant perversity are mainly responsible for the rapid degradation into which the working class is sinking." De Leon smote—and cracked his own Socialist Labor Party, while Gompers kept on reporting an increased membership in the American Federation of Labor.

The Socialist Trade and Labor Alliance started out with about 100 unions affiliated with the central bodies of New York, Brooklyn, Newark, and the United Hebrew Trades. It did not publish official figures. According to a hostile source—a member of its general executive board who joined the seceding social democrats in the split of 1899—the alliance issued 228 charters between January, and July 1898. On the latter date it had about 15,000 members. The report of the executive to the July, 1897, convention claimed that the alliance had spread to the New England textile workers, the Pennsylvania miners, the cigarmakers, bricklayers, shoeworkers, machinists, and numerous other trades, scattered all over the land. In his autobiography Gompers admitted that the alliance kept the East Side of New York in turmoil and attracted garment workers, textile workers, cigarmakers, coal miners, and glass bottle blowers outside of the metropolis. He conceded that "the activity emanating from New York constituted a potential danger . . . wherever dissension arose workers who had recently come to the United States were in the majority."

The Socialist Trade and Labor Alliance was never meant to be anything but a dual organization. It was launched as a rival to the American Federation of Labor and its avowed purpose was to destroy the older body. The report of the executive in 1897 referred to the activities of the alliance in New England in these words: "Boldly did it sound the note of secession from the

derelict of the American Federation of Labor." The dual
body came home to Gompers in his own cigarmakers'
union. A strike against a reduction of wages occurred in
Seidenberg's cigar factory in New York in March, 1898.
Local 90 of the Cigar Makers' International Union of the
federation—which local consisted in the main of socialists
—called the strike. Members of the Socialist Trade and
Labor Alliance local 141 also worked in this factory.
According to De Leon the alliance men went out with
the federation members, and only returned to work when
a settlement was made, which he claimed, left his men
"in the cold." According to the socialists of local 90,
the alliance men returned to work before the strike was
settled, and were, therefore, scabs, and the Socialist Trade
and Labor Alliance was a scab organization.

§

In the heyday of the Socialist Trade and Labor Alliance, De Leon, who dominated the alliance as he did the
Socialist Labor Party, delivered a talk to some striking
textile workers at New Bedford, on February 11, 1898.
This speech, later printed under the title, *What Means
This Strike?* embodied the intellectual weapons with
which De Leon sought to destroy Gompers and his pure
and simple unions. The leader of the alliance expected
to shatter the business union with this shot:

> Years ago, before capitalism had reached its present develop-
> ment, a trade organization of labor could and did afford protection
> to the workers, even if, as the "pure and simple" union, it was
> wholly in the dark on the issue. THAT TIME IS NO MORE.
> . . . Not only does "pure and simpledom" shut off your hope
> of emancipation by affecting to think such a state of things is
> unreachable now, but in the meantime and RIGHT NOW, the
> "good" it does to you, the "something" it secures for you "from
> the employers and from the politicians" is *lower wages.* That is
> what their "practicalness" amounts to in point of fact.

Here was a genuine test. If the workers were convinced that the business or pure and simple unions did

not protect them, did not raise their wages and prevent reductions, why did they not leave the American Federation of Labor and flock to the Socialist Trade and Labor Alliance?

The late nineties and the early years of the present century saw one of the greatest developments of American capitalism. These were also the days of Marcus A. Hanna, of Senator Aldrich and Speaker Cannon. All the conditions tallied with the thesis of De Leon, Vogt, and Sanial, that the growth of large-scale industry, concentration of wealth, rapid introduction of machinery, and dominance of the state by the capitalists, would destroy the effectiveness of the pure and simple union and its methods. Why then did the American toilers join the affiliated unions of the American Federation of Labor in greater proportionate numbers than at any other time in their history? Why did the federation rise from a membership of 264,825 in 1897 to 1,676,200 in 1904, and come through the panic of 1907 with a membership of over a million and a half, if its methods were antiquated? And why, if the Americans needed the new trade unionism, a socialist trade union purified of "labor fakers," did they ignore the Socialist Trade and Labor Alliance in the very period when American capitalism supplied all the conditions which were supposed to give the death blow to pure and simpledom and usher in the new organization which would eventually lead to the socialist commonwealth? The answer is that De Leon and his supporters were so much concerned with the supreme mission and the ultimate goal of the trade union that they ignored, for all practical purposes, its immediate objectives, its daily food. And because they were so obsessed with the final aim they narrowed the Socialist Trade and Labor Alliance until it lost all semblance of a labor organization—a mass working-class body—and it became a little sect on the economic field, as impotent as the political sect which ran it, the Socialist Labor Party.

The Socialist Trade and Labor Alliance not only antagonized the pure and simple trade unionists. It helped to destroy the unity of socialist unionists and undermined socialist unions which remained inside the American Federaton of Labor. The strike at Seidenberg's factory was but one instance. The conflict between the socialist unionists in the federation and De Leon was as real as that between him and the ordinary pure and simpler, because if one did not accept De Leon's leadership and point of view, he was an enemy, an outcast, he did not belong. The socialists in the federation had no right to hold the opinion that De Leon's method of segregating socialist unionists and carrying on a war from the outside with the American Federation of Labor was not only not good socialist tactics, but of positive detriment to the working class.

The leading socialists who were carrying on the fight inside the federation were never consulted by this extraordinary general on the advisability of launching the dual body. These socialists did not believe that the day of the pure and simple union, as a union, was over. They wanted to change the program of the old and existing unions in the direction of socialist political action. They did not believe that the alliance was the only silver lining to the black clouds hanging over American labor. They did not believe that the toilers could not improve their conditions unless they joined a trade union which emphasized the use of the socialist ballot as "the most potent and most effective" weapon of the working class. In other words, they believed that the trade unions were the natural and basic organizations of wage earners and could as such—as mass bodies—improve conditions, and that they were fighting the battles of the class struggle. As socialists they wanted to stay on the inside of these mass organizations and agitate and educate for socialism. They did not believe that a smashing policy from without would advance the cause of the wage earners or of socialism.

The Socialist Trade and Labor Alliance did not even retain the unions it chartered because it did not have as good—much less a superior—appeal for the workers, who either remained unorganized after their protest strikes or who joined the federation unions because they wanted something here and now. The alliance did not pull away from the federation those unions which contained a considerable socialist membership, because the latter did not believe in the dual body. It did not, therefore, appeal to the working class. And De Leon soon fell out with the leaders of the few organizations which remained. In 1898 the alliance lost the Central Labor Federation of New York, its backbone. The alliance was a highly centralized body, built on the model of the Knights of Labor. It allowed publishing associations and sections of the Socialist Labor Party to affiliate. It permitted an intellectual like De Leon to be its boss. And so, when the convention of July, 1898, held in Buffalo, chose a general executive board not to the "pope's" liking, he and his close co-workers promptly unseated it. It is true that De Leon charged the secretary of the Central Labor Federation with insincerity and with having used his office to promote a doubtful souvenir advertising venture, but the fact was that the Central Labor Federation seceded, and that some of De Leon's ablest and sincerest lieutenants sooner or later left him. They could not accept his type of leadership. De Leon saw the decline of his Socialist Trade and Labor Alliance. With its downfall began his own in the American labor movement.

§

Once the alliance was launched, De Leon and his supporters put the Socialist Labor Party wholeheartedly and officially behind it. At the party convention in New York, July 4-10, 1896, De Leon and Vogt presented a resolution endorsing the alliance, which the delegates adopted by a vote of seventy-one to six. As the wording of this resolution became the source of controversy in the fight which developed inside the party, it is worth giving in full:

Whereas, Both the American Federation of Labor and the Knights of Labor, or what is left of them, have fallen hopelessly into the hands of dishonest and ignorant leaders;

Whereas, These bodies have taken shape as the buffers of capitalism, against whom every intelligent effort of the working class for emancipation has hitherto gone to pieces;

Whereas, The policy of "propitiating" the leaders of these organizations has been tried long enough by the progressive movement, and is to a great extent responsible for the power which these leaders have wielded in the protection of capitalism and the selling out of the workers;

Whereas, No organization of labor can accomplish anything for the workers that does not proceed from the principle that an irrepressible conflict rages between the capitalist and the working class, a conflict that can be settled only by the total overthrow of the former and the establishment of the Socialist Commonwealth; and

Whereas, This conflict is essentially a political one, needing the combined political and economic efforts of the working class; therefore, be it

Resolved, That we hail with unqualified joy the formation of the Socialist Trade and Labor Alliance as a giant stride towards throwing off the yoke of wage slavery and of the robber class of capitalists. We call upon the socialists of the land to carry the revolutionary spirit of the Socialist Trade and Labor Alliance into all the organizations of the workers, and thus consolidate and concentrate the proletariat of America in one irresistible class-conscious army, equipped with both the shield of the economic organization and the sword of the Socialist Labor Party ballot.

The sentence, "We call upon the socialists of the land to carry the revolutionary spirit of the Socialist Trade and Labor Alliance into all the organizations of the workers," left room for those socialists who believed in boring from within to continue that policy. The convention in fact specifically urged "all socialists to join the organizations of the trades to which they respectively belonged." This last did not single out the Socialist Trade and Labor Alliance as the only organization with which socialists could affiliate. Moreover, the borers from within understood that the Socialist Trade and Labor Alliance would have as its main object the organization of the unorganized. When they found it invading the already organized trades, these socialists fought the alliance, while others did not dream that De Leon and his close followers would make the dual federation the test of loyalty to the party.

But this is what the leaders of the party proceeded to do. They started the alliance because they were determined to keep their trade unions free of "misleaders," or "labor fakers," and because they thought the political party ought to dictate the policies of the bread-and-butter organizations. They intended that the workers should be educated in their brand of socialism, and that they should do the educating. They built the alliance in such a way, therefore, that the party was directly represented in it. They planned that the alliance was to be the only and the all-inclusive federation of labor in the United States. De Leon, Vogt, and the rest made war on any individual or group who dared question the necessity for the alliance, because to them it was *the* trade union policy of the party. To argue for boring from within or to criticise the Socialist Trade and Labor Alliance was, accordingly, the same as compromising with socialism.

§

From the first days that the Socialist Trade and Labor Alliance was organized, however, at the end of 1895, the membership of the Socialist Labor Party continuously wrangled over it. There was an irreconcilable minority which refused to accept it. J. Mahlon Barnes and others active in the American Federation of Labor claimed that the alliance was foisted upon them in the first Cooper Union meeting which announced it to the world. Barnes asserted that he did not know that the question of the alliance was to be sprung at the gathering, which was

to listen to Socialist Labor Party speakers in connection
with the convention of the American Federation of Labor
which was being held at the time in New York.

Those who opposed the alliance were put into the
same category as those who were the mainstays of the
Gompers' machine—they were "trade union fakers and
would-be socialist political fakers." It was easy to stretch
the epithet "labor faker" to cover all whom De Leon,
Vogt, and the others cared to classify as enemies of the
party because they opposed the alliance. And as the
alliance made no great headway at any time, its leaders
poured forth greater and greater abuse on the heads of
those who dared differ with them.

The general executive board of the Socialist Trade
and Labor Alliance in 1897 used the following strong
language to describe the pure and simple unions: "The
very word 'union' became a stench in the nostrils of the
bulk of the working class." It paid its respects to the
"labor fakers": "From the ranks of the machinists, whom
a blatant and slick political faker has been bleeding, from
the ranks of the carpenters, whom a disreputable renegade
and inebriate has been plucking, ominous sounds have
come in response to the battle cry of the Socialist Trade
and Labor Alliance." It was very easy for those who
used such vituperation to transfer their abuse to their
foes inside the Socialist Labor Party. The national executive committee of the latter thus described an opponent who differed with them on the question of taxation, De Leon's contention being that the worker did
not pay taxes, his opponent's view that he did:

. . . . a man named Feigenbaum, a semi-lunatic, a freak with
more kinks in his head than the average well-balanced man could
ever begin to think of, and more mental dishonesty in his makeup
than could be traced with a thousand X-rays. This man Feigenbaum, who, during this taxation debate was very aptly and fitly
likened by a New York comrade to a monkey in convulsions.
. . . He promptly went off on a spree, a veritable dabauch . . .
misquoting and half-quoting. . . .

The same executive which characterized Benjamin Feigenbaum, one of the pioneers of the Jewish labor movement in the above manner, had the following to say about J. Mahlon Barnes in its report to the 1900 convention of the Socialist Labor Party—true, after the split had occurred, but still very indicative of the kind of personal abuse which it indulged in before the schism:

> J. Mahlon Barnes, secretary of an international cigarmakers' local union, a cold-blooded, crafty villain, a man without scruples of any sort, and with all the attributes that will some day, if he does not meet with some misfortune on the way, land him in the front ranks of the labor crooks in this country.

Before the revolt against De Leon's leadership took place, *The People* of May 1, 1899, justified its use of personal attacks and vituperation:

> Bitter personalities are indulged in; because the great fact is not yet generally comprehended—or is too frequently lost sight of by those even who comprehend it—that social movements, or diverging tendencies within those movements, are not the product of their so-called leaders, but that the inverse proposition is true. The existence of differences is, therefore, as a rule, wrongly imputed to those who, selected as agents or mouthpieces of the movements or tendencies to which they respectively contribute their individual efforts, sympathetically reflect in their acts or utterances, with such powers as they possess, the collective sentiment of their respective constituents.

According to this point of view it was necessary to attack those who upheld wrong tendencies, to discredit them utterly and thereby wipe out any danger to the party's principles. The premise was that the tendencies must be fought; the conclusion, that their leading spokesmen must be fought even harder in order to destroy them and their ideas. Epithets, hard names, personal abuse, what were these but weapons to better eliminate the heresy! But who decided what was heresy, and who was the heretic, and against whom the epithets were to be hurled?

Following the convention of the American Federation of Labor of 1898, where socialist resolutions were snowed under, the New York *Volkszeitung* printed an article in its issue of December 14 deploring the fact that the policy of boring from within had been given up. De Leon and his followers immediately took the matter up with the board of directors of the publishing association which issued the paper. This small body passed a vote of censure on the editor for allowing any question to be raised as to the finality of the dual union policy. When the larger membership meeting of the association met, however, on March 23, 1899, it refused to uphold the action of its own board of directors, and in addition, by a vote of nearly two to one, defeated a resolution introduced by Hugo Vogt, calling for an endorsement of the Socialist Trade and Labor Alliance. Instead of accepting defeat, the De Leonites prepared to sever relations between the party and the German daily, and kill its influence among socialists if possible.

In March of 1891 the Socialistic Cooperative Publishing Association, which ran the *Volkszeitung,* had entered into an agreement with the Socialist Labor Party whereby the association agreed to publish *The People.* By the terms of this agreement the national executive committee of the party and the board of trustees of the association elected the English paper's chief editor. In addition, the association published the official weekly German organ, *Vorwaerts,* on the same basis. De Leon, after he was defeated on the alliance, was determined that the Socialistic Cooperative Publishing Association should surrender all property belonging to *The People* and *Vorwaerts,* and that the party run these papers altogether independent of it.

The association was at first in a mood to come to some compromise but suddenly it decided to fight. It declared that it had carried the deficits of *The People* and that it did not intend giving up its share of control. It went further and took the offensive by issuing an English edition of the *Volkszeitung*, which it mailed to subscribers of *The People*. The question at issue was, who owned *The People*, the association or the national executive committee, with De Leon in control. In answer to the association's legal claim and the fact that it had borne the financial burden, De Leon said that the association "was established by the party, as a publishing committee of the party and for the party's sake." The point was that there was now a struggle for power in the party, and control over the paper was to be decided only by might and not right. This was not the first—and was not to be the last time—that socialists fought for possession of the newspaper organs of their party.

§

The German socialists were not the only ones who showed dissatisfaction with De Leon's Socialist Trade and Labor Alliance, his fierce personal attacks, and the general management of the party. The Jewish radicals also began indicating their growing opposition. On November 14, 1895, a month before the alliance was organized, the Jewish daily *Abendblatt*—under control of the party—took De Leon sharply to task for having embraced the Knights of Labor with such ardor and for his bitter onslaughts on labor leaders. The paper declared that his tactic of trying to capture the unions and of savagely denouncing their leaders was only "turning faithful trade unionists into not wholly unjustified enemies of the existing Socialist Labor Party." His methods, it charged, only made martyrs of the "labor fakers," whom the membership elected and reelected. It suggested, therefore, that the better part of reason was to educate the rank and file.

The Arbeiter-Zeitung Publishing Association, which controlled the *Abendblatt* and the weekly *Arbeiter-Zeitung*, was in the hands of the supporters of De Leon. The opposition stirred up enough dissension, however, to cause the Socialist Labor Party at its 1896 convention to decide to withdraw entirely from any connection with the Jewish press. The party elected the editors. There was no peace after the convention. There were referendums, arbitration boards, and decisions of the national executive committee of the party, but the differences were too sharp to permit of any harmonious cooperation between the two factions. Finally, the opposition bolted from the association.

Louis E. Miller, Morris Winchevsky, M. Zametkin, M. Gillis, A. Sheinberg, B. Lillienblum, M. Pine, Abraham Cahan, and a number of others thereupon launched the Jewish Daily *Forward* in April of 1897, as an independent socialist and labor enterprise. In order to get support they organized press clubs in the party's assembly branches. *The People* now began thundering against those who, previously in the monthly *Zukunft,* which Cahan had edited, and now in the daily *Forward,* were criticising the Socialist Labor Party. De Leon charged Miller, the "Bismarck of Hester Street," with being a populist and a pure and simpler; Winchevsky, with being an anarchist, and the whole *Forward* group with cooperating with the "Jewish faker leaders" of the tailors' union, as he had charged the *Volkszeitung* group with "selling out" to the German "labor fakers." He pointed out that the *Forward* men had embraced the western colonizing movement of Eugene Victor Debs— which the De Leonites considered utopian—and that they were anything but enthusiastic about the alliance. He attacked them for their statements that a bureaucratic and tyrannical machine was running and wrecking the Socialist Labor Party.

The next step, after De Leon denounced in *The People* those he sharply disagreed with, was to bring them up for expulsion. On July 4, 1897, therefore, the four assembly districts which stood by the *Forward* members found themselves suspended by the executive committee of Section Greater New York. It has never been difficult—as

the history of all organizations proves—for the powers
that be to expel the opposition. It should not be wondered at, therefore, that from 1897 to the split of 1899,
and for many years following, the De Leonites should
have managed to expel their opponents right and left.

§

In the same year that the party leaders expelled the
Forward men, they reorganized Section St. Louis. There
had been trouble for several years between G. A. Hoehn
and other St. Louis socialists—members of the party—
and De Leon and his close followers. The former had
published a weekly paper called *Labor* and had spread
out through a Socialist Newspaper Union which they
organized by issuing local editions of it in various parts
of the country. This development, plus the fact that the
sponsors were not dual unionists and did not see eye to
eye with De Leon, caused the latter to take up arms
against the rival paper and have it repudiated by the
1896 convention of the party. When Section St. Louis
in the following year re-admitted a man named Priester-
bach by a vote of twenty-eight to twenty-four, objection
was raised that a two-thirds vote was necessary to re-
admit, and upon refusal of the section to obey the executive it was re-organized. Basically, however, the differences were much the same as those that divided the
supporters and opponents of De Leon everywhere.

There was also friction between the De Leonites and
a number of sections in other parts of the country.
James F. Carey was elected a member of the city
council of Haverhill, Massachusetts, on the party ticket
in 1897. Conflict arose over Carey's voting for an
appropriation for a new armory, in which conflict Section Haverhill backed up its leader to the point of leaving
the party. The Haverhill socialists soon allied themselves with the Debs Social Democracy. In Cleveland,
prior to a municipal campaign in 1895, the section sent

delegates to a conference of the labor unions and the populists, prohibitionists, and socialists to nominate a joint ticket. The national executive committee thereupon expelled the section, although it admitted that the platform was adopted by a *bona fide* workingmen's group and was not much different from its own. However, the board of grievances over-ruled the executive and re-instated the section. It did this despite a constitutional provision that "no section shall enter into any compromise with any other political party." The action of the Cleveland section was significant, because at the time of the split of 1899 the membership in Cleveland elected the supreme body, the board of grievances, which passed on all appeals. Now the members of this board—to the utter dismay of the De Leonites—upheld the contention of the insurgents. In Chicago, Philadelphia, San Francisco, and a number of other cities, it only needed news that there was an insurrection for the anti-De Leonites to flock together and try to take things over.

§

The fight of De Leon, Vogt, and their supporters with the *Volkszeitung* group brought things to a crisis. On May 1, 1899, the national executive committee took advantage of the larger circulation of the May Day issue of *The People* to air its grievances against the association which refused to accept its orders. The men who signed the statement included Alvan S. Brown, Arthur Keep, John J. Kinneally, Charles H. Matchett, Patrick Murphy, Lucien Sanial, and Henry Kuhn, national secretary. Henry Stahl dissented. Both sides were now out campaigning for delegates to the general committee of Section Greater New York, which was to meet on July 8, 1899. Everything depended on this election, because control of New York meant domination of the national party inasmuch as the membership of the metropolis chose the national executive committee and the national secretary, and indirectly controlled the party organs,—the executive elected the editors and dictated policy to them.

As might be expected, each side accused the other of stealing the elections, of organizing bogus assembly districts, and of manoeuvring unfairly for control of the general committee. When the new delegates met on the designated day, with the supporters of De Leon in charge, the meeting got no further than the vote for election of chairman. A free-for-all fight developed when the De Leonites attempted to determine who was qualified and who was unqualified to vote. The insurgents then called together those delegates who were with them—each side claimed a majority of the general committee—and on July 10 elected Julius Gerber as local and Henry Slobodin as national secretary. They picked S. Berlin, Richard Bock, Julius Halpern, Morris Hillquit, Franz Seubert, Henry Stahl, and Robert Woodruff as the new national executive committee.

After they had done an evening's work, along about midnight their national secretary, accompanied by a goodly number of those who were strong in their faith and who wanted an opportunity to express it, marched upstairs to the headquarters of the party, in the same building which housed the *Volkszeitung,* and demanded possession. The De Leonites had already barricaded themselves in the party office and they politely informed the invaders to come and take it. This the insurgents attempted to do, and, according to the account in *The People,* "fierce did the conflict rage for fully ten minutes; blood flowed freely." The capitalist police, however, injected themselves at this point and prevented the civil war in William Street from lasting any longer. As the De Leonites held possession, the police ordered the insurgents to "move on" in the name of the law. The next day the holders of the fort transferred the party's belongings to another building. Thus ended the battle of July 10, 1899, for control of the headquarters.

The next struggles were over the title and emblem of the Socialist Labor Party, control of *The People*—each side now issued a paper by this name—,recognition by the public authorities for purposes of nominating candidates on the ballot, and adhesion of the majority of the membership in and outside of New York City. The De Leonites finally won the legal battle by which they managed to retain the old name of the party and to put their candidates on the ballot in New York, as well as issue *The People*. But they were not able to retain a majority of the membership or the socialist voters throughout the country. The split of 1899 was the beginning of the end of the old Socialist Labor Party, although it fought valiantly on and De Leon even sought a come-back through the launching of the Industrial Workers of the World six years later.

A statement of 31 members of Section New York of De Leon's party, issued after another split took place in it, declared that

. . . . . the national secretary [Henry Kuhn] and the national editor [Daniel De Leon] have come to regard their own persons as THE PARTY, just as the labor faker regards himself as THE UNION. And just as the labor faker regards every attack on himself and his management as an attack on the union itself . . . so do our managing powers regard every criticism directed against themselves and their management of the party as an attack on the party itself.

These 31 members charged De Leon with playing the role of Robespierre, Henry Kuhn that of Danton, and "that every member of Section New York has been declared a suspect and the Jacobin Club recently issued a decree for the establishment of a Revolutionary Tribunal, variously styled Committee of Inquiry, or Spying Committee, or the Holy Inquisition." The Manhattan Socialist Club—made up of more expelled members, the cream of the old party—issued its own declaration on October 20, 1902, which it styled, "The Inquisition in the Socialist Labor Party." The signers accused De Leon, Kuhn, *et al.,* with calling them "vindictive rascals," "grafters," "crooked and disgruntled individuals," and as "the slums of Section New York." Among those now on the outside and so castigated were: Lucien Sanial and Hugo Vogt, former editors of *The People* and *Vorwaerts,* two of the closest co-workers with De Leon, two-thirds of the famous triumvirate; Herman Simpson, chief editor of the Jewish *Abendblatt,* and later editor of the *New Review;* Frank MacDonald, future editor of the New York *Call;* Benjamin F. Keinard, the party's candidate for mayor in the previous election; such old standbys and De Leonites as Peter Fiebiger, Patrick Murphy, William H. Wherry, John T. Keveney, Arthur Keep, Thomas A. Hickey, Julian Pierce, Max Forker, Peter Damm, Thomas Crimmins, C. H. Vanderporten, John R. Pepin, and a host of others who had fought on the side of De Leon against the "Kangaroos."

Whatever justification De Leon, Kuhn, and their supporters had for expelling the various groups and individuals, the fact remained that they were cutting branch after branch off their own party tree and they could not hope to see their policy bear fruit. They might fulminate against the Kangaroos and Kanglets—the secessionists or those expelled, whom De Leon likened to the fly-by-night judges sitting in Texas in Civil War days—but whatever personal satisfaction they had in sledgehammering more "fakers" was obviously offset by the fact that their own ranks were becoming thinner and thinner; that they did not attract newcomers; and that they finally shrivelled up into a political sect.

The national executive committee of the opposition of July, 1899, in its statement to the membership and the public, pointed out that the editors of the party organs suppressed every form of criticism and that the party chiefs acted like those on the hunt for heresy and heretics. They made expulsions the order of the day, it claimed, and by their methods brought on one revolt after another. Their manner of attacking an opponent, it went on to say, whether inside the party or in the labor unions, was in keeping with their intolerant and bitter spirit; it evoked retaliation in kind, with no stopping place but deep and lasting hatred on both sides. In a word, altogether aside from the Socialist Trade and Labor Alliance, with the fights which it provoked between alliance men and federation members, altogether aside from other matters such as centralization, party-owned press, doctrinal purity, and tactics on the political field, which will be considered later, the leadership of the old Socialist Labor Party showed itself to be unfit to keep men and women together in an organization for successful, ongoing activity. Basically unsound in their attitude toward the trade unions, the leaders of the S. L. P. were difficult to work with or under in the same house.

§

The American political radical has been always buoyed up by knowledge of the phenomenal rise and success of the Republican Party. He has generally figured that it would be but one or two campaigns before his party would also elect a president. If a socialist, and hence a bit more modest because more conscious of the difficulties, he still believed that in twenty years he would see a president chosen on a radical labor ticket. *The People* of the nineties, when it was the organ of the fighting Socialist Labor Party, carried regularly on the editorial page in bold faced type the vote cast since the militant policy had been inaugurated in 1889. De Leon, its editor, took great pride in the upward trend. Whenever the returns from an election indicated a gain, there would appear in red a crowing cock. In one issue, December 10, 1893, the paper printed the votes of the minority parties which preceded the Republican Party of 1860, and intimated that the Socialist Labor Party would have a somewhat similar experience. The Abolition, Liberty, Free Soil, and Republican Party were the names used by the party which put Abraham Lincoln into the presi-

dency. De Leon's organ printed the following table
of their votes:

1840 James G. Birney (Liberty-Abolitionist)....	7,509	votes
1844 James G. Birney (Liberty-Abolitionist).....	62,300	"
1848 Martin Van Buren (Free Soil)............	291,265	"
1852 John P. Hale (Free Soil).................	156,149	"
1856 John C. Fremont (Republican)............	1,341,264	"
1860 Abraham Lincoln (Republican)...........	1,816,352	"

The Socialist Labor Party was, however, destined to
make no such showing. Simon Wing and Charles H.
Matchett, its standard bearers on the first presidential
ticket put up by any socialist party in the United States,
in 1892, were on the ballot in six states and polled 21,512
votes. The vote of the party up to 1898 did not show
much growth, for it was not until the populists were out
of the way that the party could make any real headway.
The returns of the congressional and state elections of
1898 warmed the cockles of the De Leonites' hearts. In
that year the party received as much as 82,204 votes for
its own candidates on its own tickets. This was more
than double the vote of 1896 and about four times that
of 1892. The party seemed to be on the march. But
in 1899 came the split. It is true that after it secured
recognition as *the* Socialist Labor Party in Greater New
York, it polled the same vote, about 15,000 in the fall
election of 1899. But it was not able to retain this or
even a large percentage of it in the metropolis, and as for
the rest of the country, when the returns were in for
the presidential contest of 1900 the De Leonites were
for all practical purposes wiped out. In rivalry with the
followers of Debs they polled only 32,751 votes, and
they were never able to rise again in any succeeding presidential contest. The vote of 1898 was their peak, and
after 1899 the Socialist Labor Party was out of the race
as a practical vote getter. It then had to and could afford
to become a party of agitation and education. There
was nothing else for it to do. It lost no opportunity,
however, of attacking the Socialist Party for doing better

what it once zealously tried to do, *viz.,* increase its vote
and elect socialists to public office.

The membership of the Socialist Labor Party in its
heyday did not reach more than six thousand. In 1889
there were about seventy sections, in 1898, about three
hundred and forty in twenty-six states. The membership, as given by Henry Kuhn, was in 1892 about three
thousand; in 1896, between five and six thousand. The
sections were largely foreign-speaking. In Chicago, for
example, *The Socialist Alliance* of July 1, 1896 reported
a preponderant number of German, Scandinavian, Polish,
and Jewish branches and clubs. The English-speaking
sub-division was often called the American branch—and
this sometimes though the majority spoke little English,
and few if any were born in this country. In New York
City, German and Jewish branches were conspicuous. The
situation varied from city to city, but the old Socialist
Labor Party certainly did not include a majority of natives. De Leon did, however, exert his every effort to
Americanize the party and did bring a number of English-
speaking persons into it.

§

The conventions of the Socialist Labor Party often
marked important points in its history. The little conference which nominated Wing for president and
Matchett for vice-president on August 28, 1892, was
composed of delegates from the state committees of five
states, Connecticut, Massachusetts, New Jersey, New
York, and Pennsylvania. The next regular convention
of the Socialist Labor Party was held in Chicago, opening on July 2, 1893, with thirty-six delegates. Daniel
De Leon was not present, being at the time in Zurich at
the international socialist congress. The convention decided to abolish the proxy system whereby delegates
represented locals of which they were not members. It
also dropped a provision allowing a labor organization the
opportunity of joining the party as a branch. In the

election of the city which was to choose the members of the national executive committee, there was a tie vote between St. Louis and New York. A referendum decided in favor of the latter.

The convention made its position clear as to the relation of the party to the populists. This attitude greatly incensed Thomas J. Morgan and many of the Chicago socialists who went along with the populists in 1894, the combined ticket polling about 30,000 votes. It was "Tommy" Morgan, a leading borer from within, a pro-labor party socialist, and an anti-De Leonite, who in his picturesque way announced in the *Workers' Call* of Chicago, as soon as he heard that the New Yorkers had declared war on De Leon, that he "believed in the dethroning of the Pope, the King, the Princes, and the Lords."

There were 94 delegates from 12 states at the July 4-10, 1896, convention of the Socialist Labor Party. This gathering paved the way for the split of 1899. After the schism had taken place, the loyal De Leonites assembled June 2-8, 1900, in New York City for their next convention, to nominate their presidential ticket, adopt a platform, and make necessary constitutional changes in view of the immediate past developments. The most radical change that this convention introduced was to strike out all immediate demands from the 1900 platform. After having fought for them for a decade, the leaders now said that these immediate demands were "nonsense and untrue." They were Kangarooish, they belonged to the infancy of the movement. This is the way they put it:

It is the navel string that connected the active fighting Socialist Labor Party with the embryo Socialist Labor Party at a time when we had to go around with our hats in our hands, and try to sugar-coat our principles, and show people what we might do. And it was very dangerous, because, by telling people what we might do—all of which things did not in any way affect the fundamental thing that we are after, namely, the abolition of the wages system—we simply notified the freaks and capitalists through what doors they could get into our citadel and knock us out.

In eliminating immediate demands from their political platform the De Leonites acted logically and in conformity with their trade union program, which stressed the ultimate and supreme mission of the economic arm. As an educational agency, on both the political and industrial fields they now found it expedient to emphasize exclusively their revolutionary goal. But once they had found and frankly acknowledged their own peculiar role, they never seemed to recognize that there was need for a mass trade union and a mass labor political party to approach the problem from the immediate bread-and-butter standpoint. This was the vital defect of the philosophy and tactics of the Socialist Labor Party.

The 1900 convention of the Socialist Labor Party also added more barbed wire to protect its citadels against the "labor faker," by the following provision:

If any member of the Socialist Labor Party accepts office in a pure and simple trade or labor organization, he shall be considered antagonistically inclined towards the Socialist Labor Party and shall be expelled. If any officer of a pure and simple trade or labor organization applies for membership in the Socialist Labor Party, he shall be rejected.

This was a splendid way of sealing up the party, and making it impossible for any socialist laborite to run the affairs of the pure and simple unions. It was dualism with a vengeance.

The convention also made changes as to the method of selecting the national executive committee, the secretary, and the editors of the official English organ, *The People,* which was now changed from a weekly to a daily. The daily was thus launched at a time when the party had just been split, and its maintenance for fourteen years after 1900 involved heavy sacrifices for the loyal supporters of the Socialist Labor Party. The national secretary and editor were to be elected by the convention, while the national executive committee of seven members was to be chosen by a general referendum vote of the party membership from among fourteen candidates nominated by the seat of the headquarters. The delegates to this convention numbered 83, with 24 alternates, from 18 states on the basis of congressional district representation. They nominated Joseph F. Malloney for president and Valentine Remmel for vice-president. The succeeding conventions of the Socialist Labor Party made no important changes in the constitution or principles of the organization.

CHAPTER VII

SOCIALIST UNITY

THE history of the Socialist Party can, in large part, be written around two men, Eugene Victor Debs and Morris Hillquit. These two figures embodied in their philosophies and personalities the main tendencies of the only significant and long-lived independent political party of the wage earners of the United States—so far. That these two men did not produce a major party of the masses in America, as did Keir Hardie and Ramsay MacDonald in England, and August Bebel and Wilhelm Liebknecht in Germany, cannot detract from their historic and enduring contribution toward that end.

Eugene Victor Debs was born on November 5, 1855 in Terre Haute, Indiana, the son of a grocer. He joined the Brotherhood of Locomotive Firemen in 1875 and five years later rose to the position of grand secretary-treasurer of the national organization. He remained at that post until 1892, although he continued to edit the official magazine for two years longer. For the four-year period, 1879-1883, he was city clerk, and in 1885 was elected to the Indiana legislature on the democratic ticket. He helped to organize the national unions of the brakemen, carmen, and switchmen. In 1892 he resigned a $4,000 annual salary—a large sum in those days—to take a job at $900 a year to work for the American Railway Union. This was the turning point in his life.

The American Railway Union was launched in Chicago in June, 1893, as an all-inclusive railway employees' organization, to cover all crafts in the industry, the skilled and the unskilled, the men and the women. In one year it had 465 lodges and claimed 150,000 members. In April, 1894, the union called its first strike against the powerful Great Northern Railway, and "won 97½ percent of the union demands, a monthly increase in wages" included. Its prestige rose. When it met at Chicago, June 9-26, 1894, for its second convention, the delegates were in a mood to hear sympathetically and take action to protect the Pullman shop employees who had joined the American Railway Union in March of that year. These work-ers had called a local strike on May 11 to bring back their wages to the level of 1893. The Pullman Company refused to meet with them or accept arbitration. The convention unanimously decided to throw the whole strength of the organization into a sympathetic strike to compel the sleeping car corporation to submit the de-mands to arbitration, and it set June 26 as the final day. If the company did not arbitrate by that time the mem-bers of the American Railway Union would not handle any Pullman cars. The Pullman Company had contracts with twenty-four railroad companies and the union soon found itself fighting not only one company but twenty-five of the most powerful corporations in the country, with nearly all the agencies of political power and public opinion on the latters' side.

The conflict was a bitter one, costly in lives lost and in millions of dollars' worth of property destroyed. Sam-uel Gompers justified the strike in these words:

From the standpoint of the American Railway Union, having no agreement with either of the railroad companies involved and expressing the inarticulate protest of the masses against the wrongs inflicted upon any of their brothers and their yearnings for justice to all mankind, yes! a thousand times yes!

The secretary of the executive committee of the Na-tional Farmers' Alliance and Industrial Union, the most powerful farmers' organization in the country, sent, in the name of his body, a resolution of sympathy with the strikers and declared that the granaries and storehouses would be opened to aid the workers. The Knights of

Labor appealed for contributions in behalf of the men. Not only did the members of the American Railway Union respond to the strike call, but many belonging to the craft and rival railroad brotherhoods downed tools also, against the orders of their officers. Then the politicians stepped into the situation.

Governor Altgeld of Illinois, the courageous liberal who a year earlier had pardoned the three surviving Chicago anarchists, refused to use the armed forces of the state to break the strike. But there was another democrat in the White House who felt otherwise. Against Altgeld's forceful pleas, President Grover Cleveland dispatched federal troops to Chicago. They entered on the day this country holds sacred to the memory of those who declared that this nation shall be dedicated to freedom— July 4th. In addition to the troops there were 3,600 deputy marshalls to do their bit. And then the courts began to issue injunctions, tying the hands of the strikers. Debs and his colleagues were arrested on July 10. At first the leader was charged with conspiracy to murder, but this was changed to contempt of court for alleged violation of an injunction. The workers in Chicago and elsewhere resorted to spontaneous walk-outs, and the strike leaders called together the chiefs of the American Federation of Labor and Knights of Labor to consider declaring a general strike. The executive council of the federation met on the 12th and decided against extending the strike to their organized workers, and at the same time issued a circular to their members to return to work. Gompers claimed that Debs himself had confessed that the strike was already a failure when the meeting of the 12th was held. There was a good deal of bitterness over the circular, however. The strike was now a lost cause. Debs was sentenced to six months in the Woodstock, Illinois, jail. Samuel Gompers at that time paid him the following tribute:

Out of all this tumult it has revealed to the world the character of one of its noblest sons, Eugene V. Debs. His earnestness, honesty and sincerity no man on this continent doubts. No one has a shadow of an excuse for doubting him and it is but right to accord him this faint measure of justice.

The corporations now have their claws ready to fasten them upon the body of Debs, not simply to try and crush him, but they hope to awe the men of labor into silence and slavish submission. That purpose cannot, dare not, and will not succeed. Debs must be defended and ably defended. In his person at this time he represents the rights of labor before the law to organize, to quit work in defense, protection and advancement of its interests.

And as to the significance of the Pullman strike, just after it ended and before Gompers became the enemy of Debs, he said.

It is true that the struggle has not been crowned with the immediate success of the objects sought to be achieved, yet it has so thrilled the hearts of the people and riveted their attention that its lessons and benefits will be widespread, deep and lasting. Like many of its predecessors, as we have said, it has failed of its immediate object, but it has accomplished more good in directing attention to the underlying wrongs of modern society than all the lectures and publications could secure in a decade.

§

The People of May 14, 1893,—some years before Debs became a socialist—already predicted his future course. Speaking of the new American Railway Union the paper said:

The new organization starts with an admirable move. It casts off the old "aristocracy of labor" pretensions and reaches the hand down to the least skilled in the railroad service. From this deliberate or instinctive recognition of the identity of the class interests of all the railroad employees golden fruits may be expected; it is a step in the direction of clasping hands with the whole working class in all other industries, of recognizing the solidarity of its interests, and of taking a position before which all false impressions must vanish, and the question, the real question, appears in its only practical light and its full grandeur—the abolition of the capitalist system of production, the establishment of the Co-Operative Commonwealth.

The People pointed out that the old craft unions, the railroad brotherhoods, were organized for the few, the costs of membership and overhead were excessive, there was "a hurtful air of mystery" about them, tremendous power was lodged in the hands of the chiefs, they were too cautious and conservative, the grievance committees were too complex and unwieldy, in a word they were unions of the labor aristocracy.

After the defeat of the Pullman strike *The People* of July 29, 1894, stated the fundamental trade union point of view of Daniel De Leon, Hugo Vogt, and their supporters:

The union of the workers that expects to be successful must recognize:

1. The impossibility of obtaining a decent living while capitalism exists; the certainty of worse and worse conditions; the necessity of the abolition of the wage and capitalist system, and their substitution by the Socialist or Co-Operative Commonwealth, whereby the instruments of production shall be made the property of the whole   people.

2. The necessity of conquering the public powers at the ballot box by the vote of the working class, cast independently.

This position—which practically precluded the need of trade unions—made it impossible for any labor leader like Debs to join the Socialist Labor Party. Moreover, the native American was not yet clear or convinced as to his own philosophy. The six months in jail helped him to understand what it was all about.

Debs referred, in an article which appeared in *The Comrade,* to the men and books that converted him to socialism:

Books and pamphlets and letters from socialists came by every mail. . . . The writings of Bellamy and Blatchford early appealed to me. The "Co-Operative Commonwealth" of Gronlund also impressed me, but the writings of Kautsky were so clear and conclusive that I readily grasped, not merely his argument, but also caught the spirit of his socialist utterance. . . . It was at this time . . . that Victor L. Berger . . . came to Woodstock . . . and delivered the first impassioned message of socialism I had ever heard.

But when Debs came out of Woodstock, greeted by hundreds, the tide of the People's Party was rising.   In

1896 occurred the memorable campaign of the democrats-populists against the republicans. The American Railway Union came out for Bryan:

We pledge our united and unwavering support to William J. Bryan for president, and appeal to railway employees and all workingmen to join with us in rebuking corporate tyranny which attempts to wrest the sacred right of suffrage from employees, in abolishing government by injunction and securing and maintaining every right of citizenship vouchsafed by the Constitution of our country.

The American workers wanted to strike hard, when their blow could do some immediate good, here, and now. Debs justified his support of the Commoner in the first issue of the *Railway Times*, on January 1, 1897:

I supported Mr. William J. Bryan and the platform upon which he stood, not because I regarded the free coinage of silver as a panacea for our national ills, for I neither affirmed nor advocated such a principle, but because I believed that the triumph of Mr. Bryan and free silver would blunt the fangs of the money power. . . . The free silver issue gave us, not only a rallying cry, but afforded common ground upon which the common people could unite against the trusts, syndicates, corporations, monopolies—in a word, the money power. . . .

The results of the 1896 election convinced Debs, however, in his own words, "that in politics, *per se,* there is no hope of emancipation from the degrading cause of wage-slavery." He declared himself a socialist and said that there was "no hope for the toiling masses of my countrymen except by the pathways mapped out by socialists, the advocates of the Co-Operative Commonwealth."

The years of depression which followed the panic of 1893 had not ended, and there were still many out of work. Debs wanted to do something for them, and he also wanted to unite the workers of the country into a grand cooperative scheme to usher in the cooperative commonwealth. He proposed, therefore, to his followers inside and outside the American Railway Union that they colonize a western state, secure political control, and then establish within its limitations as much of the socialist commonwealth as possible.

§

The American Railway Union met in convention in Chicago, June 15-18, 1897, and wound up its affairs. On June 18 began the convention of the Social Democracy, into which it merged itself. There were present at this gathering representatives of the older colonizing groups, the Brotherhood of the Co-Operative Commonwealth, labor unions, Socialist Labor Party clubs and religious associations—a motley assortment of humanitarians and idealists. The convention elected an executive board consisting of Debs as chairman, James Hogan as vice-chairman, Sylvester Keliher of the American Railway Union as secretary-treasurer, and William E. Burns and R. M. Goodwin as organizers. It provided for a national council from state units, and for the chartering of local branches under these. It adopted the following set of principles:

With a view to the immediate relief of the people, all our efforts shall be put forth to secure to the unemployed self-supporting employment. . . . For such purpose one of the states of the Union, to be hereafter determined shall be selected for the concentration of our supporters and the introduction of co-operative industry, and then gradually extending the sphere of our operations until the national cooperative commonwealth shall established.

We call upon all honest citizens to unite under the banner of the Social Democracy of America, so that we may be ready to conquer capitalism by making use of our political liberty, and by taking possession of the public power.

The declaration of principles, however, included more than a statement of fundamental purpose. It added a set of immediate demands for relief:

1. Public ownership of all industries controlled by monopolies, trusts and combines.

2. Public ownership of the railroads, telegraphs, telephone, and all means of transportation, communication, water works, gas and electric plants, and all other public utilities.

3. Public ownership of all gold, silver, lead, coal, iron, and all other mines; also all oil and gas wells.

4. Reduction of hours of labor.

5. Public works for unemployed.

6. Inventions to be free—the public to pay the inventor.

7. Postal savings banks.

8. Initiative and referendum; imperative mandate; proportional representation.

The leaders of the Socialist Labor Party had little use for the new organization and the colonizing plan of Debs. The *Socialist Alliance* of Chicago, after paying respect to the moral grandeur of the man, classified Debs as an enthusiastic and vague reformer, the failure of whose scheme would redound to the discredit of the socialist movement. Section Chicago of the Socialist Labor Party issued a statement headed: "A warning against the duodecimo edition of the New Jerusalem, known as the 'Debs Plan'." It included these sentences:

These people have dragged you through the wilderness of populism into the slough of silver, and now by a mirage of false hopes they would lead you into a thorny desert of utopianism. They are seriously proposing to you a scheme of migration, for the conquest of the political machinery of one of the smaller states, whereupon a full-fledged cooperative commonwealth is to be established therein.

There were socialists, however, who, while agreeing with this view of the Debs Plan, saw in the Social Democracy a means of advancing socialism in the United States. They were men who were to play a leading part in the Socialist Party.

The Jewish socialists of New York held a convention, July 31-August 2, 1897, with 58 delegates in attendance, claiming to represent about 1,200 members of the Socialist Labor Party, and about 10,000 trade unionists. I. A. Hourwich and Meyer London, for local branch No. 1 of the Social Democracy, explained the purposes of the new organization, and by a vote of 40 to 10 secured the adoption of a resolution approving it in these words:

All parties which have existed heretofore, have either failed to support the principles of a revolutionary class struggle, or where they have supported this principle, they were organized into a small isolated sect which was never united with the great mass of the militant proletariat.

In the evening, at a mass meeting, with Hourwich in the chair, London, Cahan, Miller, Winchevsky, and Zametkin spoke, all in favor of the western movement. The *Forward* became its unofficial organ among the Jewish workers.

The new organization received support from the Milwaukee socialists and their leader, Victor L. Berger. The latter was born on February 28, 1860, in Austria-Hungary. He studied in the universities of Budapest and Vienna—incidentally, today he has one of the largest private libraries in the country. After coming to the United States he worked at various trades, and for a time was a public school teacher. He became editor of the Milwaukee daily *Vorwaerts* in 1892 and served in that capacity until 1898. He had been a member of the old Socialist Labor Party, and in the split of 1889 showed his independence of the New Yorkers by going along with the "perambulating faction" of Rosenberg-Bushe. When the populist movement began to take hold of the American farmers and workers he and many of his fellow-socialists of Milwaukee threw in their lot with the People's Party. Hot and many were the debates that Berger held with the proponents of the Socialist Labor Party on the tactic of supporting the third party. The Milwaukee socialists were not the only ones who put their faith in boring from within the populist ranks. Berger helped to make Debs a socialist, and joined him in the Social Democracy. He and others then sought to turn the organization into more realistic channels.

The second convention of the Social Democracy opened in Chicago on June 7, 1898, with Debs as chairman. Secretary Keliher raised the first storm by declaring that eight branches had been organized in Chicago just prior to the convention in order to give control to the colonizing faction. The national executive commitee, meeting that evening, ordered the secretary to issue those charters. The anti-colonizers did not have the necessary number of votes to transform the organization in the direction they wished. On the vote for adoption of the platform the colonizers won, 52 against 37. The anti-colonizers announced a bolt and met separately.

The colonizing group, headed by John F. Lloyd of Illinois and James Hogan of Utah, argued for a program of colonization and political action; the anti-colonizers, led by Victor L. Berger of Wisconsin and Margaret Haile of Massachusetts, for political action alone. Debs at first stood by the colonizers. The platform which gave offense to the anti-colonizers read in part as follows:

Were they free of the irresponsible domination of the federal courts, the people of any state could become a commonwealth when they chose. Under the American system of government the states are the natural instruments of inaugurating socialism. The federal constitution cannot be amended . . . the power of the federal courts is at the mercy of a majority of Congress.

The colonizers had proclaimed a policy whereby they would take the field as an independent political party only when no existing party was taking practicable steps toward socialism. They also took their colonization plan seriously. In the fall of 1897, shortly after the Social Democracy was founded, the official organ, the *Social Democrat,* appealed in the name of the organization for $20 from each branch, and an individual contribution for colonization. A colonization commission was selected, consisting of Richard J. Hinton, the co-worker of John Brown the abolitionist, Cyrus Field Willard, labor editor of the Boston *Globe,* and W. P. Borland, another journalist. By June 1898, however, the commission had received only $2,430.67.

After the split, as was to be expected, the colonizers and their organization quickly went by the board. In their very brief term of existence after the bolt they fought back the attacks of the other side by declaring that "American socialist methods" had won in the convention. They added a touch of nativism and race prejudice to hit those whom they had previously welcomed with open arms: "Delegates Winchevsky, Hourwich, Barondess, Levin, Kuhn, Hunger, Moerschell, and Berger were among the bolters. Comment is superfluous." They answered the charge that they were anarchists: "Their conception of the term anarchy seems to be much perverted." The "utopians" were not anarchists, they were utopians.

§

The socialists, who had bolted at an hour when most honest men are fast asleep, 2:30 A. M., met the next morning very early—they were intense—and adopted a statement explaining the whys and wherefores of their act. They charged the colonizers with packing the convention, with opposition to independent political action, with having accomplished nothing on their colonization plan, and with having introduced "all kinds of schemes." They adopted their own declaration of principles in which they said that "the trade union movement and independent political action are the chief emancipating factors of the working class." They added a number of immediate demands including five special measures for farmers. The organization elected an executive committee consisting of Jesse Cox as chairman, Seymour Stedman as secretary, and Eugene V. Debs, Victor L. Berger, and Frederic Heath. It announced that it stood for united political action and proposed to enter the national field in the fall. Debs made his own statement. He declared that the division had to come or else the old Social Democracy would have gone on the rocks. Theodore Debs, his brother, became the national secretary of the Social Democracy Party of America, the name of the new organization. Among the founders of the purged and practical political body were:

California:
Anna Ferry Smith
Illinois:
Jesse Cox
George Koop
Seymour Stedman
Indiana:
Eugene V. Debs
Theodore Debs
Hugo Miller
Massachusetts:
James F. Carey
Margaret Haile
Missouri:
G. A. Hoehn
Mary G. Jones
C. F. Meier
New Hampshire:
F. G. R. Gordon
New Jersey:
Samuel Levine

New York:
Joseph Barondess
William Butscher
Louis E. Miller
I. Phillips
M. Winchevsky
Ohio:
W. J. Carberry
Charles R. Martin
Pennsylvania:
Walter H. Miller
Tennessee:
A. S. Edwards
William Mailly
Wisconsin:
Victor L. Berger
John Doerfler
Frederic Heath
Jacob Hunger
Chas. G. Kuhn
Oscar Loebel
George Moerschel

The platform of the Social Democratic Party no more pleased the Socialist Labor Party than did that of the Social Democracy. Herman Simpson, who reported the conventions for *The People,* wrote that "the platform adopted by the rump of the Social Democracy should be incorporated in a text book on logical fallacies and historical misconceptions." The party of De Leon could afford to crow after the election of November, 1898, and compare its 82,000 votes with the 12,411 for the party of Debs. The Social Democratic Party, however, elected James F. Carey and Lewis H. Scates to the Massachusetts legislature, and John C. Chase mayor of Haverhill. Moreover, there were a number of prominent socialist laborites who were joining such as Squire E. Putney of Massachusetts and Carl Pankopf of New Jersey. The Socialist Party of Texas affiliated on June 9, 1899. When the first national convention of the new party was held on March 6, 1900, at Indianapolis, it claimed to have 226 active branches with 4,536 members. More dangerous to the Socialist Labor Party than the losses of members or votes to the new organization was the fact that when the split occurred in its own ranks in July, 1899, the secessionists could look for unity with the western party and thus undermine the De Leonites nationally. This the insurgents proceeded to do. Their leader was Morris Hillquit.

§

The present international secretary of the American Socialist Party was born in Riga, Russia, on August 1, 1870, and came to this country when he was 15 years of age. Like Berger he worked at various trades and took part in the trade union movement from the first, being at one time secretary of the United Hebrew Trades of New York. Unlike Debs and Berger, however, Hillquit did not choose to make his living from and devote all his time to the labor movement. He was graduated from law school in 1893 and at once started on the legal work for which he is almost as noted as for his place in the socialist movement at home and abroad. He first appeared as a national figure in the old Socialist Labor Party, of which he had been a member for some years, when he submitted his letter of acceptance as candidate for member of the national executive committee on June 29, 1899. He stated the case of the insurgents in his usual logical, clear, and cogent style. Back of the steps taken by the rebels, during and after the insurrection, was his guiding hand.

In the early part of February, 1900, the opposition to the old Socialist Labor Party assembled in its first na-

tional convention at Rochester, New York, with 59 delegates. After listening to an able address by N. I. Stone,
the first editor of their rival *People*, on *The Attitude
of the Socialists toward the Trade Unions,* the convention
repudiated dual unionism and adopted the following
resolution:

Whereas, The trade union movement of the working class
is an inevitable manifestation of the struggle between capital
and labor, and is absolutely necessary to resist the superior
economic power of capital, to improve the condition of the
workingmen, and to maintain their standard of life; and

Whereas, The class struggle carried on by the trade unions
tends to develop in the workingmen the sense of solidarity
and political independence by organizing them as a class antagonistic to the capitalist class;

Resolved, That we the Socialist Labor Party in national convention assembled, fully recognize that the exploitation of labor
will cease only when society takes possession of the means of
production, nevertheless declare it the duty of all socialists to
participate in all struggles of organized labor to improve its
conditions under the present system;

Resolved, That we hereby recall any and all previous resolutions expressing preference for one body of organized labor
over another;

Resolved, That we reaffirm the resolution of the Socialist
Labor Party adopted in 1893 and readopted in 1896 recommend-
ing to all members of the party to join the organization of the
trades to which they respectively belong.

In view of the approaching presidential election the
delegates adopted a platform and nominated Job Harriman of California for president and Max Hayes of Ohio
for vice-president. They hoped that they would not have
to go it alone, however, for they elected a committee of
nine to confer with the Social Democratic Party. In
choosing the committee on unity the convention provided
that any treaty of union "including the question of party
name, platform, and constitution, be submitted to a general vote of both parties." The Rochester convention and
the Socialist Labor Party faction it represented wanted a
lasting union with the Social Democratic Party.

Three members of the Rochester committee of nine appeared at the convention of the Social Democratic Party which began its sessions on March 6, 1900, in Indianapolis. They were enthusiastically received; the delegates were in a mood for unity. Their leaders, however, were not so anxious. The latter proposed that their name be retained in the amalgamated body and that any treaty adopted be sent to referendum of the membership of each organization. These recommendations the delegates rejected by a vote of two to one, and they elected a committee of nine to confer with the similar committee of the Rochester group. The convention adopted the same platform as of the previous year. There was only one candidate for president, Eugene V. Debs. He declined, and kept on refusing, although many pleaded with him. Finally, he accepted. For vice-president the delegates picked the head of the ticket of the Rochester Socialist Labor Party, Job Harriman.

The joint committee on unity met in New York on March 25, 1900, and agreed substantially on all important matters. The candidates chosen at Indianapolis, and the Rochester platform with certain immediate demands of the Social Democratic Party tacked on, were accepted. Party headquarters were fixed at Springfield, Massachusetts, and a provisional national committee of ten was to be chosen from both parties. The only disputed point, whether the new party should be called Social Democratic Party or United Socialist Party, was to be submitted to the membership of the two bodies. Unity seemed all but achieved. On March 28 a meeting was held in Cooper Union to celebrate. Everybody was happy. *The People* —the one controlled by the Rochester group—announced that there were many present who had been prominent in past years in the work of the Social Democratic and Socialist Labor Party. It gave the following list of the local lights:

William Butscher, Joseph Barondess, N. Bendin, Peter Burrowes, S. Berlin, A. Cahan, William Edlin, Dr. C. L. Furman,

B. Feigenbaum, M. Gordon, J. Ganz, M. Hillquit, Dr. Halpern, Dr. Ingerman, Alexander Jonas, Frederick Krafft, Philip Kranz, Algernon Lee, L. A. Malkiel, John Nagel, I. Phillips, N. I. Stone, H. L. Slobodin, H. Schlueter, M. Winchevsky, besides their wives and friends.

But the jubilation was short lived. On April 2 the national executive board of the Social Democratic Party issued a manifesto repudiating the action of the joint committee. It claimed that Hayes, Harriman, and Hillquit, the three representatives of the Rochester group, had made a solemn compact agreeing to use the name Social Democratic Party, while the joint committee submitted two names for referendum; also, that the joint committee permitted a majority of all the votes to decide, and did not call for a referendum of each body separately. The executive of the Social Democratic Party also asserted that the vote of the Socialist Labor Party "would depend upon the returns made by the secretaries of local sections." It went further and charged that "political unity formed upon diplomacy, tainted with bad faith and double dealing can never stand. . . . A united Socialist Party cannot be built upon broken pledges." While Margaret Haile could write in the *Social Democratic Herald* of April 7: "Comrade Social Democrats: My pen lingers over the name as I write it. It has grown to mean more to me, within the past six weeks, than it ever did before!" the differences between the two groups were deeper—at least to the leaders of the Social Democratic Party.

§

Eugene V. Debs let himself go in the issue of April 21 to describe those with whom he was to engage in a life-long comradeship:

I take my stand against union of the parties on the basis proposed by the New York conference. . . . For years the official organ of the Socialist Labor Party [De Leon's *People*] had drilled it into their members that the Social Democratic Party consisted of a lot of freaks, frauds and fakers without a redeeming feature. They were fairly saturated with the virus of hate and contempt. Hundreds of them, members of the anti-De Leon party, and I speak advisedly, still rankle with that feeling which, to even the superfical observer is but illy concealed. It is this sort of training in the school of intolerance, fanaticism and hate which have given the party a spirit irreconcilably in conflict with that of the Social Democratic Party which by its highminded toleration has appealed so successfully to the American people in behalf of socialism that its complete supremacy as the socialist party was only a question of months, while at every step of its progress its members were derided as "halfbaked socialists" by the very men who now, we are assured, insist upon union. The spirit is still there, whatever may be said to the contrary.

He declared that the Rochester Socialist Labor Party got everything it wanted from the joint committee and that "the adoption of the majority report would simply mean the swallowing up of the Social Democratic Party and its domination by an element composed largely of men who had despised and ridiculed it."

Victor L. Berger also insisted that "the leopard has not changed its spots," and that "instead of joining us, they tried to destroy our organization and to start a new sect with the old spirit under a new name." He ridiculed the "Revolution of July 10, 1899." He pointed out that it took three Tammany policemen to quench it. He paid his respects to the *Volkszeitung* crowd, with whom he had an old score to settle because of the split of 1889:

In 1889 they had peaceable Germans to fight, who were not prepared for war. But this time they got hold of the wrong fellow. Dan was prepared, and when the *Volkszeitung's* crowd came to commit "the revolution," they found a picked lot of Irishmen and Americans to receive them. Dan made short work of the *Volkszeitung-Garde,* and the only fruit of the great revolution for the *Volkszeitung* is the capture of the Labor Lyceum Saloon. Not only this. Daniel De Leon beat them in the courts. He got the party name and the party emblem. And what's worse, he also beat them at the following state election: his party receiving about as many votes without the *Volkszeitung's* crowd as with them.

The future congressman and future co-worker of the men he taunted claimed that the new and the old Socialist Labor Party—the two factions—were one and the same in principles and tactics:

> The Socialist Labor Party is not a political party, never was one and never can be one—it is simply a political sect that adopted Marx's book *Das Kapital* as its bible. And a bible not in the modern, but in the old medieval sense, when few people could read it. . . . In all my modern experience with the Socialist Labor Party where every man constantly talks about Karl Marx as if he had attended school with him, I only found two or three men who had really read *Das Kapital*, and talked about it understandingly.

> To the average Socialist Labor Party man Marx's work is a book with seven seals. Still, the first thing the Socialist Labor Party always accomplished was to give its members a fearfully magnified idea of their importance and "science". They learn a few phrases about exploitation, surplus value, the great revolution, and especially about "class consciousness," repeat them on every occasion, and call that science. In that way the most ignorant of men becomes a "scientific socialist" in one evening without having the inconvenience of studying books and thinking about social problems.

> The rest of their tactics can be told in a very few words. It is to denounce and vilify everybody who does not entirely agree with them. . . . Especially do they say this of every reformer, labor leader, or socialist who has not joined them.

Berger did not stop at this type of attack: he began to do a bit of vilifying himself, and to indulge in personalities. He called Harriman, the candidate for vice-president on his own ticket, a "Tammany politician of the seventeenth degree," and his own "Jim" Carey, whose election in Haverhill Berger's party hailed as the beginning of the social revolution in America, a "ward politician," and Morris Hillquit—"a thorough class conscious lawyer of New York."

Max Hayes, on the other hand, took pains to throw a few "brickbats" at the leaders of the Social Democratic Party, by pointing out that they were led by intellectuals and professionals—he thought of himself as a printer and proletarian:

The anti-unionists were marshalled by Berger, a school teacher and editor; Stedman, a lawyer; Mc Cartney, a preacher; Edwards, another editor; Cox, another lawyer; Miller, another editor; London, still another lawyer; Margaret Haile, a lachrymose woman, and one or two others—all so-called academic socialists, theorists. They controlled the machine of the party and used their power as De Leon did.

To this, A. S. Edwards, the editor of the *Social Democratic Herald,* one of the few who seemed to show signs of a sense of humor about this tempest in a teapot, answered:

Comment is uncalled for, except that we might direct attention to the fact that Harriman is a lawyer and ex-preacher; Hillquit is a lawyer; Schlueter an editor; Feigenbaum an editor; Morgan, a lawyer; Jonas, an editor; Stone, an editor; Sissman, a lawyer; Benham, an editor; Taft, a lawyer; Lee, an editor; and finally, not to continue such trivialities to too great a length, Max Hayes himself is an editor—and a good one.

§

On May 6, 1900, Morris Hillquit wrote in his party organ, *The People,* that "the publication of the manifesto at that time and under those circumstances was, mildly expressed, the most puerile and mischievous act any set of officers of a socialist party could make themselves guilty of." In the socialist movement Hillquit has generally stood for unity and has gone far out of his way to achieve and maintain it. He was determined to bring about unity in this instance. Five members of the committee of nine of the Social Democratic Party helped him.

Immediately after the joint committee's meeting in March, 1900, a statement giving the basis of union and announcing the referendum on the two names appeared in the press of the Socialist Labor Party faction. It was signed by William Butscher for the Social Democratic Party, and N. I. Stone for the anti-De Leonites. The executive board of the Debsites, however, sent out their own referendum, returnable by May 7, 1900, on this proposition: Is union between the Social Democratic Party and the Socialist Labor Party faction desirable? The vote showed 939 in favor of unity, and 1,213 against. In the opposition column 365 votes were cast by Wisconsin, with only eight votes for unity, enough to determine the result.

Meanwhile, the referendum of the joint committee was being balloted on, returns to be in by June 26. On May 20 an effort was made to patch up peace at a meeting of the committee of eighteen in New York City. Berger, Mrs. Haile, Heath, and Stedman refused to go along, while James F. Carey, John C. Chase, G. A. Hoehn, William P. Lonergan, and William Butscher, secretary for the Social Democratic Party, agreed to cooperate with the nine of the Socialist Labor Party faction: J. M. Barnes, G. B. Benham, C. E. Fenner, Job Harriman, M. S. Hayes, M. Hillquit, F. A. Sieverman, W. W. White, and N. I. Stone, secretary. The fourteen canvassed the returns from the membership of the Rochester Socialist Labor Party and the pro-unity Social Democratic Party branches —they went over the heads of the executive of the anti-union party—and announced that the unity proposals were carried overwhelmingly, and that the name Social Democratic Party had received more votes than that of United Socialist Party. They thus took the very title of the party which opposed them. William Butscher was selected as temporary national secretary, with headquarters in Springfield, Massachusetts, and Debs and Harriman were chosen standard bearers for the campaign of 1900.

The Chicago Social Democratic Party, of which Theodore Debs was secretary, was invited to elect a national campaign committee to cooperate. In Illinois and New York unity was achieved for the election. The *Social Democratic Herald* for months carried the name of Debs only as the candidate for president, but finally, on September 1, capitulated and added the name of Job Harriman as candidate for vice-president. The two groups got together for the purpose of waging a common fight in the election. Debs received 96,878 votes, against about 34,000 for the candidate of De Leon's Socialist Labor Party.

After the campaign the Social Democratic Party of Chicago met in special convention on January 15, 1901, with 89 delegates representing nineteen states. It declared for a general unity convention of the two groups. Still cautious, however, it sent the matter out to its own members for approval. The latter said, "Go ahead," and finally arrangements were made with the Springfield-Rochester group to hold a common convention beginning July 29, 1901, in Indianapolis. In the spring elections of Chicago, however, there were still bitter contests between the two Social Democratic parties and the De Leon Socialist Labor Party. The unity convention buried the differences between the Chicago and Rochester factions, and the development of the party which it launched relegated into the background the uncompromising De Leonites.

§

A. M. Simons, then editor of *The International Socialist Review,* noted in his journal that at the Indianapolis unity convention "the number of young American-born delegates was a source of frequent comment." That indeed was the most striking fact about this gathering. It was made up almost entirely of young men, full of life and vigor, rich with promise, and determined to set America on fire. And unlike many other socialist gatherings of consequence in the United States hitherto, it was not dominated by German-Americans or Jewish-Americans. The Indianapolis convention represented the virile young manhood of American socialism. The program, platform, and policies it adopted served the Socialist Party basically in its subsequent career. The question of immediate demands and the party's position toward the farmer caused the warmest debates. The attitude of the socialists toward the trade unions and the type of organization to run the party did not occasion much controversy; the experience with the De Leonites was still too fresh in the minds of the delegates.

Professor George D. Herron was chairman at the opening of the convention. Of the 125 delegates seventy came from the Springfield-Rochester unity group with 4,798 votes, forty-seven represented the Chicago Debsites with 1,396 votes, and eight came from independent parties with 352 votes. The membership covered ran to about ten thousand. Committees were chosen from each of the three divisions. But from the very first the delegates forgot that they represented factions. They divided on more fundamental lines, although occasionally a die-hard of the Social Democratic Party reminded the convention that every decision still had to go to a referendum of his party. Fur flew on the question of including immediate demands in the platform. Simons, McSweeney, Saunders, and Hayes, among others, spoke against inclusion, while McCartney, Goebel, Morgan, Hoehn, Herron, and Hillquit, among a longer list, favored including proposals of reform in a socialist platform.

A. M. Simons even then prided himself on his knowledge of America; he did do later two studies, *The American Farmer,* and *Social Forces in American History.* He delivered himself of the following—in 1901:

In no other country in the world has the ground upon which those who advocate immediate demands propose to stand, grown so thin as it has grown in America. Nowhere else on the face of the earth have the interests that we propose to serve through the immediate demands grown of so little importance as here. Nowhere else in the world has the struggle between capital and labor narrowed down to as clear a point and as clear an issue as it has in America.

Simons was younger then. His next point dealt with revolutionary strategy:

You say: "Are you against ameliorative measures?" Not at all. But I say to you, I meet you again on that ground, and it devolves upon you to demonstrate that these measures are ameliorative to the working class of America. You will have made a strong point if you can demonstrate to me that these immediate demands are something of which the benefit to the laborers will be commensurate with the sidetracking of the socialist movement, with the turning aside of the forces of revolution, and with the energy that must be exerted in order to push them forward. . . . I deny that the majority of these measures would bring to the laborers more than a slight measure of relief, while they would take their attention from the things for which we stand which would bring real relief.

It is the argument that today, if we go before the laborers, we must offer them something right away. I answer to you that today, if we are to go into the field of competitive bidding for votes, either of the old political parties can outbid us . . . a handful whose demand is but a hollow cry. The Republican Party says, "We not only demand that, but we grant it to you."

McSweeny backed up Simons by this statement: "You are looking for some kind of immediate relief for the working man of this country which it is impossible to give him under a competitive system." And Saunders added:

I stand for no immediate demands, or only one immediate demand, and that a complete surrender of the capitalist class. . . . Personally, I believe we cannot get anything from the capitalist class, even though we do elect the Careys and the McCartneys and a few others. Even though we elect a whole city, it would make no difference to you or me as a workingman. Our conditions will be just the same.

Max Hayes threw in a bit of American history:

You know the trouble that they had with the Nebraska and Missouri compromise. You know it was no compromise, and you know furthermore that when the crash came the entire slave power was destroyed and all the slaves were thereupon, set free.

§

McCartney, recently elected to the legislature of Massachusetts, talked practical politics, as he saw them, in defense of including immediate demands:

We stand ready as socialists, we will not give up one iota of fundamental principle as to the collective ownership of all the means of production and distribution. . . . But in the meantime we are a political party, we are no longer a sect or a church preaching the soon-coming of the Lord. We are a political party; we have elected mayors, aldermen and representatives. . . .

Last year we [Carey and himself] introduced twenty-five bills; they all looked toward the helping of the working class, or towards the furthering of a progressive political principle. . . . If you are going to preach simply a set of principles and dwell solely upon the social revolution . . . give up this mummery of posing, this theatrical proceeding of forming a political party.

And George Goebel, a born evangelist, backed up McCartney's argument:

I don't care what kind of a Kingdom of Heaven I am going to have: I am going to look after the poor devil alongside of me and do anything in my power to help him regardless of the Kingdom of Heaven he is going to have. . . . If I can get a man's mind along the line of municipal ownership and show him that there are some good things in the movement after all, I have brought that man into the Kingdom . . . . You may talk as much as you please of the philosophy of poverty bringing men into socialism; my experience is that the man who works the fewest hours and has the best wages and the most money for books, is the man that I think from my experience I have the best chance with.

"Tommy" Morgan, who had been a machinist and a worker at the bench, but who had become a lawyer, started his speech by the remark that "It is not good to be a lawyer in the Socialist Party." He dug deep down in his experience as a veteran in the Chicago labor movement to denounce what seemed to him the goal of those who opposed immediate demands:

I want to warn you that we are approaching in the socialist movement in the United States the beginning of another era of anarchism versus socialism. . . . I heard it called out in this convention, when Comrade McCartney said, "We introduced twenty-five bills," "Did you get them passed, did you get them passed?" No, of course they did not get them passed. If you tell them, "We passed so many bills," "Did you get them enforced, did you get them enforced?" No, of course not, and there you are. "What is the good of sending them to the legislature? What is the good of having a political party?" Our soap box orators have spurned with contempt all the claims and all the history of the trade union movement.

Morgan went on to relate what happened to the anarchists of the eighties:

Their morality, their good sense and everything could not be questioned, but their desires outran their reason. Some of these men committed suicide. The editor of our socialist paper committed suicide. John Mc Auliff, one of the best agitators we have had blew his brains out. Leo Milebeck, one of our best representatives, cut his throat. William Kemke, our German agitator, one of the cigar makers' union, cut his arm off. Rudolph, our French agitator, took the morphine route; Hirth, a cigar maker and editor of the first socialist paper we had, poisoned himself in Detroit. After these men had nominated candidates and cast their votes and the candidates were elected to the legislature or city council and their votes were counted out, they gave up the struggle in despair, and went into the physical force movement and went to making bombs.

G. A. Hoehn did not hesitate to call those opposed to immediate demands anarchists:

Talk about the cooperative commonwealth, talk about scientific socialism, talk about our present state of society, and then you request the American wage working class to make a big jump, to jump from your revolutionary nonsense right into the cooperative commonwealth.

Professor Herron brought out the point that the immediate demands of the sociaists differ from any immediate reforms of the capitalist parties:

The main effort that should be before us is to get the propositions of the immediate demands so stated that there can be no mistake in the minds of the working class or in the minds of the American voters to whom we appeal,—no mistake as to the difference in the motive and the outcome of the immediate demands presented by the Socialist Party and the reform demands or concessions that shall be made by the capitalist or so-called reform party .

Morris Hillquit stated the underlying ground for including immediate demands in the Socialist Party platform. As usual he perceived the significant tendencies
of the two sides, and took a centrist position. He started
by saying that he wanted the party platform "to express
the cardinal principles of socialism, not only our ultimate
aim and views, but also our present action, our activities."
He wound up as an evolutionist:

If we ever attempt to go before the working class and promise them the cooperative commonwealth in three or four or five
years and if they wait six and ten and see no chance of its
realization, then we will be much worse off, for they will lose
faith in our propaganda. On the contrary, if you show to the
working man what we know perfectly well and understand,
that we are dealing with the complex problem of social evolution, and that we do not know whether or not the ultimate end
in which we believe and for which we are working will be
reached today, tomorrow, or in ten years or half a century—
if you show them, in other words, that all we know is the
general tendency and all we can do is to work along these
lines and that all we call upon them to do is to cooperate with
us along these lines, then real progress is begun.

The vote in favor of including immediate demands was
5,358 votes against 1,325—eighty-two delegates against
thirty. Although beaten decisively in the unity convention, the "impossibilists," as those who opposed the inclusion of immediate demands were called, brought the
question up time and again in subsequent national
and state conventions.

§

The second matter which divided the delegates was
their position toward the American farmer. In the rump
or bolters' convention which organized the Social Democratic Party in June of 1898, five demands for farmers
were adopted. A year later these proposals were eliminated by a referendum, with the extrordinary vote of
478 to 81. The unity convention wrangled and talked

a lot but got nowhere. Some of the statements of the delegates are revealing as to their knowledge of and their desire to cooperate with the producers on the land. Simons, Stedman, and Hillquit, among others, typified one viewpoint; Carey, Harriman, and Hoehn, another. Extracts from the speeches of each will indicate how the delegates divided, and continued to divide, without arriving at any real agreement in the entire history of the party.

James F. Carey and Job Harriman were generally regarded as "opportunists." Strangely enough they presented the rigid, uncompromising and class conscious point of view toward the farmer:

Carey: Every man that belongs to the possessing class, whether he be the smallest farmer or the smallest manufacturer, has an interest peculiar to the class which he belongs, and that is the purchase of labor at the lowest possible wage and the appropriation of the surplus created by those whom he may employ, and whether he may be able to exploit men to a larger or smaller degree. . . . Talk to the farm laborers, because they belong to your class, but not to the possessing farmers. . . . They belong by virtue of their economic position, to the exploiting class. . . . As such we have with them no common interest, and as such we can only appeal to them as we appeal to the men of the middle class who are affiliated with our movement, by approaching their sense of justice or desire for equality or desire for the advancement of the race.

Harriman: We are building in this convention a wage working class platform; the farmers do not belong to the working class, because the farmers own the farms. . . I know that the harder the work of the farmer is, the more intensely will he struggle to reduce the wages of his help.

G. A. Hoehn pointed to the economic conflict between the urban consumer and the rural producer, and answered the plea that the farmer was as poor as the worker:

I don't care what Marx or what anybody else says, we take conditions as they are. . . . Take the small farmer near the city here. He has to bring his products to town, and when he gets to town he has to sell them at as high a price as possible to the wage workers, and that is not an identity of interest.

Morris Hillquit proposed an amendment or substitute motion—for which he was only too well known in socialist conventions:

The interests of the farmers are not identical with those of the wage workers . . . the condition of the farmer as it is to day is practically that of a hired laborer of the capitalist class. Whether the capitalist appears as landlord or mortgagee, he virtually owns the farm. . . . If the farmers are not interested in the same immediate demands, in the same progressive steps that the workingman is, the farmer is interested alike with the working man—that is, speaking of the small farmer of course, the poor and oppressed farmer—in the overthrow of the capitalist system, for he is a victim of that capitalist system just as the wage worker is. The agencies and mode of exploitation are different.

Seymour Stedman, who had been graduated out of the populist movement, claimed that "the farmer has little more absolute control over his commodities than the laborer has over his labor power. The farmer is forced by present conditions to throw his commodities upon the market, just as much as the laborer is forced to do it." He asserted that the farmer was as much exploited as the city worker. A. M. Simons, who was respectfully listened to in socialist conventions on this question—his specialty —gave the delegates quite a historical and analytical discourse. He emphasized the fact that "the great tools of transportation, the great tools of storage, the great tools with which the larger portion of economic production is carried on," are not owned by the farmer. He noted that the average income of the farmers of the country then was between $200 and $600 a year, and asked whether that left anything to be accounted for over and above the labor cost. "If he does not get the produce of his labor, then there is nothing left to be accounted for as a capitalist." With his eyes to future victory Simons said that nearly forty per cent of the population lived on farms and that it was "absolutely ridiculous and foolish to hope that you can ever accomplish anything without the [votes of the] farmers."

The question was finally referred to a special committee which was to report to the next convention.

§

A long resolution was brought in by the committee on trade unions, and after it was boiled down, was accepted. Some of the recommendations will show how the party stood at its birth:

The formation of every trade union, no matter how small or how conservative it may be, will strengthen the power of the wage working class.

By this class struggle so nobly carried on by the trades union forces today, the exploitation of labor will only be lessened, not abolished. The exploitation of labor can only be done away with entirely when society takes possession of all the means of production for the benefit of all the people.

The socialist or cooperative system can only be brought about by the independent political organization and united action of the wage working class, and all those that recognize and sympathize with the economic and historical mission of the proletariat.

Make the members of the trades unions acquainted with the principles of socialism and induce them individually to work for and affiliate with the Socialist Party.

Trade unions are by economic and historical necessity organized on neutral grounds as far as political affiliation is concerned.

The constitution adopted provided for only one active official, a secretary, with a supervisory local quorum or executive, and a national committee. The local quorum was to be chosen by the national committee from the membership at the seat of headquarters. The national committee was to be composed of one member from each organized state or territory. Each state that was organized—that is, in which a central office was set up representing at least ten locals in different parts of the commonwealth—had complete autonomy. It was provided that no official organ was to be designated by the national committee, that all its acts were to be subject to referendum vote, and the constitution itself could also be so amended. Representation at conventions was placed on a state basis, each to be entitled to one delegate at large and one additional delegate for every hundred members in good standing. There was a close contest over the location of the headquarters. Chicago and St. Louis—rivals in many other ways—were voted on, with the former receiving 3,096 and the latter 3,517 votes. Leon Greenbaum of St. Louis, the only nominee, was made national secretary. The new party—the Socialist Party as it was named—invited the Negro to membership and fellowship. It elected a committee on municipal program, to report at its next convention. The delegates left the sessions in high spirit. Unity was achieved. They brought the message home. The Socialist Party was born. The leaders and the rank and file now set to work to make it grow.

CHAPTER VIII

THE RISING TIDE OF SOCIALISM

BETWEEN 1901, when it was organized, and 1919, when it was split, the Socialist Party of the United States increased its vote from under 100,000 to about 900,000 in 1912. At the beginning of the latter year it claimed 1,039 of its dues paying members in public office, among whom were 56 mayors, over 300 aldermen, a number of state legislators, and one Congressman. With less than ten thousand members when it was launched the Socialist Party had 118,045 in 1912 and 108,504 before the schism in 1919. This membership included men, women, and young persons: the adults in the best years of their life, the youngsters making up in enthusiasm for what they lacked in experience. It included some of the highest paid and most articulate native American wage earners, as well as the militants of all nationalities in the trade unions. It comprised not a few of the tillers of the soil and a considerable group of idealists in every walk of American life. Besides a respectable vote, a number of public officials in power, and a growing membership in the main of sterling quality, the party had a well-oiled machine for propaganda and campaigns, with literature and a press, lecturers and organizers, and a number of auxiliary bodies to carry the message of socialism into every nook and cranny of America.

Up to 1912 the socialists were putting up an increasingly successful fight for their principles and program in the trade unions. In that year a socialist leader, Max S. Hayes, received about one-third of the total vote cast in a contest with Samuel Gompers for the presidency of the American Federation of Labor. Socialist working-men and intellectuals were everywhere in the forefront of all important labor struggles.

On both the political and economic fields the tide of socialism was in truth rising in the United States, as in every other industrialized nation of the world. And if it did not continue to rise as it has in the other capitalist countries—unless checked by dictatorships or armed force —it was because of the effects of the World War and our own participation in it. This bloody contest smashed the Second (socialist) International. It precipitated the rise to power of the bolsheviki in Russia. The Russian and other communists thereupon organized the Third or Communist International. Because of the nature of the membership and voters of the American Socialist Party —after the war hysteria had helped to injure it—the conflict between communist and socialist had more disastrous results here than perhaps in any other country. Finally, America's participation in the World War did not bring desolation and ruin to the country. On the contrary, it increased as never before the tempo of economic development, until today America is the richest nation on earth and the creditor of such world powers as Great Britain, France, Germany, and Italy. The reaction during and since the war placed the greatest emphasis on the dollar and not on liberty. While the few made extraordinary material gains, the masses also participated in the spotted prosperity. As a result of these factors, together with the conservatism of the trade unions, the Socialist Party was not able to maintain its strength nor even its position as the only effective expression of militant working class protest. The farmers' Nonpartisan League, the farmer-labor parties of 1919, and the movement behind Robert Marion La Follette for president in 1924, also appeared as practical rivals to the hitherto sole independent political force of importance, the Socialist Party.

The success or failure of the socialists on the political and economic fields in this country was thus obviously not in their own hands alone. Before as well as after the extraordinary events of the years following the outbreak of the World War the Socialist Party had to meet special difficulties. Take the vote the party received for its presidential candidate in the five campaigns, 1900 to 1916:

1900	....	94,768
1904	....	402,400
1908	....	420,820
1912	....	897,011
1916	....	585,113

The American voters are a practical set, and unless stirred cast their ballots for one of the two or three probable winners at an election. It is of course evident that at no time was a candidate of the Socialist Party for president in the running. Victory was out of the question. The size of the vote—even in 1912 the party polled only 5.9 per cent of the total of 15,031,169—was not an indication of weakness, but strangely enough, of great strength. It showed that close to a million Americans were willing to give their devotion to a party or a personality, even when neither had any immediate chance. And it was more than a protest vote because most of it continued to be regularly registered. In favorable circumstances, whenever a party with a million followers has a real chance of putting itself in the running it will receive a vote altogether out of proportion to its past poll; it can, like the British Labor Party, rise quickly and be the second party and even hold forth a realistic hope of coming first. In other words, the members of a cohesive, solidly-built organization, with veterans and men of principle at its head, who know what they want and are determined to stick until they get it, able to command the vote of the Socialist Party between 1904 and 1916, can confidently believe not only that they will hold their own but also that they have good ground for expecting to win

sweeping victories. Their main task consists in preparing themselves to take advantage of favorable opportunities, holding their gains, keeping their elected officials
put, and preventing a split over theoretical questions.

Considering the loyalties and conservatism of human
beings and American voters—tied by past habit to vote
the same old ticket, by present clamor to ignore the
unpopular minority, and by the fluidity of class relations
to dream in non-socialistic terms—it is truly surprising
that a labor party, with limited means and opportunities
to make itself felt, made as much headway as the Socialist
Party did before 1919. It had, to begin with, an increasing number of faithful followers who voted the ticket in
season and out. These active socialists inside and outside the organization kept the Socialist Party alive and
growing. It was their numbers and energy, in the last
analysis, which determined the size of the Socialist Party
vote over a long period of time. They were helped or
hampered by favorable economic and political conditions.

In the gigantic upward sweep of capitalism in the
United States in the late nineties and the early part of
the present century, with escape to the West cut off by
the using up of the free land, with the decline of the
farmers' uprisings, with the extraordinary and unchecked
development of trade unionism, and with the militancy
which went with a fresh and vigorous membership, the
Socialist Party—at last on a sound basis—reaped some
of the advantages of this situation in 1902 and 1904.
On the other hand, the panics of 1907 and 1913 did not
make it possible for the party to get recruits or money in
abundance and to wage as good a campaign as during
better times. Workingmen are not militant if they are
out of work or threatened with loss of work, unless the
condition lasts for a long time. They also lose their
votes when they do much shifting about in bad years in
search of jobs. The Socialist Party made no gains in
1908 and lost votes in 1914. On the economic side, apart
from a superb organization and the cumulative results of

years of sowing, the favorable result of 1912 was again
due to the growing militancy of labor in a period of
general progressivism as a reaction to the long reign of
the Republican Party.

In the presidential contests between 1900 and 1916
there were a number who voted the socialist ticket because a progressive or radical was not heading up one
of the two or three major parties. For example, in 1900
and 1908 William Jennings Bryan was the candidate of
the Democratic Party and in both these years the Socialist
Party suffered because of his reputed liberalism. In 1904
and 1912, on the other hand, when the Democratic Party
selected a conservative easterner in the first instance and
a mild progressive in the second, the supporters of Debs
greatly increased in number. Theodore Roosevelt at first
frightened the socialists in 1912, but the radical voters
showed their good sense by seeing through the alleged
crusader and trust buster. In 1916 when Woodrow Wilson ran on his alleged pro-labor record and a camouflaged
position on the war to deceive the pacifists and radicals,
he managed to reduce the total for Allan Benson, the
relatively weak candidate of the Socialist Party, to 300,-
000 below the 1912 total for Debs.

§

With the exception of but one campaign while he lived,
the presidential candidate of the Socialist Party was
Eugene Victor Debs. His running mate in 1904 and 1908
was Ben Hanford. The Socialist Party was indeed fortunate in having such men in its ranks, especially its
standard bearer for the office which voters in America
pay most attention to. Debs was indeed not the best
strategist. He was often in disagreement with the
majority in the party, and not infrequently too far ahead
of the American masses. But for all that there was a
nobility about 'Gene Debs that made him one of the
greatest labor leaders America has produced. His out-

standing quality was his sublime devotion to the working
class as its foremost and most fearless champion, as it
was Ben Hanford's unique contribution to be its leading
Jimmy Higgins—the representative of the unkown
soldiers in the socialist army, the men who do the "dirty
work" behind the scenes and "deliver the goods." Debs
and Hanford simply could not dream of leaving their
class, much less betray it as did Powderly, or follow
numberless labor leaders nurtured in the philosophy of
pure and simple trade unionism into the old parties. They
could not enter the employ of a corporation as superin-
tendents, act as negotiators for the other side, or set
up in business for themselves.

It must, in all fairness, be said of Samuel Gompers
that he was honest and a fighter for the workers. But
one leader after another among the iron and steel workers, the miners, and any number of the other trade unions
which Gompers stamped with his philosophy left the labor
movement to enter politics or business. Some also "sold
out" their rank and file. This, as Robert F. Hoxie pointed
out in his work, *Trade Unionism in the United States,* is
the greatest weakness, the Achilles heel, in pure and simpledom. It sprouts business unionism and predatory unionism, in which the rank and file and their leaders are
absorbed in more, more, more, now, for themselves, and
have little practical idealism. As a direct result of the
teachings of Gompers and his pure and simple trade
unionism, apart from basic causes in American economic
and political life, we have but one-ninth of the wage and
salaried workers organized, one of the lowest percentages
in any industrialized nation in the world. Moreover, in
addition to their small numbers, the American unions are
relatively restricted to the best paid and the most highly
skilled workmen and, with exceptions, to untrustified industries, where capitalism is least developed. Their feeling of labor solidarity is weak, their social vision is
limited, and their present labor philosophy cannot and will
not meet the needs of the hour in a country where capital-

ism has made greater strides than in any other. The leaders of the A. F. of L. are themselves becoming worried at their impotence—a healthy sign.

The Socialist Party was fortunate in having Debs as its outstanding leader because he hailed from the ranks of labor. As a party it has always appealed primarily to the working class, to the organized toilers, to the proletariat. And Debs knew how to put the message of socialism and of his party into words which the ordinary wage earner could understand. He was an eloquent orator, a trenchant writer, and a fiery evangelist. None carried greater conviction when he spoke and none evoked such warmth of response. The Socialist Party had no one in its ranks whom it could present to the voters of the country with greater pride, joy, and confidence. There was devotion almost bordering on worship toward this man who began and ended his career in prison, and who died with head unbowed, a free man who called his soul his own. Among the pioneers of the socialist movement throughout the world, among the leaders of the lowly in all ages, there is none more entitled to be chronicled than Eugene Victor Debs.

§

The candidate of the Socialist Party for vice-president in the banner year of 1912 was Emil Seidel. When in April, 1910, it was announced that he had been elected mayor of Milwaukee, the first large city captured by the socialists, there was unbounded joy in the hearts of the comrades throughout the land. Abraham Cahan, editor of the *Forward,* described the feelings of those present at the mayor's inauguration, in a dispatch to the New York *Call*:

A thrill passed through the socialists present. It was one of those moments which are a landmark in one's life. There were tears in some eyes, tears of the highest joy known to man. That which had been cherished as a dream was beginning to look like reality. It almost seemed too good to be true. As Comrade Simons subsequently put it, "Is this the United States?"

In the fall of 1910 Victor L. Berger was elected as the first congressman on the socialist ticket in this country. In 1911 and 1912 socialist victories continued, until the elected officials could be counted in four figures, and they covered a majority of the states of the Union.

Robert F. Hoxie made two studies of these victories. From the returns to his questionnaire and with the co-operation of J. Mahlon Barnes and William J. Ghent, Hoxie analyzed the successes before and after the 1911 election. He classified the municipal gains in the first period into seven types:

1. There is first the clean-cut victory of a broad, liberal, opportunistic, moderate type of socialism, of comparatively slow and solid growth. This type appears mainly in the Middle West, especially in Wisconsin and the states grouped immediately around it. The communities in which it occurs are for the most part manufacturing cities and railroad centers both large and small. These cities generally have a strong foreign element in the population; and Germans, especially, foster and guide the movement, which has a working-class basis and strong trade union support, but also a good deal of backing from the well-to-do and middle classes. This type of triumphant socialism appears to stand immediately for honest and efficient city administration, the equalization of tax burdens, the curbing of corporations, direct popular control of legislation and officials, the improvement of labor conditions and of the housing, education, and amusements of the working people, and the greatest practicable extension of municipal ownership and control.

2. The second type of socialist victory is also the immediate result of long-continued "organization, agitation and education," but represents a more class-conscious socialism which places, perhaps, more emphasis on the ultimate socialist ideas. It occurs mainly in a line extending through the Middle West and on into the Rocky Mountains. The most significant thing about it is that it is characteristically to be found in mining communities and apparently owes its existence mainly to the mineworkers' union. It rests, therefore, very largely on the support of men with European blood in their veins, but the leadership in this case seems to come most largely from the English, Scotch, Welsh, and Americans.

3. . . . a third type based mainly on socialist organization and agitation but occurring for the most part in small agricultural or semi-agricultural communities. . . . The brand of socialism which they represent tends to be in outer seeming of the ultra-theoretical, blood-and-thunder variety; but an examination of the party membership in these cases often discloses a surprisingly large proportion of farmers and small business men. It is in fact neither well-rooted nor working-class socialism. It is mainly but the outcome of the policy of the Socialist Party in maintaining a permanent corps of speakers and organizers. . . .

4. A fourth type of socialist triumph . . . was the outcome mainly of temporary industrial conditions. Every contest of magnitude between the employers and trade unions is a socialist opportunity and no such opportunity is neglected. Socialist organizers and newspapers throw themselves strenuously into the fight. The occasion is made use of for the preaching of socialist doctrine and the pointing of socialist morals. The outcome usually is a clear demarcation, for the time at least, of class lines, and an occasional socialist success. . . . A substantially similar situation sometimes develops out of local business collapse. . . .

5. A fifth and more important type of socialist success grows out of the generally deplorable state of American municipal politics and government. It is in the boss-ruled, corporation-ridden, tax-burdened city, with its poorly-paved, ill-lighted dirty streets, its insufficient water supply and air-filled gas mains, its industrial fire-traps, its graft-protected vice district, its fat politicians, untaxed wealth, crooked contracts, and wasted resources, that socialism finds its best object-lessons and has won some of its most significant, if not most numerous, successes. . . .

6. The sixth type of socialist success which may be distinguished is in a sense the obverse of the fifth. It results not so much from a desperate attempt to escape the present evils of city government as from a positive desire to uplift and ennoble it. . . . It makes its appeal to all good people, is apt to elect ministers and physicians as mayors, and makes combinations with the church-goers and anti-saloon advocates. Its support is prevailingly American. . . .

7. Finally, there is a type of recent success which so far as significant socialism is concerned must be regarded as altogether trivial and fortuitous. In such cases the socialists have won not because of any special virtues or strength in themselves but as the result of factional squabbling, personal likes and dislikes, lack of opposition, petty local and personal issues.

Hoxie concluded his observations on the successes in the first period with this generalization:

There seems to be a definite law of the development of socialism which applies both to the individual and to the group. The law is this: The credalism and immoderateness of socialism, other things being equal, vary inversely with its age and responsibility. The average socialist recruit begins as a theoretical impossibilist and develops gradually into a constructive opportunist. Add a taste of real responsibility and he is hard to distinguish from a liberal reformer. It is the same with the movement. These socialist successes in general, therefore, are a training school of constructive democracy.

When in November, 1911, the Socialist Party made its sweeping gains in Pennsylvania, Ohio, and the industrial states generally, Hoxie declared that a "far more serious and formidable movement" had now at last developed. He felt that there was "a distinct tendency toward the establishment of a characteristic or predominant type of socialist victory." It was due more to immediate economic conditions than to mere political circumstance or theoretical idealism. He described it as follows:

It appears in industrial and transportation centers both large and small, prevailingly, however, in those of moderate size. Territorially it is characteristic neither of the East nor the West, but prevades the whole industrial area. The cities in which it appears are not ethnically peculiar, though the dominant element in their population is prevailingly Anglo-Saxon, Teutonic, or Scandinavian. . . . Locally it is in part a revolt against the whole range of political, social and economic evils foisted upon American cities by self-seeking, corrupt, and inefficient political bosses and gangs and by greedy corporations; but in part also the evidence of a healthy growth of working-class organization and ideals. Generally, it rests upon a growing discontent among the workers and an ethical awakening among representatives of the well-to-do classes, induced by the feeling that high cost of living, industrial depression, and unemployment are rendering economic conditions intolerable, and that the old political parties have nothing worth while to offer toward the improvement of these conditions and have proved themselves utterly incapable of coping with them. The forces which stand back of such socialist success and make it possible are in part proletarian and in part middle class. It is the immediate outcome of socialist party "organization, agitation and education," which is, however, not necessarily long continued, plus the support of a strong contingent of malcontents and sympathizers unattached to the party and largely of the middle class. . . .Its sponsors claim adherence to the general theory of socialism: it gains the working-class support largely through the preaching of socialist doctrine; but to all practical intents and purposes it is moderate, opportunistic and reformatory. Such, in its municipal manifestation, is the type toward which American socialism seems to be swinging.

§

The states showing the largest number of communities in which socialists were elected in the first period—before November, 1911—and those in the second, after that campaign, according to Hoxie's charts, were in their order of successes, as follows:

Before November, 1911.

Wisconsin	Montana	New Jersey
Illinois	Iowa	Indiana
Kansas	Nebraska	Texas
Missouri	Idaho	Utah
California	West Virginia	Virginia
Minnesota	Oklahoma	Maine
Michigan	Colorado	Connecticut
Washington	Vermont	Mississippi
Pennsylvania	South Dakota	Oregon
Arkansas	Massachusetts	Florida
North Dakota	Ohio	New York

Immediately After November, 1911.

Pennsylvania	North Dakota	New York
Ohio	Iowa	South Dakota
Wisconsin	West Virginia	Connecticut
Minnesota	Nebraska	Massachusetts
Illinois	Montana	Wyoming
Missouri	Arkansas	Vermont
Utah	Oklahoma	Maine
Kansas	Idaho	Virginia
California	New Jersey	Florida
Washington	Colorado	Kentucky
Indiana	Oregon	Mississippi
Michigan	Texas	Rhode Island

The representation of the socialists in 1910-1912 was mainly in the smaller cities, villages, and townships. On the other hand, there were dozens of cities of 10,000 or more where the socialists scored successes. Of the places where conspicuous victories were won, regardless of size, the following might be mentioned:

Adamston, West Virginia	Milwaukee, Wisconsin
Berkeley, California	Mineral City, Ohio
Butte, Montana	New Castle, Pennsylvania
Cardwell, Missouri	O'Fallon, Illinois
	St. Mary's, Ohio
Coeur d'Alene, Idaho	Schenectady, New York
Davis, Illinois	South Frankfort, Michigan
Edmonds, Washington	Star City, West Virginia
Flint, Michigan	Thayer, Illinois
Granite City, Illinois	Two Harbors, Minnesota
Greenville, Michigan	Victor, Colorado
Martin's Ferry, Ohio	Wymore, Nebraska

In subsequent elections, before the entrance of the country into the World War, the socialists elected in addition mayors in Hamilton, Ohio, Minneapolis, Minnesota, and Barre, Vermont, and a congressman from New York City. At the beginning of 1915 the party had 31 representatives in 13 state legislatures as follows:

Los Angeles, California, 2; Adams County, Idaho, 1; Chicago, Illinois, 2; Girard, Kansas, 1; Haverhill, Massachusetts, 1; Minneapolis, Two Harbors, Minnesota, 2; Butte, Montana, 2; Tonopah, Yerington, Nevada, 2; Curry County, New Mexico, 1; Cestos, Elk City, Ringwood, Roll, Seiling, Snyder, Oklahoma, 6; Reading, Pennsylvania, 1; Tooele, Utah, 1 and Milwaukee, Wisconsin, 9.

Paul H. Douglas made a survey of the socialist vote in the elections of 1917, after war was declared by this country against Germany. He discovered that in fifteen cities from which he had accurate election returns, casting a total vote of about 1,450,000, the socialists polled 314,000, or 21.6 per cent of the whole. He declared that this was over "four times the proportion of the vote usually polled by the socialist candidates in these cities. Had the socialists polled an equal proportion in the presidential election of 1916, their total vote would have been approximately 4,000,000." Some of the striking successes occurred in Buffalo, Chicago, Cincinnati, Cleveland, Dayton, Evansville, Marion, New York City, and Toledo—some of the leading cities of the land. The percentage of the vote received by the socialists in some of these cities was:

City	Percentage in 1917	Municipal Election Before 1917
Buffalo	25.4	13.9
Chicago	33.8	3.6
Cincinnati	11.9	2.9
Cleveland	19.3	5.7
Dayton	44.1	
Evansville	17.3	15.3
Marion	30.8	
New York City	21.7	5.1
Civilian vote	22.1	
Soldier vote	12.9	
Bronx	31.5	
Manhattan	20.9	
Brooklyn	20.1	
Queens	19.6	
Richmond	9.7	
Toledo	34.8	

In this 1917 election the Socialist Party of New York City scored the greatest success in its history. It sent ten assemblymen to Albany—a gain of eight—and elected representatives for the first time to the city board of aldermen to the number of seven. It elected Jacob Panken for a ten-year term as municipal court judge. Outside of the metropolis the party carried five Chicago wards by a majority vote, and elected public officials in Allentown, Cleveland, Elkhart, Fort Wayne, Sandusky, and Toledo, besides a large number of smaller places.

§

While the socialists of Massachusetts started the ball rolling as early as 1898 by electing James F. Carey to the legislature and sent the state vote up to 33,629 in 1902, they were not able to hold their position in one of the most important industrial states of the Union after about twenty years of activity before the split of 1919. The old Socialist Labor Party polled a fair sized vote in this commonwealth in the nineties. De Leon's party received 10,778 against 8,262 votes for the Social Democratic Party in 1899. In 1900 the De Leonites dropped to 2,591 and did not cut much figure thereafter. The Socialist Party received 10,671 votes for its candidate for governor in 1901, 11,500 for the same office in 1912, 12,615 for Debs in the same year, and 11,058 for Benson in 1916.

A. M. Simons, after the state made such a fine show-ing in 1902, explained the vote in terms of the low per-centage of illiteracy: "When we combine highly devel-oped capitalism with an intelligent proletariat the result is socialism." When the vote dropped he declared that the voters had never been properly educated in socialism. In the *New Review* for January 25, 1913, Rev. Roland D. Sawyer claimed that it was the incoming of the newer immigrants which helped to lower the vote. Massachu-setts suffered most from the agitation of Martha Moore Avery, David Goldstein and F. G. R. Gordon, former socialists, the first two of whom carried on a persistent campaign among Catholics and religious people against socialism. An important cause for the decline in the vote was the presence of two rival unions of shoe workers, the Boot and Shoe Workers' Union and the Shoe Workers' Protective Union. The contests between these two organizations involved some of the leaders of the party and weakened the labor movement on both the eco-nomic and political fields. In the far West, particularly Montana, internal division among the metal miners had the same result. Again, since the days of the Knights of St. Crispin and the Knights of Labor there had not been a strong trade union movement in the state. In the rural centers the socialists could not make much headway among the individualistic, conservative, and puritanical

Yankees. In the cities, especially the larger centers, they faced the political machines of the Irish-Americans, who cooperated closely with the leaders of labor and the various racial and religious groups. In some of the smaller towns, however, the Socialist Party was always able to elect several of its members to the legislature and to municipal office, notwithstanding fusion, nonpartisan elections, and the action of officials elected on a socialist ticket repudiating their party.

§

The socialists of the Empire State polled only 63,381 votes in 1912. Of the 46,102 votes given Benson in 1916, New York City contributed 31,763. At no time before the spectacular run of Morris Hillquit for mayor in 1917 did the socialists of the leading city of the Union make a good showing for the metropolis as a whole. Again and again William Randolph Hearst cut into what strength the party had. In Chicago, Cleveland, and Toledo, as well as elsewhere, real or alleged reformers also had the same effect. Following the 1909 election for mayor, the New York *Call* editorialized as follows:

The ability of Hearst to cut heavily into the socialist vote every time he chooses to be a candidate for office must be a source of bitter humiliation to every sincere socialist.

Meyer London was elected to Congress for the first time in 1914 from the 12th district, Manhattan, on the lower East Side. He received about four times the vote secured by the rest of the socialist ticket in his district. When John C. Kennedy and William E. Rodriguez were elected in the spring of 1915 as aldermen of Chicago, their vote was 11,873 and 6,265, while Seymour Stedman, running for mayor, only got 2,183 and 1,703 votes respectively in the two wards. Next to Debs, one of the best beloved men among socialists, Meyer London was born on December 29, 1871, in Russia, and came to this country when he was 19 years old. He was admitted to the bar

in 1898. His campaigns on the East Side of New York,
backed up by his brothers, an army of socialists and
sympathizers, the leaders and rank and file of the growing
Jewish garment trades which he helped to organize, and
the influence of the *Call* and especially the Jewish Daily
Forward, were marvels of industry, enthusiasm, and a
will to win which bowled over some of the worst elements that Tammany Hall contributed to the glory of
American politics. London was elected for a third and
last term in 1920—in 1922 the republican and democratic
legislators of the state gerrymandered his district.

§

The New York socialists were never able to put such
men as Morris Hillquit, Algernon Lee, or any other of
their ablest spokesmen, gifted as parliamentarians, into
Congress. In Europe these would be the legislative representatives of a labor or socialist party. The New York
socialists did wage, however, some of their hottest campaigns in favor of their leader. Into these campaigns
they threw every ounce of their energy, every penny,
every bit of brains they possessed and what they could
introduce from the outside. They drafted their ablest
organizer, Julius Gerber, to manage one of the congressional contests. Despite all their efforts they could not
elect Hillquit, although on one occasion they came very
close. In New York City it is not easy to beat Tammany
Hall or, whenever a socialist has a real chance, the fusion
candidate of both the old parties. There is a good reason
for the reputation of the 14th Street organization.

In 1919 Edward F. Cassidy and Algernon Lee were
officially reported defeated in their race for aldermen of
New York City on the Socialist Party ticket. The party
appealed to the board of aldermen for a recount. This
board, made up overwhelmingly of Tammany Hall democrats, referred the matter to the committee on elections and privileges. The committee, also made up in

the main of Tammany Hall aldermen, refused to hold a meeting for one year. The socialists were compelled to secure a state supreme court order forcing the Tammany Hall committee to meet and open the ballot boxes. Thereupon the committee assembled and proceeded to spend the city's money and supply jobs to their henchmen for nine months, to do what could be done in one evening. The recount showed that Cassidy and Lee were elected. But by this time their term of office was up.

That is Tammany Hall. During elections voters are bought with money, they are registered when they have no business in the district, and they are voted more than once. Every device is used to prevent a fair election and to intimidate the voters and watchers of the opposition party—if it is really in opposition as the Socialist Party is. Every form of economic pressure is used to get votes or prevent the opposition from having any: peddlers are told that they will not have their licenses renewed or secure places for their push-carts, storekeepers are made to understand that they will be denied privileges or rights, workingmen are kept from employment, and henchmen are given sinecures at the government's expense. On the day of the election and the evening-night-morning-afternoon of the count, clerks and judges of polling places have been known to violate practically every provision of the election law, with the aid of gangsters who prevent interference.

The Socialist Party never made any real headway in any section of New York City not dominated by Jewish-Americans. Outside of the metropolis the socialists elected Herbert M. Merrill to the state legislature from Schenectady and bent its constitution to make George R. Lunn mayor of the city in 1911. Lunn went back on the party later and became a leading democratic office holder. There were a number of other good strongholds, particularly Buffalo, which also elected socialists to office.

In a speech on June 6, 1910, following the election of
Seidel as mayor of Milwaukee, Victor L. Berger explained to New Yorkers the methods that made the
Cream City victory possible. First, he claimed, was the
fact that they used literature in abundance and they had
a weekly paper with a good circulation. There was relatively little public speaking, but there was a good deal of
house to house canvassing, systematically done, with literature left in each voter's home. Then the Milwaukee
socialists were loyal trade unionists and had the closest
contacts with the labor organizations. In fact the leaders
of the movement on the economic and political fields were
practicaly the same. The party was a proletarian affair,
with relatively few intellectuals or professional men.
Again, the Milwaukee comrades stressed opportunist socialism and did not tolerate any "I'm a bum" tactics of
the Industrial Workers of the World, with their free
speech fights. He emphasized the slow and steady growth
of the party.

The *Milwaukee Leader* of November 18, 1916, after
Stafford beat Berger, declared:

Mr. Berger undoubtedly would have been elected if it had
not been for the racial politics cultivated by the *Free Press* and
the *Germania-Herold,* which urged German voters in the strongest German district in the United States, to vote for Stafford
to "reward" him for what he had done for "our cause."

The success in Milwaukee was thus due to the hard,
persistent educational work of the socialists, their friendly
relations with the unions, their opportunism, the ability
and integrity of their leaders, the devotion of their rank
and file, and above all, to the fact that they had a stable,
German proletarian element as the backbone of their
movement. The socialists there were fortunate in possessing an outstanding leader who knew the game of practical politics and jealously guarded his bailiwick. When
America entered the war in 1917, the socialist mayor,
Daniel W. Hoan, was in office and no hysteria could destroy the party in the state of Wisconsin where the sym-

pathies of the people were not violently in opposition to
the anti-war position of the national Socialist Party. The
communists could not make a dent in Milwaukee either,
because Berger's followers were too firmly grounded in
opportunist socialism, and there was already in existence
a genuine and responsible mass movement.

The state of Oklahoma which gave the socialists the
highest percentage of votes in 1912 and 1916, 16.4 and
15.6 per cent, with 42,262 in the first and 45,190 votes
in the second presidential year, was a new state, and
almost exclusively agricultural in make-up. The vote
showed a steady and continuous increase up to Benson's
run; it fell in 1916; it practically disappeared after 1920.
George Gilbert Hamilton, writing in the *American Socialist*, emphasized the point that the best socialist centers
were in the most prosperous farming sections of Oklahoma and Texas. The Oklahoma socialists started the
plan of holding encampments, with farmers gathered
from miles around. They made great headway at these
get-togethers. They also had some of the ablest, clever-
est, and most energetic propagandists in a party which
was known for its orators, writers, and evangelists.

§

In the reports of the national secretaries to the conventions of the Socialist Party mention would be made
of the size of the socialist press. The *American Labor
Year Book, 1916,* published the result of a questionnaire
sent out to determine the number of socialist papers in
that year. The situation in 1912, when the party was at
its height, and in 1916, was as follows:

Dailies	*1912*	*1916*
English	5	2
Foreign	8	13
Weeklies		
English	262	42
Foreign	36	22
Monthlies, etc.		
English	10	12
Foreign	2	9

The party had in 1912 the following English dailies: the *Chicago Daily Socialist,* the *New York Call,* the *Milwaukee Leader,* the *Alarm* of Belleville, Illinois, and the *Daily Register* of Lead, South Dakota. By 1916 only the *Call* and the *Leader* survived the almost insuperable task of maintaining a daily, and at the end of 1923 the *Milwaukee Leader* was the only English socialist daily in the United States.

When the *Year Book* made its study of the socialist press in 1916 it found the following dailies, weeklies, monthlies, and quarterlies with an approximate circulation of 4,000 or more:

English	*Approximate circulation*	*Controlled or published by*
Dailies:		
Milwaukee Leader	37,000	Pub. Assn.
New York Call	15,000	Pub. Assn.
Weeklies:		
American Socialist, Chicago	60,000	Party
Appeal to Reason, Girard	500,000	Private
Citizen, The, Schenectady	4,000	Pub. Co.
Cleveland Citizen	14,000	Pub. Co.
New Age, Buffalo	5,000	Party
New England Socialist, Boston	5,000	Party
New Times, Minneapolis	5,000	Private
Rebel, The, Hallettsville, Texas	20,000	Private
Voice of Labor, Camden, N. J.	5,000	Party
Wheeling Majority, Wheeling, W. Va.	8,000	Pub. Co.
Monthlies:		
Fool-Killer, Boomer, N. C.	40,000	Private
International Socialist Review, Chicago	40,000	Pub. Co.
National Rip-Saw, St. Louis	200,000	Pub. Co.
Nebraska Worker, Lincoln	10,000	Pub. Co.
Party Builder, Everett, Wash	4,000	Party
Rip Saw, Boston	40,000	Party
Quarterly:		
Intercollegiate Socialist, New York	4,000	Pub. Assn.

Foreign languages	Approximate circulation	Controlled or published by
Bohemian:		
Spravedlnost (daily), Chicago........		Party
Finnish:		
Dailies:		
Raivaaja, Fitchburg, Mass.	10,000	Pub. Co.
Sosialisti, Duluth	....	Pub. Co.
Toveri, Astoria, Ore.	4,000	Pub. Co.
Tyomies, Superior, Wis.	7,000	Pub. Co.
Weeklies, Monthlies, etc.		
Lapatossu, Superior, Wis.	10,000	Pub. Co.
Pelto ja Koti (Farmer's Journal) ..	5,000	Pub. Co.
Sakenia, Fitchburg, Mass.	10,000	Pub. Co.
Toveritar, Astoria, Ore.	7,000	Pub. Co.
French:		
L'Union des Travailleurs, Charleroi, Pa. (weekly)	....	Pub. Co.
German:		
Dailies:		
Arbeiter-Zeitung, Chicago	....	Party
Tageblatt, Philadelphia	....	Private
Volkszeitung, New York City	15,000	Pub. Assn.
Weeklies:		
Vorwaerts, Milwaukee	4,600	Pub. Assn.
Hungarian:		
Elore (daily), New York City.......	10,000	Party
Italian:		
La Parola Proletaria (weekly), Chicago	5,500	Party
Japanese:		
Heimin (monthly), San Francisco....	....	Private
Jewish:		
Daily:		
Jewish Daily Forward, New York City	200,000	Pub. Assn.
Weekly:		
Die Naya Welt, New York City....	10,000	Party
Monthly:		
Die Zukunft, New York City.....	10,000	Pub. Assn.
Lithuanian:		
Keleivis (weekly), South Boston.....	15,000	Private
Laisve (semi-weekly), Brooklyn......	10,000	Pub. Co.
Naujienos (daily), Chicago	15,000	Pub. Co.

Foreign languages	Approximate circulation	Controlled or published by
Polish:		
Bicz Bozy (God's Whip) (weekly), Chicago	20,000	Pub. Co.
Dziennik Ludowy (daily), Chicago....	18,000	Pub. Co.
Russian:		
Novy Mir (daily), New York City....	15,000	Pub. Co.
Russkaja Sjisn (weekly), Detroit.....	6,000	Private
Scandinavian:		
Social-Demokraten (weekly), Chicago	7,000	Party
Svenska Socialisten (weekly), Chicago	7,000	Party
Slovak:		
Rovost Ludu (weekly), Chicago......	9,000	Party
South Slavic:		
Radnicke Straza (weekly), Chicago..	4,200	Party
Ukrainian:		
Narordna Wola (tri-weekly), Scranton	7,500	Pub. Co.

A number of socialist publications of 1916 are not included because their circulation either was not given or was under 4,000. Among the English papers which ought to be mentioned, however, were the following:

Weeklies:

Christian Socialist, Chicago

Miami Valley Socialist, Dayton

Reading Labor Advocate, Reading

St. Louis Labor

World, Oakland, California

Monthly:

Masses, New York City

Significant socialist publications listed in the report of J. Mahlon Barnes to the 1910 national socialist congress, which had disappeared by 1916, were:

Weeklies or Monthlies:

Comrade, Erie, Pennsylvania

Evolutionist, Chicago

Harp, New York City

Progressive Journal of Education, Chicago

Progressive Woman, Girard

Wilshire's Magazine, New York City.

The *Social Democratic Herald,* edited by Victor L. Berger, was the predecessor of the *Milwaukee Leader,* just as the *Worker,* edited by Algernon Lee, preceded the *New York Call.*   In addition to all these papers, mention should be made of the two *Coming Nations* and the host of trade union journals, such as the *Miners' Magazine* of Denver, which ran socialist propaganda and news.   In 1912 the Socialist Party sent out each week mimeographed articles to about 400 socialist, union, and other papers, and maintained a news service in Washington with a daily release to the labor press.

§

It should be noted that in 1912 the percentage of English to foreign language socialist papers was very much greater than in 1916.   Not only were there many more English publications but their circulation was far in excess of the foreign language periodicals.   The *Chicago Daily Socialist* was the first English daily of the Socialist Party, having been launched in the two weeks preceding the November, 1906, election.   Started as a temporary campaign publication it was made permanent, only to be thrown into bankruptcy on December 5, 1912, under its new name, the *Chicago Daily World.*   As the result of a lockout and strike on the capitalist newspapers in 1912 the circulation of the *World* went up to 300,000—this was the year that William A. Cunnea, socialist candidate for state's attorney, made his phenomenal run and was counted out.   But the paper became involved after new outlays were made beyond its capacity to meet them. It was already on the verge of failure before the strike occurred.

The *New York Call* first appeared on May 30, 1908, and heroically managed to survive until October 1, 1923, when it became the *Leader.*   The Workmen's Cooperative Publishing Association was then succeeded by the Labor Press Association, as the new owner of the *Leader* was called.   The radical unions of New York City and the American Fund for Public Service, Inc. (the Garland Fund), gave $92,000 in cash to finance the new paper. While it stressed labor news, the *Leader* featured sports and comic strips, and tried to compete with the metropolitan dailies. On November 12 the experiment ended in the death of the only English daily in the East devoted to the labor and socialist movement. What the socialists had managed to maintain after so much heart-breaking sacrifice for fifteen years was killed in a few months. The *Milwaukee Leader,* now the only English daily, was started on December 7, 1911.

Of the English weeklies the *Appeal to Reason,* the *National Rip-Saw,* and the *American Socialist* were the most important before 1917, although the old and new *Coming Nation* and *Wilshire's Magazine* also had a national circulation. Only the *American Socialist* was owned by the national party. The *Appeal to Reason* with its 500,000 circulation was by all odds the greatest single unofficial organ of the movement. Its chief object and contribution were to spread the gospel among the people living in the smaller cities and in the agricultural areas. It built up its huge circulation by special inducements to militants and locals to distribute the paper at a low subscription rate and at reduced cost in bundle orders. It also offered prizes, some of which were of doubtful value to the recipient and to the Socialist Party. With its immense circulation the independent and privately owned *Appeal* could and did mold policy in the party and movement, sometimes to their detriment. It was, however, one of the greatest engines of socialist propaganda. It ran special articles of a sensational character and made itself famous by its little paragraphs with catchy and telling illustrations and arguments for socialism. J. A. Wayland, Fred D. Warren, and Louis Kopelin, as well as a number of writers, and above all the *Appeal* army of Jimmy Higginses, built up the enormous circulation of the paper.

The *Coming Nation* and *Wilshire's Magazine* were private ventures of Fred D. Warren and Gaylord Wilshire. A. M. Simons edited the first and quarrelled with Warren when the latter suspended the paper. Wilshire was in part interested in promoting his own business schemes and called forth vigorous protest, particularly from Thomas J. Morgan in the little *Provoker*. Kate Richards and Frank O'Hare and others were largely responsible for the 200,000 circulation of the *National Rip-Saw*. The *American Socialist*, edited by Louis Engdahl, was the only national publication owned by the party. Its first number appeared on July 18, 1914, and was denied the use of the mails soon after the United States entered the World War.

§

The *International Socialist Review*, a monthly magazine, was started in 1900 and ended, like the *American Socialist*, in 1917. Simons edited it for eight years and made it a scientific socialist publication, according to his lights. Max Hayes ran a regular section on labor. It was Charles H. Kerr's medium for promoting the distribution of his socialist classics. In 1908 a new policy was inaugurated, to please, in the words of Kerr, workers not college professors. It then became and remained the most outspoken organ of the revolutionary and syndicalistic wing of the Socialist Party.

The *Masses* saw the light in January, 1911. Its first editor was Thomas Seltzer, with Eugene Wood as president of the publishing company. In 1912 Piet Vlag became managing editor, to be succeeded in 1913 by Max Eastman. Andre Tridon was secretary for a time. The *Masses* described itself as an "illustrated magazine of art, literature, politics, and science devoted to the interests of the working people." It was generally to the left of the majority in the party. Its cartoons and comments, its daring drawings and poetical bits, were caviar to the young intellectual or artistic radical and to the Jimmy Higgins, over-burdened with party work. It had a sense of humor and believed—in its own words—in enjoying the revolution. The contributors to the spicy *Masses* could express in it their most honest selves. Genevieve Taggard has listed some of the poets and compiled their better verse in a volume. Among the artists were:

Maurice Becker	Robert Minor
George Bellows	Alex. Popini
O. E. Cesare	Boardman Robinson
K. R. Chamberlain	Robert Robinson
Glenn O. Coleman	John Sloan
Jo Davidson	Horace Taylor
Arthur B. Davies	H. J. Turner
Cornelia Davis	Frank Van Sloun
Stuart Davis	Ryan Walker
Anton O. Fischer	Frank Walts
Hugo Gellert	Alice Beach Winter
H. J. Glintenkamp	Charles A. Winter
	Art Young

Among its contributing writers could be counted:

Sherwood Anderson	Emanuel Julius
Konrad Bercovici	Walter Lippmann
Edwin Bjorkman	Jack London
Howard Brubaker	John R. McMahon
	Ernest Poole
Arthur Bullard	John Reed
Arthur W. Calhoun	Thomas Seltzer
George Creel	Upton Sinclair
Floyd Dell	Lincoln Steffens
Max Eastman	Louis Untermeyer
W. J. Ghent	Mary Heaton Vorse
Arturo Giovanitti	Charles Erskine Scott Wood
Will Irwin	Charles W. Wood
Ellis O. Jones	Eugene Wood

A third magazine of consequence was the *New Review,* edited by Herman Simpson and Louis B. Boudin. It first appeared on January 4, 1913. It was much more critical and scientific than either the *International Socialist Review,* with its primary appeal to the proletariat, or the *Masses,* with its literary flair. Like both of these, it stood to the left of the majority of the Socialist Party.

There were other periodicals of lesser note and shorter duration on evolution, education, woman, Christian socialism, Jewish and Irish nationalism, and what not. Again, there were newspaper chains in such states as Ohio and

Pennsylvania. During campaigns special editions of the dozens of socialist papers would be gotten out, besides little make-shifts with all sorts of amusing names to cover the particuar electoral district.

The press of the socialist movement in this country as well as throughout the world not only educates the workingmen and their sympathizers in socialism. It also keeps them in touch with developments in almost every field of human knowledge. Socialist publications are not merely Marxian journals, devoted to teaching the dismal science. They contain the out-pourings of the hearts and minds of those who see in socialism the regeneration of the race in every field of human activity. Hence scientists, educators, and economists, as well as poets, artists, and writers contribute; the genius and the lowly rank and filer add their mite to the richness of a socialist publication and each learns to know the joy of working side by side for a common human end. The socialist and labor movements develop men and women, they give as much as they receive, and they make real such things as human solidarity.

§

Socialist literature published in America was as broad as the international socialist movement. Almost every socialist classic produced in any part of the world was translated or imported into the United States. Charles H. Kerr did yeoman service with his company in publishing a splendid list of books. Not only did he spread extensively the writings of Karl Marx, Friedrich Engels, Karl Kautsky and the other masters, but he published the works of radicals, as in the case of several written by Gustavus Myers before that author fell for the idealism of Calvin Coolidge and Otto H. Kahn. In addition to publishing a solid reading list, Kerr got out ten-cent pamphlets and little vest pocket booklets which sold at the rate of three for five cents. These spread the gospel in a telling way. It was a piece of literature or a periodical that generally did the most effective work in converting a person.

There was also an enormous output of pamphlet material by the various sections of the party from the national office down, and by the auxiliaries of the movement such as the Rand School of Social Science and the Intercollegiate Socialist Society. Of the better known socialist writers who contributed larger books to the literature of the American party might be mentioned Allan L. Benson, Louis B. Boudin, Joseph Cohen, W. J. Ghent, Morris Hillquit, I. A. Hourwich, Jessie Wallace Hughan, Robert Hunter, Edmond Kelly, Harry Laidler, Gustavus Myers, Scott Nearing, James Oneal, Walter Rauschenbusch, I. M. Rubinow, Charles Edward Russell, Hermann Schlueter, Vida Scudder, A. M. Simons, John Spargo, Upton Sinclair, Ernest Untermann, William English Walling, Maurice William, and John M. Work. The journalists, whose output was not put between covers, frequently wrote more than did these authors. It is impossible even to mention the hundreds of men and women who often dipped their pens in their hearts' blood to win support for the cause to which they gave their all. Typical of their spirit and hardly exceptional was Charles W. Ervin, who stuck to the socialist movement during and after the war hysteria, when the party was being attacked on all sides and who saw the New York *Call* through that difficult period.

§

The Rand School of Social Science is the oldest and the pioneer enterprise in America in workers' education, having been established in 1906. "Its object," as stated in one of its bulletins, "is to offer to the general public facilities for studying the principles, purposes, methods, and problems of socialism and organized labor." It was started as a much more modest affair than it has grown to, and was at first directed by W. J. Ghent. In 1909 Ghent was succeeded by Algernon Lee and Bertha H.

Mailly. The People's House and the Rand School of Social Science which it houses are the center of socialist activity in New York, as were a number of similar buildings in other cities, Chicago, Detroit, and elsewhere.

While the Rand School of Social Science served as high school, college, and professional training school for the workers, the Intercollegiate Socialist Society—today the League for Industrial Democracy—made its task that of promoting an intelligent interest in socialism among college men and women. It was founded in 1905 and included the leading intellectuals of the socialist movement. Its conferences and discussions, lectures and symposia, helped to bring fellowship as well as light to the assembled socialists, students, and college alumni. Its organizers and speakers are constantly on the road addressing those behind academic walls. It issued two magazines, the *Intercollegiate Socialist,* which began in March, 1913, and after that suspended, the *Socialist Review* in the post-war period. Harry W. Laidler has been director of the society and of the League for Industrial Democracy for the greater part of their existence. Norman Thomas became co-director in 1918.

On the religious side the Christian Socialist Fellowship, founded in 1906, was re-organized in 1909 as the Christian Socialist League of America, and later revived under its original name. As given by the League, its objects were "to carry to churches and other religious organizations the message of socialism; to show the necessity of socialism to a complete realization of the teachings of Jesus; to end the class struggle by establishing industrial and political democracy, and to hasten the reign of justice and brotherhood upon earth." It published in its prime several weekly and monthly organs. While the socialist movement was accused of being atheistic and materialistic, the Christian socialists found little difficulty in working with and taking a prominent part in the Socialist Party. The socialism they preached differed in no way from that of the international socialist movement.

As in England where socialism received a tremendous impetus from the religiously minded workers, so in America the writings and teachings of the Christian socialists were of help among religious people.

Sunday schools for children, young people's socialist leagues, special departments for work among women, sport clubs, and other agencies spread socialism among special groups.

§

On June 26, 1911, the lyceum department was established in the national office of the Socialist Party under the direction of L. E. Katterfeld. The *Chicago Daily Socialist,* the *Appeal to Reason,* and other papers before and since also conducted lecture bureaus to promote their circulation, but the lyceum department was the first national and party-owned effort along this line. The plan was to issue a special combination subscription ticket to a series of lectures, including with it one or more subscriptions to socialist newspapers and books. The locals of the party took the collections and managed the sales of literature at the meetings. The lyceum department furnished speakers, advance agents, and advertising free, and got the pledged $300 sale of combination subscriptions plus 60 per cent of all subscriptions sold above this amount. It had its own arrangement with the publications for which it obtained subscriptions.

In his report to the 1912 convention Katterfeld claimed that over 1,500 lyceum lectures had been given in less than one year, with 309 locals participating. Up to April 15, 1912, his department had, he claimed, secured over 50,000 subscriptions to socialist papers, and sold about 45,000 cloth and paper bound books. Over 2,000,000 pieces of advertising matter had been used. About 10,000 new members, he reported, had been brought into the party. The department was discontinued after one year's activity.

In addition to the lyceum department, the national office, the state organizations and the locals maintained organizers and lecturers. There was a host of full-time, paid officials in party offices at a time when there were over 5,000 locals and 120,000 members paying dues and active. And in addition to the regular officials there were many who devoted all their time to and were compensated per piece for writing, lecturing, and organizing. Trade union officials also contributed a great deal while they were being maintained by their organizations.

There were a number who did not work directly for the party. They preferred to free-lance. It is difficult to compile a list of the hundreds of speakers and organizers. Many have already been mentioned in other connections. Among the lecturers given by Katterfeld as having worked for the lyceum department in the one year, 1911-1912, were the following:

Walter J. Millard	Arthur Brooks Baker
N. A. Richardson	Frank Bohn
A. W. Ricker	George D. Brewer
W. F. Ries	Phil H. Callery
	Janet Fennimore
Charles Edward Russell	George H. Goebel
May Wood Simons	Ralph Korngold
John W. Slayton	Lena Morrow Lewis
W. Harry Spears	Anna A. Maley
Ernest Untermann	James H. Maurer
Ben F. Wilson	Mila Tupper Maynard
Engene Wood	R. A. Maynard

If to this group such names as Arthur Morrow Lewis, Oscar Ameringer, and August Claessens be added—to mention only three of the great number that could be appended—it will be understood that the Socialist Party had a large body of fairly talented and energetic propagandist speakers. The writers and editors, the party secretaries and prominent volunteers, together with the paid lecturers, comprised the intellectual vanguard of the socialist army. For taking subscriptions, for securing members, for making collections in meetings, for selling books and pamphlets, for hard, persistent, conscientious, and untiring work in converting individuals and groups, these men and women were possibly unmatched by any socialists in the world. If Arthur Morrow Lewis is signalled out it is because he was an extraordinarily successful distributor of socialist literature and a lucid speaker to the multitude, to whom he transmitted the lessons of socialism and science. And if Oscar Ameringer is mentioned, it is because he is one of the wittiest and most facile writers in the movement. His pamphlets and his articles in the many papers which he edited deserve a place in the best of American humor. Claessens is an extraordinarily appealing soap-boxer and lecturer. Again, if George H. Goebel and Lena Morrow Lewis are picked out of a very long list it is because they were hardly to be surpassed in increasing the circulation of the socialist press.

§

In the eighteen years that elapsed between the unity convention of 1901 and the split of 1919 the party had six different national secretaries. As the quality of the man at national headquarters had much to do with the success or failure of the party, the fact that no official served for more than six years indicated some difficulty on the part of the national executive committee, the national committee, or the membership in a referendum, to secure and retain the right man for the position. In sharp contrast with the Socialist Party, for example, the American Federation of Labor was fortunate from the point of view of pure and simple trade unionism, in having a continuous leadership. The party was not lucky enough to have such on-going leadership in its national office, to express its own socialist position to the American people.

The Indianapolis unity convention selected St. Louis as the seat of the headquarters and chose Leon Greenbaum of that city as national secretary. He tried to make the autonomous state organizations aware of the existence of the national body. Because he flatly took sides with the local quorum—made up of sound trade unionists—in refusing to encourage dual unionism and in cooperating with the labor party movement of his day, he and the St. Louis local quorum were gotten rid of in January, 1903. By a close vote the members of the national committee selected William Mailly as the new secretary and located the party headquarters in Omaha, Nebraska. The westerners, agrarian and impossibilist, were responsible for fixing the location of the national office in an out-of-the-way place in an agricultural state, remote from industrial centers. The office could not remain there, however, and it was soon removed to Chicago, where it has continued down to the present.

William Mailly was "a son of the people" and started life as a coal miner. In the rump convention which organized the Social Democratic Party he represented Tennessee. When he was called to take charge of the party office he already had had considerable experience as an organizer and administrator in the socialist movement. He remained as secretary only for about two and a half years, having to give up the office on account of his health. He saw the party through its first important campaign of 1904, and helped to build up a national organization and to systematise the national office. He made carrying on easier for his successors. After Mailly left the national party office he edited a number of socialist papers, among them the New York *Call*. At the time of his death he was writing for the *Metropolitan Magazine*. George D. Herron, shortly after he passed away on September 4, 1912, paid a tribute to him in the *Coming Nation,* "as a socialist type."

The man who followed Mailly was probably the ablest national official the party ever had, and played a most prominent part in the American labor movement on both the industrial and political fields for thirty years. John

Mahlon Barnes, national secretary of the party from 1905 to 1911, and campaign manager in 1912 and 1924, was like Samuel Gompers a cigarmaker by trade. Despite the fact that he was a militant socialist, he was delegated by the Cigar Makers' International Union to twenty-seven conventions of the A. F. of L. to oppose the pure and simple trade union policies of George W. Perkins and Gompers. The exchange of bitter invective between Gompers and Barnes, with Gompers generally more personal, characterized many a convention of the A. F. of L.

Barnes was a member of the old Socialist Labor Party from 1891 until the split of 1899. In those days he was one of the outstanding leaders of the Philadelphia movement, and when he declared, after an investigation, in favor of the Kangaroos or insurgents, Daniel De Leon could not find words harsh enough to abuse him with. During the 1908 campaign of the Socialist Party, which Barnes directed, he originated the Red Special Campaign Train which toured Debs through the country. In his six years in the national office Barnes saw the party grow and prosper. But because of attacks upon him, matters concerning his private life and personal habits, he left in 1911. The following year, however, when the Socialist Party received the highest vote in all its history, he was through Hillquit's influence made campaign manager. There was considerable controversy at the time as to whether the eastern socialist leader had not "put over" Barnes in the 1912 convention in too hurried a fashion. The record of the 1912 convention shows that no opposition was raised to his nomination. The syndicalist wing of the party failed to make its point against the more opportunistic wing, with Hillquit as the target, and Barnes remained.

The fourth secretary was John McClelland Work. He had been a member of the national executive committee between 1903 and 1910, and had also been a lecturer for the party in that period. He was a college graduate and had practiced law. He was primarily a propagandist, writer and lecturer. He occupied the office for a few years until 1913, when he was succeeded by Walter Lanfersiek, who was unfortunate enough to be secretary during the time the party had to go through the strain of the early days of the World War, prior to America's joining it. There were losses in membership and voting strength, retrenchment, a business depression, and considerable internal squabbling. Louis Engdahl, editor of the *American Socialist,* the official national organ, Ralph Korngold, and Carl D. Thompson, employed by the party, appealed to the national committee to recall Lanfersiek. The petitioners were censured, but it was only a short time after they made their plea that Lanfersiek was defeated in the first party referendum to elect a national secretary.

There were four candidates on the first ballot, the results of which were announced on March 18, 1916:

Adolph F. Germer	10,894
Carl D. Thompson	11,790
Walter Lanfersiek	5,283
L. E. Katterfeld	3,558

Inasmuch as none of the contestants received a majority there was a second ballot, on which Germer received 14,486 and Thompson 11,900 votes. In this referendum Katterfeld, from stormy and ever-divided Washington, represented the left wing; he is today a member of the Workers' (Communist) Party. Carl Dean Thompson had been city clerk of Milwaukee in 1910-1912, director of the information and research department of the national party between 1912 and 1916, and was probably the best man for the position, in experience and equipment. Against him were raised the objections that he was a former Congregational minister and that he was alleged to be a prohibitionist. Some of the foreign language federations were accused of actively promoting Germer's candidacy because of their anti-religious and wet sympathies. The fact that Germer was a worker helped him.

Adolph F. Germer was the son of a German miner and went to work in the Illinois coal mines at the age of eleven. He took an active part in the miners' union and rose to be vice-president of the Illinois coal diggers' organization in 1915. He, Duncan MacDonald, John Walker—before he left the Socialist Party to support the democrats—, and a number of other Illinois leaders of the United Mine Workers helped to make the largest union in the A. F. of L. sympathetic to socialist ideas. Germer acted as national secretary when the Socialist Party adopted the St. Louis anti-war resolution; he was indicted and sentenced to twenty years—which sentence was later reversed— and he occupied the office at the time when the left wing created such havoc in the party. He resigned at the 1919 convention.

§

It is true that the leaders of the party, the candidates, the party officials, the speakers, organizers, and writers, in a word, the "shining lights," stamped the Socialist Party with their philosophies and personalities and contributed heavily to its success. But what made it possible to build up a socialist movement in the first place and to keep it alive for fifty years in the United States, what makes it possible to maintain and push it in America today, is the faith of those who bear the socialist torch, the rank and file. They believe that they as workers have a historic mission, and that they are unconquerable. They firmly believe that time and tide are on their side and nothing can prevent their victory. Veterans of the socialist faith go to their death with the last words of Ben Hanford:

I would that my every heart's beat should have been for the working class, and through them for all mankind.

The rank and file of the Socialist Party in truth made, and then, unfortunately, unmade it. But it was not altogether the same rank and file.

In 1898, when the Social Democratic Party was cutting its first teeth, James F. Carey was elected a delegate to the convention of the American Federation of Labor, and Seymour Stedman, secretary of the executive committee of the party, traveled to Kansas City where the labor men met. A resolution was introduced by John F. Tobin of the shoe workers urging trade unionists to vote only for such political parties as stood for the trade unions and socialism. It was beaten by a vote of 1,971 to 493. Samuel Gompers was reported by the socialists to have told them he would vote the Social Democratic Party ticket. The leaders of the new party felt at the time that in a few years the American Federation of Labor would swing around to their point of view. They believed that their policy of friendship and cooperation would undo the damage of Daniel De Leon's opposite policy, and would soon bear fruit.

The following year Max S. Hayes introduced the famous resolution which the A. F. of L. adopted: "That this convention call upon the trade unionists of the United States and workingmen generally to carefully study the development of trusts and monopolies, with a view to nationalizing the same." As he realized that many of the delegates were suspicious of anything coming from him, the Cleveland socialist in discussing his proposal said that there was nothing political in it. Nevertheless, the 1900 convention got rid of the dangerous proposal and declared that the organization of trade unions was the best means of checking the encroachments of the trusts. It also declared, by a vote of 4,169 to 685, that "it is not within the constitutional or any other power of the A. F. of L. to legislate, resolve, or specify to which political party members of our unions shall belong, or for which party they shall vote." On the socialist resolution to commit the federation in favor of collective ownership of the means of production, delegates from the following organizations voted in favor:

International Unions:
  Boilermakers
  Boot and shoe workers
  Brewery workmen
  Carpenters and joiners
  Amalgamated carpenters
  Wood carvers
  Electricians
  Amalgamated engineers
  Lathers
  Metal polishers
  Pattern makers

  Pressmen
  Stove mounters
  Tobacco workers
  Upholsterers
  Wood workers
State Federations:
  Wisconsin
City Central Bodies:
  Alton and Chicago, Ill., Cleveland, Erie County, N. Y., Milwaukee, Omaha, St. Louis, and Youngstown.

In the 1902 convention of the A. F. of L. there was a battle royal, with the supporters of Gompers badly split. Hayes had introduced a proposition reading as follows:

Resolved, That this twenty-second annual convention of the A. F. of L. advise the working people to organize their economic and political power to secure for labor the full equivalent of its toil and the overthrow of the wage system and the establishment of an industrial, cooperative democracy.

William B. Wilson of the miners, later made Secretary of Labor under President Wilson, amended by dropping all that followed "the full equivalent of its toil." Although Gompers was later compelled to enter politics actively in 1906, he fought the resolution even with Wilson's amendment. He made the following absurd charge: "In the German Parliament there are nearly a hundred socialists, and there we find the most backward of all European countries in the interest of labor. . . . Marx denounced the socialists as the worst enemies of the laboring classes." This was not the first nor the last time that Gompers made unscrupulous attacks on socialists. The vote was very close, only a few hundred deciding the result in favor of the pure and simple trade unionists.

At this same 1902 convention the delegates adopted by a vote of 90 to 85 the committeee's report against Victor L. Berger's resolution in favor of old age pensions. In 1908 the A. F. of L. reversed itself and endorsed Berger's pet legislative proposal. Again, in 1902 the Milwaukee

socialist and trade union leader proposed that the salaries
of Gompers and Morrison be increased. On a point of
personal privilege, Berger denied that he was trying to
win the officers to socialism, but stated that "as a matter
of justice and fairness" they were entitled to the raise
and he wanted to show that he could forget differences.
On the other hand, after the convention, Berger wrote in
his *Social Democratic Herald* that "well meaning observ-
ers predict that the A. F. of L. will have to change its
structure, or it will go to pieces within a few years."
Following the 1903 convention, with its decisive defeats
for the socialists, Eugene Victor Debs wrote in Berger's
weekly: "Between the pure and simple labor leaders
and civic federationists and the socialist agitators there
is war and the place to fight it out is not in an Alamo
where they out-number us a dozen to one, but out in the
hearing of the working class."

§

Feeling between the socialist leaders in the trade unions
and the pure and simplers ran high in the 1904 convention. Just prior to the gathering the Socialist Party polled
its record vote. Max S. Hayes accordingly delivered
himself as follows:

The statement was sent out that the socialists were crushed
by the Boston convention [1903]; so far as the rank and file
of the labor movement of the United States is concerned the
edict of the Boston convention had practically no effect, as was
proven by on the eighth day of November.

We care not what the act of this or any other convention is in
regard to such resolutions . . . it is the constant, continuous
agitation carried on by the socialist element, so-called . . . among
their fellow workers and the diffusion of education that produces
socialists, and that alone.

In the next two or three years, without the slightest doubt,
the rank and file will have become so thoroughly impregnated
with the principles of socialism that a great many of the leaders
who pose as having been appointed guardians, perhaps, of the
working class, will either get in line with their constituents or
perhaps they will go up in air.

There was considerable happening in the labor world to back up the predictions of Hayes. A referendum of the machinists at the end of 1903 declared in favor of socialism and for the repudiation of Gompers, although their delegates in the convention of the A. F. of L. paid little attention to it. There was a western labor federation—the American Labor Union—bidding for the support of dissatisfied elements. And the young and vigorous Socialist Party was making inroads among the members of the conservative unions. But Samuel Gompers knew how to cement the opposition inside A. F. of L. convention halls—where the higher officials gathered—and in the 1904 gathering he made much of a leaflet that emanated from Berger's bailiwick asking if Gompers and John Mitchell, the president of the miners, were not traitors. They were accused of dining with President Eliot of Harvard. The latter was said to have remarked that "the scab is a very good type of the modern hero." The pure and simplers rode rough-shod over the socialists. Berger in his paper called them "socialist killers;" he styled Gompers the "savior of the existing capitalistic order of society," and added that "a final settlement cannot be reached on the basis of the old trade union autonomy, which the leaders of the large national unions advocate or violate, just as suits them best." The results of the 1905 convention were also so unsatisfactory to Berger that he let himself go: "All its proceedings are senile and show symptoms of marasmus. Sam Gompers . . . has more and more developed into an empty, self-complacent old fool, who does not see or does not wish to see that the A. F. of L., from inertia and lack of movement, is hastening before his very eyes to a fatal apoplexy." Notwithstanding, Berger later refused to join a new organization, the Industrial Workers of the World.

By authority of the executive council Samuel Gompers
invited the presidents of the international unions affiliated
to the A. F. of L. to a conference early in 1906. The
heads or representatives of the 117 unions met and
drew up the Bill of Labor's Grievances which they presented in a body to President Roosevelt and to the presid-
ing officers of the Senate and the House on March 21,
1906:

1. An effective eight-hour law. Said Gompers: "Labor has,
since 1894 urged the passage of a law so as to remedy the defects, and for its extension to all work done for or on behalf of
the government. Our efforts have been in vain."
2. Protection from the evil of convict labor.
3. Some immigration restriction and enforcement of existing
laws.
4. Freedom and safety for the sailor.
5. Perversion of the anti-trust law against labor organizations.
6. Writ of injunction abused.
7. Committee on Labor in the House opposed to unions. "In
the past two Congresses this committee has been so organized as
to make ineffectual any attempt labor has made for redress."
8. No progress made upon legislation demanded of Congress.
9. Executive order denying right of petition to government
employees.

The American Federation of Labor, through its leading spokesman, Samuel Gompers, now more emphatically than ever declared:

We will stand by our friends and administer a stinging rebuke
to men or parties who are either indifferent, negligent or hostile;
and, wherever opportunity affords, secure the selection of intelligent, honest, earnest trade unionists, with unblemished paid-up
union cards in their possession.

The Bill of Grievances was nothing new. The nonpartisan method was as old as the federation itself. But
what was different was the greater determination of the
pure and simplers to bring pressure to bear upon hostile
legislators. The attitude of the republican and reactionary
Congresses, the growth of the Socialist Party, the success of the British Labor Party in 1906, the organization
of the I. W. W., and above all, the menacing power of
the courts and the employers' lobbies in legislative halls,

awakened the A. F. of L. out of its lethargy. The federation leaders decided to show that they were not "bluffing" by throwing their resources into the fight against the reelection of Congressman Charles E. Littlefield, considered one of labor's worst foes. The election in Maine occurred before the general election in other parts of the country and would constitute a trial of strength. Littlefield was reelected. But against a plurality of about 5,500 in 1904 he received only 1,000 in 1906. Some of the leading republicans of the nation invaded the district to prevent his defeat. Littlefield later resigned while in office.

Into the November election of 1906 Gompers and his followers put considerable energy to teach their foes a lesson. They were limited by finances, men, and lack of a political organization. Despite the 1,500,000 members in the American Federation of Labor Gompers could only raise $8,225.24, and he did not have the speakers and propagandists nor the well-oiled political machine of the Socialist Party. These facts caused him to make unwarranted attacks on the socialists. He accused the *Worker,* the socialist weekly of New York, of receiving money from Littlefield sources, because the socialists refused to endorse an old-party candidate and instead ran their own man. Again, in 1908, when Gompers was receiving very little money or support from organized labor for his nonpartisan campaign, he printed the following in his *American Federationist,* attacking Debs and the socialists for successfully raising enough money to tour their presidential candidate in a special train, called the Red Special:

We note the "socialists' Special" train is to make a tour of the country, carrying Mr. Debs with all the luxurious accessories which modern transportation can accomplish. The train is said to cost $23,000 for the campaign. Now we would like to inquire who finances the socialist campaign? It seems hardly probable that such luxurious style of transportation would be authorized by those voters of small means whose contributions are alleged to be the chief support of the socialist campaign. Why not publish a list of your campaign contributions, Mr. Debs? It would be interesting to know who contributes the $23,000 campaign train. There is a strong suspicion in the minds of many that the money has the same similarity of source as the abuse. In other words, that the interests behind the Parry-Post-Van Cleave-Taft-Debs opposition to unions furnishes the money for any branch of the campaign where it is expected to do the most harm to the unions and their friends. Come out into the open, Mr. Debs. Where does your party get the money? What is the real reason of your virulent hostility to the A. F. of L. political campaign?

In the 1907 convention Gompers made a statement that a representative of the National Manufacturers' Association had attempted to bribe him. Thereupon Victor L. Berger moved a vote of confidence in the leader of the A. F. of L. and urged his unanimous reelection as president. J. Mahlon Barnes, national secretary of the Socialist Party, added his opinion on the floor that the expose of the employers constituted "the greatest day's work of the American Federation." When he was attacked by the common enemy, the socialist trade unionists did not hesitate to declare their loyalty to their bitter foe, and their faith in his honesty and devotion to the working class. However, when in the 1908 convention a group of delegates from a half dozen organizations introduced a resolution to investigate the truth of Gompers' charge that anti-union employers paid for the Red Special which toured Debs, Frank Duffy of the Carpenters had the proposition sidetracked by tacking on an amendment calling upon its sponsors to say whether or not they were willing "to vouch for the truth and accuracy of the articles published in socialistic papers in reference to the officers of the A. F. of L."

Despite the Danbury hatters' case which brought the unions under the ban of the Sherman anti-trust law, despite the growth of the militant employers' associations and the set-backs of labor on the economic and political field, and despite the meagre support that the workers gave to its selected candidates, the American Federation of Labor continued to adhere to its nonpartisan policy.

Its leaders were lukewarm toward the candidacy of Woodrow Wilson in 1912 but after his first term they felt that their method was justified. In fact, they declared that it had been crowned with success. Labor has really gained little by following the weak and hopeless policy of nonpartisan political action.

During all the struggles of the socialist unionists to swing the A. F. of L. toward independent political action, they continued to organize unions and to do their share of the work of conducting the business of the unions to which they belonged. The socialists inside and outside the unions helped with money, voice, and pen whenever a strike took place, regardless of how conservative or radical the union was which ran it.

§

One of the sore points of dispute between Gompers, Mitchell, and the pure and simple trade union leaders on one side and the socialists on the other was the affiliation of the former with the National Civic Federation. This body was organized in 1901 and counted among its supporters the leaders of big business and the conservative unions besides a number of influential old party politicians. Morris Hillquit stated the socialist point of view in his remarks before the Commission on Industrial Relations in 1914:

The Civic Federation is an organization founded by employers for the purpose principally and primarily of deadening the aggressive spirit of the American labor movement, and I think it is succeeding marvellously. . . . It maintains an elaborate office. It pays salaries to a secretary and to a large staff of workers. It has various departments. It spends very large sums of money. . . . I should like to know . . . where that money comes from? Does the American Federation of Labor contribute any part to it, and if it does not, who does? And if it is all contributed by our capitalists and their friends in the National Civic Federation, I should like Mr. Gompers to say whether in his opinion, such contributions are made solely and single-mindedly for the benefit of the workers?

Samuel Gompers replied as follows:

There is no such thing as cooperation between the leaders of
the labor movement and the leaders of the National Civic Fea-
eration.   So far as I am concerned, I can go anywhere where
men assemble, and where they consider questions affecting the
working people.   I can meet with them and bring the message
of labor to them, and argue and contend as best I can with them
for the rights of the working people, and if I can influence them
to an act of helpfulness toward any one thing in which the
working people are interested, I have accomplished something.

Then Hillquit asked him:

And you think it is perfectly feasible and possible for a labor
leader to influence the large employers and capitalists in the
National Civic Federation to take measures for the benefit of
organized labor?

And Gompers answered:

This is not the question.   I will appeal to the devil and his
mother-in-law to help labor, if labor can be aided in that way.

The United Mine Workers in 1911 adopted a resolution to compel John Mitchell, its former president, to
sever his relations with the Civic Federation, if he wanted
to remain inside the union.   It went further and put up a
vigorous fight in the 1911 convention of the A. F. of L.
for the repudiation of the National Civic Federation and
the withdrawal from it of the officers of the trade union
federation.

Duncan MacDonald spoke on the question.   He was
the miners' leader from Illinois and a socialist, one who
has not "sold out" or gone over to the other side as did
Frank Farrington.   MacDonald said he hoped that personalities would not be indulged in.   He was referring
to the way Gompers had of draping the banner of the
A. F. of L. around himself, dragging in the Socialist
Trade and Labor Alliance and the Industrial Workers
of the World which were maintained by men violently
opposed to the Socialist Party, fishing up ancient history
to discredit socialism and socialists, and thus stirring up
enough heat and hate to win his point—and incidentally

reelecting himself president of the federation. For Gompers at times managed to keep alive the opposition to socialism as a substitute for a constructive program. Others used the opposition to socialism as a shield for reactionary and predatory purposes.

It was Max S. Hayes who pointed out that some of the leaders of the A. F. of L. and the Socialist Party retarded the natural development, whereby the rank and file was slowly but surely accepting the socialist position and gradually unhorsing the conservative leadership. If it were not for the election of Woodrow Wilson in 1912, the outbreak of the World War and America's entrance into it, with the hysteria and the post-war reaction, not even Gompers could have stopped the growth of socialism among the trade unionists of America. For it was in the unions, among the American workingmen, the highest paid and the best skilled, the most militant and the best informed, that socialism had some of its most ardent, determined, able, and sound elements. Only when a labor party has its roots deep down in the unions can it hope to make any real headway in the United States. It is not among the unskilled, the foreign-born, the poorest paid—however vital they are—where the greatest hope lies. It is when the better paid and higher skilled feel the need, that a labor party will come to stay.

The miners had several spokesmen besides MacDonald in the 1911 convention. They were bitter because they knew that their fellow-workers went through hell to make a living, and to organize and maintain their union against the coal operators, some of the largest of whom were allied with the same interests which dominated the National Civic Federation. E. S. McCullough put the case of the coal diggers as follows:

Take the history of every strike and every settlement that has been made in this country and you will find that the employer of labor never was willing to go into the halls of peace and fight it out there until he had been licked to a standstill on the economic field, or had measured the strength and power of organized labor on the economic field. They will only arbitrate, they will only grant to us those things our power allows us to take.

I have no faith in these great employers giving anything to the wage working class, only a sufficient amount to keep them quiet and from rising in their might and strength and power and shaking off the shackles that have bound them for so many years.

The defenders of the National Civic Federation repeated the argument of Gompers in his reply to Hillquit in 1914—that it served as an agency to bring employers and workers together during labor disputes, that it promoted collective bargaining. They hotly denied the charge that they were "chloroformed" or made any concessions. They said they wanted every opportunity to present labor's point of view before the public, to meet with the large employers who were not opposed to unionism, and to work with them against the militant employers' associations which were out to smash the unions altogether. The socialist unionists replied to all these arguments by saying that the class struggle was a fact, that the employers respected nothing but economic and political power, and that the pure and simplers could win no concessions but were being cleverly taken into hand by the capitalists and by their agents who appeared in the false role of representatives of the so-called public.

The vote on the resolution was 4,294 for, 11,851 against —more than two to one to permit Gompers and the others to continue their membership in the Civic Federation. The list of organizations whose delegates voted for the resolution showed pretty well how strong the socialists were inside the federation of labor at their peak. Whole or part delegations from the following unions voted against the National Civic Federation:

International Unions:
  Brewery Workmen
  Cigar Makers [Barnes]
  Coal Miners
  Cloth Hat and Cap Makers
  Garment Workers
  Glove Workers
  Iron, Steel, and Tin Workers
  Journeymen Tailors
  Machinists
  Metal Miners
  Painters
  Potters
  Quarry Workers
  Railway Carmen
  Typographical Union
State Federations:
  Arkansas, Michigan, Montana,
    Oklahoma, Pennsylvania,
    Tennessee, Washington,
    Wisconsin, Wyoming
City Central Bodies:
  Butte, Chattanooga, Chicago,
    Jacksonville, Jersey City,
    Kalamazoo, Milwaukee,
    Philadelphia, St. Louis,
    Springfield, Mo., Vancouver.

An opposition movement getting this vote and the support of these organizations in the American Federation of Labor was in truth a power in the labor movement. Apart from all the successes of the Socialist Party on the political field, whether on a liberal reform or a revolutionary program, apart from all its intellectuals, writers, speakers, and propagandists, apart from its magnificent press and literature, apart from its idealists and zealots, in the last analysis its strength and hope rested on an organized and class-conscious working class. In truth, the tide of socialism was rising in the United States because it was making headway in the old trade unions and among the native American wage earners.

CHAPTER IX

THE SOCIALIST PARTY PROGRAM

IN the twenty years that the Socialist Party occupied the center of the stage of the independent political movement of the producers of America there were two sharply divided tendencies represented by two groups within the organization. They called each other impossibilists and opportunists, reds and yellows, revolutionists and reformists. On some of the more fundamental party issues they were divided as follows:

Revolutionists	*Reformists*
A violent revolution is inevitable.	There is a possibility of a peaceful transformation.
The final conflict should be chiefly emphasized.	The immediate demands must receive most attention.
The proletariat must be made class conscious.	All classes and groups must be aroused, in addition to the wage earners.
The party must emphasize the class struggle.	The intensity of the class struggle is not so great in the United States.
The party must advocate industrial and revolutionary unionism.	The party must be neutral, although industrial unionism is preferable.
The party must support the I. W. W. and opposition unions.	The party must be neutral; it should help sound, progressive unions.
The party must be thoroughly democratized by placing all power in the hands of the rank and file.	The party must be democratic and also efficient; the voice of the people is not the voice of God.
The party must be run by proletarians, with rotation in office; low salaries to party workers.	The party must be run by those most competent regardless of class origin, to continue in office, if fit; adequate compensation.

The party must teach the materialistic basis of religion.

The party must not make any concession to the property-owning, exploiting, decaying small farmer.

The party must demand absolutely no restrictions on immigration.

There must be no compromise with a labor party.

There must be complete autonomy for each state branch

There must be strict construction of and rigid adherence to the teachings of the founders.

Elected public officials must be completely controlled by the party.

There must be no infractions of the rule requiring several years' membership for elected party officials and candidates for public office.

The party must insist that its candidates and elected public officials adhere rigidly to socialist platforms and principles.

The party press must at all times rigidly adhere to socialist platforms and principles.

The party must allow its members freedom to advocate sabotage, mass action, and illegal means.

The party must regard religion as a private matter.

The party welcomes the poor and small farmer; does not demand the nationalization of his land.

The party cannot represent the American workers without demanding protection for their standard of life and their unions; in favor of restriction.

Whenever the trade unions organize a *bona fide* labor party on a national scale the party must support it.

No national party can be built up unless its needs are supreme.

Socialism is an evolutionary science. The spirit and not the letter of Marxism is important.

The party should not unduly control the acts of responsible public officials.

There should be exceptions made even for the highest party posts for certain individuals; equally so for candidates for office.

There must be a certain leniency if the party is to succeed and retain within its ranks certain types of individuals.

There must be a certain leniency, if freedom of the press is to be maintained and heresy hunting avoided.

The party must advocate legal methods; it can grow and succeed only by emphasizing political and trade union action.

The party must insist that all its officials, members and organs oppose preparedness for war on pain of expulsion.

The party must take all means to oppose all wars but the class war; it must try to convert imperialistic wars into civil wars; no civil peace.

The party must teach that the worker has no country, and emphasize international socialism.

The party should not require expulsion as a penalty for infractions; the individual office holder should be allowed a certain leeway.

The party must take all legal steps to oppose war. It is not against all wars. It should emphasize the preservation and improvement of labor standards during wars.

The party does not deny that the worker has a country worth fighting for; international socialism does not preclude working class nationalism.

The revolutionists and reformists were not always consistent. They did not formulate or carry through all the points in their programs, but they tended to take the positions outlined above on these questions as they arose in the history of the Socialist Party. There were centrists, too, who leaned toward the revolutionists but generally acted with the reformists.

§

The unity convention of 1901 definitely relegated the impossibilists to the rear. It decisively defeated their proposal of excluding immediate demands. It appointed committees on a farmers' and a municipal program. It adopted an opportunist attitude toward the trade unions and a form of organization which permitted of considerable efficiency.

The second convention of the party met in Chicago, May 1-6, 1904, with 184 delegates from 35 states and territories. According to socialist custom the delegates elected all committees and the chairman for the day. This is in contrast with the policy of the American Federation of Labor where the president occupies the chair throughout and appoints all the committees of the annual convention. The Socialist Party gathering of 1904 made this concession to the left wing: it buried and condensed the immediate demands into a single paragraph in the platform. It added a section to the constitution providing that "no member of the party, in any state or territory, shall under any pretext, interfere with the regular or organized movement in any other state." It made its position of no compromise plain with reference to any union labor party:

No state or local organization shall under any circumstances fuse, combine or compromise with any other political party or organization, or refrain from making nominations in order to favor the candidate of such other organizations, nor shall any candidate of the Socialist Party accept any nomination or endorsement from any other party or political organization.

The question of the salaries to be paid party officials came up for discussion. Delegates from the Washington state branch pointed out that they paid $40 a month to their state secretary, $480 a year. They did not see why the national secretary—William Mailly at the time—should have his salary increased from $1,000 to $1,500 a year. Morris Hillquit made the following attack upon—and concession to—their point of view:

We are not going to hire a hod-carrier now, nor are we going to hire a miner. . . . I am opposed to extravagant salaries. I am opposed to high salaries with all my soul, because they may have a tendency to attract to our movement people who are out for salaries.

The convention adopted a resolution putting the party on record as follows:

This body declares itself opposed to paying speakers or other workers employed by the party exorbitant fees or salaries, placing them above the standard of the working class the party represents.

By almost unanimous vote the delegates declared against an official national party organ. The national committee was specifically prohibited in the constitution from publishing or designating such a paper. In 1904 the experience of the former members of the Socialist Labor Party with the *People* was still too fresh. They were afraid of dictation, heresy hunting, and statements *ex cathedra* from the organ of a small centralized executive. But in addition to this group there were the editors of local and private papers who feared the prestige and circulation of a national organ. The weak opposition could only ask one honest question: Who is more to be trusted, the private editor or the national executive committee of the party? The answer in 1904 was that the former was to be preferred.

The convention adopted a resolution on the attitude of the party toward the trade unions in conformity with its action of 1901. Nevertheless, there was an opposition from the West, where the machine process had not penetrated and where individualism and populist agrarianism dominated the socialist movement. Irene M. Smith of Oregon was typical. She made the following remarks:

> The trades unionist is leaning upon his little crutch and until that crutch is broken entirely under him, he will have to lean upon it, whether we preach socialism or not. . . . As class conscious revolutionary socialists—yes, I use the combined term—we have no business with those temporary movements.

Frederick W. Ott of Wyoming introduced a resolution denouncing craft unionism, and putting the party on record for industrial unionism. Other speakers said that the party should not cater to trade unionists, for they were only a part of the working class, while the ballot was more powerful than the strike. The opposition— those behind Ott's resolution—received 52 votes, against 107 for the majority. In the minority were Eugene Victor Debs, James Maurer of Pennsylvania, and Ernest Untermann. The majority also favored industrial unionism but were opposed to having the party interfere in internal union affairs.

Chicago was again the place of the 1908 convention, May 10-17, with 215 delegates from 45 states. There had been a healthy growth since 1904. There were now about 2,500 locals with 41,000 members. The socialists also had behind them the splendid vote of four years back. In view of the menace of the Industrial Workers of the World, which had been organized in 1905, and which was now becoming anti-political, the convention adopted two important constitutional amendments:

Any member of the party who opposes political action as a weapon of the working class to aid in its emancipation shall be expelled from membership in the party.

All persons joining the Socialist Party shall sign the following pledge: "I, the undersigned, recognizing the class struggle between the capitalist class and the working class and the necessity of the working class constituting themselves into a political party distinct from and opposed to all parties formed by the propertied classes, hereby declare that I have severed my relations with all other parties, that I indorse the platform and constitution of the Socialist Party, including the principle of political action, and hereby apply for admission to said party."

These provisions pretty definitely put the party on the wheels of parliamentary as against direct action, as preached by the syndicalist I. W. W.

By a vote of 99 to 51 the delegates appealed to the farmers to ally themselves with the party of their class— the Socialist Party—but pledged them nothing except complete socialization of the industries, including all land. The convention did this unrealistic and inconsistent thing despite the fact that it snowed under the opposition to including immediate demands and the proposal for taking sides in the trade union struggle in favor of industrial unionism. This convention continued the supposedly proletarian flavor of the party by refusing to allow any expenses to delegates for Pullmans.

By only one vote, 79 to 78, the following proposition was carried as to the relation between socialism and religion and the home:

The socialist movement is primarily an economic and political movement. It is not concerned with the institutions of marriage or religion.

Many of the delegates who voted in the negative did so because they were opposed to making any declaration whatever, while the majority definitely wanted to hit at the same time the atheists within their own ranks who, they felt, abused the privilege of a socialist platform or periodical, and those opponents who unfairly attacked the socialist movement because some of its leaders were irreligious.

When it came to the nomination of candidates for president it was discovered that Debs was no longer the unquestioned and unanimous choice of all delegates. In 1900 and 1904 there was no thought of any other. But in 1908 there was opposition, although relatively insignificant and not based on a clear-cut issue. In 1912, however, it was much more active and organized. By 1916 Debs was off the ticket. The special circumstances of 1920 made Debs again the inevitable choice.

The men who ran against Debs in 1908 were James F. Carey of Massachusetts, Carl D. Thompson of Wisconsin, and A. M. Simons of Illinois. Strangely enough, apart from such veteran trade unionists as "Barney" Berlyn, William M. Brandt, and Gottlieb A. Hoehn, Carey's supporters were from out-of-the-way states, such as Montana, Maine, Minnesota, and Louisiana. Thompson and Simons received scattering votes also, but drew in addition on their own state delegations. Debs obtained 159, Carey sixteen, Thompson fourteen, and Simons nine votes.

§

The first national congress, as contrasted with a presidential nominating convention, was held in 1910, once more in Chicago, May 15-21. This time there was a smaller and a more selected list of delegates. The purpose of the conference was to thrash out party policy and program, free from the pressure of a campaign. There were about 100 delegates, plus the representatives of the lusty and growing foreign language federations. The man who customarily occupied the chair at the first day's proceedings of a Socialist Party convention, Morris Hillquit, ruled, and he was sustained in his ruling, that the spokesmen of the language federations were to have no votes in the convention and no representation on its committees. He held that to do otherwise would be to make them privileged characters, because the members of the federations had already had a hand in electing the delegates to the congress.

The two most important matters that were considered in 1910 were immigration and the attitude of the party toward the farmer. Ernest Untermann, Victor L. Berger, and Joshua Wanhope, for the majority of a committee on immigration which had been studying the question for some time, made one report, John Spargo submitted another. The convention accepted neither but by the close vote of 55 to 50 adopted a substitute of Morris Hillquit, about which the following took place between "Tommy" Morgan and the eastern socialist leader:

Morgan: I desire to ask the comrade whether he pressed his substitute upon either the majority or the minority or has it been formulated since we adjourned last night?
Hillquit: It has been formulated, if that is of any interest, within the past half hour.
Morgan: I thought so.
Hillquit: Does it bear the marks of hasty preparation?

The majority report included the following observations:

. . . . the working class of each nation has first to settle matters with its own ruling class . . . the principle of national autonomy prevents the international congress of the socialist parties from laying down specific rules for the carrying out of the general principles recognized as valid by all socialists [a resolution of the International forbade exclusion of specific races] . . . any measures which do not conform to the immediate interests of the working class in the United States are fruitless and reactionary. . . . Such a measure or measures would place the Socialist

Party in opposition to the most militant and intelligent portion of the organized workers of the United States, those whose assistance is indispensable to the purpose of elevating the Socialist Party to political power. . . .

We advocate the unconditional exclusion of these races [Chinese, Japanese, Koreans and Hindus] not as races per se— not as peoples with definite physiological characteristics—but for the evident reason that these peoples occupy definite portions of the earth in which they are so far behind the general modern development of industry, psychologically as well as economically, that they constitute a drawback, an obstacle and menace to the progress of the most aggressive, militant and intelligent elements of our working class population.

The proposition discussed did not involve restrictions upon any immigrants but the races mentioned above, the Asiatics. John Spargo, for his own minority report, significantly pointed out, however, "that if today you vote Asiatic exclusion, next time you will be voting Italian exclusion or Hebrew exclusion." The man who is today busily attacking international socialism, could in 1910 deliver himself as follows:

There is coming over the minds of the capitalist class of America a consciousness that the revolutionary temper is by no means the exclusive proprietary possession of those whose forefathers came over and landed at Plymouth Rock, but that there is good fighting material among our alien proletariat.

Victor L. Berger took the opportunity to answer the European socialists who criticized the Americans for excluding even Asiatics. He mentioned the fact that the German Social Democrats had threatened a general strike if their capitalists imported coolie laborers. Untermann added that the German workers had raised a hue and cry against the immigration of the Poles into Germany during harvesting time. Berger, in his characteristic way, put the matter bluntly: "It is easy to stick to nice phrases when the issue does not concern you directly." Adolph Germer, a man who had battled for the miners and who could speak on the question of the fighting qualities of foreigner and native born in America, remarked that "the protest of the foreigner on the economic field has been spasmodic and not of long endurance," while Gaylord asked if Asiatics would help to build up a trade union and political movement in the United States.

The note of violent protest was struck by Eugene V. Debs, who later wrote that the majority of the immigration committee had sacrificed principle and ought to leave the Socialist Party. Ernest Untermann replied in the *Call* of August 2, 1910, that Debs was a poor general and was surrounded by bad advisors. In the congress itself Fraenckel of Illinois said:

If we are to go on record as being in favor of the exclusion of any particular races I say that the Socialist Party from that time on is no more the place for me, is no more the place for a socialist of the world.

The representatives of the foreign language federations, which did not yet have the influence that they had in 1919, opposed all restrictions, in part for sentimental reasons, and also because they were afraid that the bars would be extended to cover the peoples from their home lands, as well as the Asiatics. There was considerable nationalism inside the Socialist Party which masqueraded as internationalism.

The substitute of Morris Hillquit, which was barely carried, read as follows:

The Socialist Party of the United States favors all legislative measures tending to prevent the immigration of strike breakers and contract laborers and the mass importation of workers from foreign countries brought about by the employing classes for the purpose of weakening the organization of American labor and lowering the standard of life of American workers. The party is opposed to the exclusion of any immigrants on account of their race or nationality, and demands that the United States be at all times maintained as a free asylum for all men and women persecuted in their countries on account of their politics, religion or race.

The farmers' program adopted did not include the error of the 1908 convention by calling for the socialization of all land. It embodied the following statement on this matter:

Only to a very small extent is the land now, only to a very small extent is it likely to be for many years to come, a socially operated means of production. Even to declare in any dogmatic manner that all the land must eventually become social property is somewhat utopian; to demand that the ownership of all land shall be immediately socialized is to make ourselves ridiculous.

The program demanded the nationalization of the railways, public warehouses, the encouragement of cooperation, the extension of state credit without the intervention of private banks, government insurance against diseases of animals, pests, and natural calamities, and the taxation of all lands to their full rental value, "the income therefrom to be applied to the establishment of industrial plants for the preparing of agricultural products for final consumption, such as packing-houses, canneries, cotton gins, grain elevators, storage, and market facilities." The party's proposals included this one concession to those who advocated nationalization of the land:

We should include in our immediate demands the retention by the nation and by the state respectively of such lands as they still own, and such as they may hereafter secure by reclamation, purchase, condemnation or otherwise; such land to be organized into model state farms and various forms of collective agricultural enterprises, as far and as fast as practical under capitalistic development.

§

The last regular convention before the historic emergency St. Louis gathering of 1917, was held in the city where the party was founded, Indianapolis, May 12-18, 1912. Every state but one was represented, including all the foreign language federations. The prosperity of the party was now evident. Without a murmur the delegates decided to include in their expenses—which the party paid—accommodations for Pullmans. Berger threw this *bon mot* to the gallery: "I believe that those have the best right to ride in sleeping cars who build the sleeping cars."

Karl Legien, secretary of the International Trade Union Secretariat and a German Social Democrat, a leading member of the most powerful socialist party in the world, addressed the convention—to help crush the I. W. W. element. He stated a commonly held belief of that day when he said "that the United States may possibly be or become the first nation of practical socialism as a result of the rapid concentration and growth of capitalism and the privileges and possibilities that are open to the workers of this country." According to the socialists—as contrasted with the communists of our own day—a country must first be thoroughly prepared by the capitalists, their historic mission must be fulfilled, before the wage earners are able, after organizing on the political and economic fields, to take control of the means of production and distribution.

The one overshadowing issue in the 1912 convention was that of syndicalism, as typified by the program and methods of the Industrial Workers of the World. Karl Legien took pains to say that in Germany they had "no room for sabotage and similar syndicalist and destructive tendencies." The left wing succeeded after a strenuous fight in having a telegram sent to the I. W. W., which was then conducting one of its spectacular free speech struggles in San Diego. But they got no further in this memorable convention. By a vote of 191 to 90 the delegates inserted in the constitution the famous article II, section 6, which read as follows:

Any member of the party who opposes political action or advocates crime, sabotage, or other methods of violence as a weapon of the working class to aid in its emancipation, shall be expelled from membership in this party. Political action shall be construed to mean participation in elections for public office and practical legislative and administrative work along the lines of the Socialist Party platform.

Despite the fact that the committee on labor organizations adopted a unanimous report, the left wing did not win any victory. William Haywood, its leader, could say that he was satisfied, and a diverse committee made up of the three "red" Toms, Clifford, Hickey and Lewis, as well as Oscar Ameringer, Job Harriman, Algernon Lee, William E. Rodriguez, and Dan A. White, could come to agreement. The fact remained that the report did not specifically endorse industrial or dual unionism and merely brought out the implications of previous resolutions of a similar character adopted at former socialist conventions. The resolution read:

That the party has neither the right nor the desire to interfere in any controversies which may exist within the labor union movement over questions of form of organization or technical methods of action in the industrial struggle, but trusts to the labor organizations themselves to solve these questions.

That the socialists call the attention of the brothers in the labor unions to the vital importance of the task of organizing the unorganized, especially the immigrants and the unskilled laborers, who stand in greatest need of organized protection and who will constitute a great menace to the progress and welfare of organized labor, if they remain neglected. The Socialist Party will ever be ready to cooperate with the labor unions in the task of organizing the unorganized workers and urges all labor organizations who have not already done so, to throw their doors wide open to the workers of their respective trades and industries, abolishing all onerous conditions of membership and artificial restrictions. In the face of the tremendous powers of the American capitalists and their close industrial and political union the workers of this country can win their battles only by a strong class-consciousness on the economic field, a powerful and militant party on the political field and by joint attack of both on the common enemy.

That it is the duty of the party to give moral and material support to the labor organizations in all their defensive or aggressive struggles against capitalist oppression and exploitation, for the protection and extension of the rights of the wage workers and the betterment of their material and social condition.

That it is the duty of the members of the Socialist Party who are eligible to membership in the unions to join and be active in their respective labor organizations.

The more conservative delegates to the 1908 convention, according to the account of Robert F. Hoxie, were able to prevent William D. Haywood from even announcing himself as a candidate for president. They did not put up much of a fight against Debs in that year. In 1912, however, they strenuously campaigned to prevent his nomination. They were divided between pushing Charles Edward Russell and Emil Seidel. Both together obtained only 110 votes, Seidel 56 and Russell 54, against 165 for Debs.

Eugene Victor Debs never fully belonged to the left wing, for when the real test came in 1919 he refused to go along with those who adopted the communist program of preparation for armed struggle and civil war. Throughout the history of the party Debs played with and was supported by the left wing, but at many a critical juncture and occasion where a decision was to be made Debs broke with the left wing and repudiated their major demands. He helped to launch the Industrial Workers of the World but soon abandoned it. He unreservedly condemned the methods of sabotage. He did not change in any essential when he left Atlanta prison on December 23, 1921. However militant and courageous, Debs was from the first until the last a social democrat, not a communist. He believed that parliamentary and trade union action made a decisive difference and could win improvements and final emancipation for the working class. The man who led the left wing in the Socialist Party for the half dozen years that he was prominent in it, was William D. Haywood.

The I. W. W. leader was born in Salt Lake City in 1869, the son of a miner. He worked underground himself from 1885 to 1901. He joined the Western Federation of Miners in 1896 and became its national secretary treasurer in the year when the Socialist Party was born, 1901.

The metal miners' organization of the West was formed in 1893 and, until it re-affiliated with the American Federation of Labor, was a highly militant union. Its bitter strikes at Cripple Creek, 1894 and 1903-1904, at Coeur d'Alene in 1899, and in the Michigan copper district in 1913-1914, compelled the attention of the nation. The Western Federation of Miners was the heart of the dual trade union movement in the United States between 1898 and 1908. Its officers were the center of one of the most famous cases in labor history, the Moyer-Haywood-Pettibone case of 1905.

§

Although the Western Federation of Miners joined the American Federation of Labor immediately upon its formation in 1893, it seceded in 1897. The following year it launched the Western Labor Union, which changed its name to that of the American Labor Union in 1902, indicating a wider jurisdiction and a menace to the American Federation of Labor, as a dual trade union body. The preamble of the Western Federation of Miners stated "that an industrial union and the concerted political action of all wage workers is the only method" of achieving the emancipation of the working class. The support of the metal miners' union was welcome to all socialists, but the spreading out of the American Labor Union, with a threatened repetition of the fight between a socialist trade union federation and the American Federation of Labor, was not altogether welcome to many. Apart from the western miners' union, which gave them what life they had, the American Labor Union and its predecessor were never much more than paper organizations. Nor did the adoption of a socialist preamble win Colorado for the Socialist Party.

The American Labor Union came home to the new Socialist Party when the latter's management committee, or local quorum as it was called, located in St. Louis, was asked to issue an organizer's commission of the party to a general officer of the union. The experienced trade unionists, William Brandt and G. A. Hoehn, the secretary, Leon Greenbaum, together with the other members of the local quorum, refused to grant the commission on this ground:

While the Socialist Party in national convention has solemnly pledged itself to the unification of the trade unions, yet a contrary policy has been set up in the West by comrades acting in a dual capacity as organizers of the American Labor Union and the Socialist Party, thus misrepresenting the attitude of our party and compromising it in their attempts to build up a rival organization to the American Federation of Labor.

G. A. Hoehn wrote an article in the *International Socialist Review* at the time, headed "The American Labor Movement." His remarks will easily stand the test of time:

Many years' experience has convinced me that the relationship between trades unionism and socialism, *i. e.,* the attitude of the politically organized socialists towards the trade union and general labor movement, is the most vital question in the American socialist movement.

It is significant to know that the socialist movement develops in about the same manner and ratio as the trades unions . . . the same economic causes that produce trades unionism also produce socialism.

While theoretically the Socialist Party adopted an entirely new policy, in reality the everyday practice of many of our party members differs but little from the Socialist Labor Party methods.

Debs took occasion to defend the western labor federation in the November, 1902, issue of Kerr's magazine. His position was never more clearly stated in favor of class unionism and dualism:

Why did they start a dual organization? This is made the burden of the opposition to the western unionists who refused to be assimilated by Mark Hanna's Civic Federation. . . .

And this objection may be dismissed with a single sentence. Why did not those who urge it remain in the Socialist Labor Party and carry on their agitation there? Why split the socialist movement?

It is not wiser to curry favor with numbers than to stand by principles.

When the American Federation of Labor sheds its outgrown pure and simple policy, when it declares against the capitalist system and for union, class conscious action at the ballot box; when it relegates leaders to the rear who secure fat offices for themselves in reward for keeping the rank and file in political ignorance and industrial slavery, when it shall cease to rely upon cringing lobbying committees. . . .

Socialists boring from within will not object to a little help from the outside. In time the two progressive forces will meet and the work of redemption will have been accomplished.

A. M. Simons, in an editorial, criticized the St. Louis committee. He said that they seemed to feel "that the Indianapolis convention organized not a Socialist Party, but an annex to the American Federation of Labor." He threw out a most suggestive explanation for the revolutionary character of the miners' union and the westerners—whether miners or farmers on the newest frontier:

They are . . . made up of freedom-loving, whole-souled people who are not tied down by bigotry and ignorance and made cowardly by fear of losing a six-dollar-a-week job. They are more free than is the worker of the East, and they see that the conditions under which the eastern mill and factory and mine worker labors is liable to overtake them and they are ready to fight it. . . . The western wealth producer will not allow himself to be subjected to the degrading and humiliating servitude of the eastern wage slave.

And after saying this Simons could not see how unreliable and objectively, how reactionary the westerners were, considering the march of the machine process. He did not see that the individualism of the westerner was not the soil in which socialist oaks could grow.

When the national committee of the party met on January 29-31, 1903, to get rid of the St. Louis quorum and Leon Greenbaum as secretary, it declared that the Socialist Party would continue to solicit the sympathy and support of all trade organizations of labor without allowing itself to be made the ally of any one division of the trade union movement as against another.

The men who launched the Industrial Workers of the World were committed to the socialist movement as represented by the revolutionary trade unions, such as the Western Federation of Miners, and the political parties, the Socialist Labor Party and the Socialist Party. Their criticisms of the American Federation of Labor and its constituent unions were as follows:

1. They are built on the craft union system; each craft has its little union and fights its own battles in the main, for relief, but not for the ultimate overthrow of the whole wage system.

Craft unionism shatters the ranks of the workers into fragments, rendering them helpless; it compels union men of one craft to scab upon unionists of another; it fosters hatred of worker for worker instead of promoting industrial and class solidarity; craft jealousies lead to attempts to create trade monopolies; also to efforts of employers to monopolize the product and make the bulk of the workers pay in higher prices, to the advantage of the favored employers and employees; finally, craft divisions foster political ignorance, by not elevating the struggle above the petty issues of the trade and not instilling the feelings of class solidarity to be expressed at the ballot box and on the economic battlefield.

2. The leaders of the craft unions have the limited vision of pure and simple trade unionists; many are corrupt and "sell out" the rank and file to the employers; not having any ultimate goal, not believing in independent political action, not caring about the interests of the mass of workers, apart from their own craftsmen, they make contacts with old party politicians to their own advantage, and above all, they "bind and deliver the working class into the hands of its enemies," such organizations, for example, as the National Civic Federation. The revolutionary unionists charge that "the American Federation of Labor in its last analysis is little more than a clique of labor politicians whose main service is on the parade ground, and who are seldom or never seen on the field of battle." Hence, say the revolutionists, they do not organize the unorganized, they do not amalgamate existing craft unions into industrial bodies, they do not fight the employers energetically; their main occupation is to see that the per capita tax comes to headquarters and that their salaries and expenses are amply taken care of in increasing measure.

The Industrial Workers of the World was accordingly placed squarely on the class struggle and in the preamble it was stated:

Between these two classes [the working class and the employing class] a struggle must go on until all the toilers come together on the political, as well as on the industrial field, and take and hold that which they produce by their labor, through an economic organization of the working class, without affiliation with any political party.

The members of the I. W. W. were all to have the same rights, and the workers were to be admitted freely to any and all of the industrial unions to which they were eligible. There were to be no closed books, high initiation fees or high dues, nor insurance features. That the industrial unionists might bring their united strength to bear on the powerful corporations and trusts, the related unions, and if need be the entire organization, could be called out on strike. The highly centralized body was to issue but one official organ. No contracts were to be signed with employers, tying the hands of workers or unionists and compelling them to refrain from militant and sympathetic class action.

§

At the second convention of the I. W. W., in 1906, there was a serious split, and two years later, in the 1908 convention, the organization was again rent asunder. Thereafter it had a checkered career until 1917 when most of its leaders were imprisoned. Today its main strength is found among the migratory workers and it offers little hope of ever becoming a mass organization or a serious rival of the American Federation of Labor. Neither Daniel De Leon, A. M. Simons, Eugene Victor Debs, nor Ernest Untermann among the socialists fully grasped the difficulties and needs of such a labor organization as the I. W. W. on the economic field. They were propagandists. They tended to stress the ultimate goal of trade unionism, the class struggle and the importance of the ballot, but they did not know how to keep workingmen permanently organized for bread and butter and yet educate them up to socialist ideals.

Offsetting the politically minded socialists were the industrial unionists, such as St. John and Trautmann, westerners, who at first compromised with the "pure and simple" leaders of the Socialist Party, but broke with them in a short time. And then in 1908 the "proletarian rabble" finished the job by cutting loose from Daniel De Leon, and put the I. W. W. on its present basis as an anti-political organization, committed to industrial unionism and the emancipation of the workers by direct action alone. All the high hopes of its founders —especially De Leon, who took the I. W. W. and St. John to his bosom as he had done with the Socialist Trade and Labor Alliance in 1895—were smashed on the rocks of the vagaries of the syndicalists. The Western Federation of Labor, the only *bona fide* affiliated organization with any power, left the I. W. W. soon after the 1906 split.

Vincent St. John, William D. Haywood, and hundreds of known and unknown members of the I. W. W. led some splendid battles for the organization and betterment of the workers. They went where none other dared enter. They showed capacity to galvanize public attention to their strikes and to hold the foreign born workers in stubborn fights. They kept the red flag flying and asserted the right of free speech and peaceable assemblage at the peril of their liberty and lives. But for all that, they failed of their real tasks. They did not keep the workers they enrolled, they did not organize industrial unions, they did not develop a substitute for the American Federation of Labor, and worst of all, they harnessed the militant unionists to the hopeless chariot of dual unionism, and left a clear field to the pure and simple trade union leaders to entrench themselves in their own organizations. The I. W. W. also helped to undermine the faith of the workers in political action, in constructive day-by-day unionism, and in educational processes. It never reconciled itself to the machine process and the necessity of organizing a slowly evolving mass movement. Instead, it put a premium on decentralization, rank and file and isolated job control, irresponsibility of the individual member, and guerilla warfare. It stressed spectacular strikes and spasmodic revolts. It raised up the martyred leader who today is scattered to the four winds. The I. W. W. lacked stability. It was a rebel band of foot-loose fighters.

§

Eugene Victor Debs said of the Socialist Trade and Labor Alliance at the time the I. W. W. was launched: "I concede that their theory is right." He added:

I find myself breaking away from some men I have been in close touch with and getting in close touch with some men from whom I have been widely separated. . . . I now stand ready to take by the hand every man, every woman that comes here, totally regardless of past affiliations. . . .

Max Hayes was not quite so ready to forgive and forget. The latter represented the borers from within. He said:

The day that De Leon has long prayed for has come at last. The Socialist Party can be split.

Already in a score of places dissension has developed in the Socialist Party and we find our own members parroting the phrases coined by De Leon a dozen years ago, writing articles for his disreputable organ, and attempting to revive his malevolent and repudiated policies.

Hayes overlooked the fact, however, that there were revolutionary and dual unionists inside the Socialist Party who saw eye to eye with Daniel De Leon. Several state branches, to say nothing of locals, endorsed the I. W. W. Prominent socialists were identified with it. The members of the Socialist Party overwhelmingly supported both the borers from within and the dualists in their propaganda for industrial *versus* craft unionism. There were also those in the party who nicknamed it the "Slowshulist" party, and who agreed with the I. W. W. and

De Leon that "dropping pieces of paper into a box" did not insure the revolution; that an economic organization was essential to "take and hold" the industries on the day of the final victory, when the party and the capitalist state were to be adjourned *sine die*. There was also a growing number who believed in a party-owned press. The Socialist Labor Party and the Socialist Party were drawing together. Demands were made and maneuvers started for unity.

Apart from the left wingers, there were centrists and right wingers, too, inside the Socialist Party who wanted unity. They believed that unity was desirable because it meant added strength when both were relatively weak; that the existence of two parties confused the workers and voters; and that it prevented individuals and foreign language groups from affiliating themselves with either. The questions of immediate demands, centralization, industrial unionism, a party owned press, and even the personality of De Leon did not seem insurmountable to them.

Unity was never achieved, however. Early in 1908 Berger moved in the national executive committee that members and sections of the Socialist Labor Party be invited to join the Socialist Party. This motion—which prevented unity—was carried. In the May, 1908, convention the matter was thoroughly aired, and by a vote of 131 to 48 the delegates opposed any steps being taken looking towards amalgamation. The majority felt that De Leon would bore from within and wreck the party, they did not believe that the differences were any less real in 1908 than in 1899, and a number could not overlook and forget the past. Between 1905, the year that the I. W. W. was launched, and 1916, when the first real effort was made to achieve unity, some of the states and localities did arrive at agreement, but it was without national official sanction.

The national move for unity did not occur until nearly two years after De Leon's death in 1914. Committees of the two parties met in 1916. On January 7, 1917 they announced their disagreement on the question of their attitude toward the unions. The Socialist Labor Party stood out for a specific condemnation of craft unionism and the endorsement of industrial unionism. This the Socialist Party committee refused to accept.

§

Starting in 1909, after its victory at McKees Rocks, Pennsylvania, where it won a strike and better conditions for the unorganized steel workers, the I. W. W. received a new lease on life. William D. Haywood was now also giving it strength. After being kidnapped and held in jail for fifteen months, charged together with Moyer and Pettibone with the murder of ex-Governor Steunenberg of Idaho—Senator Borah was the prosecuting attorney and Clarence Darrow the defendants' lawyer in this famous case—he was finally acquitted. He toured the country several times, with the backing of the *International Socialist Review*. He found a ready response from the left wingers in the Socialist Party. His star rose when at the end of 1911 he was elected to the national executive committee of the party, the third highest in the list. In 1912 he led the Lawrence strike. This was the peak of the I. W. W. The convention of the Socialist Party of that year passed its anti-sabotage clause, and in February, 1913, its membership, by a referendum vote, recalled Haywood from the national executive committee.

The party refused to put up with his views. He expressed himself very fully and frankly in Cooper Union —his speech is printed in full in the February, 1912, issue of the *International Socialist Review*:

I am going to speak on the class struggle, and I am going to make it so plain that even a lawyer can understand it. I am going to present the class struggle so clearly here tonight that even a preacher will know its meaning. . . . The lawyer and the preacher have never fought with the underdog. For the ages agone they have been the mouthpieces of the capitalist class.

We will have control . . . of whatever forces government can give us, but we will not use them to continue to uphold and advance this present system. But we will use the forces of the police power to overthrow this present system. And instead of using the powers of the police to protect the strike-breakers, we will use the powers of the police to protect the strikers. That's about as far as I go on political action. But that's a long way. And the reason that I don't go into the halls of parliament to make laws to govern the working class is because the working class is working with machines, and every time some fellow has a thought, inspiration, the machine changes, and I don't know that laws can be made quick enough to keep up with the changing machinery.

. . . when these soldiers dispersed the deputies, the miners went into session in their union hall and passed an eight-hour law. Just think of the impudence of those miners. And that law proved to be court-decision proof. It's never been declared unconstitutional by any supreme court.

. . . having contended with all the bitter things that we have been called upon to drink to the dregs, do you blame me when I say that I despise the law and I am not a law-abiding citizen. And more than that, no socialist can be a law-abiding citizen. When we come together and are of a common mind, and the purpose of our minds is to overthrow the capitalist system, we become conspirators then against the United States government.

As before, the mine owners brought in deputies, and there was another mill blown up. . . . It is said that there were 3,000 pounds of powder put under that mill. Naturally, when that powder went off the mill went up.

I again want to justify direct action and sabotage . . . I don't know of anything that can be applied that will bring as much satisfaction to you, and as much anguish to the boss as a little sabotage in the right place at the proper time. Find out what it means. It won't hurt you, and it will cripple the boss.

. . . a Christian socialist is one who is drunk on religious fanaticism and is trying ot sober up on economic truth.

. . . a trade unionist who becomes a party to a contract takes his organization out of the columns of fighting organizations; he removes it from the class struggle and he binds it up and makes it absolutely useless.

In a pamphlet on industrial unionism, written by Haywood and Frank Bohn, who, like a number of others, was so "red" or revolutionary that the Socialist Party was "pink" and "yellow" when he was a member, and who later left it, there was a passage which was the source of much conflict in connection with the attack on Haywood. It read as follows:

> When the worker, either through experience or study of socialism, comes to know this truth, he acts accordingly. He retains absolutely no respect for the property "rights" of the profit-takers. He will use any weapon which will win his fight. He knows that the present laws of property are made by and for the capitalists. Therefore he does not hesitate to break them.

§

The action of the 1912 Socialist Party convention in amending its constitution with article II, section 6 was the result of a long and bitter discussion. Louis B. Boudin endorsed the much discussed passage in the Haywood-Bohn pamphlet:

> We have no more respect for law than we have for brute force. We submit to both as a matter of expediency, and only as long as we find it expedient.

Debs agreed in part with Boudin:

> For my own part I believe the paragraph to be entirely sound. . . . This does not imply that I propose making an individual law-breaker of myself. . . . If I had the force to overthrow these despotic laws I would use it without an instant's hesitation or delay, but I haven't got it, and so I am law-abiding under protest—not from scruple—and bide my time.
>
> Here let me say that for the same reason I am opposed to sabotage and to "direct action." I have not a bit of use for the "propaganda of the deed." These are the tactics of anarchist individuals and not of socialist collectivists. . . .
>
> My chief objection to all these measures is that they do violence to the class psychology of the workers and cannot be successfully inculcated as mass doctrine.
>
> To the extent that the working class has power based upon class-consciousness, force is unnecessary; to the extent that power is lacking, force can only result in harm.

The outstanding leader of the Socialist Party pointed out that the use of sabotage and violence made for guerilla warfare, demoralized those who employed these methods, and opened the door to the agent provocateur, the conspirator, and the madman, the anarchist and the careerist. He said that sabotage could not and did not appeal to the American worker, who is fundamentally law-abiding. "Direct action will never appeal to any considerable number of them while they have the ballot and the right of industrial and political organization." This is where Debs always stood. That is why he always was a socialist and turned his back on the communist method of preparation for armed struggle and civil war.

The Sunday editor of the *New York Call* at the time had some telling comments on Haywood and sabotage. He pointed out first, that Haywood

. . . bases all his concepts on a personal experience, his idea of the class struggle is a series of disassociated class broils . . . those desperate clashes in the mining regions of the West. Well, they are not. It is in that very region that the old-time individualistic possibility of successful enterprise has its greatest opportunity.

Then, as to sabotage, the editor showed that its weakness lay in its impossiblity of accomplishment. He correctly defined it as "an attack upon property held by the master class, and the method of attack consists of impairment of machinery, deliberate lessening of output, or spoiling of product."

In the sharp controversy between the socialists and the pure and simple trade unionists during the McNamara case in 1911, the former insisted that the McNamaras, with their blowing up of the Los Angeles *Times* building, were a logical product of a philosophy which did not rest its case on working class solidarity and independent political action; that the pure and simplers were at bottom anarchists and ultimately and inevitably their only argument was physical force. Direct action, whether employed by the conservative business unionist or the revolutionary syndicalist, led to the use of violence; this was the claim of the socialists.

Morris Hillquit presented the case of the evolutionary socialist:

> We maintain that modern law is in the main class law, capitalist law made to enslave the workers, and we urge a complete change of the juridical system along the lines of the socialist program. But we advocate the introduction of such change by the regular and lawful methods established for that purpose. To preach to the workers lawbreaking and violence is ethically unjustifiable and tactically suicidal. . . . Whenever any group or section of the socialist movement has embarked upon a policy of "breaking the law" or using "any weapons which will win the fight," whether such policy was styled "terrorism," "propaganda of the deed," "direct action," "sabotage," or "anarchism," it has invariably served to demoralize and destroy the movement by attracting to it professional criminals, infesting it with spies, leading the workers to needless and senseless slaughter, and ultimately engendering a spirit of disgust and reaction.

In this discussion, however, Morris Hillquit did say that if the powers that be stole a decisive election or prevented the elected officials of the people from taking office, that the socialists would "fight like tigers and mount the barricades if need be."

The international secretary of the party also made clear at the time his position toward the dual federation: "I have no love for the I. W. W., which has no corporeal existence in the labor movement and is merely a sort of masonic formula for cantankerousness and disruption within the Socialist Party." When Haywood was recalled in 1913 from the national executive committee, the editor of the *Call* expressed the feelings of the center and right wing generally:

> The self-starting imbecilities of both the *Industrial Worker* and *Solidarity* [I. W. W. papers] are equalled only by the persistence with which they insist on it as the duty of the Socialist Party unquestioningly to give money to their strikes, space to their claims, acquiescence to their assaults and credence to their falsehood.
>
> [The *Industrial Worker* of Spokane] publishes a cartoon representing a mangy, starveling cur, tagged "Socialist Party Proletarian," tail between legs, tethered to a stake labeled American

Federation of Labor, and with a big ball chained to one leg. It is hungrily regarding a bone marked "sabotage."

The Socialist Party had endless trouble with the I. W. W., and was glad to get rid of Haywood and his supporters. While leading socialists had helped to launch the industrial union body, they had withdrawn soon after the first split of 1906. Nevertheless the party as an organization and its membership contributed considerable sums to I. W. W. strikes and defense funds.

The Socialist Party and the I. W. W. had little in common. The former advocated political and trade union action, the latter stressed direct economic action exclusively. The first emphasized the use of the ballot, the second would have none of it. The I. W. W. was a dual trade union federation. The trade unionists of the Socialist Party were opposed in the main to dual trade unionism, although Debs and others differed with the majority. The I. W. W. made its primary appeal to the unskilled and foreign born, the unorganized and poorly paid workers. The Socialist Party also addressed itself to these toilers, but it placed its main reliance on the workers and unions already organized. The syndicalist I. W. W. envisaged a general strike as the means of winning final victory. The socialist political body put its hopes in an electoral sweep, backed up by a powerful trade union movement. The I. W. W., finally, did not build lasting unions. It conducted spasmodic revolts. The Socialist Party, or for that matter any labor party, rests its case on the march of the machine process; the organization and education of the working class to take an ever increasing share in the control of the means of production and distribution; and the active participation of the producers in all governmental activities.

§

Notwithstanding the fact that the Socialist Party and the majority of the trade unionists within its ranks were opposed to dual unionism, and notwithstanding the failures of the Socialist Trade and Labor Alliance, the American Labor Union, and the Industrial Workers of the World, early in 1914 Engene V. Debs proposed a split in the American Federation of Labor. He urged the amalgamation of the Socialist and the Socialist Labor Party on the political field. He favored the merging of the unions of the coal and metal miners, the secession of both from the A. F. of L. and the setting up of a revolutionary industrial union federation on the economic field. Nothing came of his suggestion. In the same year Morris Hillquit publicly declared his disagreement with the dual trade union position of Debs. The former said he wanted the A. F. of L. to adopt more progressive policies, but he emphasized his point of view that the A. F. of L. was *the* trade union federation. And yet, when in 1914 the Amalgamated Clothing Workers seceded from the United Garment Workers and indirectly from the A. F. of L., and thus set itself up as a dual union in the men's clothing trade, the New York *Call,* the organ of the eastern socialists of whom Hillquit was the outstanding leader, supported the organization headed by Sidney Hillman and Joseph Schlossberg, and broke with one of its editors in order to do so.

In its conventions the Socialist Party stated that it did not interfere in internal union matters such as the question of industrial *versus* craft unionism. The fact remained, however, that the socialist trade unionists conducted an energetic and persistent fight in favor of industrial unionism. Gompers replied by pointing to the departments in the building, metal, mining and railway industries, besides the numerous amalgamations which he helped to bring about. At the same time, by his fixed opposition to the industrial union resolutions of the socialists, Gompers helped to retard the development toward the industrial form.

The socialists in the unions were equally responsible, however, for holding up the process of amalgamation, by their undue optimism as to the ease with which the change could be achieved, and the benefits to be obtained. They did not realize that the officials and the rank and file often simply refuse to merge themselves, and this regardless of how reactionary, conservative, or revolutionary they are. Organizations hang on with the tenacity of life itself, they strive to continue because of such human traits as habit, love of power, fear of change, jealousy of others, and desire for self-expression.

The socialists also did not realize sufficiently that industrial unionists of and by themselves are no more class conscious than craft unionists, and that they are often no more effective in combatting powerful corporations, as shown in the case of the United Mine Workers. The industrial union is a better fighting weapon, it is line with the development of the machine process, it is in accordance with the concentration of control, and it tends to organize more workers. But the industrial union can be truly effective only when its leaders and rank and file believe in and act upon a labor philosophy that stresses working class solidarity and power. Jurisdictional disputes, high initiation fees, closed books, refusal to accept colored folk, refusal to organize the unorganized, bureaucratic or corrupt leadership, and a privileged rank and file, all these may go along with an amalgamated as with a craft union. It is the spirit and point of view of the leaders and members that count. If the unionists are intelligent, militant, and progressive, then and only then can the industrial form of organization come into its own.

§

The Socialist Party which favored amalgamation on the economic field did not achieve unity on the political. It did not make any effort to secure harmony with the Socialist Labor Party until 1916. With almost no exceptions prior to 1921 the party took official action to prevent any of its division from cooperating with a labor party.

In the days of the Social Democratic Party the New York section sent delegates in September, 1899, to a local Independent Labor Party convention, which grew out of a trolley strike. The national executive ordered the New Yorkers to recall their representatives:

We consider the trades union movement an economic movement only for the purpose of maintaining and possibly elevating the standard of living of the wage workers; and as such, we consider it our duty to uphold it and assist it in every way possible. But the trades unions are by necessity made up of men of all parties, and therefore, cannot lead the proletariat politically. The trades unions must be supplanted on the political field by the Social Democratic movement, which contains the political philosophy of the struggle of the proletariat for the emancipation from wage slavery. The Social Democratic Party —that is, its members—cannot follow the trades unions in their zigzag course in the political field, and they can least of all follow them when that course is capitalistic or semi-capitalist. . . .

The New York section protested but accepted the ruling of the national executive committee. It found it easier to comply inasmuch as the trade union convention seated delegates from a group affiliated with the Chicago Platform Democrats.

In 1902, after a strike on the water front, the labor organizations of San Francisco put up a trade union ticket headed by a musician named Eugene Schmitz as candidate for mayor. The unions launched labor parties in other cities. The socialists of California united with the trade unionists and carried through an amendment to the state constitution of the Socialist Party which permitted locals to refrain from making nominations whenever a *bona fide* labor party was in the field which demanded the abolition of the wage system and put up working class candidates. The matter did not end there. The local quorum or management committee of the national Socialist Party, then located in St. Louis and almost entirely made up of trade unionists, showed a sympathetic attitude toward the policy of those socialists who cooperated with the labor parties. Cameron H. King of California presented in the *International Socialist Review* the point of view of those who favored unity on the political field between the socialists and trade unionists:

The fundamental mistake of the utopians is their assumption that the ultimate interest of men of living under the ideal conditions of a cooperative commonwealth has a sufficient binding or cohesive force to be used in building up a powerful political party. It certainly does attract a certain percentage of idealists and zealots and holds them, inspired and militant, for a considerable time; from others it exacts a temporary allegiance and service; from others, mere intellectual acquiescence. But the vast body it fails utterly to move.

The Socialist Party must become a workingman's party, flesh of their flesh, bone of their bone. It will not do to regard the working class and its immediate interests as something separate from the Socialist Party and its interests and ideals. They must be one . . . it is labor that must be it.

It followed, according to King, that when the unions organized a *bona fide* labor party, the socialists ought to cooperate closely with them, and thus not present the spectacle of a dual, idealistic, and utopian organization, actively or passively opposed to the workers in their struggles on the political field.

It was because the St. Louis local quorum openly expressed its sympathy for a labor party that when the national committee met at the end of January, 1903, it adopted the following resolution calling for expulsion of any local or member "compromising" with a labor party:

Whereas, The history of the labor movement of the world has conclusively demonstrated that a Socialist Party is the only political organization able to adequately and consistently conduct the political struggles of the working class; and

Whereas, All "radical and reform" parties, including the so-called "union labor parties" have, after a brief existence, uniformly succumbed to the influence of the old parties and have proven disastrous to the ultimate end of the labor movement; and

Whereas, Any alliance, direct or indirect, with such parties, is dangerous to the political integrity and the very existence of the Socialist Party and the socialist movement; and

Whereas, At the present stage of development of the socialist movement of this country there is neither necessity nor excuse for such alliance; therefore be it

Resolved, That no state or local organization, or member of the party shall under any circumstances fuse, combine, or compromise, with any political party or organization, or refrain from making nominations in order to further the interests of candidates of such parties or organization.

This was the uncompromising and fixed policy of the Socialist Party until 1921.

§

Notwithstanding the official position of the Socialist Party, socialist trade unionists looked with favor at times upon a labor party. The Milwaukee Federated Trades Council, under socialist leadership, attempted in 1902 the old plan of the Central Labor Federation of New York of welding together the central bodies of the A. F. of L., and thus promoting independent political action and socialism. The executive council of the A. F. of L. had no delusions as to what such a national alliance of city centrals might mean to its own control, and it forced the Milwaukee body to give up its ambitious scheme on the ground that it was treading on the jurisdiction of its parent, the American Federation of Labor, which could revoke its charter if it did not toe the line.

In the 1906 convention of the A. F. of L., when the aggressive non-partisan political policy was adopted, the socialist delegates urged independent political action. Max S. Hayes could write in the same year, however, after the exposure of the odorous and corrupt leaders of the San Francisco Union Labor Party, in a very critical vein of so-called labor parties:

No labor political movement amounts to a hill of beans that does not accept the principles of socialism. This fact has been proven over and over again and only late in California, where the so-called Union Labor Party in San Francisco is in disintegration. Schmitz, Reuf & Co. were merely republicans in disguise and are handing out franchises and special franchises to their capitalistic masters just like other boodle politicians have done before them.

The socialists in the cities had seen so-called labor parties, such as that of the San Francisco stripe, act no differently from the corrupt old parties or the predatory unions, both of which contributed their leadership at times to the far-western city's misnamed labor party.

In the Norfolk convention of the A. F. of L. in 1907, when a moment of good feeling prevailed and socialists and pure and simplers united against the common enemy, a minority of the delegates introduced a resolution calling for the organization of a labor party. The socialist delegates did not support it. In the following year the Danbury hatters' case was decided, in which the union and its members were held to be a conspiracy in violation of the Sherman anti-trust law, and fined triple damages. Gompers, Mitchell, and Morrison were also held in contempt of court in the Buck's Stove and Range boycott case the same year. Some of the socialists prayed that the union leaders would go to jail and come out for a labor party. Said Max S. Hayes:

> Let us sink our differences of the past, as we did in fact at the Norfolk convention and get together in a national conference, as is the desire of the rank and file everywhere, and proceed along the lines of the British socialists and trade unionists, and include the farmers, if they will come, and organize a political combination. . . .

There was a stormy discussion of the question in the A. F. of L. convention of 1908, the socialists putting up a gallant fight for a labor party. By 1913, however, they had changed again and did not support George L. Berry —the president of the pressmen and an aspirant for the vice-presidential nomination in the democratic convention of 1924—when he introduced in the A. F. of L. convention of that year a resolution calling for the very thing that Hayes proposed in 1908.

The action of the British trade unionists in 1906, and the policies of the British Labor Party which they founded, did not receive universal acclaim from the socialists of the United States. William English Walling could say in March, 1909: "Let us all hope that there will never arise a British Labor Party in the United States." It was too conservative and not sufficiently revolutionary for him. John M. Work, otherwise hardly a left winger and one who would give much to see an American labor party today, had little use even for the British Independent Labor Party, the tail of the dog which was supposed to wag the latter, and which was founded as a socialist organization. Work exclaimed:

The Independent Labor Party has started out with a bastard socialism and diluted it with three parts of pure and simple trade unionism.

The Labor Party of Great Britain is less independent and farther from socialism than the so-called Labor Party of San Francisco and farther than a hundred other abortive attempts of the kind we have had in the United States—attempts which have been indignantly cast aside by the good sense of the American working people.

The American socialist press was so full of hostile articles from the pen of Henry M. Hyndman of the Social Democratic Federation and Th. Rothstein, a London correspondent for the radical papers in the United States, that Keir Hardie and Ramsay MacDonald, Philip Snowden and others had to write repeatedly reiterating their socialism and answering specific attacks and charges and explaining alleged deals which they had made with liberals and non-socialist trade unionists. That stalwart Scotch militant, Robert Smillie, records in his autobiography that when he was in Chicago in 1912 the impossibilists there accused him of being a rank opportunist and a conservative labor leader.

§

In 1909 there was a real debate among the socialist leaders on the position of the Socialist Party toward a possible labor party. A. M. Simons wrote his famous letter to Walling on November 19, 1909, after he had attended a session of the American Federation of Labor:

The Socialist Party has become a hissing and a by-word with the actual wage workers of America. . . . I believe that there have been most ridiculous exaggerations of the work of the I. W. W. in Pennsylvania [at McKees Rocks] and of the French syndicalists. . . . I do not like the English policy, but I say frankly it is better than the present Socialist Party. . . . Above all else we must have the union men. No one has denounced the defects of the A. F. of L. more than I, but I am forced to recognize that it comes much nearer representing the working class than the Socialist Party and unless we are able to so shape our policy and our organization as to meet the demands and incarnate the position of the workers we will have failed of our mission.

Following this letter of Simons there was an interchange of correspondence between Morris Hillquit and J. G. Phelps Stokes. The "revolutionist" Stokes warned Hillquit against "compromising too much with the working class," by his sympathetic attitude toward a labor party. Debs was drawn into the fight. He had no love for the A. F. of L. leaders and he wrote:

The Socialist Party has already catered far too much to the A. F. of L., and there is no doubt that a halt will have to be called. . . . If the trimmers had their way, we should degenerate into bourgeois reform. But they will not have their way.

Back of the labor party talk among the leaders was the fact that the Socialist Party had made no gains in 1908 as compared with 1904; that in 1909 the New York socialists suffered a bad slump in their city vote when Hearst ran again; that the courts were hammering the unions; that the British Labor Party had shown how a combination of forces, each retaining its identity, could function and win signal successes; and finally, that there were a number on the national executive committee who were friendly to the idea. When Milwaukee went socialist in 1910 Berger joyfully wrote that all talk of a labor party was over. The Socialist Party successes in the years 1911 and 1912 clinched the matter.

In 1909 there was a national election on for the highest body of the party, the national executive committee, when the labor party issue was raised. The *International Socialist Review,* the organ of the left wing, took it upon itself through Charles H. Kerr, its editor, to telegraph the candidates and request a statement from them as to where they stood on the labor party controversy. The *Review* expressed its own position as follows:

Whether the Socialist Party of America should encourage the formation of a labor party here, and become a part of it, is a vital question to us. To this question the Review's answer is an emphatic NO. For the American trade unions today are as yet conservative rather than revolutionary. They are too much concerned with holding what little advantages skilled laborers still have over unskilled laborers, to realize that the important thing for the working class is to get control of the machinery of production and keep the full value of what they produce.

Among the candidates for the national executive committee who replied was Robert Hunter. In the history of the American Socialist Party, although he did not occupy a commanding position as a theoretician, much less as a political or organizational leader, his healthy attitude toward the trade unions and his position on the relationship between the political and economic arms of the movement, entitle him to signal recognition. He came as close to F. A. Sorge's point of view as it was possible in a succeeding generation. Hunter's work on *Violence in The Labor Movement,* his excellent brochure on *Labor in Politics,* and his copious writings for the socialist and labor press did much to clarify the atmosphere and minimize the influence of the impossibilists and the so-called revolutionists.

In answer to Kerr's telegram Hunter replied as follows:

. . . there is no immediate likelihood of a labor party. . . .
As a socialist I should want to wait until I see what kind of a labor party was formed. In any case I doubt if I should think it advisable for the Socialist Party to merge itself with any other

organization. Certainly before taking any action a socialist would want to have the labor party declare itself distinctly on the following lines:

It would have to be a truly class-conscious labor party. It would have to declare itself absolutely opposed to any fusion or alliance with capitalist parties. It would have to place in its constitution a declaration that any members of the labor party that advocated the election of any capitalist candidate would thereby be excluded from the labor party. In other words, I, as a socialist, would want to know whether or not the labor party intended to be absolutely independent and to carry out actually on the political field the class struggle.

Hunter on another occasion quoted Frederick Engels to the following effect: "I think all our practice has shown that it is possible to work along with the general movement of the working class at every one of its stages without giving up or hiding our own distinct position and even organization." In the New York *Call* of August 17, 1909, he stated the only possible mission of socialists so far as politics is concerned:

The work of socialism is to organize the workers into an independent political organization. We must do here what has been done in every country of Europe; carry the class struggle on to the political field.

To make the working class the arbiter of its own destiny, to make it conscious of its role in social evolution, to make it fearless, independent and self-reliant, is all conscious socialists can do.

Morris Hillquit's position was practically the same as Hunter's. In one of his letters to Stokes he admitted that the Socialist Party "has so far not succeeded" in organizing the working class politically. His reply to Kerr's wire was as follows:

The main object of the Socialist Party is to organize the workingmen of this country into a class-conscious independent political party. If our movement is to succeed at all, this object must be accomplished, and I am not worrying very much about the manner and form of the accomplishment. It would of course be preferable to organize the working class of America within the Socialist Party; this would ensure permanent soundness and clearness of the movement.

If, however, the organized workers of the country, independent of our desires and theories, should form a party of their own, a *bona fide* and uncompromising working class political party on a national scale, I believe the logical thing for our party to do, would be cooperate with such a party. I would not favor a complete merger in any case, because as long as the assumed labor party would not be thoroughly socialistic, our party would still have an important mission to perform, even more so than now.

No national labor party was formed. State and city labor parties, however, were organized. The national executive committee suspended the Arizona branch for helping to start a labor party in 1910. The Washington state branch suspended locals and members for alleged participation in a labor party convention. The Socialist Party did make one important exception, when it asked the support of the A. F. of L. in the fight of Job Harriman for mayor in Los Angeles on a joint labor and socialist ticket in 1911. This was during the time that the McNamara brothers were in prison, charged with the bombing of the Los Angeles *Times* building. On the very eve of the hot city election, with the socialists and laborites lined up on one side and their opponents on the other, the McNamaras confessed. Four days later, on December 5, Harriman polled 50,827 votes against George Alexander's 87,165.

CHAPTER X

1917

ON the occasion of the visit of Karl Liebknecht to the United States in 1910 the New York *Call* ran the following editorial in its issue of October 12:

Karl Liebknecht comes here as a representative of the mighty socialist movement of Germany, the most powerul and most enlightened socialist movement on earth. And this sense of resistless power, of invincible might, finds a most eloquent expression in the words of Karl Liebknecht.

Feeling as it did about the German socialists the eastern socialist daily naturally raised the question four years later as to what "the most powerful and most enlightened socialist movement on earth" was going to do on the very eve of the World War:

What will the voice of labor say in the European crisis? Austria has declared war on Servia, but—? The world has not yet heard from the socialists of Europe. The most important factor in Europe, the factor which the world most wants to hear from, is the great socialist party. What is the powerful Social Democracy of Germany going to say? What is the Socialist Party of France going to say?

When the socialists of Europe, and particularly those of Germany, threw themselves into the war on the side of the governments—with some important exceptions—there was deep disappointment among the socialists of America. The movement in the United States did not make the progress that it was making in Europe, and the socialists here had drawn inspiration and confidence from the victories on the other side. Many of the socialists of America had come to have a very high personal regard for their western European comrades. They

301

read the literature of the movement abroad in the original. The socialists here sadly overestimated the strength and exaggerated the quality of the internationalism of their co-workers across the Atlantic.

The Socialist Party of the United States was far to the left of the more successful European parties. Its absence of control over the trade unions with their bread-and-butter demands, its lack of political strongholds and a large organization to conserve, all this made the American party primarily a party of propaganda and education. And as such it tended to stress Marxian concepts and international socialism. Finally, the Americans, whether socialist or bourgeois, were thousands of miles removed from the conflict, they were not caught in the volcanic eruption, and they did not have their emotions stirred by the hot issues of the bloody contest. They could coolly condemn.

Algernon Lee wrote in the *Call* of December 27, 1914, that in none of the neutral countries was hatred of Germany so intense and so prevalent as in the United States. The pro-ally sentiment affected the American socialists, except those nationalists who wanted Russian Czarism crushed, some pro-Germans, and the true internationalists. Lee explained that the socialists of Germany believed that they were menaced by Russia. He deplored the lining up of Americans into two camps. He appealed to socialists to hold fast "to the ideal of international solidarity." Morris Hillquit declared himself forcefully in the official party weekly, the *American Socialist,* of January 9, 1915:

American socialists should not take sides with the allies as against the Germans. The assertion that the forces of the allied armies are waging a war of democracy against militarism is a hollow catch-phrase devoid of true sense and substance. . . . From the true socialist viewpoint the most satisfactory solution of the great sanguinary conflict of the nations lies in a draw, a cessation of hostilities from sheer exhaustion without determining anything.

There were socialists, however, who wanted Germany decisively defeated and said so. Allan L. Benson, the party's candidate for president of the United States two years later, who left the party because of its anti-war stand after America entered the World War, wrote on August 6, 1914:

> The best thing that can happen to the German people will be to be defeated. First, they need to be taught a lesson, if not as to the rights of others, at least as to the great danger of invading those rights. Secondly, the crushing defeat of the German arms will give the German people an opportunity to throw off the medieval institutions under which they live.

The national executive committee of the Socialist Party, in its appeal to the European socialist parties to consider the immediate holding of an international congress, which it issued a few months after the outbreak of the World War, said: "We do not presume to pass judgment upon the conduct of our brother parties in Europe. We realize that they are victims of the present vicious industrial, political, and military systems and that they did the best they could under the circumstances."

In the first official manifesto issued on August 14, 1914, by the party's national committee on immediate action, the demand was made "that the exportation of money and of munitions of war to the European nations be prohibited. The United States must not aid the powers of Europe to continue their fratricidal strife." Meyer London, then the sole congressman of the party, went so far in May of 1915 as to advocate a general strike to stop shipments of food and ammunition. The national committee of the party, meeting at this time, drew up an extensive peace program, which, in defining the causes of the European war, said that "capitalism, inevitably leading to commercial rivalry and imperialism and functioning through the modern state with its vast armaments, secret diplomacies, and undemocratic governments, logically leads to war." As summarized by Alexander Trachtenberg in his little pamphlet, *The American Socialists and the War,* this program called for no indemnities, no annexations, and free development of the nations. It demanded the formation of an international federation, the United States of the World, "with legislative and administrative powers over international affairs," international ownership and control of strategic waterways and neutralization of the seas; universal disarmament as speedily as possible; and extension of political and industrial democracy. Without prejudice toward any of the warring European socialists, the party statement also said: "We proclaim our determination to join our comrades in the task of rebuilding the Socialist International upon such a basis that henceforth it cannot be shaken by the most violent storms of capitalist conflicts."

§

With the continuation of the World War the eyes of the American socialists became opened to the possibility and even danger of American entry into it. In 1915 a lively propaganda was started in the United States for military preparedness. The socialists were almost unanimously opposed. The national committee meeting of May, 1915, proposed a new section to the party constitution, which went to a referendum and was adopted by 11,041 votes in favor, with only 782 against:

Any member of the Socialist Party, elected to an office, who shall in any way vote to appropriate moneys for military or naval purposes, or war, shall be expelled from the party.

Writing at the time in the *Call,* of which he was associate editor, William M. Feigenbaum expressed the typical socialist attitude:

"Security," "preparedness," "national defense"—these are the sinister words that are on the lips of every one. It is no longer called militarism. It is no longer called war. It is "national defense."

The minority was small, but it was articulate and included a few of the leading figures of the movement. W. J. Ghent, former director of the Rand School of Social Science and a trenchant writer, characterized the new provision providing for expulsion as "an attempt at party suicide." Charles Edward Russell, the idol of the New York socialists, was reported in the *Call* of December 5, 1915, as having declared in a speech delivered in San Francisco:

I hate war. I loathe war. I stood for peace once. I am disillusioned now. I know that we've got to have war and that we've got to get ready the tool for war unless we wish to see, instead of democracy, German autocracy dominate the world for the next two or three hundred years.

Russell's utterance staggered many of the socialists. Eugene Victor Debs came to his rescue. In a statement in the *American Socialist* of January 29, 1916, he pleaded that Russell should not be denounced nor asked to leave the party. Debs added: "I think there is no doubt that but for his utterance on the question of preparedness, on the very eve of the nomination, he would have been chosen as the standard bearer of the party in the coming campaign."

Victor L. Berger, who was known for his opportunism, and who, regardless of how the majority voted, often expressed himself without mincing words, this time dissented sufficiently from the party's position so that a local asked for his recall from the national executive committee. In his statement in the *American Socialist,* during the discussion, Berger said that preparedness was a *fait accompli,* and he proposed that all young men give one year of service to the nation, during which time they were to be taught how to use a machine gun and to be properly educated for American citizenship.

§

In the congressional elections of November, 1914, the American socialists advanced the slogan: "Every socialist ballot is a protest against war." When the presidential campaign of 1916 loomed, the preparedness issue had taken the center of the stage, and the question of America entering the World War faced the voters. The Socialist Party platform of 1916 vigorously opposed both preparedness and war. The party's candidates, Allan L. Benson and George R. Kirkpatrick, were noted for "their conspicuous opposition to war and militarism," and millions of pieces of literature were distributed explaining the party's position. Notwithstanding, in this election the Socialist Party lost about one-third of its vote of 1912.

Benson was not as strong a candidate as Debs. But it is problematical whether even the latter would have made a very much better showing, although he would have reached more people with his magnetic personality and golden voice. Woodrow Wilson's record in office was not yet as repugnant as that of William Howard Taft's. The trade unions were much further from the party than in 1912. The size and quality of the membership was not the same in 1916 as it was four years previously. Above all, the American people voted in 1916 on a burning question of war and peace.

Benson was nominated by referendum, the only time the standard bearers were chosen directly by the rank and file. He ran against James H. Maurer and Arthur Le Sueur, the attorney for the Nonpartisan League, and at that time a left-winger. Debs declined to be a candidate. If a convention had selected the standard bearers, it is quite possible that the president of the Pennsylvania State Federation of Labor would have been the candidate. The more experienced and able parliamentarians, the adroit managers of socialist conventions, hailed from the states which gave Maurer his heaviest support in the referendum, while it was the agricultural and western states which put Benson in the lead. The delegates from these sections were not generally so influential in socialist gatherings as those from the older eastern and industrial states which supported Maurer. What undoubtedly helped Benson was his popularity as a writer of the *Appeal to Reason.*

The agrarian and western states made a fetish of the referendum. A good bit of the space in party bulletins and official organs was taken up by all sorts of propositions, because of the ease with which referendums could be presented to the membership.

§

The attitude of the Socialist Party toward America's entrance into the World War, expressed in the majority report adopted at the St. Louis convention in April of 1917, was due primarily to the fact that unlike the parties of Europe the Socialist Party of the United States in 1917 was not a mass movement. In 1912 the socialists and their sympathizers polled one-third the vote cast in an American Federation of Labor convention. But between 1912 and 1917 the party had lost considerable ground in the unions. The Democratic Party's victory in 1912 and the clever compromises of Woodrow Wilson—called pro-labor bills, the Clayton act, and the like, helped to undermine socialist strength. When the American unions were called on to declare their attitude toward America's participation in the World War, the leaders of the American Federation of Labor and of the unaffiliated railroad brotherhoods, all, with no exceptions, offered their services and pledged their loyalty to the United States on March 12, 1917, that is, before war had even been officially declared against Germany.

One of the methods talked of by radicals to prevent war is the use of a general strike, or at least a strike in the vital war industries, including transport, in order to paralyze the government. In 1917 the American trade unions decided in advance to support the war. The I. W. W. controlled no important industries and its strength was negligible. If the Socialist Party and the trade unions had been as close together in this as in all the other warring nations, the position that the party here took on the war would have reflected it. The labor leaders were all loyally behind Wilson and for bettering the conditions of the workers during the war. The Socialist Party did not in 1917 feel any loyalty to Wilson nor overwhelming concern merely for the bread and butter—and *plus*—of the wage earners on the economic field.

The Socialist Party had also suffered a loss of one-third of its voting strength in 1916 and was not in 1917 the virile party of promise of 1912. It had not kept men in office in nation and state for a sufficient number of years, it had not built up constituencies which it could regard as its own, in the same sense as the European parties had. It did not, therefore, have to face the practical problem of the conservation of a political organization and political strongholds. The party had not become so large and so cautious through success and responsibility, that it needed to weigh carefully the losses in terms of the material welfare of its supporters. The American party had not in reality become integrated in the government and life of the country.

Moreover, the European socialists were caught in the storm. The American socialists had about three years to watch the none-too attractive spectacle of socialist killing socialist. And there were things happening in April, 1917, which encouraged the comrades here to adopt a left wing position. The majority socialists of the leading warring nations were never popular in the United States. News of the growing strength of the opposition was featured in the American socialist press. In March of 1917 came the momentous Russian revolution.

Of the 193 delegates in the St. Louis convention and of the fifteen elected on the committee on war and militarism, only a small number were born abroad. Victor L. Berger, of Austrian antecedents, was chosen thirteenth on the committee and occupied a minor place in the convention. There was an active, although not very large German language federation in the party, but this federation toured the present bolshevik leader, Alexandra Kollontai,

to lecture in this country, it applauded the acts of such
men as Karl Liebknecht and Friedrich Adler, and it
opposed the stand of the majority socialists in Germany.
It was because the opportunists, centrists, and revolutionists all got together for the first time on this question,
it was because the delegates were acting as international
socialists, and not as pro-Germans or aliens, that they
adopted the St. Louis anti-war resolution.

§

It was not until the fifth day that the committee on
war and militarism, which had had protracted and spirited
sessions, made its reports to the convention: Morris
Hillquit for the majority, Louis B. Boudin for one minority, and John Spargo for another. The majority report
was accepted as the basis for further consideration by a
vote of 140, against thirty-one for the Boudin statement
—which differed only slightly from Hillquit's—and five
for the Spargo report. The convention was thus nearly
unanimous. There was an element, however, which
wanted a much more forceful statement than even that
brought in by the majority of the committee.

When the nominations were originally made for the
committee, L. E. Katterfeld of Washington moved that
each nominee be asked the question and required to answer "Yes," or "No:" "Are you opposed to all militarism
and to all war, either offensive or defensive, except the
war of the working class against the capitalist class?"
This motion was defeated only by a vote of 96 to 66,
showing how great was the sentiment against war as such,
except the class war, among the delegates. The Katter-
feld-Ruthenberg group kept on raising amendments to
the document brought in by the committee, but they were
defeated in about the same ratio that Katterfeld's proposition was. Nevertheless, the document presented to the
convention already contained their point of view in the
statement: "The only struggle which would justify the
workers in taking up arms is the great struggle of the

working class of the world to free itself from economic exploitation and political oppression," to which the convention added, on the motion of Kate Richards O'Hare, "and we particularly warn the workers against the snare and delusion of so-called defensive warfare."

§

A minority report was gotten up by those delegates who were in disagreement with the anti-war stand of the party or who wanted the membership to pass on it. Both it and the majority report were submitted to the rank and file. The opposition to the majority statement, by those who took part in the referendum, was negligible. James Oneal states that "every section of the majority report but one received over 21,000 votes, while the "nay" votes with one exception averaged 350." Inasmuch as these reports throw light on the history of the socialist and communist parties, they are worth quoting in full.

MAJORITY REPORT

The Socialist Party of the United States in the present grave crisis solemnly reaffirms its allegiance to the principle of internationalism and working class solidarity the world over, and proclaims its unalterable opposition to the war just declared by the government of the United States.

Modern wars as a rule have been caused by the commercial and financial rivalry and intrigues of the capitalist interests in the different countries. Whether they have been frankly waged as wars of aggression or have been hypocritically represented as wars of "defense," they have always been made by the classes and fought by the masses. Wars bring wealth and power to the ruling classes, and suffering, death and demoralization to the workers.

They breed a sinister spirit of passion, unreason, race hatred and false patriotism. They obscure the struggles of the workers for life, liberty and social justice. They tend to sever the vital bonds of solidarity between them and their brothers in other countries, to destroy their organizations and to curtail their civic and political rights and liberties.

The Socialist Party of the United States is unalterably opposed to the system of exploitation and class rule which is upheld and strengthened by military power and sham national patriotism.

We, therefore, call upon the workers of all countries to refuse
support to their governments in their wars. The wars of the
contending national groups of capitalists are not the concern of
the workers. The only struggle which would justify the workers
in taking up arms is the great struggle of the working class of
the world to free itself from economic exploitation and political
oppression, and we particularly warn the workers against the
snare and delusion of so-called defensive warfare. As against
the false doctrine of national patriotism we uphold the ideal of
international working class solidarity. In support of capitalism,
we will not willingly give a single life or a single dollar; in support of the struggle of the workers for freedom we pledge our
all.

The mad orgy of death and destruction which is now convuls-
ing unfortunate Europe was caused by the conflict of capitalist
interests in the European countries.

In each of these countries the workers were oppressed and
exploited. They produced enormous wealth, but the bulk of it
was withheld from them by the owners of the industries. The
workers were thus deprived of the means to repurchase the wealth
which they themselves had created.

The capitalist class of each country was forced to look for
foreign markets to dispose of the accumulated "surplus" wealth.
The huge profits made by the capitalists could no longer be profit-
ably reinvested in their own countries, hence they were driven to
look for foreign fields of investment. The geographical bound-
aries of each modern capitalist country thus became too narrow
for the industrial and commercial operations of its capitalist class.

The efforts of the capitalists of all leading nations were, therefore, centered upon the domination of the world markets. Imperialism became the dominant note in the politics of Europe.
The acquisition of colonial possessions and the extension of
spheres of influence became the object of diplomatic intrigues
and the cause of constant clashes between nations.

The acute competition between the capitalist powers of the
earth, their jealousies and distrusts of one another and the fear
of the rising power of the working class forced each of them to
arm to the teeth. This led to the mad rivalry of armament, which
years before the outbreak of the present war had turned the leading countries of Europe into armed camps with standing armies
of many millions, drilled and equipped for war in times of
"peace."

Capitalism, imperialism and militarism had thus laid the foundation of an inevitable general conflict in Europe. The ghastly war
in Europe was not caused by an accidental event, nor by the policy

or institutions of any single nation. It was the logical outcome of the competitive capitalist system.

The six million men of all countries and races who have been ruthlessly slain in the first thirty months of this war, the millions of others who have been crippled and maimed, the vast treasures of wealth that have been destroyed, the untold misery and sufferings of Europe, have not been sacrifices exacted in a struggle for principles or ideals, but wanton offerings upon the altar of private profit.

The forces of capitalism which have led to the war in Europe are even more hideously transparent in the war recently provoked by the ruling class of this country.

When Belgium was invaded, the government enjoined upon the people of this country the duty of remaining neutral, thus clearly demonstrating that the "dictates of humanity" and the fate of small nations and of democratic institutions were matters that did not concern it. But when our enormous war traffic was seriously threatened, our government calls upon us to rally to the "defense of democracy and civilization."

Our entrance into the European war was instigated by the predatory capitalists in the United States who boast of the enormous profits of seven billion dollars from the manufacture and sale of munitions and war supplies and from the exportation of American foodstuffs and other necessaries. They are also deeply interested in the continuance of war and the success of the allied arms through our huge loans to the governments of the allied powers and through other commercial ties. It is the same interests which strive for imperialistic domination of the Western Hemisphere.

The war of the United States against Germany cannot be justified even on the plea that it is a war in defense of American rights or American "honor". Ruthless as the unrestricted submarine war policy of the German government was and is, it is not an invasion of the rights of the American people, as such, but only an interference with the opportunity of certain groups of American capitalists to coin cold profits out of the blood and sufferings of our fellow men in the warring countries of Europe.

It is not a war against the militarist regime of the Central Powers. Militarism can never be abolished by militarism.

It is not a war to advance the cause of democracy in Europe. Democracy can never be imposed upon any country by a foreign power by force of arms.

It is cant and hypocrisy to say that the war is not directed against the German people, but against the Imperial Government of Germany. If we send an armed force to the battlefields of

Europe, its cannon will mow down the masses of the German people and not the Imperial German Government.

Our entrance into the European conflict at this time will serve only to multiply the horrors of the war, to increase the toll of death and destruction and to prolong the fiendish slaughter. It will bring death, suffering and destitution to the people of the United States and particularly to the working class. It will give the powers of reaction in this country the pretext for an attempt to throttle our rights and to crush our democratic institutions, and to fasten upon this country a permanent militarism.

The working class of the United States has no quarrel with the working class of Germany or of any other country. The people of the United States have no quarrel with the people of Germany or any other country. The American people did not want and do not want this war. They have not been consulted about the war and have had no part in declaring war. They have been plunged into this war by the trickery and treachery of the ruling class of the country through its representatives in the National Administration and National Congress, its demagogic agitators, its subsidized press, and other servile instruments of public expression.

We brand the declaration of war by our government as a crime against the people of the United States and against the nations of the world.

In all modern history there has been no war more unjustifiable than the war in which we are about to engage.

No greater dishonor has ever been forced upon a people than that which the capitalist class is forcing upon this nation against its will.

In harmony with these principles, the Socialist Party emphatically rejects the proposal that in time of war the workers should suspend their struggle for better conditions. On the contrary, the acute situation created by war calls for an even more vigorous prosecution of the class struggle, and we recommend to the workers and pledge ourselves to the following course of action:

1. Continuous, active, and public opposition to the war, through demonstrations, mass petitions, and all other means within our power.

2. Unyielding opposition to all proposed legislation for military or industrial conscription. Should such conscription be forced upon the people, we pledge ourselves to continuous efforts for the repeal of such laws and to the support of all mass movements in opposition to conscription. We pledge ourselves to oppose with all our strength any attempt to raise money for payment of war expense by taxing the necessaries of life or issuing bonds which

will put the burden upon future generations. We demand that the capitalist class, which is responsible for the war, pay its cost. Let those who kindled the fire, furnish the fuel.

3. Vigorous resistance to all reactionary measures, such as censorship of press and mails, restriction of the rights of free speech, assemblage, and organization, or compulsory arbitration and limitation of the right to strike.

4. Consistent propaganda against military training and militaristic teaching in the public schools.

5. Extension of the campaign of education among the workers to organize them into strong, class-conscious, and closely unified political and industrial organizations, to enable them by concerted and harmonious mass action to shorten this war to establish lasting peace.

6. Widespread educational propaganda to enlighten the masses as to the true relation between capitalism and war, and to rouse and organize them for action, not only against present war evils, but for the prevention of future wars and for the destruction of the causes of war.

7. To protect the masses of the American people from the pressing danger of starvation which the war in Europe has brought upon them, and which the entry of the United States has already accentuated, we demand—

(a) The restriction of food exports so long as the present shortage continues, the fixing of maximum prices and whatever measures may be necessary to prevent the food speculators from holding back the supplies now in their hands:

(b) The socialization and democratic management of the great industries concerned with the production, transportation, storage, and the marketing of food and other necessaries of life;

(c) The socialization and democratic management of all land and other natural resources now held out of use for monopolistic or speculative profit.

These measures are presented as means of protecting the workers against the evil results of the present war. The danger of recurrence of war will exist as long as the capitalist system of industry remains in existence. The end of wars will come with the establishment of socialized industry and industrial democracy the world over. The Socialist Party calls upon all the workers to join in its struggle to reach this goal, and thus bring into the world a new society in which peace, fraternity, and human brotherhood will be the dominant ideals.

MINORITY REPORT

Congress has declared that a state of war exists between this nation and Germany. War between the two nations is a fact.

We opposed the entrance of this republic into the war, but we failed. The political and economic organizations of the working class were not strong enough to do more than protest.

Having failed to prevent the war by our agitation, we can only recognize it as a fact and try to force upon the government, through pressure of public opinion, a constructive program.

Our aim now must be to minimize the suffering and misery which the war will bring to our own people, to protect our rights and liberties against reactionary encroachments, and to promote an early peace upon a democratic basis, advantageous to the international working class.

Furthermore, we must seize the opportunity presented by war conditions to advance our program of democratic collectivism. Every one of the other belligerent nations has discovered through the war that capitalism is inherently inefficient. To secure a maximum of efficiency, whether for military or civil needs, it has been found necessary to abandon the essential principle of capitalist industry. The warring nations have had to give up the organization and operation of industry and primary economic functions for profit, and to adopt the socialist principle of production for use. Thus the war has demonstrated the superior efficiency of collective organization and operation of industry.

Guided by this experience, we would so reorganize our economic system as to secure for our permanent domestic needs the greatest possible results from the proper utilization of our national resources.

In furtherance of these aims we propose the following:

1. We propose that the Socialist Party shall establish communication with the socialists within the enemy countries, to the end that peace may be secured upon democratic terms at the earliest possible moment.

2. We demand that there be no interference with freedom of speech, freedom of the press, and freedom of assemblage.

3. We demand that dealings between the government and the workers in all of the industries and services taken over and operated by the government shall be conducted through their organizations with due regard to the right of organization of those not yet organized.

4. We demand that conscription, if it comes at all, shall begin with wealth. All annual incomes in excess of $5,000 should be taken by the government and used to pay the current expenses

of the war. If it is just to conscript a human being, it is just to conscript wealth. Money is not as sacred as human life.

5. We demand that there shall be no conscription of men until the American people shall have been given the right to vote upon it. Under the British Empire the people of Australia were permitted to decide by ballot whether they should be conscripted. We demand for the American people the same right.

6. We demand that the government seize and operate for the benefit of the whole people the great industries concerned with production, transportation, storage and marketing of the food and other necessities of the people.

7. We demand that the government seize all suitable vacant land and have the same cultivated for the purpose of furnishing food supplies for the national use.

8. We demand that the government take over and operate all land and water transport facilities; all water powers and irrigation plants; mines, forests and oil fields; and all industrial monopolies; and that this be done at once, before the nation shall suffer calamity from the failure of their capitalist direction and management under war pressure.

§

The adoption of the majority report against the war caused a number of prominent socialists to leave the party. Some of these were hardly consistent in their attitude, before and after the St. Louis anti-war resolution was made party policy. John Spargo, for example, who had protested against the Boer War at the risk of his life, though he later became violently pro-ally, said in 1915 when the preparedness debate was going on:

It is easy to affirm international solidarity in times of peace, when the skies are unclouded, but the test of our faith comes with war and the threat of war. And now more than ever we need to affirm our faith unshaken, to set our faces and our hearts against hatred, against war, against militarism, and trust in the sword.

A. M. Simons had repeatedly given vent to utterances which helped to build up the sentiment which resulted in the St. Louis declaration:

There is no room in the same world for militarism and socialism (*American Socialist* of November 21, 1914).

We should quit asking for votes on the ground of our superior administrative ability (which we do not possess), of our greater anxiety to lower taxes (which it would be a bad thing to possess), of our nationalistic patriotism (of which we should be ashamed). . . . It is not knowledge we lack but courage (*American Socialist* of February 6, 1915).

The first ray of light from the bloody darkness of Europe has come in the call issued by the International Socialist Conference in Switzerland [Zimmerwald]. Out of the cowardly compromise, insane jingoism, and contemptible desertion of socialist principle that has turned cold the enthusiasm of those to whom socialism was something more than office-seeking, vote-counting and bureau-cratic-supporting, has come a call that shows that the old faith is still there (*American Socialist* of October 23, 1915).

Furthermore, Simons did not leave the Milwaukee *Leader,* where he wrote side by side with Victor L. Berger, until the early part of 1917. And yet, despite his vehement protestations, Simons could say after the St. Louis anti-war resolution was adopted, that it was "technically and insultingly treasonable," and that the party had been scuttled by "German nationalistic jingoes and anarchistic impossibilists."

Together with Simons who left the party for its anti-war stand were other "revolutionists," whose attacks on the "reformists" while they were members made them conspicuous as "reds." There were, of course, a number who had been consistently to the right of the party and quite naturally left it after St. Louis. In addition to these "shining lights," the Socialist Party by its declaration against the war lost a goodly group of trade union leaders. But these losses of individuals were not so important, after all. It was the attacks of governmental and unofficial agencies, which began soon after the St. Louis convention adjourned, that hurt the organization vitally.

The press of the party was hardest hit. The official weekly, the *American Socialist,* was barred from the mails soon after the espionage act was approved on June 15, 1917. The *Appeal to Reason* with its immense circulation had become pro-war under another name, *The New Appeal.* On November 13, 1917, the New York *Call* was deprived of its second class mailing privileges. According to Roger Baldwin's compilation, during the first year of the war most of the socialist papers were either held up by the Post Office Department or had their second class mail privileges revoked. Without its press the party was greatly handicapped.

The organization could not conduct its business without fear of official or non-official interference. In May the Indiana state headquarters at Indianapolis was raided. In September the national headquarters in Chicago was occupied for three days and "samples of all literature on hand, files of socialist publications, financial records, and letter files, in addition to much other matter was taken." The Ohio state headquarters in Cleveland, and several other party offices, were invaded. A Socialist Party convention at Mitchell, South Dakota, in January, 1918, was broken up. Private mail was tampered with. In the smaller cities and rural areas local socialists, if they were militant at all, ran economic, social, and even personal risks.

§

Eugene V. Debs delivered at Canton, Ohio, on June 16, 1918, his anti-war speech for which he was sentenced to ten years' imprisonment. There were dozens outside and inside the Socialist Party who paid the price of their convictions. Among the prominent members of the party who were sentenced to prison and who served part or all of their terms, were, in addition to Debs, J. O. Bentall, Stanley J. Clark, Joseph M. Coldwell, Emil Herman, Frederick Krafft, Kate Richards O'Hare, Charles E. Ruthenberg, A. L. Sugarman, Alfred Wagenknecht, and Hulet M. Wells. On February 2, 1918, the national officials of the Socialist Party were indicted, tried, found guilty and sentenced on February 20, 1919. The men who were then given twenty years in prison included Adolph Germer, secretary, Louis Engdahl, editor of the official organ, William Kruse, secretary of the Young

People's Socialist League, Irwin St. John Tucker, author of the pointed bit, "The Price We Pay," and Victor L. Berger, one of the leading members of the national executive committee. Two years after they were convicted, during which the sentence had hung over their heads, the United States Supreme Court set the convictions aside. The prejudice of Judge Kenesaw Mountain Landis, who tried the case, was given as one reason. He is reported to have said:

It was my great displeasure to give Berger twenty years in Fort Leavenworth. I regretted it exceedingly, because I believe the laws of this country should have enabled me to have Berger lined up against a wall and shot.

It was by this same judge in Chicago that the 100 leaders of the I. W. W., including William D. Haywood, were tried in April, 1918, and sentenced to long prison terms. In the Sacramento case many of the I. W. W. members conceded the bias of the court and populace and refused to put up any defense whatever. It was in the prejudiced atmosphere of 1917 and 1918 that the socialists, pacifists, rebel I. W. W.'s, and other opponents of the war were tried and convicted.

The editors of the *Masses* were tried twice but each time the jury disagreed and finally the indictments were dismissed. In the first case Max Eastman, Floyd Dell, and Art Young, the editors, and Merrill Rogers, the business manager, were the defendants; in the second, John Reed, who had meanwhile returned from Russia, was included. Scott Nearing and the Rand School of Social Science were also indicted and tried, the former for writing and the latter for publishing his pamphlet, *The Great Madness*. Nearing was acquitted but the school was fined $3,000. In the fall of 1918 Mollie Steimer, twenty years old, was sentenced to fifteen years in prison for distributing leaflets against intervention in Russia. A number of professors in the universities were dropped, including Carl Haessler who went to jail, while many teachers in the public schools in New York and elsewhere were

dismissed. Attorneys were disbarred. Where meetings
were allowed and halls not closed to the socialists, stenog-
raphers were present, and spies abounded. Reports came
to the national office of the party that in the southern
and northwestern states it was practically impossible for
the locals to function.

In his study, *The Conscientious Objector in America,*
Norman Thomas does not list, among the young men
who preferred to go to jail rather than serve in the armed
forces of the United States, those who were or became
socialists. There were dozens, however, who were opposed to all wars and to the war against Germany on
socialist grounds. It was not cowardice nor was it a
relief to go to jail and take its consequences in war days.
The conscientious objectors were often treated worse than
ordinary criminals. Thomas records that they were confined "in unsanitary guardhouses—sometimes in unheated
cells during winter months, without blankets . . . men
were forcibly clad in uniform, beaten, pricked or stabbed
with bayonets, jerked about with ropes around their necks,
threatened with summary execution, tortured by various
forms of the 'water cure'." Guards dug their thumbs
into the eyes of the objectors who were thrown into
solitary cells, and subjected to physical tortures worthy
of medieval days. Some of the prisoners resorted to
suicide and strikes in order to compel humane treatment.

§

Within a year of the St. Louis convention of 1917 the
position of important sections of the Socialist Party had
changed. The seven socialist aldermen of New York
City, the center of anti-war feeling, when they were
elected in the previous November, came out in April of
1918 in support of the third liberty loan. Algernon Lee,
leader of the aldermanic delegation, explained that the
results of the Interallied Socialist and Labor Conference,
the attacks by Germany upon Russia which had had its

second revolution, and above all, the support that Wilson gave to the terms of peace which socialists in America and abroad favored, made it unnecessary to oppose the war as such; that, by supporting the liberty loan, encouragement would be given the president to continue his negotiations for a settlement that the radicals desired.

The Illinois socialists held a state convention in May, 1918, and it was only by the close vote of 31 to 27 that the minority was beaten, which advocated support of the war in order to defeat Germany and promote a Wilsonian peace. In June a convention of the Massachusetts socialists by a vote of 72 to 46 urged support of the Russian Soviet Republic and commended Wilson's 14 points. The strikes and revolts in the central powers, the second Russian Revolution, the publication of the war aims of the British Labor Party, and the 14 points of Woodrow Wilson, were responsible for a real shift in the position of the party.

There was considerable discussion among leading socialists, therefore, of the desirability of restating the party position and holding a special convention for the purpose. The newly elected national executive committee, the state secretaries, representatives of the foreign language federations, and some others did, accordingly, get together on August 10, 1918. A national convention, it was said, was out of the question because of the espionage act and the fact that many of the socialists were either in jail or under indictment. The national executive committee adopted a resolution strongly endorsing the Russian soviet government, which it described as being "of the workers, by the workers, and for the workers." On the war itself, the highest governing body of the Socialist Party merely said:

Our record of opposition to the German Kaiser was consistent, continuous and uniform before the war. It will continue until the Kaiser is dethroned. We shall attack the institutions of kaiserism, no matter where they appear, until they are banished from the face of the earth.

The party even modified its position within a month or two after the St. Louis convention in one important respect. The People's Council of America for Democracy and Peace was organized with the help of leading socialists. Its first local conference was held on May 30-31, 1917, in New York; similar local meetings were organized in a number of other cities, until a call went out for a national gathering for September 1, 1917. This congress was prevented from assembling in Minneapolis, and when it did get together in Chicago, Governor Lowden sent troops to break it up. The program of the People's Council was not that of the Socialist Party of 1917. To that extent the latter had given up the St. Louis anti-war resolution. The Council merely called for an immediate announcement by the government in concrete terms of its war aims, and stressed a peace which met only part of the demands of the American socialists. It made no mention whatever of opposing the war, nor did it even discuss its causes and the necessity of eradicating them. In truth, then, both as an independent socialist body, and through the liberal and pacifist People's Council which it sponsored and supported, the Socialist Party did not stand in 1918 where it stood in April, 1917. Whatever the reasons, the fact remained that by the middle of 1918 important sections of the party were no longer seriously, if at all, opposed to the war. By this time also the socialist needle trades unions came out quite openly in favor of the war.

§

In the April and November elections of 1917 the Socialist Party made extraordinary gains in a number of the largest cities of the country. It played up its anti-war position and made it practically the only issue of the campaigns. In New York City the socialists made their greatest showing in November, 1917, with their outstanding leader, Morris Hillquit, as candidate for mayor. They had an organization then that they have never matched since. In the heat of the campaign they were able to fill Madison Square Garden a half dozen or more times to its capacity of 15,000. They caught Tammany Hall napping and there was no fusion. Accordingly, the party sent ten assemblymen to Albany and seven aldermen to the City Hall.

The situation in the other cities where the socialists scored in 1917 was as extraordinary as in New York: the old parties were caught unawares and the people were in a mood to respond to the socialist anti-war cry. In some of the leading cities, however, such as New York, Chicago, and Cleveland, the anti-war vote of 1917 came from certain nationalities preponderantly.

The socialist vote did not slump much in the spring of 1918, but in the November, 1918, congressional campaign it fell badly, except in Wisconsin. Meyer London was defeated for reelection to Congress, and instead of ten assemblymen, only two were reelected in the Jewish-American socialist strongholds of New York City. These two survived because they did not face the combined opposition of the Republican and Democratic Parties, which fused on one candidate in the remaining eight assembly districts. The eight defeated socialist candidates made good showings but were not able to get a majority in the uneven contest.

Outside of the larger cities the Socialist Party organization had suffered severely because of the St. Louis anti-war resolution. The remaining and healthy part of the movement was now to undergo a terrific internal crisis. The armistice of November 11, 1918, was not half as significant for the American socialists as the second Russian Revolution of November 7, 1917, when the bolsheviki seized power.

CHAPTER XI

COMMUNIST VERSUS SOCIALIST

THE Socialist Party had about 40,000 members when in 1908 its national office published some figures as to the countries of birth of the dues-paying adherents. It revealed the fact that over two-thirds of the membership were natives:

Country of Birth	Per Cent	Country of Birth	Per Cent
United States	71	Great Britain	4
Germany	8½	Finland	2
Denmark, Norway and Sweden	5	All Other	9½

Of the foreign born members, many, if not most, were from lands with advanced labor and socialist movements. From 1909 to 1917 also, the Socialist Party was a party of natives and assimilated immigrants. The delegates to its conventions in 1901, 1904, 1908, 1910, 1912, and 1917 were not of the foreign quarters of the United States. In appearance, language, tradition and outlook they were Americans of at least several generations.

In the nineties and continuing through the present century there was a tremendous influx of immigrants into the United States from the eastern and the southern countries of Europe. These newcomers were chiefly peasants and proletarians from areas which were relatively undeveloped industrially. They were toilers whose standard of living was low and who did not have much contact with a modern labor movement in their home countries. They were unused to democratic government. Some were planning to stay here only long enough to accumulate sufficient money to return and spend it in their mother countries. It was next to impossible to reach these proletarian immigrants through the regular English party branches. The Socialist Party tried to attract them through special language federations, where those speaking the same language could belong to their own organization.

The 1910 congress of the party supplied the constitutional framework for these language federations by providing that 500 or more members of a foreign language speaking group could organize a national federation with the right of having a translator-secretary in the headquarters of the party, whose salary was to be paid by the party. In the 1912 convention the question of the relation of the non-English organizations to the party proper came up for considerable discussion. Charles E. Ruthenberg, later the leader of the left wing and secretary of the Workers' (Communist) Party, stated that the local units of the foreign language federations hardly ever came in touch with the regular party branches. This convention decided that the federations were to continue as autonomous bodies, except insofar as they had a translator-secretary in the national party office, and paid 50 per cent of the regular dues to the state branches. In other words, they could have their own officers, their own organizers, their own conventions, their own dues, and their own press and literature. They were allowed to continue as wheels within the party machine, practically independent of and without any supervision from the party. Their activities would be known, at best, to but a few of the regular party officials.

According to James Oneal's table in his book, *American Communism,* the national language federations were admitted to the Socialist Party in the following years:

Finnish	1907	German	1913
Lettish	1908	Polish	1913
South Slavic	1911	Jewish	1913
Italian	1911	Slovak	1913
Scandinavian	1911	Ukrainian	1915
Hungarian	1912	Lithuanian	1915
Bohemian	1912	Russian	1915

In their reports to the 1912 convention the translator-secretaries claimed for the Finnish federation 11,483 members, the South Slavic, 1,266, the Italian, 1,200, the Bohemian, 1,164 the Scandinavian, 1,000, and the Lettish, 983.

In a membership of 118,045 for the year 1912 the total of those in the foreign language bodies, under 16,000, could not seriously affect the character or program of the Socialist Party. It should be noticed, however, that after 1912 there was a sharp drop in the party's membership:

1903...15,975	1908... 41,751	1913...95,957	1918... 82,344
1904...20,763	1909... 41,479	1914...93,579	1919...108,504
1905...23,327	1910... 58,011	1915...79,374	1920... 26,766
1906...26,784	1911... 84,716	1916...83,284	1921... 13,484
1907...29,270	1912...118,045	1917...80,379	1926... 12,000

In 1913 four new language federations were admitted. By 1915 the number of dues-paying socialists was down to about 80,000, one-third less than in 1912. But of more serious consequence was the fact that of the 80,000, between 25,000 and 30,000 were in the foreign language federations. In 1919 the Socialist Party of the United States had about 110,000 members, over half of whom, however, belonged to non-English-speaking bodies, to the autonomous and practically independent language federations.

§

The foreign language federations were supposed to devote themselves exclusively to agitation, education, and organization among their own people who did not speak or read English. They were supposed to keep their members informed of the problems of America and the American Socialist Party. In practice, however, the language federations did not confine themselves to propaganda, and many of them, according to Oneal, "constituted small national Socialist Parties attached to the American organization." In the 1912 convention some of the federations were accused of spreading literature against religion. The fraternal delegate from the Bohemian organization declared that they were fighting the churches which attacked socialism. In its report to this convention the Lettish federation advocated a vigorous fight on the church where it interfered in the labor movement. In the Lettish report, seven years before the split of 1919, these revolutionary socialists had already declared in favor of mass action.

During the disastrous internal fight among the metal miners of Butte, Montana, Mayor Lewis J. Duncan, elected on the socialist ticket, had his troubles with the Finnish socialists. Eric Lantala, leader of the local Finns, stabbed Duncan, and the mayor shot the Finnish socialist. When the Industrial Workers of the World were riding high, there were many members of the foreign language federations, as among the recent immigrants generally, who were only too ready to embrace a rival to the American Federation of Labor, which they distrusted.

After the World War broke out there was a split in the Polish federation over supporting the volunteer legions to fight on the side of Austria against Russia. There were serious differences in a few other federations. Resentment was expressed at the interference of some of the federations in the national referendum for election of the secretary of the party in 1916—when Germer won out. But apart from these relatively unimportant cases, the federations were generally praised for their good work and their loyalty to the American Socialist Party. For, despite their smaller numbers, their lower wages, and their own needs—to maintain a press and various institutions—the foreign-speaking socialists came through handsomely in aid of the regular party papers and campaigns.

One of the most generous in the past and one of the mainstays of the Socialist Party at present is the organ of the Jewish socialists, the *Forward*. It has contributed hundreds of thousands of dollars to the labor and socialist movement of this country. Started in 1897, the paper reached a circulation of 200,000 before 1917, which despite the cutting of immigration it has retained down to the present day. This circulation was built up largely through the efforts of one man, Abraham Cahan. In his hands, said Harry Rogoff, it became "the literary guide, the dramatic criterion, the scientific preceptor, the socialist agitator, the domestic court of the great masses of immigrant Jews in this country." A membership corporation, to which the leading Jewish socialists belong, controls the paper. B. Charney Vladeck is its present manager.

The Finnish socialists also gave large sums to the party, despite the fact that they had more newspapers, publishing plants, libraries, cooperatives, and buildings to maintain than any other of the foreign socialist groups. The various federations contributed not a few dollars besides to the socialist parties of Europe, and raised sums for touring the leaders of the latter in the United States. The language federations helped in immeasurable ways toward the education of their own and other party members in socialism and trade unionism. The influence of the *Volkszeitung* in this respect, when it was edited by a scholar like Hermann Schlueter, was as valuable to the Socialist Party as any financial contributions.

§

On January 5, 1919, a mass meeting of Chicago socialists was held to further the municipal campaign. A correspondent of the New York *Call* described the scene in these words:

Eight thousand socialist voices shouted until they were hoarse at the Coliseum this afternoon at every mention of the word "bolsheviki." The occasion was the launching of the mayoralty campaign. . . . Kate Richards O'Hare and Ella Reeves Bloor were the principal speakers.

John Collins, candidate for mayor, brought down the house first by an accidental mention of the Russian bolsheviki. From that moment until the close the attention of the vast audience seemed directed more to the present happenings in Siberia . . . than it was on the municipal platform as outlined by the socialist candidate for mayor of Chicago.

This was the temper of the socialists at the opening of the year 1919. Some of the most ardent supporters of the bolsheviki were the leaders and members of the rapidly increasing language federations. Between December, 1918 and April, 1919, the membership of the Russian federation jumped from 2,373 to 7,824; the South Slavic, from 1,200 to 3,115. As has been stated, prior to the split in 1919 the Socialist Party officially claimed 108,504 members, of which 57,248 belonged to the language federations, or 53 per cent of the total.

In the organization of the left wing, in the formation of the first two and subsequent communist parties, in the underground and in the legal communist movement of America, it was the old language federations of the Socialist Party, however transformed, which played a leading part, and which still predominate in the Workers' (Communist) Party today. The communist movement in the United States was and is, of course, of the same cloth as that in the rest of the world, but with this one striking difference. In this country it started out and has remained, up to the present at least, as an expression in the main of radical immigrant workmen. It is today where the socialist movement was in the eighties and nineties, when it was dominated by German-Americans.

The last published membership figures of the Workers' (Communist) Party cover the first six months of 1925, before it abolished the language federations and adopted the shop and street form of organization. There have been changes, but it is doubtful if there has been any radical shift in the composition of the party. At that time, of the 16,325 members claimed, only 2,282 were given as in the English-speaking branches. Not all of these, of course, were born in this country. The over-whelming proportion of the membership was in the language federations. The following table gives the picture for 1925:

Language Federation	Membership
Armenian	132
Czechoslovak	295
Esthonian	70
Finnish	6,410
German	350
Greek	256
Hungarian	509
Italian	331
Jewish	1,447
Lettish	434
Lithuanian	815
Polish	121
Rumanian	47
Russian	870
Scandinavian	211
South Slavic	1,109
Slovenian	14
Ukrainian	622
English	2,282
Total	16,325

One of the interesting points about the foregoing table is the fact that almost two-thirds of the members of the Workers' (Communist) Party in 1925 were born in countries which were either part of the old Russian empire or which are inhabited by Slavs. The total membership of the language federations of the Finns, the Jews, the Russians, the Ukrainians, the Lithuanians, the Letts, and the South Slavs amounted to 11,707. In Europe there are powerful indigenous communist parties in Russia, Germany, Czechoslovakia, and France, to mention only leading nations. But in the United States the Workers' Party has not yet attracted any considerable body of natives. The split in the Socialist Party in 1919 was the result of forces which divided the socialist move-

ment throughout the world, the *raison d'etre* of the Workers' Party is the same here as elsewhere, but it can be
fully understood at this stage of its history only in terms
of the foreign-born elements which led the left wing
in 1919 and which dominate the communist party today.

§

The germs of communism were lodged in the body of
the socialist movement from its inception in 1848 when
the *Communist Manifesto* was given to the world. They
were active in practically every socialist party of the
world at one stage of its career, or among certain of its
adherents at all times. They played havoc with the
socialist movement soon after the World War broke out
because nearly all the parties of the warring countries
turned nationalist. Oppositions developed with a more
or less communistic philosophy, stressing internationalism
and revolutionary socialism, with the out-and-out communists demanding the conversion of the imperialist into
civil war, with the goal of domination or dictatorship
by the proletariat.

On November 7, 1917, occurred the bolshevik Russian
Revolution. The moderate socialists seized power in Austria and Germany in 1918. The left wing socialists set
up soviet governments in Bavaria and Finland, and in
1919 the communists established a dictatorship in Hungary. The spartacans now attempted to repeat in Germany the success of the bolsheviks in Russia, and by an
uprising take power from the socialists. They failed.
The soviet governments of Finland, Hungary, and Bavaria were overthrown. The communists were not strong
enough to retain power anywhere outside of Russia.

The Second (socialist) International had been destroyed in 1914. Representatives of the leading communist and near-communist groups gathered in Moscow,
March 2-6, 1919, and established the Third (communist)
International. They declared in no uncertain words their
undying hatred and opposition toward the majority social-

ists who had fought on the side of their governments. They also pointed out, however, that they could not cooperate with the independents who had broken away from the majority groups. They attacked, for example, the British Independent Labor Party, the German Independent Social Democratic Party, and other opposition socialist parties. They declared that these centrist groups were unwilling to accept their communist program and adopt their revolutionary tactics.

The second congress of the Communist International, held in 1920, drafted the famous twenty-one points as conditions for affiliation. Successive congresses and executive committees have drawn up voluminous theses— rather long-winded for Americans—but the twenty-one points still give a good clue to what was in the minds of the communist and near-communist elements the world over, including the United States, in 1919-1920, and what is in their nerve cells today.

These theses made clear the irreconcilable conflict between communist and socialist. In the United States the native and foreign born members of the Socialist Party who turned left wing and communist organized their forces in 1919 and set out to capture or split the old organization, or tear away what groups they could and establish a party to carry out the communist program in accordance with these theses of the Third International.

§

TWENTY-ONE POINTS OF THE COMMUNIST (THIRD) INTERNATIONAL

1. The entire propaganda and agitation must bear a genuinely communistic character and agree with the program and the decisions of the Third International. All the press organs of the party must be managed by responsible communists, who have proved their devotion to the cause of the proletariat.

The dictatorship of the proletariat must not be talked about as if it were an ordinary formula learned by heart, but it must be propagated for in such a way as to make its necessity apparent to every plain worker, soldier, and peasant through the facts of daily life, which must be systematically watched by our press and fully utilized from day to day.

The periodical and non-periodical press and all party publishing concerns must be under the complete control of the party management, regardless of the fact of the party as a whole being at that moment legal or illegal. It is inadmissible for the publishing concerns to abuse their autonomy and to follow a policy which does not entirely correspond to the party's policy.

In the columns of the press, at public meetings, in trade unions, in cooperatives, and all other places where the supporters of the Third International are admitted, it is necessary systematically and unmercifully to brand, not only the bourgeoisie, but also its accomplices, the reformers of all types.

2. Every organization that wishes to affiliate with the Communist International must regularly and systematically remove the reformist and centrist elements from all the more or less important posts in the labor movement (in party organizations, editorial offices, trade unions, parliamentary groups, cooperatives and municipal administrations) and replace them with well-tried communists, without taking offense at the fact that, especially in the beginning, the places of "experienced" opportunists will be filled by plain workers from the masses.

3. In nearly every country in Europe and America the class struggle is entering upon the phase of civil war. In such circumstances the communists can have no confidence in bourgeois legality.

It is their duty to create everywhere a parallel illegal organization machine which at the decisive moment will be helpful to the party in fulfilling its duty to the revolution.

In all countries where the communists, because of a state of siege and because of exceptional laws directed against them, are unable to carry on their whole work legally, it is absolutely necessary to combine legal with illegal activities.

4. The duty of spreading communist ideas includes the special obligation to carry on a vigorous and systematic propaganda in the army. Where this agitation is forbidden by exceptional laws it is to be carried on illegally. Renunciation of such activities would be the same as treason to revolutionary duty and would be incompatible with membership in the Third International.

5. It is necessary to carry on a systematic and well-planned agitation in the country districts. The working class cannot triumph unless its policy will have insured it the support of the country proletariat and at least a part of the poorer farmers, and the neutrality of part of the rest of the village population. The communistic work in the country is gaining greatly in importance at the present time.

It must principally be carried on with the help of the revolutionary communist workers in the city and the country who have connections in the country. Renunciation of this work or its transfer to unreliable, semi-reformist hands is equal to renunciation of the proletarian revolution.

6. Every party that wishes to belong to the Third International is obligated to unmask not only open social patriotism, but also the dishonesty and hypocrisy of social pacifism, and systematically bring to the attention of the workers the fact that, without the revolutionary overthrow of capitalism, no kind of an international court of arbitration, no kind of an agreement regarding the limitation of armaments, no kind of a "democratic" renovation of the League of Nations will be able to prevent fresh imperialistic wars.

7. The parties wishing to belong to the Communist International are obligated to proclaim a clean break with reformism and with the policy of the "center" and to propagate this break throughout the ranks of the entire party membership. Without this a logical communist policy is impossible.

The Communist International demands unconditionally and in the form of an ultimatum the execution of this break within a very brief period. The Communist International cannot reconcile itself to a condition that would allow notorious opportunists, such as are now represented by Turati, Kautsky, Hilferding, Hillquit, Longuet, MacDonald, Modigliani, et al., to have the right to be counted as members of the Third International. That could only lead to the Third International resembling to a high degree the dead Second International.

8. In the matter of colonies and oppressed nations a particularly clear-cut stand by the parties is necessary in those countries whose bourgeoisie is in possession of colonies and oppressed other nations.

Every party wishing to belong to the Communist International is obligated to unmask the tricks of "its" own imperialists in the colonies, to support every movement for freedom in the colonies, not only with words but with deeds, to demand the expulsion of its native imperialists from those colonies, to create in the hearts of the workers of its own country a genuine fraternal feeling for the working population of the colonies and for the oppressed nations and to carry on a systematic agitation among the troops of its own country against all oppression of the colonial peoples.

9. Every party wishing to belong to the Communist International must systematically and persistently develop a communistic agitation within the trade unions, the workers' and shop councils, the consumers' cooperatives, and other mass organizations of the workers.

Within these organizations it is necessary to organize communistic nuclei which, through continuous and persistent work, are to win over the trade unions, etc., for the cause of communism. These nuclei must be completely under the control of the party as a whole.

10. Every party belonging to the Communist International is obligated to carry on a stubborn struggle against the Amsterdam International of the yellow trade unions. It must carry on a most emphatic propaganda among the workers organized in trade unions for a break with the yellow Amsterdam International. With all its means it must support the rising international association of the Red trade unions which affiliate with the Communist International.

11. Parties wishing to belong to the Third International are obligated to subject the personnel of the parliamentary groups to a revision, to cleanse these groups of all unreliable elements, and to make these groups subject to the party executives, not only in form but in fact, by demanding that each communist member of parliament subordinate his entire activities to the interests of genuinely revolutionary propaganda and agitation.

12. The parties belonging to the Communist International must be built upon the principle of democratic centralization. In the present epoch of acute civil war the communist party will only be in a position to do its duty if it is organized along extremely centralized lines, if it is controlled by iron discipline, and if its party central body, supported by the confidence of the party membership, is fully equipped with power, authority, and the most far-reaching faculties.

13. The communist parties of those countries where the communists carry on their work legally must from time to time institute cleansings (now registrations) of the personnel of their party organization in order systematically to rid the party of the petit bourgeois elements creeping into it.

14. Every party wishing to belong to the Communist International is obligated to offer unqualified support to every soviet republic in its struggle against the counter-revolutionary forces. The communist parties must carry on a clean-cut propaganda for the hindering of the transportation of munitions of war to the enemies of the soviet republic; and furthermore, they must use all means, legal or illegal, to carry propaganda, etc., among the troops sent to throttle the workers' republic.

15. Parties that have thus far still retained their old social democratic programs are now obligated to alter these programs within the shortest time possible and, in accordance with the particular conditions of their countries, work out a new communist program in the sense of the decisions of the Communist International.

As a rule the program of every party belonging to the Communist International must be sanctioned by the regular congress of the Communist International or by its executive committee.

16. All decisions of the Congresses of the Communist International, as well as the decisions of its executive committee, are binding upon all the parties belonging to the Communist International. The Communist International, which is working under conditions of the most acute civil war, must be constructed along much more centralized lines than was the case with the Second International.

In this connection, of course, the Communist International and its executive committee must, in their entire activities, take into consideration the varied conditions under which the individual parties have to fight and labor, and only adopt decisions of general application regarding such questions as can be covered by such decisions.

17. In connection with this, all parties wishing to belong to the Communist International must change their names. Every party wishing to belong to the Communist International must bear the name: communist party of such and such a country (section of the Third International). The question of name is not only a formal matter, but is to a high degree a political question of great importance.

The Communist International has declared war upon the whole bourgeois world and all yellow social democratic parties. It is necessary to make clear to every plain workingman the difference between the communist parties and the old official social democratic and socialist parties that have betrayed the banner of the working class.

18. All the leading press organs of the parties of all countries are obligated to print all important official documents of the executive committee of the Communist International.

19. All parties that belong to the Communist International, or that have applied for admission to it, are obligated to call, as soon as possible, but at the latest not more than four months after the second congress of the Communist International, a special convention for the purpose of examining all these conditions.

In this connection the central bodies must see to it that all the local organizations are made acquainted with the decisions of the second congress of the Communist International.

20. Those parties that thus far wish to enter into the Third International, but have not radically changed their former tactics, must see to it that two-thirds of the members of their central committees and of all their important central bodies are comrades who unambiguously and publicly declare in favor of their parties'

entry into the Third International before the second congress of the Communist International.

Exceptions may be allowed with the approval of the executive committee of the Third International. The executive committee of the Communist International also has the right to make exceptions in the cases of the representatives of the center tendency named in paragraph 7.

21. Those party members who, on principle, reject the conditions and theses laid down by the Communist International are to be expelled from the party.

The same thing applies especially to delegates to the special party convention.

§

The Socialist Party of the United States had opposed America's entrance into the World War in 1917 and had adopted the St. Louis anti-war resolution. The left wing claimed that the right wing and centrist leaders had not carried out the terms of this resolution. In the September-October, 1917, number of the *Class Struggle,* Louis B. Boudin ridiculed the People's Council, with which the Socialist Party leaders were identified.

Ludwig Lore attacked Meyer London because he claimed the congressman had "neglected every opportunity of manifesting serious opposition to war—in direct violation of the wording of our St. Louis program and resolution." Boudin also demanded the recall of Victor L. Berger from the national executive committee of the party. He charged the Milwaukee leader with being pro-German and not anti-war. Boudin also held that Hillquit had not taken an international socialist position against war. He quoted him as follows:

If I had believed that our participation would shorten the duration of the world war and force a better, more democratic and more durable peace, I should have favored the measure, regardless of the cost and sacrifices of America.

The left wing attacked the New York socialist aldermen for endorsing the third liberty loan in 1918.

Leon Trotsky was in the United States just prior to America's entering the war. At a special meeting of

Local New York of the Socialist Party he presented a minority report along communist lines eight months before the bolshevik revolution in Russia. His program called for active opposition to the war through strikes, mass resistance to conscription, and intensification of the class struggle.

As early as 1915 S. J. Rutgers presented to the readers of the *International Socialist Review* the declarations of those minority and communist groups who convened in Zimmerwald, Switzerland, in September, 1915. When the Communist or Third International was established in March, 1919, the left wing demanded that the American Socialist Party affiliate with it, and condemn the Berne conference, where socialist as distinguished from communist parties gathered in February, 1919, to attempt to re-create a socialist international. The national executive committee of the American party sent delegates to the Berne conference. To the left wing this was capitulation to the "traitors" and "social patriots," as well as to the wavering and untrustworthy centrists. The spokesmen of the communists called the leaders of the right wing and center "Noskes," "Scheidemanns," "Kerenskys," and "Kolchaks." They accused these socialists of being ready to do what they charged Noske and Scheidemann had actually done in Germany, kill communists of the type of Karl Liebknecht and Rosa Luxemburg.

Through the *New International* and the *Class Struggle,* and later in the *Revolutionary Age,* Louis C. Fraina, a young man in his middle twenties, helped to disseminate the important documents of the communists of Europe, especially those emanating from Moscow. He and Rutgers wrote voluminously, explaining and popularizing the new tactics of mass action, revolutionary trade unionism, and preparation for armed conflict in civil war. They paved the way for the manifestoes of 1919.

"The left wing," wrote Dr. Morris Zucker in the *Call* of April 11, 1919, "believes that a revolutionary outbreak in America is not a matter of the far and distant future."

In truth, with its revolutions and soviet governments, Europe was cracking in 1919. Zucker declared that there was developing throughout the capitalist world

. . . the clean-cut, death struggle between capital and labor, between the Entente group and the Bolshevist group. We in America do not yet feel the hot breath of this titanic struggle, due to our geographical situation. But it is only a question of time, a short time until it reaches us here as inevitably as the great war finally reached America. The capitalist world is a single organism with various parts and America is today an important part.

If the world, including America, was going through a period of revolution it followed, from the left wing point of view, that all emphasis should be placed on preparation for it. To pay attention to ameliorative measures, such as cheaper food, better housing, or protection against unemployment, sickness, or old age for the masses, to stress the immediate demands of the movement was stupid and futile. Zucker exclaimed for the left wingers generally:

Work for immediate demands? Today our immediate demand can only be the unconditional surrender of the capitalist class and the establishment of a proletarian state.

The left wing charged the right wing and centrist elements with cooperating with non-socialist groups and individuals for a labor party and for amnesty. Jay Lovestone, at present joint secretary with Foster of the Workers' (Communist) Party, wrote in the *Call* of February 6, 1919 that the left wingers would

. . . not devote their energy to the organization of a political party opposed to the Socialist Party—even though it be a "Labor Party," engineered by the labor fakers in particular and the most bitter opponents of socialism in general.

The left wing charged the right wingers with making personal campaigns for office, with cooperating with liberals like Dudley Field Malone, and advocating petty reforms, such as cheap milk, in the memorable 1917 campaign in New York City. They maintained that the party leaders were associated with pacifists in the amnesty drives, and attacked them for not simply coming out with

a declaration in favor of using the revolutionary might
of the working class to compel the powers that be to open
the prison gates to the political and class war prisoners.
They asserted that some of the right wing and centrist
leaders lacked courage and had gone back on the St.
Louis resolution and international socialism by their hesi-
tating defenses when tried in courts of law.

§

Even prior to our entrance into the World War some
Boston left wingers had organized on November 26, 1916,
the Socialist Propaganda League with a program not essentially different from that contained in the manifestoes
of 1919. In February and March of the latter year, however, the New York and the Chicago left wingers got
together on a much more substantial basis and organized
their forces. The New Yorkers adopted a manifesto and
program of the left wing which they sent out broadcast
to the various state and local branches of the party
throughout the country. The left wingers everywhere
bombarded the socialist press and assemblies with their
new slogans.

They did not stop at education and propaganda. They
issued membership cards to their supporters, they tied
them up through caucuses, they instructed them in military fashion, and they went about capturing socialist locals
and state branches in a thoroughly organized manner. In
New York City, one of the storm centers, they captured
the Brooklyn, the Bronx, and Queens locals. Outside of
the metropolis they won quite a number of state branches
and city locals. Those foreign language federations which
had turned left wing cooperated with them. A national
left wing conference was the next step. It was held in
New York on June 21, 1919.

At this conference there were two factions, one that
wanted the immediate organization of a communist party,
another that wished to continue to bore from within the

Socialist Party, hold a convention at the same time as it did, and capture or split it. The delegates of the foreign language federations were the backbone of the first group, and when they were defeated by a vote of fifty-five to thirty-eight, withdrew. They issued a call for a convention to launch a new party, committed to a communist program. The elements which refused to accept their tactics also sent out a call for a convention. The Socialist Party had already issued an official call for an emergency convention to be held on August 30, 1919, in Chicago. While some of those, who in the June conference had refused to go along with the language federations later changed their minds and endorsed their program, the rest of the left wingers went ahead on their original plan. All three conventions were now set for the same time and place. The socialists were out to keep their party intact and under their control, the left wingers who opposed the dictation of the foreign language federations wanted an "American" communist party, while the leaders of the federations and those natives who saw eye to eye with them were determined to keep the communist movement in their hands, in order, as they saw it, that it might be genuinely bolshevik.

§

The right wing and centrist leaders of the Socialist Party did not sit idly by while the left wing organized its forces. Wherever they were in control of the party press they used it to present their own point of view, although they gave space to the opposition. They felt that it was absurd to advocate mass action and preparation for civil war in America in 1919, that there was no revolutionary situation here, and that those who said that there was were either fanatics, fools, or spies. The *Call* repeated time and time again that America was not Europe:

We have no vast laggard hordes stricken with famine, made desperate by the war and ready for working-class control. We have no economic structure almost wrecked by the war. We have no great casualties, no great swarms of crippled and discontented soldiers returning with the more or less vague intention of overthrowing capitalism.

The editor referred to the conservatism of the trade unionists, the relative prosperity of the American workers and the weakness of socialism in the United States. One of the common remarks of those opposed to the left wing was that there were "too many socialists who board in this country but really live in Europe."

Cameron H. King of California expressed his fears for the party's future, if the left wing captured the organization:

> I oppose the left wing policy of advocating at this time "revolutionary mass action" for the "armed conquest of the state," because under the criminal syndicalist law it is punishable by . . . imprisonment. Our officers will be jailed; our membership intimidated; our meetings suppressed; and our funds consumed in lawyers' fees.

The right wingers pointed to the fact that a mild labor party was only beginning to take hold in 1919, and that against the desires of the trade union leaders. They asked, if American workers would not even support the Socialist Party on a moderate program, if they would not cast *ballots* in their own behalf, what prospect was there of them mounting the barricades and resorting to *bullets*?

The opposition to the left wing answered the latter's specific attacks. The right wingers and centrists denied that they had gone back on the St. Louis anti-war resolution by demanding terms of peace which socialists throughout the world asked for, or by cooperating with anti-war liberals and pacifists in the People's Council to compel Woodrow Wilson to announce his fourteen points. They claimed that they had done all they could as international socialists to prevent the war, to oppose it after it was declared, and to bring it to a close, using all possible legal and constitutional means. They believed that to employ illegal tactics would get nowhere. They argued that it was impossible to secure amnesty for the political prisoners—among whom were right wingers and centrists as well as left wingers—by merely passing resolutions and calling upon the American working class to display its power. They felt that the American workers would not even listen, much less go out of their way to strike or take any action to put pressure upon the authorities in favor of amnesty. They claimed that they had cooperated with whatever persons would actually help open the doors to those who were languishing in jail.

They denied that they had supported or cooperated with the rising reformist labor parties. They stated their position as to a new international: that they were glad to include the Russian and German communists but they could not see how a world federation worthy of the name could possibly be set up excluding every party that was not communist. Finally, and most important, the old leaders of the Socialist Party in the United States made it very clear that they were willing to modify program and tactics, but they were not willing to abandon democratic and peaceful methods, they were not willing to wipe the immediate demands out of the platforms of the party, and they were not willing to swallow whole the Russian communist program and tactics for America. They insisted that they were socialists and Marxians and were unalterably oposed to what they regarded as unsocialistic and un-Marxian theory and practice.

§

The right wingers and centrists did not stop at argument and persuasion—any more than the left wingers did —to meet the phalanxes of the latter. Wherever the rights lost a branch or local, after protracted and bitter fighting in meetings running to all hours of the night and consequent discouragement of those not intensely interested, they promptly "re-organized" it without the opposition. There was a good deal of "re-organization" work to do. The rights controlled the national executive committee, the supreme body of the party. They used their power to keep the machinery in their own hands and get rid of the lefts. Conversely, wherever and whenever the lefts were in control, they used their authority in bolshevik fashion to build up a monolithic machine and crush the rights. It was a struggle for power between communist and socialist.

In May, 1919, the national executive committee suspended the seven left wing language federations, Hungarian, Lettish, Lithuanian, Polish, Russian, South Slavic, and Ukrainian. By this operation it cut off about one-third of the party membership. It also revoked the charter of the Michigan state branch. The following June it eliminated the regular Massachusetts body, and in August it severed the Ohio state branch, one of the largest in the party. What with the "re-organizations" by local and state divisions, together with the drastic suspensions by the national executive, the Socialist Party was in a much-weakened condition when the emergency convention opened on August 30, 1919, in Chicago.

The members of the party had voted in the spring of the year for new officers, a national and international secretary, delegates to the international congress, and a national executive committee. When the old executive met in May, although the left wing candidates—on the face of the returns—were the victors, it instructed the secretary not to tabulate the vote. Instead, it appointed a committee to investigate the alleged irregularities which the convention of the party in August was to finally pass upon. It also decided that until this gathering no referendums on controversial questions would be allowed. The executive continued in office and made its report to the delegates of the emergency convention.

This report pointed out that the left wing had participated in the election of delegates to the very Berne conference which they later attacked. It added that the leaders of the party had no more defended the results of this poor attempt at re-establishing an international than had the communists. It stated that the left wing had slandered the party officials as "Kolchaks" and "Noskes," when they had come out again and again for wholehearted support of the soviet government of Russia, and had condemned "the actions of those in Germany who have betrayed the working class of Germany and the socialists of the world."

The national executive committee said of the left wing that "they were dominated by the one persistent motive of securing power." As a result:

An astounding state of affairs resulted. Veterans and pioneers of the movement, who had served the party in many ways for ten, twenty and thirty years, suddenly found they had no rights within the party but to pay dues. Members of the left wing, some of them never having joined the Socialist Party, some of them having only a card of the Left Wing, some of them being members only a few weeks, usurped all rights within the party organization.

In a supplementary report, gotten up at the request of the convention, the executive committee stated the grounds on which the federations and the state branches had been suspended. Massachusetts and Ohio had definitely declared for the dual left wing, as the executive viewed it, and the party officials wanted to prevent them from adding their strength to those on the inside who were bent on capturing the organization. Michigan had adopted a platform without immediate demands. The language federations, through their translator-secretaries, their press, and officials had heaped abuse upon the party, its leaders, and its policies; they had committed frauds in the referendum election and they had declared they would not abide by the decisions of the regular party branches. The executive held that "either the national executive committee had to accept the offending federations as a self-constituted supreme court with power to veto our decisions, or else suspend the federations."

In 1899 the right wing and centrist leaders of the Socialist Party had split the old Socialist Labor Party, as in 1889 the Jonas-Schevitsch faction had split it previously. In 1919 the left wing attempted to do to the old

Socialist Party leaders what the latter had done twenty and thirty years ago to the Socialist Labor Party. Regardless, then, of the legal or constitutional grounds, regardless of the tactics employed by the left wing, the important fact remained that the division between the factions in 1919 was so deep that they could not occupy the same house. In these circumstances it was inevitable that the communists and the socialists should separate and organize their own parties.

§

The regular Socialist Party convention opened in the machinists' union hall of Chicago on August 30, 1919. Before the national secretary, Adolph Germer, called it to order, however, there was a physical encounter between some of the right and left wing leaders. According to the version of Julius Gerber, one of the mainstays of the rights in the convention:

He stated that a typewritten circular was being distributed in which he was accused of having called the police to eject a number of delegates who were in the hall in the morning. He branded that statement as being untrue . . . he was at the hall . . . assisting the janitor in getting the hall in order . . . a number of people came up and took seats in that part of the hall reserved for delegates. He asked one of them whom he was sure was not a delegate (John Reed of New York) what business he had to enter the hall reserved for the delegates. . . . Reed tried to shove him aside, and when he tried to prevent Reed from entering the hall, there was an altercation. . . . During this altercation the police entered the hall, and he (Gerber) never called the police or had anything to do with ordering the police in ejecting the people in the hall.

The main business before the convention was the passing upon the credentials of delegates, the report of the special committee on the irregularities in the referendum election for party officials, the acts of the national executive committee in suspending the federations and the state branches, the taking of a stand with reference to a new international, and the adoption of a program in accordance with the conditions of post-war America.

The right wingers and centrists were in control of the convention. They tried to be lenient toward those left wing delegates against whom objections had been raised on various grounds. But despite the fact that they seated nearly all of those who applied, the left wingers, who were prepared to bolt, did not continue long in the regular party convention, some not even taking seats. There was an element, however, which later seceded from the Socialist Party, which stuck throughout this convention because it was not ready in 1919 to join the communist forces.

The convention approved the findings of the special committee on the referendum election and the acts of the national executive committee, thus giving the *coup de grace* to the dying efforts of the left wing to capture the party machinery. The delegates provided, however, that hereafter the convention was to elect the members of the national executive committee and that a board of appeals was to be set up to hear charges in case of future suspensions of federations and state branches.

Among a large number of resolutions adopted at this gathering one indicated the fact that the party of 1919 had gone considerably to the left. This resolution unqualifiedly endorsed industrial unionism. Morris Hillquit, who was unable to attend the convention on account of illness, which prevented him from functioning very actively for a year or more, advocated in the *Call* of May 21, 1919, not only amalgamation into industrial bodies but also one working class union.

There was little real disagreement among the delegates as to what kind of an international the Socialist Party of the United States favored. Nevertheless, a minority brought in a demand that the convention endorse the Third International, regardless of its programs and methods, which it did not approve, and "whatever we may have to say to 'Moscow' afterwards." The majority report opposed endorsing the Communist International and called for a new world federation which would be more inclusive, which would include the communists, certainly, but would not keep out those parties which declared "their strict adherence by word and deed to the principle of the class struggle." Both factions were agreed that "no party which participates in a government coalition with parties of the bourgeoisie shall be invited." The question went to a referendum. The minority report received 3,475 votes, against 1,444 for the majority statement of the convention. There were still many left wingers inside the party, despite the suspensions and withdrawals.

§

The national executive committee did not announce the results of the spring referendum for the election of party officials, when in May of 1919 it declared the election null and void on account of the frauds which it claimed the federations had practiced to win it. The lefts, however, obtained the returns from twenty-six states and the District of Columbia, and broadcast the fact that they had won a sweeping victory, electing Alfred Wagenknecht national secretary and an executive of their tendency. On July 26, accordingly, the "new" secretary, Wagenknecht, demanded possession of the national office. He was turned down. The left wingers went ahead, however, on the assumption that they were now *the* party.

They rented another hall in the machinists' union building, just below the meeting place of the regular Socialist Party. A number of them, prior to the opening of the convention of the latter, tried to capture it physically. Julius Gerber and the police dissuaded them from attempting to carry out any "direct action" tactics. They then decided to try the credentials committee and the convention itself. They found that they did not have the majority. Thereupon they called their own convention with those delegates who did, and those who did not apply for admission to the regular Socialist Party gathering, who were of their point of view.

Representatives from the seven suspended foreign language federations, the Michigan state branch, and some other minor groups were in Chicago also to hold their own convention to establish a pure communist party, in "Smolny Institute," the headquarters of the "reds" of the Windy City. They numbered 137 delegates, representing, according to their figures, 58,000 members. The left wingers' meeting in the machinists' union building had 92 delegates from 22 states and claimed more than 30,000 members. The only important matter before both these communist conventions was the question of unity. The machinists' union hall gathering was much more anxious to achieve it than the "Smolny" group.

The Smolny Institute gathering was dominated by the leaders of the federations. It refused even to consider the request for a conference with the left wingers until threatened with a bolt by some of the English-speaking elements within its ranks. The exchange of documents and the negotiations were fruitless. The "Smolny" group contrasted its own delegates with the "heterogeneous bolting delegates" of the left wing. In one of its documents it made this interesting statement:

There are delegates with you on the basis of objection to "foreign" control, thus showing inability to grasp the first principle of communism. Think of such an objection against an organization which is to be the American branch of the Communist International.

It attacked the left wingers as not understanding communist principles and tactics and as being united in opposition to the Socialist Party chiefly, on legalistic, personal, or other grounds. It would accept only those delegates who passed through the sieve of its credentials committee.

The left wing convention answered:

We shall probably never find ourselves in agreement with the tactic of hopping from one position to another at the rate of nearly twice a week, in direct violation of the mandates of higher governing bodies and agreements.

It was referring to the original plan adopted in June to
capture the Socialist Party which some of the "Smolny"
folk broke faith on. It also took pains to attack the in-
congruity of the opportunistic Michigan body being tied
up with the dyed in the wool communist federations. Notwithstanding, it stood ready to meet the communist group
"on the basis of equality." This attitude it maintained to
the end.

After the left wingers found the "Smolny" crowd ad-
amant, they went ahead and organized a party which they
called the Communist Labor Party. The purists carried
out their original scheme and founded the Communist
Party. In its resentment against the autonomous language
federations which had helped wreck the Socialist Party—
and might destroy them, too—and which stood in the way
of communist unity, the Communist Labor Party adopted
a constitution providing that such bodies were to be solely
propaganda affairs—a pious wish—with their local
branches tied up with and subordinate to the regular party
organizations. The Communist Party decreed, in order
to keep itself proletarian, that no one who received his
entire livelihood from rent, interest, or profit would be
admitted as a member.

In the matter of platform and program, the Communist
Labor Party put more emphasis on the political struggle,
although it came out for "only one demand: the establishment of the dictatorship of the proletariat," and advocated
revolutionary trade unionism and political strikes. The
Communist Party declared that "participation in parliamentary campaigns . . . is of secondary importance,"
while "the great industrial struggles of the working class"
would be "its major campaigns, in order to develop an
understanding of the strike in relation to the overthrow
of capitalism." It stated that in these general mass strikes
which it proposed to participate in, the workers would be
prepared for "the complete assumption of industrial and
social control." It came out for a dual union federation
as opposed to the American Federation of Labor, and for

revolutionary industrial unionism. In spite of differences, the programs of the Communist and the Communist Labor Party were both communist. The former simply placed more emphasis on trade union and mass action and less on the political struggle than the latter. This division has continued until the present day in the Workers' (Communist) Party.

The Communist Labor Party elected A. Wagenknecht as secretary, and chose the following five, regardless of geographical location, as its national executive committee: Alexander Bilan, Jack Carney (now in Ireland), L. E. Katterfeld, Edward Lindgren, and Max Bedacht. On the important conference committee with the "Smolny" group Ludwig Lore (later expelled from the Workers' Party but still the editor of the *Volkszeitung*) was a member. In addition, Benjamin Gitlow, John Reed (buried beside the Kremlin in Moscow), and Louis Boudin represented New York. According to Max Eastman's account, Boudin fled the convention when it adopted a communist as against a "centrist" program, by a vote of 46 to 22. Ruthenberg, the head and fount of the communist movement of America and for many years secretary of the Workers' Party, now dead, and like Reed buried in the sanctuary of Moscow, sat in at first in the Communist Labor Party convention, but left it. Margaret Prevey (now deceased), and Charles Baker, besides Ruthenberg, came from Ohio. William Bross Lloyd, who has given up carrying the red flag, Edgar Owens, and Charles Krumbein were delegates from Illinois, Arne Swabeck from Washington, and J. M. Coldwell from Rhode Island.

C. E. Ruthenberg was made executive secretary of the Communist Party, while Louis C. Fraina (mysteriously gone, about whom all sorts of rumors persist) was elected international secretary. I. E. Ferguson, (today outside the movement), was assistant editor of the official organ, *The Communist*. Three of the most influential delegates in the Communist Party convention were Alexander Stoklitsky and Nicholas I. Hourwich (both now in Russia) and Joseph V. Stilson, all of whom spoke for the language federations. John Keracher (now the mainstay of the Proletarian Party) came from Michigan to the "Smolny" gathering, and John J. Ballam from Massachusetts.

§

In describing the opening of the Communist Party convention in Smolny Institute, Max Eastman wrote in his magazine *The Liberator,* which replaced the *Masses*:

The Chicago police supplied the best of all arguments in favor of the communist convention. The right wing was protected by the police, the left wing was ignored, but the hall of the communist convention was raided, photographs taken, decorations and revolutionary placards destroyed, and two men arrested. Perhaps this argument is a little crippled by the fact that one of the men arrested was a lawyer, and the other was Dennis Batt of Detroit. . . .

What the Chicago police inaugurated the authorities of the federal, state, and city governments throughout the country finished. By raids, brutality, arrests, indictments, sentences to prison, deportations, break-up of meetings, denials of free press, and ruthless suppression generally, they drove both the Communist and the Communist Labor Party underground,—exactly as predicted by the right wing and centrist leaders of the Socialist Party.

The lawyer Swinburne Hale, writing in the *American Labor Year Book, 1921-1922,* summarized the national offensive against the communists:

A period of governmental terrorism unparalleled in American history began in August, 1919, under the leadership of A. Mitchell Palmer, Attorney General of the United States. Becoming intensified in November it reached its climax in January, 1920, then gradually declined under liberal and labor opposition, and may be said to have been finally broken about the month of June. Its aftermath extended to March 3, 1921, the day before Mr. Palmer ceased to be Attorney General.

In their "report upon the illegal practices of the United States Department of Justice," twelve leading lawyers of the country affixed their signatures to the following opening statement:

To the American people: For more than six months we, the undersigned lawyers, whose sworn duty it is to uphold the Constitution and laws of the United States, have seen with growing apprehension the continued violation of the Constitution and breaking of those Laws by the Department of Justice of the United States government.

Under the guise of a campaign for the suppression of radical activities, the office of the Attorney General, acting by its local agents throughout the country, and giving express instructions from Washington, has committed illegal acts. Wholesale arrests both of aliens and citizens have been made without warrant or any process of law; men and women have been jailed and held *incommunicado* without access of friends or counsel; homes have been entered without search-warrant and property seized and removed; other property has been wantonly destroyed; workingmen and working-women suspected of radical views have been shamefully abused and maltreated. Agents of the Department of Justice have been introduced into radical organizations for the purpose of informing upon their members or inciting them to activities; these agents have even been instructed from Washington to arrange meetings upon certain dates for the express object of facilitating wholesale raids and arrests. In support of these illegal arrests and to create sentiment in its favor, the Department of Justice has also constituted itself a propaganda bureau, and has sent to newspapers and magazines of this country quantities of material designed to excite public opinion against radicals, all at the expense of the government and outside the scope of the Attorney General's duties.

The men who signed the foregoing were: R. G. Brown, Zechariah Chaffee, Jr., Felix Frankfurter, Ernst Freund, Swinburne Hale, Francis Fisher Kane, Alfred S. Niles, Roscoe Pound, Jackson H. Ralston, David Wallerstein, Frank P. Walsh, and Tyrell Williams.

Extensive raids were made on the communists' meeting places and homes in November and December, 1919. "Through the night of January 2, 1920, the white terror reached its climax," in the words of Hale:

It is estimated in the evidence before the Senate Committee, which a year later investigated charges against the Attorney General, that approximately 10,000 persons were arrested, that 6,530 Labor Department warrants were applied for either before or after the arrests (mostly after) and that about 3,000 people among those arrested were actually "fitted up" to the warrants and held for deportation hearings.

On December 21, 1919 the Buford sailed from America to Russia with 249 deported persons "whose cases," according to Hale, "had been rushed through the Department of Labor with little pretense of evidence or process of law." William B. Wilson, secretary of labor, decided on January 24, 1920, that the Communist Party was illegal,. Louis F. Post, assistant secretary of labor, however, ordered the release of at least 75 per cent of the prisoners, and on April 10 decided in effect, "that although membership in the Communist Party was sufficient ground for deportation, certain rules for due process of law must be observed." Secretary Wilson had meanwhile ruled that the Communist Labor Party, as distinguished from the Communist Party, was not illegal, and membership in the former, of itself, not enough for deportation. Between December, 1920, and March, 1921, according to the figures of the lawyer Walter Nelles, 295 persons were deported to Russia.

While the raids were being conducted to intimidate, deport, or scatter the rank and file supporters of the two communist parties, the criminal anarchy and criminal syndicalism laws were utilized to throw their leaders into jail. In November and December, 1919, James Larkin, Benjamin Gitlow, Harry Winitsky, C. E. Ruthenberg, and I. E. Ferguson were indicted in New York, found guilty, and sentenced to prison. Charlotte Anita Whitney was indicted in California and likewise sentenced. Thirty-eight national leaders of the Communist Labor Party were also indicted in Illinois and given prison sentences. While not many actually went to jail—they were mostly pardoned before they entered—the costly litigation, the concentra-

tion upon their defenses, and the uncertainties prevented
the outstanding communists from devoting all their energy
to building up the communist movement, not to speak of
their handicaps of carrying on secretly in an underground
organization.   Even worse for the communists, however,
than the raids and the indictments, was the fact that they
were badly divided.   Until the legal and above-ground
Workers' Party emerged at the end of 1921, which
brought a semblance of unity and peace, there was the
fiercest kind of fighting between the numerous communist
parties in America.   Despite their small numbers and
isolation, there were in the United States between September, 1919, and December, 1921, in the words of James
Oneal, "more communist organizations than in any other
country of the world."

§

"Sometime recently, somewhere between the Atlantic
and Pacific, between the Gulf and the Great Lakes, two
groups of elected delegates assembled at the unity conference of the Communist Party and the Communist
Labor Party."   Thus did the United Communist Party
announce its birth in *The Communist* of June 12, 1920.
It did not, however, represent a united movement, for
only a fourth of the Communist Party joined.   The
secretary of the latter wrote that only about 3,500 members had left it to become part of the United Communist
Party.   Of his own membership of 8,350, he gave the
Lithuanian federation in it 2,500, the Russian, 2,000, the
Ukrainian, 1,500, and the Lettish, 1,000, thus showing
conclusively that the Communist Party was a Russian
colony on American soil.

It may or may not have been the same kind of a party,
however, after the Workers' Party was organized.   For
when it met in secret convention in August, 1922, almost
a year after the legal party had been formed, and when

the delegates were trapped by a spy in their midst in the sand dunes near Bridgman, Michigan, the leaders of the Workers' Party were found. On April 7, 1923 the underground Communist Party announced its liquidation.

The Proletarian Party, another communist offshoot, held its first convention in June, 1920. It declared that it was the only *bona fide* communist organization. Despite its claims and efforts it has remained an isolated educational body in a few cities, not recognized by Moscow or by the overwhelming majority of the communists in the United States. The Industrial Communists also set up claims to be the genuine article. They went quickly by the board. Then came the Rummagers' League, with an ambitious program "to rummage the field of history and science so as to develop the keenest intellect possible. Special consideration given to present-day problems." They also disappeared.

Early in 1921 arose the American Labor Alliance, the legal counterpart of the illegal and underground United Communist Party. Its innocent name did not indicate its program to achieve unity and bring the communists together. Despite this purpose, however, it attacked the Committee for the Third International, and the Workers' Council, groups which were boring from within the Socialist Party along communist lines. Many of the foreign language federations which had not been suspended or had not withdrawn from the parent Socialist Party were also very restive and were coquetting with communism. When they finally seceded or split, part remaining, they had no home. There were now any number of communist organizations but no unity among them. Finally, however, they got together in a convention in December, 1921, and organized the Workers' Party. By the time they held their second meeting in 1922 they were all practically united, with the exception of the small Proletarian Party and a few other minor groups. But the program of the Workers' Party is not altogether that of the left wingers and communists of 1919 and 1920.

Unlike their fiery and romantic predecessors of the years of epoch-making events, the more realistic and prosaic leaders of the Workers' (Communist) Party of 1928 do not unduly stress the dictatorship of the proletariat, mass action, preparation for civil war, formation of soviets of workers, farmers, and soldiers, and illegal activity among the armed forces, and they do not call on the capitalist class of America to surrender forthwith. They do not think that there is much immediate likelihood of a revolution or civil war in the United States. Their platform in 1928 includes immediate demands and petty reforms. It stresses the need for a reformist labor party, built along the lines of the British Labor Party with the "faker-ridden" unions as its backbone. It urgently demands the organization of the unorganized into the old American Federation of Labor unions and it does not talk of revolutionary industrial unionism, mass and political strikes, defensive and offensive warfare, rising to armed conquest for the control of the state. The Workers' Party cooperates today with all persons and groups, however bourgeois or counter-revolutionary, however liberal or reactionary, even with the hated socialist, in all its auxiliary work, such as defense, amnesty, protection of the foreign born, anti-imperialism, strikes and relief, and delegations to Russia. In truth, times have changed.

And yet the Workers' Party is the American section of the Communist (Third) International. It is the representative of the communist movement in the United States. It is communist, as thoroughly so as the Communist Party of Russia, operating in accordance with conditions here, and as Leninist as its own leaders and those of the world communist movement can make it. For the Workers' Party follows the decisions of the whole international. The program of the party must be judged, accordingly, from that all-important fact.

Whatever his immediate program may in reality or in pretense be, the communist is primarily and exclusively concerned with the revolution, to be achieved in the main according to the Russian model of 1917. The American socialist of today, the farmer, the pure and simple trade unionist, the progressive generally, on the other hand, may or not be in favor of a new order, but they are chiefly interested in the "immediate demands," the ameliorative measures for the ills of the present situation. In that they fundamentally differ from the communist. That is why, with his eye fixed on his revolutionary goal, the communist can never fully cooperate with non-communist groups, except for his own purposes.

The communist finds his only *raison d'etre* in the belief that the development of capitalism in America will force the working class—prepared and educated by his propaganda—to turn to him for substantial relief and a way out; that whatever other methods and reformist agencies the workers use, short of those of the communist, they will discover to be insufficient and deadly; that the toilers will simply have to adopt the communist tactics of organizing and preparing themselves for the armed struggle and the inevitable civil war, win power by their might after they have built up revolutionary unions and a revolutionary political party, set up a dictatorship of the proletariat for a shorter or longer transitory period, and put through the communist program with an iron hand. The communist feels, therefore, that he must open the eyes of the workers to the futility of any methods short of his.

Why then does he advocate immediate demands, a labor party, organization of the unorganized into unions? Only for so long and insofar as these slogans enable him to reach the masses in the United States, permit him to drive the whole working class movement further to the left, and thereby increase his own following, which will continue to drive the whole further and further to the left, until he hopes to control it entirely.

The communist is perfectly willing to use workers, farmers, unionists, and progressives, socialists and all others whom in his heart or openly he classifies as "counter-revolutionists," "enemies and traitors to the working class," and "fascists." The communist, however, will abandon them, their projects and all their works—if he has the chance; he will attack and destroy them—if he can, whenever it suits his purposes. He has no more use for the non-communist, or for that matter for the communist faction with which he disagrees—note the treatment accorded Trotsky and his followers by Stalin and his group in Russia—than he has for the bourgeois. In America he favors the organization of a labor party and will gladly cooperate with whatever "innocents" will help bring it about, under his direction. In Great Britain and Minnesota, however, he is the open foe of a flourishing party of this nature and nominates candidates in opposition. The British Labor Party now stands in the way of his own program of civil war and dictatorship. The communist demands working class unity and a united front. In England as elsewhere he is continuing to divide the forces of the producing classes. He wants a labor party in the United States so that he may get into it, drive it into communist channels, capture or split it, and carry on thereafter upon its ruins.

The communist claims that he favors the organization of the unorganized into unions, advocates progressive union policies, demands the election of honest, capable, energetic, and class-conscious officers, and calls for the best possible conditions for the workers inside and outside the unions. But here as in the case of his advocacy for a labor party there is the drop of poison which brings death, not life, to his plans.

The communists can hardly undertake alone such tremendous tasks as the organization of steel, automobile and other workers in basic industries. By their ruthless warfare against the leadership of the unions in and outside the American Federation of Labor, they have com-

pletely isolated themselves. When William Z. Foster led
in the organization of the packinghouse and steel workers, he was favored by unique war-time conditions, and
he had the support of John Fitzpatrick and Edward
Nockels, as well as some sort of backing by most of
the international unions involved. He had the enthusiastic
help of all of the progressives and socialists. The Amalgamated Clothing Workers sent $100,000 to fill the war-
chest. The organization of the unorganized depends on
something more than the adoption of a resolution by the
Workers' Party or its limited efforts.

In 1928 the Workers' Party started building a national
coal diggers' union apart from and independent of the
United Mine Workers. Its leaders took steps to launch
dual national organizations of ladies' garment workers,
furriers and textile workers. William Z. Foster has thus
gone back on practically everything he once stood for.
He used to say that dual unionism was one of the greatest
errors of the radicals. Now he is as much a dualist as
any of his forerunners. For years Foster advocated the
getting together of all militants to put up a common fight
against the reactionaries. Today, he opposes himself to
every man who is not a member of or willing to take
orders from his political party. The former leader of the
steel strike, finally, used to be impatient of scholasticism.
And yet today he is heading a group which receives and
hands down voluminous theses, which are as interesting
and significant to American toilers as Kant's *Critique of
Pure Reason*. William Z. Foster is going the way of
Daniel De Leon.

De Leonism is not Leninism. The leader of the old
Socialist Labor Party, in the first place, pinned his faith
on the use of the ballot as a civilized weapon, backed up
by the might of the economic organizations. He did not
picture a socialist state continuing beyond the day of the
final victory. He believed that the industrial unions would
constitute the framework of the cooperative common-

wealth. He did not advocate boring from within the
unions and he never stressed immediate demands. Daniel
De Leon, whatever else may be said of him, did not constantly jump from one position to another, nor did he
declare to his followers and the world that the end justified the means.

The communists, on the other hand, do not conceive
of the possibility of a peaceful transition to a socialist
society. Hence they lay chief stress on building up an
organization to carry through the revolution, set up a
dictatorship, and put over the communist program. In
their every-day struggles, however, they employ many of
De Leon's weapons. When defeated in their efforts to
impress an agressive policy on the unions by boring from
within, they are, as has been seen, ready to set up dual
organizations. In their vehement and personal attacks
on "labor fakers," "misleaders," and "crooks," and in
their determination to dictate the policies of the unions
by a political party, they resort to methods which De Leon
used. In their party centralization, discipline, ownership and control of the press, orthodoxy, and admixture
of romanticism and Marxism, they come close to the
organization ruled by De Leon.

As for the communist's demands for militant union
policies, the election of courageous officers, and better
working conditions, he is hardly fair, honest or consistent. No matter how decent, progressive or militant
a trade union leader or rank and filer is, the communist
will try to destroy him if he does not take orders—whatever they are at the moment—from the Workers' Party
leadership in America and Moscow, or become a member
of the organization. As for those leaders in the American
Federation of Labor or the unaffiliated bodies, who may
be corrupt, reactionary and determined at any cost to
retain their power, the communist cannot establish a
united front against them. His case loses its otherwise
sound appeal because he makes no distinction between

reactionary and progressive, between corrupt and honest leader or rank and filer. The non-communist feels, therefore, that—barring exceptional circumstances—it is suicide for him and his policies to cooperate with the communist.

CHAPTER XII

NONPARTISAN LEAGUE AND FARMER-LABOR PARTY

WHEN the former Senator from Wisconsin, Robert Marion La Follette, ran for president in 1924 on an independent ticket, he carried but one state, his own. But he lost North Dakota by only 5,066, Montana by 13,033, South Dakota by 25,752 and Minnesota by 81,567 votes. These were the strongholds of the National Nonpartisan League, when it was a power to be reckoned with in the Northwest. The man who led the progressives ran second in Idaho, Iowa, and Washington, and polled a fair vote in Colorado, Kansas, Nebraska, Oklahoma, and Texas. Altogether, with Wisconsin added, La Follette received a good slice of his popular vote of about 5,000,000 in those thirteen agricultural or mixed agricultural and industrial states which Nonpartisan League organizers had cultivated.

The league contributed only in part to make 1924 a reality. Of far greater importance were the activities of the Conference for Progressive Political Action, the American Federation of Labor, the Committee of Forty-Eight, the Farmer-Labor Party, and the Socialist Party. The Conference for Progressive Political Action brought the railroad unions together and acted as the central agency around which nearly all the groups could gather. The American Federation of Labor, for the only time in its history, threw its prestige behind a third party candidate. The radicals and liberals contributed experience, self-sacrifice, and finances to build up that for which they had been praying and working for two generations. The campaign of 1924 was not planned. The union of forces was as unexpected as it was pleasing to the supporters of independent political action.

Back of it were a set of circumstances which made the Nonpartisan League a factor in thirteen states from 1915 onward, which produced the labor and farmer-labor parties and the Committee of Forty-Eight between 1918 and 1920, which created the Conference for Progressive Political Action in 1922, which determined the uncompromising Socialist Party to forego nominating its own candidates, and which made even the American Federation of Labor join hands for the first time with supporters of independent political action on a national scale. The 1924 campaign truly has historic interest, if it is merely for the one fact that workers, farmers, progressives, and socialists actually did get together, independent of the old parties, on a program which they could all, with justice to their own position as well, fully and wholeheartedly accept. What has once been can be again.

§

In his study of the organization which he knew so well, Herbert E. Gaston observed that "the vital thing" about the Nonpartisan League "was the creation and the existence of the organization itself. That was, in fact, something new, and built upon new lines." He explained how it was done:

The league idea has not been merely "taken up" by the northwestern farmers [Gaston wrote in 1920, when the league was still flourishing]. It has been "sold" to them. Practical salesmanship, a program of immediate and forceful action and the use of the Ford automobile are the factors principally explaining the rise of the Nonpartisan League.

The super-salesman, the man who conceived the National Nonpartisan League idea in a head filled with socialist formulae, the farmer who knew his group and how to sell them a program, Arthur C. Townley was by common consent of friend and foe alike, in the words of

H. G. Teigan, secretary of the league, "a man of remarkable genius as an organizer." He was born in 1880 and was thirty-five when he launched the league. His parents were farmers and natives. Before Townley became the leader of the agricultural producers he himself had been a practical farmer and had had his ups and downs in North Dakota. Equally valuable to him had been his membership in the Socialist Party, for which he had been an organizer for a while. He acquired many of his economic ideas and not a bit of his organizational technique from this connection. When Townley happened to be a spectator and saw how the state legislature treated the demands of the agricultural producers in 1915, he was fully equipped to undertake the task of organizing the farmers' body.

The crusader-entrepreneur had fertile soil to work in. In his monograph, *The Agrarian Movement in North Dakota*, Paul R. Fossum noted that between 1903 and 1915 the price of wheat was going up, and yet

. . . the farmer was the recipient of diminishing profits, due to the added expense of conditioning his land, the diminishing acre yield of his wheat crop and the increased capitalization of his land . . . the farmer had increased both the amount of his land and the number of his horses and . . . these additions seemed to fail to realize for him an increase in his net profits.

The farmer of North Dakota was restive because wheat was his money crop, most of his acreage was planted in it, and despite an increase in price he was not augmenting his net income. But more important, because it drove him to seek a political remedy, was this fact, as stated by Fossum:

The state of North Dakota was developed subsequent to the location of the industry for which she produced a great part of the raw materials, and that those industries together with the market which they created lie outside the jurisdiction of her government.

The farmers of the northwestern state were, in other words, dependent upon the grading practices and prices fixed by the terminal elevators in the states of Minnesota and Wisconsin, to which they shipped their grain. The North Dakota wheat growers charged that the elevator men gave them short weight and cheated them of large sums by unfair grading. They would be paid on the basis of low or no grade wheat, and yet the elevators would ship out practically all the wheat classified in the highest grades, thus making a large profit for themselves by mixing and grading the wheat after it was once in their hands. They tried to prevail upon the outside elevators and the legislatures of the two states to remedy the evils complained of. Failing here, they turned to their own state legislature to give them relief.

As early as 1906 the bankers' association of North Dakota urged the farmers "to cooperate for the purpose of building home and terminal elevators." In the next eight years two constitutional amendments were adopted giving the state authority to own elevators inside and outside the state. A terminal elevator fund tax was inaugurated to raise the money. Notwithstanding the action of several legislatures and popular votes of ratification, the 1915 legislature went ahead and repealed the law calling for a tax for the elevator, and refused to vote any appropriation for the purpose.

The North Dakota Union of the American Society of Equity—a cooperative buying and selling agency, dominated at the time by George S. Loftus—was holding its annual convention while the legislature was in session. The equity delegates tried to bring pressure upon the legislators to go through with the elevator program. Whether out of defiance to Loftus and his threats, or because they were opposed to the proposition, the members of the legislature turned a deaf ear to the pleadings of the farmers. A. C. Townley was an interested spectator of the proceedings. The action of the legislature "registered." He was now out to build up a political organization and a "machine" which would give political power to the farmers and executive direction to himself. The league was born.

Townley had something to sell. His program comprised five points:

State ownership of terminal elevators, flour mills, packing houses and cold storage plants.
State inspection of grain and grain dockage.
Exemption of farm improvements from taxation.
State hail insurance on the acreage tax basis.
Rural credit banks operated at cost.

The first demand aimed a body blow at the middleman, the ancient enemy of the farmer from the days that the Grange and the Alliance of the seventies and eighties organized their cooperatives to eliminate him. The second sought, in the words of Gaston:

. . . to provide a new system of marketing which would give the state control over grades, insure fair grading and weighing, to guarantee to the farmer the full milling value of his grain, to enable him to hold for higher prices and still, by borrowing on warehouse receipts, get the bulk of his money out of the crop, and to create within the state a market for its own products which would build up diversified farming to replace the one-crop system.

The third intended to tax land held for speculative purposes and presumably reduce the burden on the working farmer. The fourth was an obvious step to cut the costs of hail insurance. The fifth was to lower the interest rate and protect the farmers against seizures. It is true that these reforms "were not original with Townley." But what Townley did was to organize the farmers on the basis of them. He created a political organization in an effort to put them on the statute books of North Dakota and elsewhere.

Townley's methods for selling his program were business-like. He would convert a substantial and trusted farmer in a neighborhood and have him act as the local "booster." The Nonpartisan League organizer, or Townley in the first instance, would then have the benefit of the personal introduction of the "booster" in canvassing a new prospect. If necessary, a hired farm hand would do the work left undone while the farmer was listening to the league solicitor. Like Gompers, Townley believed in high dues. At first he fixed them at $2.50 a year. This figure he raised to $6.00 and within a year again to $9.00. By the end of 1916 he standardized it at $16.00 for two years, from one election to another. At its prime there were hundreds of league organizers in the field. Their expenses and the overhead had to be met, and money was necessary for the many enterprises of the organization.

What helped Townley in his first year, the trial year, of 1915 was the abnormally large crop and the high price for it, due to the demand of the warring countries of Europe. The North Dakota farmer had the money with which to pay dues to the league. In 1916, on the other hand, there was a "light and shriveled crop. . . . It gave impetus to the demand for state-owned mills, for much of the wheat sold on 'feed' grades, and it developed that this 'feed' wheat, bought by the millers for less than half the price of No. 1, actually was milled into a rich and nourishing flour, the extra profit going to the millers." In both good and bad times, and at all seasons of the year, league organizers took postdated checks to relieve the farmer of the burden or impossibility of paying cash.

To meet the attacks of his opponents Townley launched the *Nonpartisan Leader,* a weekly, on September 23, 1915. Later he acquired two dailies, one in Fargo, the other in Grand Forks. State *Leaders* were established. A publishing association was set up which planted about 100 county newspapers all over North Dakota and the adjoining states. Cooperatives and banks, owned and run by farmers, were started. The Nonpartisan League was more than a political organization.

§

When Townley won Fred B. Wood as his first convert he made him vice president. By virtue of his own act he became president. He selected three others and called the five the executive committee. There never was an election until several years afterward when the *Nonpartisan Leader* conducted some sort of a referendum. An office was opened in St. Paul and the National Nonpartisan League was born. Articles of association were later adopted in a national convention on December 3, 1918, which gave Townley, or at best one other besides himself, practically unlimited power over the national and the state organizations.

In these articles a state committee, a national committee, and a national executive committee were provided for. The first state committees, consisting of from three to five resident members, were to be appointed by the national executive. Thereafter the state membership was to elect. The national committee comprised the chairmen of the state committees. A majority of this national committee could amend the articles or remove the members of the national executive committee. The national committee, however, met only once a year or on call of the chairman or two members of the supreme executive body.

The all-important national executive committee was named in the articles: A. C. Townley, chairman, to serve two years from January 1, 1917; William Lemke, four years from that date, and Fred B. Wood, six years. Every two years this group of three was to nominate one member. They could perpetuate themselves in office, if they so wished. In case of any vacancy they filled it. The executive had "full and complete power and authority"—so the articles read—"to fix, collect, and disburse the membership fees and other funds." It had complete control of the organizing work, with appointive and removal power over the state executive secretaries and managers. The state committees did not dictate to the highest officer in their territory. He was answerable to the national executive. Finally, the latter made all rules and regulations for the affiliation of other political and industrial organizations. Truly the league was highly centralized and dominated by one or two men. Its structure represented Townley's idea of a fighting weapon, efficient, disciplined, quick, and elastic, in a word, possessed of the virtues of a military "machine," or of a dictatorship of the post-war type. Townley was out to win power for the farmers, and to prevent the enemy from destroying or crippling the organization from without or within. That was his justification for the extreme centralization.

The farmer was not, however, merely the "sucker" who paid "the freight." He contributed the money, yes, but he also owned the league, and in the last analysis dictated to Townley. If he stopped paying the latter was through. The striking and distinguishing fact about the league, as about all the *bona fide* labor and farmer parties of the last hundred years, was and is that the workers and farmers owned and controlled them by contributing the money to run them. The obvious fact about the old parties, likewise, has been and is that they were and are owned by the men and interests which finance them. This is not a journalistic generalization nor a radical outburst. It is literal truth. The farmers chose wisely and dug down in their own pockets to match with their pennies the dollars of those opposed to them and their program.

Townley dominated the league. But all political power rested with the farmers. The league was founded and remained on a democratic basis. It gave the farmers the means by which they could enforce their will, the will of the overwhelming majority in North Dakota. In other industrial-agricultural states it gave the chance to the farmers and workers, likewise the overwhelming majority, to make their demands felt. The farmers gathered in their localities and nominated their own candidates, they selected their own delegates to conventions embracing larger areas than their district, and they functioned in a democratic way, without politicians or paid agents of their opponents cajoling or dictating to them. When they elected farmers, not paid officials of the league, to the legislature or Congress, barring those who turned against them, they had representatives in the most literal sense of the word. These public officials caucused with the leaders of the league and hammered out a program which would carry out the mandates of the farmers and workers who had chosen them. It was because the league was so eminently democratic, regardless of Townley's iron grip upon it, that it appealed to the farmers. And it was because they belived in the league that their opponents desired to smash it. Had Townley more vision and deeper understanding, he could have made it more than a temporary instrument, however effective at the time, that it was.

§

In his debate with Morris Hillquit on the question, *Shall A Labor Party Be Formed in America?* Edward F. Keating, editor of *Labor,* the railway unions' weekly, made what he believed his strongest argument against the necessity for one in these words:

We have something in America that they have in no other country in the world, and that is the primary.

This is a tremendously important fact which should never be overlooked by those who are anxious to "drive special privilege out of government."

The primary law renders the formation of new parties unnecessary for the reason that whenever the people wish to renovate one or both of the old parties they may do so by the simple expedient of taking advantage of the primary.

A. C. Townley put all his trust in and based his organization on this device which was to democratize American politics—the direct primary. The Nonpartisan League started out by being nonpartisan, *i.e.,* by entering the primaries in an organized fashion and putting its own slate over, regardless of whether its candidates were on the republican or democratic tickets, or both. In the first electoral test of its strength in the state-wide primaries of North Dakota on June 28, 1916, the league nominated Lynn J. Frazier for governor by a vote in excess of the total for all his three opponents. A year later, in a special election, it put J. M. Baer into Congress. It followed up these victories in 1918 by capturing the primaries again and electing a majority of the members of the state legislature and sending three congressmen to Washington. According to Teigan's figures, after this November, 1918, election, apart from the small number elected in Colorado and Nebraska, and barring North Dakota where it had a majority in each house, the league had the following representation in the various legislatures of the Northwest:

State	Senate	House	State	Senate	House
Idaho	7	14	Montana	3	18
Minnesota	12	34	South Dakota	6	12

In 1918 and 1920 the democrats and republicans combined to oppose the league in North Dakota, thus putting the organization into the position of being a party whether it liked to or not. And on October 28, 1921, in the recall election in North Dakota the opposition candidate for governor, Nestos, beat Frazier by a vote of 111,434 to 107,332. In 1922 Nestos repeated his victory by defeating Lemke, 110,321 to 81,048. In this election the winner ran as the regular republican. And how did Lemke ever run at all, when he was not the party candidate? He stood as the independent in the election. In other words, once the league failed to win at the primaries it did not support the victor, the choice of the party voters, it bolted. And when the league captured the Republican Party primaries, those opposed to its domination left the Grand Old Party and combined with the democrats to defeat it at the election which followed the primaries. The league was a party in spite of itself, in spite of its supposed nonpartisanship, and in spite of its pretense of entering the primaries.

The strength of the league did not consist in capturing the name, the prestige, or the machinery of an old party. It did not consist in having its candidate on a ticket which voters habitually supported. The power of the Nonpartisan League rested in its leadership, its organized and militant membership and its program, and that alone. Had Townley realized that, and had others like Keating understood it, they would not have raised false hopes. The task of driving special privilege out of government cannot be accomplished by what Keating suggests, unless there is an organized army of workers and farmers and progressives ready to do it. And even if there is, they can only achieve lasting and valuable results by and through a party of their own, financed and completely controlled in every respect by themselves.

It is because the present leaders of organized labor and the farmers' associations have no fundamental social program and have no politically educated army to achieve it, that they must perforce resort to the weak and hopeless policy of nonpartisan politics, of rewarding friends and defeating enemies. They are not anywhere nearly as strong as the Nonpartisan League which at least picked its own candidates in the primaries, in the sense that farmers selected them in the first instance. The nonpartisans of the American Federation of Labor merely endorse candidates chosen for them by one or the other of the capitalist parties. Unlike the Nonpartisan League the American Federation of Labor does not write the platforms of the candidates it endorses, does not finance and conduct their campaigns, and does not control them in case they are elected.

§

At the end of 1918, using Teigan's figures, there were 188,365 members in the National Nonpartisan League, of which 131,443 lived in these four states:

Minnesota	50,162	South Dakota	24,669
North Dakota	35,062	Montana	21,550

The balance of 56,922 were in nine other states, of which Idaho and Washington were two. What was the history of the league in these states, so far as the non-partisan method was concerned?

In Minnesota where it had the largest membership, the league threw its hat in the ring in the gubernatorial election of 1918. It entered the primaries in this year of war hysteria in a state where it was at a high pitch, with Charles A. Lindbergh, the father of perhaps the most popular living mortal today, the youthful "lone eagle" of America. In the tributes paid to the son the father is never mentioned, nor is his book, *Why Is Your Country at War, and What Happens to You After the War, and Related Subjects.* The league lost in the primaries. Did it give up its fight? No, a joint convention of organized workers and farmers nominated a candidate on an independent ticket, called Farmer-Labor. The Minnesota experience repeated that of North Dakota. What mattered it if the organization or group was called nonpartisan, independent, or farmer-labor? It functioned as and was a political party in every sense of the word, separate and apart from the old parties. Furthermore, and very significant, the only state where league ideas can today be said to function at all as a political force among the farmers and workers, a living thing and not a tradition or a past influence, is Minnesota, where the Farmer-Labor Party as an independent party has carried on for the last ten years as a virile producers' party.

South Dakota had a strong league following. By 1920 the farmers had to put up a ticket of their own, when they were beaten in the primaries, under the name of Nonpartisan Party, which they later changed to Farmer-Labor Party. In Idaho the league captured the democratic primaries in 1918 but by 1922 the workers-farmers-progressives had their own Progressive Party. In Montana and Washington there were strong independent parties and there was a weaker one in Colorado.

The old party "machines" defeated the league in the primaries, except in the first few elections in North Dakota and Idaho. But they did not stop at that. It was troublesome and costly to go through a primary contest. They proceeded to abolish the primary or render it useless. In the words of Charles Edward Russell, a writer for the league:

In Idaho, where the league had been making great inroads, the reactionaries succeeded in abolishing the primary.

In Nebraska the plans seem to have been to wreck the primary without abolishing it. . . .

In Montana . . . the old political machine had no difficulty in slipping through the legislature of January, 1919, a bill that practically abolished the primary and returned to the old convention plan for the nominating of state candidates.

In Minnesota the legislature was called in special session on September 9, 1919, for, among other purposes, the repeal of the primary law. It found it inexpedient to do so, however. There was practically an independent party in the field anyway. In truth, "special privilege" did not sit idly by and let the league go ahead on its plan of capturing primaries. And where the league actually did win in the primary, the agents of the old parties "knifed" its candidates in the election. In other words, in nearly every state where the league amounted to something and where it really tried its nonpartisan method, boring from within, it was forced, whether it liked to or not, to come out as an independent party of its own.

§

The league was in complete control of North Dakota for a short time. The sweeping victories of 1918 gave it real power for the next two years. But betrayal by a few officials that it put into office, court action, misrepresentation in the press, and opposition by the financiers within and without the state, hampered it at every step. No impartial study has been made of the state enterprises, associations, and commissions set up. When the league lost control of the legislature it was in no position to see that the state enterprises were given a fair chance. That it did pass legislation in the interests of the

farmers and the workers, there is no doubt. Those
wedded to private management and "special privilege"
condemn their projects, in principle, while others—os-
tensibly unprejudiced—find fault with nearly all of them
for one reason or another. On the other hand, defenders
of the league and of state ownership praise their schemes.
How they actually worked, when controlled by agents
of the league, is not usually discussed.

After the defeat of Governor Frazier in the recall election of 1921 the league began to decline in North Dakota.
It had already lost considerable ground in the rest of the
Northwest. In 1922 Townley resigned. After 1920 the
league cut its dues to $6.50 for two years. In the seven
good years of the league's history, 1915-1921, it accumulated close to $2,000,000 of unpaid postdated checks. The
official national organ suspended in July, 1923. In October of the same year the Nonpartisan League of North
Dakota severed relations with the national body—which
had practically disappeared. *The Farmer-Labor State
Record,* official spokesman of the North Dakota Federation of Labor, commenting on the action of the League
in quitting the national, wrote:

. . . there is no Townleyism in this state any more. . . . The
farmers' Nonpartisan League has been reorganized from the
ground up. . . . It is now absolutely democratically organized
and democratically managed; all the former leaders that stood
for autocracy in management have been dismissed; all the schemers
of the type of men that organized and wrecked the Consumers'
Stores Company, the newspaper ventures, and the banks have
been kicked out.

While the Nonpartisan League elected congressmen on
the old party tickets in North Dakota and elsewhere, it
took no part in the national presidential contests of 1916
and 1920. Its members supported Wilson and Harding,
except in Montana, South Dakota and Washington, where
they threw their votes in the main behind Parley P. Christensen, the candidate of the Farmer-Labor Party, or in
some cases where they supported Debs on the socialist

ticket. Townley refused to cooperate with those who were trying to organize a labor, farmer-labor, or labor-farmer-progressive party in 1920. He gave no encouragement to the Committee of Forty-Eight or the Chicago leaders of the Farmer-Labor Party. He wanted a coalition of the workers and the farmers and he achieved it in North Dakota and Minnesota. But he insisted on a nonpartisan organization to make its fight in the old party primaries. The independent party movement carried on without him.

§

When the workers of the world were turning to the left in the epoch-making year of 1919 it was inevitable that those in the United States should also move—a little. The labor party movement of 1918-1920 in America was part of the stormy world scene. It belonged to the volcanic eruptions of the World War and the Russian and European revolutions. It represented in this country what the Webb reconstruction program and the Triple Alliance meant to the labor movement of Great Britain, what their rise to power signified to the German and Austrian socialists, and what the consolidation of their dictatorship implied to the Russian bolsheviks. Hope filled the common man's breast everywhere. He felt a kinship for his fellow-worker. He thought in group and class terms. He believed, in the words of Eugene Victor Debs, that the day of the people had arrived.

The year 1919 was the year of the American steel strike, the coal strike, the Boston police strike and the Seattle general strike. More men were involved in the labor disputes of this year than in the next six years put together. Unorganized workers felt the power and joy of being organized, toilers who had not struck for a lifetime downed tools as men, and trade unionists who had only responded to craft interest entered upon class action. On the political field socialists turned to the left, while others became communists. And those who had voted old party tickets began to incline to the candidates of the rising labor parties.

To the bleeding world of 1918 and 1919 Woodrow Wilson's fourteen points seemed like manna from heaven. The common people believed that he had come to deliver them from bondage to the war-makers. They felt that he would fulfill his pledge to make the world safe for democracy. What was more natural than that in the United States there should be those who would seize upon the magic of the figure fourteen and draw up Labor's Fourteen Points, to do for the relations between the classes what the original fourteen were to accomplish in the intercourse between nations? These fourteen points of labor served as the first program of the budding labor party movement. They embraced the immediate demands and underlying philosophy of those trade unionists and intellectuals who inspired the independent political agitation.

The Labor Party that was organized at a national convention on November 22, 1919, and the Farmer-Labor Party which succeeded it in 1920, adopted a declaration of principles and a presidential platform, which included thirty-two principles in the first and nine planks in the second. But the fourteen points, the principles and the platform embodied only one fundamental idea of the leaders of the new movement: all power to the workers and farmers. To be sure, the labor and farmer-labor parties were not called socialist, their official statements did not demand the overthrow of the capitalist system, they did not declare that the present order was breaking down, and they did not assert that the cooperative commonwealth was the only and inevitable solution for the basic and unsolvable ills of our society. But nevertheless, the labor parties were socialist, in the sense that the British Labor Party was.

Number two of the fourteen points called for democratic control of industry, while point ten demanded public ownership of public utilities and basic natural resources. The last point stressed internationalism; it urged "a league of the workers of all nations pledged and organized to enforce the destruction of autocracy, militarism, and economic imperialism throughout the world." The opening paragraphs of the declaration of principles of the Labor Party of 1919 stated in simple language the Marxian position:

The Labor Party was organized to assemble into a new majority the men and women who work, but who have been scattered as helpless minorities in the old parties under the leadership of the confidence men of big business.

These confidence men, by exploitation, rob the workers of the product of their activities and use the huge profits thus gained to finance the old political parties, by which they gain and keep control of the government. They withhold money from the worker and use it to make him pay for his own defeat.

Labor is aware of this and throughout the world the workers have reached the determination to reverse this condition and take control of their own lives and their own government.

In this country this can and must be achieved peacefully by the workers uniting and marching in unbroken phalanx to the ballot boxes. It is the mission of the Labor Party to bring this to pass.

The immediate demands of the declaration included an extensive program of nationalization and socialization, hardly to be excelled in the ordinary Socialist Party platform:

We demand nationalization of railroads, mines, forests, water power, telegraphs, telephones, stock yards, grain elevators, natural gas and oil wells, cold storage and terminal warehouses, elevators, packing plants, flour mills and of all basic industries which require large-scale production and are in reality on a non-competitive basis; these to be democratically managed.

The citadel of special privilege today is the private bank. We demand the banking business, including the right to issue money and credit, be placed exclusively in the hands of the federal government.

We demand nationalization of unused land, including reclaimed tracts in swamp and arid areas, such nationalized lands to be kept in use by lease to citizens who will cultivate them for production, title to remain public forever.

In the much-debated platform of the Farmer-Labor Party, when the representatives of the Committee of Forty-Eight and of Robert Marion La Follette endeavored to water it down, the leaders of the Labor Party insisted on the inclusion of the following plank:

The right of labor to an *increasing* share in the responsibilities and management of industry; application of this principle to be developed in accordance with the experience of actual operation.

And no stopping place was mentioned.

The labor party platforms of cities, states, and nation of 1918-1920 did not use the phraseology of the Marxians or socialists. They spoke of industrial, political, and social democracy. But the all-important fact is that the men and women behind the movement had come to think in terms of the necessity of changing the present system in fundamentals; they envisaged an increasingly powerful labor movement on both the economic and political field to accomplish immediately the task of forcing basic reforms and ultimately of so altering existing society as to warrant the work being called a revolution.

§

The first president of the National Labor Party and the candidate for vice-president of the Farmer-Labor Party in 1920, was Max S. Hayes. He was nothing if not a socialist, regardless of the fact that he had quit the Socialist Party after Charles Emil Ruthenberg and the left wingers captured the Cleveland local. On the national committee were Duncan MacDonald and William Kohn. They also had dropped out of the Socialist Party, but they were still socialists. MacDonald was president of the Illinois Federation of Labor and threw his influence behind the independent labor party movement. William Kohn spoke for the Central Federated Union of New York, the largest central body in the country. He had helped to establish and maintain not a few Socialist Party locals and enterprises before he tied up with the labor party movement.

Men like John Fitzpatrick, Edward N. Nockels, Robert M. Buck, Toscan Bennett, Abraham Lefkowitz, and a host of others were not and had never been members of the Socialist Party nor were they known as socialists. But between 1917 and 1919 they acquired a point of view which was as much socialist as that of the followers of Marx in any of the great socialist parties of the world.

Take the outstanding leader and central figure of the labor party movement, John Fitzpatrick, president of the Chicago Federation of Labor. He delivered the keynote addresses in the national conventions of 1919 and 1920. It was his powerful influence, plus that of his close friend and co-worker, Edward N. Nockels, that kept the new party in the foreground and helped to maintain it against the opposition of the American Federation of Labor. Fitzpatrick is a born rebel and defender of the underdog. His Irish republicanism and his love of liberty, his granite-like integrity and unwillingness to bend the knee to Samuel Gompers, his profound sense of justice, above all, his courage to enter the battlefield, made him the center of many a progressive cause in behalf of labor in the United States.

It was he who eliminated the influence of "Skinny" Madden in the central body of Chicago. He lined up behind the Amalgamated Clothing Workers in its efforts to survive against the United Garment Workers, thus winning the warm friendship of Sidney Hillman and Samuel Levin. He helped the women teachers, the printing trades, and a number of others to wage many a good fight under the greatest difficulties, with international union and public officials against him. He did not hesitate to speak up on the floor of the convention of the American Federation of Labor, nor to help elect delegates from Chicago who would oppose the standpat policies of Gompers. He fought the entrance of the United States into the World War. Nor did he become hysterically pro-war after April, 1917. He did not assist the "American Alliance for Labor and Democracy" to weaken liberty at home, while its leaders traveled abroad to keep war-weary Europeans in the trenches. While Wilson and others talked about making the world safe for democracy, Fitzpatrick listened to William Z. Foster, accepted him despite his I. W. W. and syndicalist past, and helped his campaign to make the United States safe for the workers by unionizing the stockyards and the steel mills. While others fought the Kaiser, he attacked Gary. Nockels and Fitzpatrick took up the Mooney case and made it an international issue. Fitzpatrick never failed to speak of the great achievement of the Russians in overthrowing their masters, and he said repeatedly that he wished the American workers would do as thorough a job in accordance with our traditions and opportunities. Fitzpatrick was of the workers, and has remained one of them. He never aspired to be a leader. He has been such a pillar of strength to the militant working class movement, because in trying to serve his fellows he forged to the front, in a country where there are so few labor leaders like him.

When Fitzpatrick was converted to the labor party idea in 1918, he added independent political action to a labor philosophy which was basically radical. The man who helped organize the steel workers and who was willing to demand Tom Mooney's release with a general strike was prepared to lead the fight on the political field when the opportunity offered itself.

§

The labor parties of the post-war period were organized by local trade union officials and the rank and file. At no time did the international union leaders give them encouragement. After an unsuccessful strike in the spring of 1918 the munitions workers of Bridgeport, Connecticut, built up the first of the local labor parties in September of 1918. In February there was a state labor party in Connecticut. In the month of the armistice the Chicago Federation of Labor took a referendum vote of its affiliated unions on the question of establishing an independent labor party. The following December the Illinois State Federation of Labor decided to canvass its affiliated bodies on the same matter. On January 11, 1919, delegates from unions of the leading city of the land launched the American Labor Party of Greater New York. In May, 1919 the Pennsylvania State Federation of Labor, and in September the Indiana state body declared in favor of independent political action. The time was ripe for a national get-together.

The convention which launched the National Labor Party on November 22, 1919, in Chicago, was one of the largest rank and file gatherings, with wage earners straight from their work places, in the history of the American labor movement. The delegates came from local unions overwhelmingly, although those from city central bodies, railroad system federations, district councils, and the like, besides representatives from local labor parties, constituted a goodly number of the assembly. Illinois, Indiana, Iowa, Kansas, Kentucky, Michigan, Missouri, New York, Ohio, and Pennsylvania contributed the bulk of the delegates from about forty states. The first two states accounted for hundreds, among whom those from the coal fields were conspicuous. Although the American Federation of Labor was vigorously opposed, delegates were present from subordinate units of over half of the international unions affiliated with it. The men and women who started the National Labor Party were among the most militant trade unionists of America in 1919.

Founded by local unions, the labor party organizations reflected it in their structure, from the bottom up. The county or city labor party received its main income from affiliated unions, representatives of whom dominated its counsels. The state labor parties also obtained their chief revenue from the unions in unorganized territory and from labor bodies which embraced more than one local labor party's jurisdiction. It is true that local, state, and national parties admitted individuals to membership and received dues from them. But the money received in this way did not amount to much. In the city, state, and national committees, in the conferences and conventions, it was the representatives of the local unions that constituted the majority or controlling influence.

There were intellectuals and business men in high places. But even many of these belonged to labor organizations. Abraham Lefkowitz a d Toscan Bennett, leaders of the New York and Connecticut parties, were members of the teachers' union. Bennett was a retired lawyer but his connection with Brookwood Labor College made him eligible to the American Federation of Teachers, as his editing of a couple of labor papers in Bridgeport and Hartford admitted him to the International Typographical Union. Robert M. Buck, editor of the Chicago *New Majority,* official organ of the movement, was probably a member of the newswriters' union, as was Parley Parker Christensen, although he practiced law. Nicholas Klein of Cincinnati was a lawyer, as was William E. Rodriguez of Chicago. Lillian Herstein of the Windy City was a teacher. There were also some liberal ministers. Alcan Hirsch of New York, who contributed heavily to make the party a going concern in the eastern state, was a man of large means, in business for himself. Ben Howe had been president of a manufacturing company and city buyer for Louisville, Kentucky, before he settled in New York to engage in social work, such as community and cooperative organization. West of the Hudson River the labor party movement was dominated almost entirely by trade union leaders.

In the first plan of organization of the American Labor Party of Greater New York, there occurred these significant lines on candidates:

No candidate of the Labor Party shall accept endorsement of either the democratic or the republican parties, nor any other parties that stand for private ownership of public utilities; nor shall the Labor Party endorse any candidates of the above-mentioned parties.

In the first constitution adopted by the National Labor Party in November, 1919 there was this provision:

> No members of the Labor Party shall permit their names to be placed in nomination by any political party other than the Labor Party, and no branch of the Labor Party shall endorse the nominee of any other party. Provided, that nothing herein contained shall prevent a working alliance between any branch of the Labor Party and any organized farmers' group, which shall endorse the principles and platform of the Labor Party, or other progressive organization or party which shall subscribe to and support the principles and platform of the Labor Party. The National Committee shall expel any member or organization offending against the foregoing provisions.

Everywhere, in city, state, and nation, the Labor Party declared its complete independence of the two old parties, and at the same time specifically provided against fusion or nonpartisan political action. On the other hand it very definitely left the door open for cooperation with the farmers or progressive political organizations.

In nearly every convention that was held to establish a local, state, or the national party, the prevailing opinion was expressed that the labor party should not split the vote, help defeat candidates of the Socialist Party, nor spend much time organizing where the latter had any strength. The labor party men and women were not on the war-path. On the contrary, they held an olive branch in their hands, and invited the socialists to cooperate with them.

The schooled and practical trade unionists of the labor parties were not anxious for a fight either with the heads of the American Federation of Labor or with the chiefs of the international unions. From the start they excluded discussion of union matters. As stated by Robert M. Buck at the time:

> The party scrupulously refrains from trying to dictate to the unions as to how they should run themselves. The Farmer-Labor

Party has no theories for the conduct of the labor movement, nor any criticisms to make of the conduct of unions or union personnel. It is concerned only with the politics of labor.

But in thus concerning itself with "the politics of labor," the labor party leadership brought on a conflict with the higher officials of the federation and its affiliated internationals. The latter were wedded in theory to the nonpartisan political policy and in practice to the two old parties. They were vigorously opposed to independent political action. They made their influence and power felt to prevent the development of the labor parties and to hamper and destroy them after they were once started in spite of their efforts.

§

Before the New York unionists launched their local labor party, Samuel Gompers called them to a conference and preached to them on the error of their ways and cautioned them against taking the step. Daniel J. Tobin, president of the teamsters' union and treasurer of the American Federation of Labor, appeared at the Indiana state labor party convention to urge the nonpartisan plan. While the Central Federated Union of Manhattan and the Bronx in New York persisted in supporting the American Labor Party, the Brooklyn central body was persuaded to withdraw and become the agency through which the leaders of the C. F. U. were replaced by those in sympathy with the so-called nonpartisan political policy, in actuality, a program of supporting Tammany Hall in New York City. In the Central Federated Union just before it was "re-organized," delegates from organizations hostile to the labor party "packed" several meetings to compel a change of policy.

In Harry Bird Sell's unpublished manuscript on *The A. F. of L. and the Labor Party Movement,* he cites the correspondence between the president of the federation and William A. Mitch, secretary-treasurer of the miners of Indiana, and a leader of the labor party of that state.

He quotes Gompers as saying that the organization of the independent party constituted an attack on the trade union movement. In the *New Majority* of March 27, 1920 John Fitzpatrick came out with the blunt statement that "the A. F. of L. is trying to scare everyone to death who dares to rise up and oppose its political ideas."

Paralleling the opposition of Gompers and the A. F. of L. heads to the departure from their nonpartisan program was the indifference or open sabotage of the leaders of some of the most powerful unions. The 1919 convention of the United Mine Workers, for instance, representing 400,000 members, unanimously adopted the following resolution:

Whereas, We hold that the composition of the present Congress of the United States furnishes conclusive proof that the efforts of labor politically in this country have been a miserable failure; and

Whereas, We have nothing to lose politically and everything to gain by abandoning the political policy of the labor movement, as expressed by the American Federation of Labor; and

Whereas, The need of the times so far as labor is concerned is to organize our forces so that labor will be represented as it should be in the Congress of the United States and the legislatures of the various states, and we feel that this can be accomplished only by the organization of a labor party that will be representative of and under the control of the workers of hand and brain of the United States; and

Whereas, Such a party cooperating wherever possible with the progressive poltical forces of the organized farmers could wield a tremendous power and assure the enactment of legislation for nationalization of coal and other basic industries in the interest of the workers; therefore be it

Resolved, That this convention favor the organization of such a labor party and instruct the officers of the international organization and the international executive board to call a conference of representatives of the labor movement from the various national and international unions to meet at a time and place to be determined by the executive board for the purpose of taking action on the question of organizing and launching a national labor party. And that such conference be held prior to the convening of the next American Federation of Labor convention; and be it further

Resolved, That the cooperative movement, the Nonpartisan League and farmers' organizations be requested to have representatives at said conference; and be it further

Resolved, That the American Federation of Labor and its various affiliated state branches be invited to have representatives at said conference.

The executive board of the coal diggers' union, despite the unanimous vote and the specific wording of this resolution, in no way promoted the independent labor party movement. One year after the Cleveland convention of the miners had declared for a labor party, the painters' union, then the tenth largest in the federation, carried a referendum in favor of the proposal. With the possible exception of the secretary, who was a former socialist, the officials of the painters gave little encouragement to the national labor party.

In the course of the next several years—some unions do not meet oftener than once in three or more years— there were a number of other internationals which adopted resolutions favoring the new step. The molders' union, of which John P. Frey is a prominent member, decided by a vote of 185 to 158 in its September, 1923, convention —after long and exhaustive debate—in favor of wiping out the nonpartisan political policy of the American Federation of Labor, and instructed its delegates to the federation's convention to work toward that end. The resolution pointed out that the power of the government was "used on the side of the bosses, as witnessed by the infamous Dougherty injunction against the railroad shopmen, the abolition of the federal child labor law, and women's minimum wage law." It compared the situation in this country with that in Great Britain, where the workers have built a powerful labor party which exerts tremendous influence on the government. Notwithstanding the adoption of this resolution, such an outstanding leader as Frey did not throw his intellectual ability on the side of a labor party. In fact, the spokesmen of the American labor movement—and the leaders here compare favor-

ably with those in other countries—did nothing to initiate
a new political policy in 1919, a golden year for it.

There was genuine labor solidarity then. The unions
were stronger than ever. Men believed. And yet the
higher officials of the unions missed their opportunity.
Gompers and the A. F. of L. advanced nothing more than
the nonpartisan political policy, which was about as stimu-
lating as his slogan of "more, more, more, here and now."
When Gompers wrote to Fitzpatrick, "it is to be hoped
that we shall live at least until after the close of the coming campaign when we, too, may be in a position to compare notes as to who will have the excuses and the regrets
to feel and express," he might have added as a postscript,
that he intended using his power of removing A. F. of L.
organizers who were presidents of central bodies and
opposed to his policies, of re-organizing central bodies
that favored the labor party idea, and of using paid
officials on the staff of the federation and of the internationals to see to it that there would be "regrets" sooner
or later. That despite the active opposition of Gompers
and the higher union officials the labor party men held
their ground was a credit to their independence. That
they did not make greater headway in their electoral campaigns was due to their inexperience and shortsighted
radicalism, the indifference of the Socialist Party, and
external factors beyond their control, which swept Harding into office in 1920.

§

The professional and business men and intellectuals
who constituted the Committee of Forty-Eight came from
every state in the Union, as their name indicated. They
were the inheritors of the Progressive Party of 1912.
They spoke in terms of old-fashioned American civil
liberties, they were deeply sympathetic toward labor's
struggles, and they favored a government ownership program to include at first the public utilities and basic
natural resources. Among them were able publicity work-

ers and students of social problems, as well as men of some means. They were not hardened politicians but they loved the game of politics. They believed in a short and effective platform of a few planks. They stressed the importance of leaders in American political life. Magazines like the *Nation* and the *New Republic* unofficially represented their point of view. J. A. H. Hopkins was one of their outstanding spokesmen, a man who gave liberally of his time and money to build up a third party in the United States.

The forty-eighters knew that they had to have the cooperation of the rising labor parties and the Nonpartisan League. With Townley they got no further than did the Chicago labor men. It was natural, then, that when the National Labor Party called a presidential nominating convention to meet at Chicago in July, 1920, the forty-eighters should also send out an appeal to their followers to convene in the Windy City at the same time. The collision and wrecking of the Committee of Forty-Eight that occurred could have been predicted, for at no time before the two conventions met had the two groups arrived at any working agreement.

The National Labor Party convention of 1920, like that of 1919, was dominated by the local unions. There was quite a drop in their number. The sharpest decline, however, was in the number of central bodies. These directly affiliated organizations are very vulnerable in the A. F. of L. structure, because their charters can be revoked without much ado by the executive council of the federation, and the leaders of the central bodies are frequently tied up with the old parties. Notwithstanding the poorer showing, there were still 171 unions from Illinois, 69 from Indiana, 25 from Pennsylvania, and several others which sent delegates. This was a remarkable demonstration of strength. For, while the labor party movement began with a rush in 1919, it was already subsiding by the middle of 1920, due to the opposition of the American Federation of Labor, the supporters of the old parties inside and outside the unions, the Socialist Party and the communists, and the fact that the labor parties did not achieve instantaneous victory. Unions which sent delegates to an organizing convention did not follow this up by supporting the labor party. In New York, for example, there were some 884 delegates to the convention of January, 1919, which established the American Labor Party, but by July, 1920, there was only a handful of unions affiliated with it. It was the same everywhere, especially in the larger cities.

The Labor Party leaders won the day in July, 1920. The membership represented by their delegates was far in excess of that of the Committee of Forty-Eight men, who spoke in nearly every case only for themselves. The unionists were quite willing to go it alone, while the forty-eighters were anxious for unity. The labor men had greater physical endurance, they controlled the delegates in their own assembly, they were used to gatherings in which there were clashes, they were rough and tumble, and they knew how to steer in stormy waters. They had a sense of working class consciousness in their instinctive opposition to the middle class leaders of the Committee of Forty-Eight. Robert M. Buck could write in the *New Majority* as follows:

Some think that this organization [the Committee of Forty-Eight] will try to make the Labor Party change its name, modify its platform and merge in a harmless liberal outfit like the old Bull Moose outfit. Others think that the Committee of Forty-Eight has more genuine intentions and will affiliate with the Labor Party. This is a question for the delegates to decide.

In all the conferences of the forty-eighters and the Labor Party leaders, before and during the hectic July days, the former tended to be less radical or more liberal, while the latter tended to be more radical and scorned to be liberal. Buck had been graduated out of the old Progressive Party of 1912, in fact had been elected an alderman on this ticket, but he was anxious to forget his liberal past. He and some other intellectuals of the labor party movement thought of themselves as "reds," of a constructive type. They did much to influence the trade unionists to adopt their point of view. The differences between the forty-eighters and the leaders of the National Labor Party were, however, more apparent than real. In many ways the latter bent over backward in their anxiety to appear and to be radical. There was after all but little in a name, the all-night wrangling over a platform was largely meaningless in terms of organizational or voting strength, and the lack of unity was more costly than any kind of factional or personal victory. In 1924, name did not matter much, the platform was acceptable to all, and unity was achieved. The presence of Robert Marion La Follette did not need to complicate matters any more in 1920 than in 1924. In both years he and his immediate supporters were out to run things. They were amenable to reason and to cooperation from an organization in 1924 —the Conference for Progressive Political Action—and they would also have been in 1920, from the Labor Party and the Committee of Forty-Eight.

§

The delegates to the convention of the Committee of Forty-Eight "walked out on" their leaders. After listening to their many reports which indicated that they had reached no agreement with the labor party men, the delegates got up *en masse* and marched in a body to the meeting hall of the trade unionists. The Labor Party thus did not swallow up the organization which J. A. H. Hopkins had labored so hard to build up, by any effort of its own. And inasmuch as the delegates from the unions and local labor parties outnumbered those from the Committee of Forty-Eight in the merged convention, the leaders of the Labor Party could run things their own way.

Robert Marion La Follette was the choice of the delegates for the presidential nomination. But there was the same conflict between him and the labor men as there was between the latter and the forty-eighters. He proposed a platform and presaged a kind of leadership which seemed fatal to the radical leaders of the Labor Party. In 1920 La Follette was nowhere in so strong a position as he was later in 1924 to dictate to the third party supporters. His representatives in Chicago tried to stampede the delegates into nominating him, and their effort fizzled out. In the endless sessions of the platform committee the leaders of the Labor Party fought like Trojans against the forty-eighters and the supporters of La Follette. They had already trimmed their sails in the unhappy process of arriving at some sort of a working agreement with the followers of Hopkins who descended upon them. They refused to compromise further when La Follette's platform was the issue.

Specifically, they opposed "pussyfooting" on the question of the Negro's equality, they were intent on including the plank calling for an increasing and not merely an equal share for labor in the management of industry, and they refused to budge on the matter of democratic management in the operation of publicly owned utilities and natural resources. But in addition to these matters the Labor Party leaders were not anxious to have La Follette step in, reap where they had sown, and possibly run the campaign and organization pretty much as he saw fit. From their standpoint they were even willing to lose the vote-getting senator in order to build a lasting and growing party on the broad base of the labor unions and farmer associations.

With La Follette eliminated, the convention had the real problem of finding a man who could head the ticket. The delegates picked Parley Parker Christensen of Utah. He was a tall, striking figure, and pleased both the forty-eighters, from whose convention he came, and the Labor Party men, by the effective way in which he presided and by his genial personality. He appealed to the trade unionists because he was a genuine radical, he had defended the I. W. W. in his law practice, and he did not hesitate to accept the platform which was adopted. On

the first ballot Dudley Field Malone of New York polled
a good vote. On the second the westerner won out. Max
S. Hayes was prevailed upon to run for vice-president.
The delegates changed the name to that of Farmer-Labor
Party in the hope of appealing to the agricultural producers. They were glad at last to leave the hectic sessions of a supposedly amalgamated convention to return
home, those in sympathy with the party, ready to work;
those not converted, to go their own way. The results of
the July gatherings did not promise too much for the new
party.

§

Beside the divisions in the convention, the Farmer-
Labor Party did not have the necessary money, the numbers, the experienced men, the organization, nor the candidate to wage a very good campaign. The process of
merely getting the ticket on the ballot is costly, if there
is no army of volunteers available. In New York it
costs about $10,000 to pay notaries and solicitors to go
up and down every county in the state gathering signatures. Election laws are not passed to assist new parties.
A Farmer-Labor Party, or for that matter any minority
party, gets practically no publicity in the newspapers. It
must have a self-sacrificing membership to reach the
voters. The average worker expects to receive something,
not give his money and energy to a party. Finally, the
Farmer-Labor Party men were not so adept on the political as on the economic field. They did not know how to
raise money, organize meetings, distribute literature, rally
their followers, and keep them at work so efficiently as,
for example, the Socialist Party veterans.

Parley Parker Christensen was not an outstanding personality in the sense that he was known through any
crisis or event in labor history. He was not the orator
like Debs, he was not the writer like Benson, he was not
the public figure like La Follette, and without a powerful
organization he could not be put over in a big way. The

vote he received came mainly from those states where the movement for independent political action had made some headway. In all he obtained about a quarter of a million votes, scattered over the following states:

Colorado	3,016	New Jersey	2,173
Connecticut	1,947	New Mexico	1,097
Illinois	49,630	New York	18,413
Indiana	16,490	Pennsylvania	15,642
Iowa	10,321	South Dakota	34,707
Maryland	1,645	Utah	4,475
Michigan	10,372		
Missouri	3,291	Washington	77,246
Montana	12,204	Wyoming	2,180

It will be seen that Christensen received his support from Washington, South Dakota, Illinois, New York, Indiana, Pennsylvania, Montana, Michigan, and Iowa, nine states in all. He made a good showing only in Washington, South Dakota, and Montana.

§

When J. B. S. Hardman was editing the interesting *American Labor Monthly* some years back, John C. Kennedy wrote an article for it, in which he characterized Washington as "a logical farmer-labor party state." In 1920 this far western state led the country in the independent political movement. Seattle startled the powers that be with a thorough-going general strike on February 6, 1919. Its immediate cause was as non-revolutionary as that behind the British general strike. Both were sympathetic walk-outs on behalf of a union in a wage fight. The Seattle craft unions struck for five days to secure an increase for the mass of unskilled shipyard workers. Behind the two general strikes were radical labor movements prepared to take the step. During the Seattle tie-up, which was complete, an unarmed labor guard patrolled the streets. The unionists improvised eating places and milk stations, and they gave permits to garbage wagons and funeral cars. Mayor Ole Hanson threatened to place the city under martial law but did not go so far. On February 11 the labor men declared the strike off.

One of the leaders of the Seattle general strike and secretary of the central labor body, James A. Duncan, ran for mayor on a labor ticket in the spring of 1920 and polled the remarkable vote of 35,000 against 51,000 for the victor. In the November, 1920, election the Farmer-Labor Party candidates for state offices received an average vote of well over 100,000, about half of that for the winning republicans.

In Washington, where I. W. W. propaganda had left its mark, where socialists and industrialists had stamped the craft unions with their philosophies, and where long-shoremen refused to load ships with supplies for Kolchak, it was natural that the A. F. of L. unionists, railroad men, and farmers should organize the only Triple Alliance in the country. This formidable body held a convention in July, 1920, and threw its support behind the Farmer-Labor Party. But after the election, when the shipyard industry was on the decline, when the old-line A. F. of L. leaders began vigorously to oppose the new party, the alliance broke up. John C. Kennedy explained the scattering of its component elements:

After the enthusiasm of the first campaign was over and it was apparent that victory for the Farmer-Labor Party could be won only by an arduous and extended campaign—who stood by the ship? Not the Gompers type of labor officials, who looked upon political action solely as a means of getting political jobs or minor legislative concessions for organized labor; not the officials of the Nonpartisan League, who wanted a large dues-paying membership in the league and who feared that if the Farmer-Labor Party were too successful the league might lose its identity; not the liberals, who considered that the party was dominated too largely by a radical "labor crowd" . . . The real support for the Farmer-Labor Party had shrunk to the radical industrial workers and farmers together with a sprinkling of intellectuals who were interested in winning substantial advantages for labor as a class,— in a word, to those who wanted fundamental changes in the social, political and industrial system.

Outside of Washington Christensen received 50,000 in Illinois and less than 20,000 votes in New York. Of the poll in the middle western state only 5,000 came from the second largest city in the land. In the spring of 1919 John Fitzpatrick as candidate for mayor received 56,000 votes in Chicago. Inside a year and a half the Cook County Labor Party was through as a vote-getter. Down-state the party fared much better, and held its strength throughout the two years of 1919 and 1920. In New York City the labor party men put up a ticket in the November, 1919, election but partly through their ineptitude and partly through the obstacles placed in their path by the Tammany election board, they were not able to have their candidates on the regular ballot. It probably mattered but little for they would not have made much of a showing. The following year, after they organized a state labor party, they nominated Dudley Field Malone as candidate for governor and Rose Schneiderman for United States Senator. Malone took advantage of the bitter feeling of the Irish in New York City to stir up their republicanism at a time when British "black and tans" were "pacifying" the home land. As a result of his personal appeal he obtained 69,908 votes. He was, however, disappointed and withdrew from the movement. The leader of the Women's Trade Union League, Miss Schneiderman, polled only 27,934, and the presidential candidate 18,413.

CHAPTER XIII

THE CONFERENCE FOR PROGRESSIVE POLITICAL ACTION

In the year the World War started the membership of the American Federation of Labor was two million, six years later it was four million. In 1914 the affiliated unions which had all or some of their members working in the railroad industry numbered 219,500 adherents, in 1920 they counted 1,425,000, more than one-third of the national body:

Union	1914	1920
Blacksmiths	16,700	103,000
Boilermakers	9,600	48,300
Carmen (Railway)	28,700	182,100
Clerks (Railway)	5,000	186,000
Electricians	30,800	139,000
Firemen and oilers	16,000	29,600
Machinists	75,400	330,800
Maintenance of waymen	6,500	200,000
Sheet metal workers	17,800	21,800
Signalmen	700	12,300
Switchmen	9,800	14,000
Telegraphers	2,500	48,700

Between 1914 and 1917 there had been some increase in these twelve unions, particularly those also engaged in the metal trades. But their extraordinary gains were almost entirely due to the policies of the United States Railroad Administration and of William Gibbs McAdoo after 1917. Together with the Big Four—the engineers, firemen, conductors, and brakemen—they were given official recognition and allowed to organize freely. Before the railroads were turned back to their private owners by the signing of the Cummins-Esch law on February 28, 1920, the sixteen standard unions in the industry had a cohesiveness, membership, and unity previously unknown in their history.

The largest single union in the railroad group was that of the machinists, whose president was William H. Johnston. To the extent that any one created the Conference for Progressive Political Action it was Johnston's interest, strategic position, and contacts which accounted in large part for the origin and development of this political organization. From the days in 1911 when he, a known socialist, was elected president of the machinists' union, until he voluntarily left the office in 1926 on account of ill health, Johnston was generally to be found in opposition to the Gompers administration.

Johnston made his peace with the conservative executive council of the federation in 1917-1918, but he openly and vigorously opposed them after the armistice. In the Montreal (1920) convention he gave Jacob Fischer of the barbers a hard fight for the seventh vice-presidency and lost only by the vote of 19,920 to 18,195. In the post-war period he was not as radical as John Fitzpatrick, nor as ready as the Chicago leader to enter the arena. But in his own way he preferred to cooperate closely with the international officials, trying to swing the entire labor and progressive movement to more advanced policies. The odds were against him. The leaders of American labor would not march forward. The alliance of the railroad shop crafts and the railroad brotherhoods became a rope of sand. The Plumb plan was discarded. The Montreal and Denver resolutions of the A. F. of L. for government ownership and democratic management of the railroads were not pushed. The railroad strike was ineffective. The amalgamation program of federating the crafts into industrial unions, which had been given some lip service, was dropped. And the Conference for Progressive Political Action passed into oblivion. The chiefs of the railroad brotherhoods and the presidents of the internationals refused to leave the old beaten tracks.

§

It has been the commonly accepted opinion that American labor resorted to political action only in times when the trade unions, because of industrial depression or untoward causes, were weak and unable to achieve results on the economic field. How erroneous this opinion is, was shown in 1866 by the immediate plunge into politics of the new-born National Labor Union, formed as a federation of national craft unions which themselves had their origin in a wave of industrial activity. It was shown again in 1886 by the nation-wide formation of local labor parties when the Knights of Labor was at its peak and the American Federation of Labor was making its first strides. It was shown once more, and most strikingly, in the years between 1897 and 1904 when a socialist party got its first permanent foothold among the union rank and file at the period of the greatest industrial and trade union development the country had yet witnessed. Again the same fact was demonstrated in 1919-1920 by the emergence of state labor parties and finally of the National Labor Party while the unions were at a pinnacle of strength never attained previously or since. Finally, in 1922, when the Conference for Progressive Political Action was born, the unions engaged in politics not when they were weak, nor when they could not wield effectively the economic weapon. On the contrary, they marched into the political arena because they felt their power, because they had a heightened sense of labor solidarity, because they had a vision of larger things. The railroad shop crafts' strike did not occur until July, 1922, four months after the first sessions of the C. P. P. A. The latter included the representatives of the brotherhoods, which did not suffer from the strike at all. On the basis of this history, it seems clear that the workers have generally resorted to political action not because they cannot strike and use direct action, as in a period of depression. The fact is just opposite. They turn to politics because in a period of prosperity and growing union power they are awakened to a labor philosophy which is broader than the creed of pure and simpledom.

Industrial democracy, Plumb plan—the promise of a share in control offered by these proposals meant more to the railroad workers than the prospect of the continuation of the favorable conditions granted when the common carriers were run by the government. In 1919-1922 the rank and file on the railroads as well as in other industries had the feeling that the workers should share in management, that the private owner should not run industry like a Czar or a Kaiser. In periods of upheaval this democratic demand, often leaderless, inchoate, and short-lived, nevertheless is the most vital urge of the hour. The conservative railroad brotherhood chiefs talked of the necessity of political action in 1922 because even they felt the undercurrent for more power, more control to labor. The unity session of the Conference for Progressive Political Action on February 20-21, 1922 in Chicago, with representatives present of trade unions, progressive political, and farmer groups, was the expression of the underlying desire of those with even a little vision, to forge the instrument to attain more say in the affairs of government and life for the producing classes, for the farmers, for labor.

A committee consisting of Johnston, Martin F. Ryan of the railway carmen, Warren S. Stone of the engineers, E. J. Manion of the telegraphers, Timothy Healy of the stationary firemen, and L. E. Sheppard of the conductors sent out the call for the conference, at which 124 delegates appeared. Besides the railroad unions, the needle trades and the miners, to speak of only the largest bodies, were represented, as well as nine state federations of labor. Every progressive political organization except the extreme radicals was there, the Socialist Party, the

Farmer-Labor Party, the independent state parties, the Nonpartisan League. The largest farmers' associations were represented. The National Catholic Welfare Council and the Methodist Federation for Social Service had delegates. It was the most significant get-together in decades.

The first and organizing session of the Conference for Progressive Political Action was a love-feast. The leaders of the railroad unions, the backbone of the movement, saw a national organization grow up to carry out their policies through nonpartisan political action. They were all put on the national committee of fifteen and they would steer the ship in their own way. The supporters of independent political action, the delegates from the Socialist and Farmer-Labor Party and the radical unions, were also content. They were glad to be on the same boat with the chiefs of the powerful unions of America, even if they travelled second or third class. They were especially happy becaues they thought they saw the inevitable storm which would drive the pilot and captain to steer for "Labor Party Land." The plan of action provided that each state was free to adopt whatever political method it preferred, nonpartisanship or independent party. The national organizing committee included J. G. Brown of the Farmer-Labor Party and Morris Hillquit of the Socialist Party. The *Address to the American People* scored the old parties without mercy and as bitterly as the platform of any radical party. Finally, there would be another conference in December, 1922, and probably others after that, and who could tell what the C. P. P. A. would finally do?

§

The second conference was held in Cleveland, December 11-12, 1922, a month after the congressional elections. The national committee reported that it was well satisfied with the number of progressives elected and the work of the state and local organizations which had been formed in thirty-two out of the forty-eight states. The executives of the railway labor organizations had sent out instructions to the local lodges, special state editions of *Labor* totalling over 1,000,000 copies were distributed, and about $15,000 expended. The next step was to perfect and make permanent the subordinate units of the C. P. P. A. in every state of the Union.

But the spokesmen of the Farmer-Labor Party did not share the enthusiasm of the railroad chiefs nor the quiet hopefulness of the Socialist Party leaders. The delegates of the Farmer-Labor Party introduced a resolution which precipitated the first real clash and split in the C. P. P. A. They wanted it to declare for independent political action. They did not have the support of all elements who genuinely wanted the same thing they did. The Socialist Party men openly stated their opposition. James Oneal declared that he did not think the organized masses were yet ready for an independent party. Morris Hillquit, previously in an address to the conference, pointed out why he was in the assembly:

We are convinced that we have made the initial step. But these gains or these victories in the old party primaries, we are convinced, are temporary. We are convinced that the workers of this country will eventually go by the road which has brought power and progress to the workers and the farmers of the other countries of the world. . . .

I want you to know that this is my sentiment, my hope and inspiration. But personally I take the position that progress is always made safely and slowly, step by step. We can go no faster than we are allowed to go; and so I say, let us continue being helpful to each other; let us make progress step by step, day by day, year by year; let us increase our power; let us increase our facilities for political power, and the right way will undoubtedly be found.

From the standpoint of the socialists it was unwise to force something upon the union men at an unpropitious time.

Representatives of the Missouri and Wisconsin Federations of Labor, the delegates from the Minnesota Farmer-

Labor Party, and a few from the farming states, as well as the leaders of the party which introduced the resolution for independent political action, spoke in favor of it. Bert M. Jewell of the railway employees' department of the A. F. of L. and E. J. Evans of the electrical workers, as well as Edward Keating, advanced the arguments against it, backed up by a delegate from the Nonpartisan League of North Dakota. The large number present from the radical unions and the national and state political parties in favor of independent action— the delegates of the Socialist Party supported the resolution when it came to a vote—accounted for the total of fifty-two for the Farmer-Labor Party's resolution. It was beaten by sixty-four delegates, on a show of hands. Had a roll call been taken, the railroad organizations would have defeated it badly. Under the rules the international unions cast one vote for every 10,000 members, while the political bodies had only as many votes as the number of delegates to which they were entitled. The needle trades and the other radical unions did not have more than 300,000 members as against three or four times that number in the railroad bodies plus the miners. But aside from the question of whether the resolution could have been carried, no effective action could be taken by the C. P. P. A. if the leaders of the transportation unions were against it. In February, 1925, when they declared against independent political action once more, the C. P. P. A. disappeared.

The Farmer-Labor Party men had tried to swing the organization their way. They failed. Henceforth they were through with it. The Workers' Party was not even allowed to participate, much less start anything. The credentials committee made no mention of the delegates from the communist party. C. E. Ruthenberg, who was present, protested that his credentials had been handed in. Edward Keating thereupon moved that they be not received. He charged the Workers' Party with being un-American, that it did not stand for the constitution and the flag, that its leaders were disrupting the unions, and that the party was manned by private detectives and spies.   His motion was brushed aside and the matter was referred back to the credentials committee.

The latter reported that the delegates of the Workers' Party be not seated. The Farmer-Labor Party spokesmen favored their inclusion, while the Socialist Party delegates demanded their exclusion. Otto Branstetter, their secretary, read the following statement for the socialist delegation:

We do not believe that the representatives of the Workers' Party are agents of the employers. Nor can we agree with the sentiment that the Workers' Party or any other organization should be excluded because it is alleged to be "un-American." It ill becomes any member of a labor organization to resort to the phrases used by the most reactionary interests in creating prejudice against organized labor.

The Socialist Party delegation therefore does not share the views offered by the delegate in question as a reason for excluding the delegates of the Workers' Party. It does believe, however, that actual experience has shown that the disruptive tactics of the Workers' Party justify the expulsion of this party from representation. It further believes that by rejecting the principles of democracy in favor of dictatorship the Workers' Party is recorded against the declared principles of the Conference and hence is not entitled to representation.

There was practically no debate on the matter. The Workers' Party was not admitted.

The Cleveland conference adopted a permanent plan of organization, a short platform with a number of additional planks to be added by the enlarged national committee, a few resolutions, and adjourned.

§

Before the Conference for Progressive Political Action held its third session in St. Louis, February 11-12, 1924, some interesting developments had taken place as far as the Socialist Party was concerned, and also as far as the candidacy of William Gibbs McAdoo on the democratic ticket was a matter of importance to the railroad union leaders. The socialists had experienced their first hard blow in New York state when they tried to carry out their plan of boring from within the new organization, and the nonpartisans in the C. P. P. A. were in a quandary because their favorite, the man who had helped to give them prestige, power, and favorable working conditions, had been smeared with oil.

Under the plan of organization adopted in the December, 1922, session of the C. P. P. A., state conferences were called with all organizations invited which had representation in the national body. In other words, the subordinate units of the railroad and other unions, progressive political parties, cooperatives, farmers' associations, and the like, were to be included in a state organization of the conference. In the Empire State, however, the local leaders of the railroad unions went ahead and called a state organizing convention of the C. P. P. A. by and for themselves. This was obviously contrary to the rules. As a result of pressure put upon them by the national officials the New Yorkers modified the call and sent invitations to the radical unions—the needle trades—of New York, and to the Socialist and the American Labor Party.

The date of the convention was July 29, 1923; the city, Albany. When the delegates from the organizations which had been invited—outside the railroad unions—arrived, they were presented with the spectacle of having their admission considered by their hosts. They were finally allowed to participate. Then there were many speeches and the note of harmony was struck. The conference looked like a repetition of the first session of the national C. P. P. A. in February, 1922. After a day and a half, however, the outstanding leaders of the railroad unions, influenced and backed up by some old party politicians who took an important part in the proceedings, decided that the play had continued long enough. Without much ado they carried a motion to adjourn the gathering. They rang down the curtain on any performance where socialists and those in favor of independent political action were there to participate, persuade, or pray for anything but nonpartisan political action. They were not going to give them any chance to bore from within. The socialists and supporters of independent political action declared that they were willing temporarily to accept nonpartisanship as the official policy of the conference, as they had in the national C. P. P. A., but they asked that in May, 1924, another conference be held to decide permanent political policy. They did not say, however, that they would endorse so-called friends or condemn so-called enemies of labor in the two old parties and enter the primaries. In July, 1923, the New York railroad union leaders dampened the hope of the labor party men. In February, 1925, the national spokesmen of the transportation unions buried it for some time to come, despite the magnificent showing that La Follette made in the presidential election. The leaders were opposed to a labor party and would do nothing to promote one.

Before the St. Louis conference of 1924 opened, the labor leaders who dominated the national committee of the C. P. P. A. had met in Washington. They undoubtedly discussed the bursting of the presidential boom of McAdoo, due to the oil disclosures, and they must have raised the possibility of an independent race by Robert M. La Follette. The St. Louis gathering in February could not have taken the action it did, of calling a nationwide convention for July 4 at Cleveland "for the purpose of taking action on nomination of candidates for the offices of president and vice-president of the United States," unless the railroad union chiefs were ready for it. Furthermore, the conference added a section to its plan of organization by which state branches which organized independent parties could continue affiliation. It took a slap at the New York railroad union officials who had excluded the socialists and radicals, by providing for expulsion of such bodies conducted in violation of the

rules of the national body. It even accepted a resolution
on the British Labor Party—which had just taken office—
including some remarkable concessions to the point of
view of those supporting independent political action:

> Whereas, The British Labor Party, through its intelligent and
> forceful program for economic justice at home and for justice in
> international relations has deservedly attained its present power,
> and . . .
> Resolved, That we welcome the success of the British Labor
> Party as conclusive evidence that workers in any country having
> universal or general suffrage may come into peaceful control of
> their government whenever they have the intelligence and the will
> to do so.

Well might the St. Louis conference adjourn on this
note:

> Delegate Hillquit moved that a vote of thanks and appreciation
> be extended to Mr. Johnston, the chairman. The delegates re-
> sponded with a rising vote of thanks.

§

Close to 600 delegates flocked to the nominating convention of the Conference for Progressive Political Action
on July 4, 1924. The larger representation was due to
the fact that the state branches of the Socialist and
Farmer-Labor Party, of the Committee of Forty-Eight,
and of the Women's Committee on Political Action were
for the first time invited, that the unions sent heavier
delegations, and that a host of miscellaneous groups were
included. William H. Johnston made the keynote address. Senators Lynn Frazier of North Dakota and
Hendrik Shipstead of Minnesota, and Congressmen
John M. Nelson of Wisconsin and Fiorello La Guardia
of New York for the progressives in office, Morris Hillquit and Harriot Stanton Blatch for the socialists, Andrew
Furuseth for the seamen, and several others spoke. The
delegates were in a hopeful mood.

The first note of discord arose when the credentials
committee refused to seat William Mahoney of Minnesota for his active participation in the St. Paul convention

of June 17, 1924, which the national committee of the
Conference for Progressive Political Action and Robert
Marion La Follette had previously condemned. Mahoney
had practically no defenders. The next clash came when
after Robert M. La Follette, Jr., finished reading his
father's message a leader of the engineers jumped up and
nominated the senator from Wisconsin for president.
Those who were there merely to nominate La Follette
were not interested in what happened to the C. P. P. A.
The supporters of independent political action demanded
that the convention be first organized—the credentials
committee had not reported—and the regular committees
bring in their recommendations. Precipitate action was
thus prevented.

E. J. Manion of the telegraphers, and chairman of the
committee on organization and campaign, read a unanimous report: it endorsed La Follette for president on his
own platform; it authorized the national committee in
consultation with the presidential candidate to pick his
running mate; and it instructed the executive to call a
special national convention in January, 1925, to consider
the formation of a permanent independent political party.

In the platform he submitted to the convention La Follette declared that the paramount issue was "to break the
combined power of the private monopoly system over the
political and economic life of the American people." The
first plank of the independent platform adopted by the
convention also demanded that the federal government
crush private monopoly. In only two industries did the
campaign document call for public ownership: water
power and the railroads. The labor leaders and La
Follette were still thinking in terms of individualized,
competitive business, and were fighting shy of a policy
of nationalization. In that they differed sharply from the
more radical sponsors of the National Labor Party.

In addition to that on private monopoly, the separate
platform of the C. P. P. A. had three planks among its
fourteen—one on taxation, another on the courts, the

last on foreign affairs—which will indicate fairly well how progressive or radical it was:

Retention of surtax on swollen incomes, restoration of the tax on excess profits, taxation of stock dividends, profits undistributed to evade taxes, rapidly progressive taxes on large estates and inheritances, and repeal of excessive tariff duties, especially on trust-controlled necessities of life and of nuisance taxes on consumption, to relieve the people of the present unjust burden of taxation and compel those who profited by the war to pay their share of the war's cost, and to provide the funds for adjusted compensation solemnly pledged to the veterans of the World War.

Abolition of the tyranny and usurpation of the courts, including the practice of nullifying legislation in conflict with the political, social or economic theories of the judges. Abolition of injunctions in labor disputes and of the power to punish for contempt of court without trial by jury. Election of all federal judges without party designation for limited terms.

We denounce the mercenary system of degraded foreign policy under recent administrations in the interests of financial imperialists, oil imperialists, and international bankers, which has at times degraded our State Department from its high service as a strong and kindly intermediary of defenseless governments to a trading outpost for those interests and concession seekers engaged in the exploitation of weaker nations, as contrary to the will of the American people, destructive of domestic development and provocative of war. We favor an active foreign policy to bring about a revision of the Versailles treaty in accordance with the terms of the armistice, and to promote firm treaty agreements with all nations to outlaw wars, abolish conscription, drastically reduce land, air and naval armaments and guarantee public referendum on peace and war.

There was no discussion of the platform on the floor of the convention, as there was no sharp division in the committee which reported it out. There was no other candidate for the presidency than La Follette, and there was no objection to the unusual procedure of letting a small group nominate the candidate for vice-president. At least, none was expressed, although the socialists would have probably advanced James H. Maurer as their choice if any balloting had taken place. The statement of La Follette that the time had come "for a militant political movement independent of the two old party organizations," and his prediction that a new party would be born after the November election, because the people would "register their will and united purpose by a vote of such magnitude that a new political party" was inevitable, cheered those delegates who were boring from within the C. P. P. A. On the other hand, his immediate policy, which he emphasized, of heading up a campaign with candidates only for president and vice-president, and his endorsement of those progressives running for Congress on the two old party tickets, enabled the supporters of the nonpartisan political policy in the C. P. P. A. and the A. F. of L. to work for him.

Stepping for the only time out of its traditional nonpartisan attitude, the executive council of the American Federation of Labor specifically approved La Follette and Senator Burton K. Wheeler of Montana, the vice-presidential candidate, on the ground that both "have, throughout their whole political careers, stood steadfast in defense of the rights and interests of wage earners and farmers," and "have proffered a platform in which the economic issues of the day are met in a manner more nearly conforming to labor's proposals than any other platform." What made it comparatively easy for the heads of the A. F. of L. to endorse an independent national ticket for the only time in the history of the federation was the fact that conservative Coolidge the republican was out of the question, John W. Davis the democratic candidate had resigned from the House of Morgan in order to run for office, and La Follette had fought so strenuously and so courageously for labor for a lifetime that it would have been base ingratitude not to have given him some encouragement. Finally, the A. F. of L. leaders saw quite a genuine and significant mass movement behind La Follette. They rode with the tide. They also must have known that they were not giving up their nonpartisan policy for good. They never intended to do that when they officially endorsed La Follette.

The baking of the La Follette pie was a labor of many willing hands. The trade unionists, the socialists, the awakened farmers, and the progressives contributed generously of their time and money. It was comparatively easy, therefore, to put the ticket on the ballot in every state but one, Louisiana. In California the state election officials took advantage of technicalities to compel the La Follette presidential electors to appear only under the Socialist Party name. In Wisconsin, by mutual agreement, Coolidge electors were put in the Republican Party column. The Liberty Bell was chosen as the only emblem, while such designations as Progressive Party, Independent Party, Farmer-Labor Party or Labor Party were used.

About a quarter of a million dollars was raised for the campaign. The Scripps-Howard chain was the only group of daily newspapers to support the independent ticket, in addition to the labor, radical, and liberal press which was almost entirely made up of weeklies and monthlies with a limited and specialized circulation. Not all the subordinate labor organizations followed the example of the executive of the American Federation of Labor. International union officials and state federations of labor, local leaders and central labor bodies throughout the country, supported the republican or the democratic nominees. George L. Berry, president of the Pressmen's Union, had himself been a contender for the vice-presidential nomination of the Democratic Party. Men like John L. Lewis of the miners and William Hutcheson of the carpenters were well known republicans. Terrence V. O'Connor, former president of the Longshoremen's Union, and appointed to the United States Shipping Board in part at least for his support of Harding in 1920, issued several absurd public statements attacking La Follette. The Central Trades and Labor Council of Greater New York officially endorsed the progressive, but a very short while before the election its executive came out for the Democratic Party nominee.

The Republican Party had little to fear from so conservative and unpopular a candidate as its rival John W. Davis, and from so shattered a party as that which emerged from a convention of record-breaking length and futility. In order to weaken La Follette in his industrial and agrarian strongholds the party of big business *par excellence* attacked his proposal to have Congress pass upon the Supreme Court's power of declaring laws unconstitutional, and charged him with undermining the foundations of the American government and endangering property relations. The republican chiefs saw to it that La Follette appeared as a radical, a very near relative to a bolshevik. They took advantage of the business depression to intimidate wage earners in ways that the 1896 campaign had shown were effective. They threatened those with jobs that they would lose them if they did not vote for Coolidge, and they appealed to the unemployed to cast their ballots for prosperity. Despite the oil scandals, the agricultural and industrial depression, the reactionary policies of the party, and the colorlessness of Calvin Coolidge, the latter lost only Wisconsin to LaFollette and rode into power hands down.

The leader of the progressive forces got what little comfort he could from running second in eleven states, apart from capturing his own: California, Idaho, Iowa, Minnesota, Montana, Nevada, North Dakota, Oregon, South Dakota, Washington, and Wyoming. Some of La Follette's supporters talked of ten million votes, while others, in their little knowledge of the forces arrayed against them, predicted his election. The agricultural states which had suffered from the deflation did not fall into the La Follette column because the farmers had been improving their condition since 1921. Between 1923 and 1924 the price index of all grains had risen from 114 to 129, while the index of non-agricultural prices in the same period had dropped from 171 to 162. The republicans were lucky because in 1924 the purchasing power of the farmers' products went up. Moreover, the progressives had but little organization outside of North Dakota and Minnesota, they did not have the money or newspapers to reach the farmers, and they could not build up their strength inside of three or four months in forty-eight states. If consideration is given to his limited resources, La Follette made a remarkable run in the farming states.

He polled an extraordinary vote, also, in the large cities. He obtained the support of many Irish, German, and Jewish voters. Districts in New York which are inhabited heavily by these nationalities showed a substantial vote for the senator. He appealed to the Irish because the Democratic Party had turned down Alfred E. Smith, because he was not a defender of Great Britain, because he had fought for Irish independence, and because he had always stood for the common and poor people. La Follette undoubtedly drew to himself many German-American voters because of his anti-war stand. In part for the same reason, and especially for his known progressivism, he made a clean sweep of those Jewish districts which the Socialist Party had cultivated for a quarter of a century. Interestingly enough La Follette carried practically every assembly district—in some cases by a majority—which once had been a socialist stronghold, and yet the candidates of the Socialist Party for state and local offices in the same sections came out generally at the bottom of the poll. Everywhere in the city and country La Follette benefitted from the hard and continuous propaganda work of the labor and farmer parties which had preceded and continued through the 1924 campaign. But despite the vote of 5,000,000 which La Follette received, the army behind him melted away soon after the election and the C. P. P. A. went up in smoke.

§

The result of the La Follette campaign was a disappointment to political romanticists, to those who required a mental earthquake to unsettle their conviction in favor of nonpartisan political action, and to those who needed a tidal wave to float them into sure political berths to replace those they held as appointees or elected officials by their connection with the old parties. The so-called progressive congressmen who backed La Follette feared that they could not be reelected on an independent or third party ticket. They were only too glad, therefore, to abandon the ship. They had no fundamental program for which they needed an independent party. Nor did Senators La Follette and Wheeler do much if anything to hold the office holders, the labor leaders, and the rank and file in line for a new political party. They gave up the struggle without a murmur.

The representatives of the American Federation of Labor and the railroad unions never intended to assist seriously in the upbuilding of a third party and they fell back on the excuse that the vote was a disappointment. One of the arguments which they have generally advanced against a labor or independent party has been that it does not get the backing of the voters. Now when La Follette polled about 5,000,000 votes, a percentage of the total comparable to that of some of the leading labor and socialist parties in Europe at the time, they refused to view it as a splendid beginning and a remarkable demonstration of the unity of the opposition to the old parties. They were simply not ready ideologically for labor solidarity at the ballot box along independent lines, and some were even prepared to prevent the formation of a labor-farmer-progressive party because it endangered their influence and position in the two old parties. It is not easy to make the headway otherwise possible among the unions if the international officials are opposed to a third party movement.

When the national committee of the C. P. P. A. met on December 12, 1924, accordingly, the result was a foregone conclusion. The railroad union leaders declared they were opposed to holding the January or February, 1925, convention to consider the formation of a new party. They were outvoted, however—30 to 13. The individuals who constituted the majority did not represent the membership that the thirteen did, and it was a pyrrhic victory. On February 21-22, 1925, when the last convention of the C. P. P. A. was held in Chicago, L. E. Sheppard, president of the conductors, introduced a resolution, which was supported by E. J. Manion of the telegraphers and David B. Robertson of the firemen, calling for a continuation of the C. P. P. A. along nonpartisan lines. No vote was taken on this proposition. Instead, a motion to adjourn *sine die,* with the provision that those who wished to organize a new party could reconvene as individuals, was carried. With this vote the Conference for Progressive Political Action passed out of existence. Subsequently the efforts of the socialists and progressives to get together into one party failed. The organization which the liberals set up did not survive the conference which planned it. In 1925 there now remained some independent and farmer-labor parties in the states, the homeless progressives and the Socialist and the Workers' Party. There was no unity among them. And apart from Minnesota and Milwaukee, there was little strength left in the Farmer-Labor or the Socialist Party.

§

When the American Labor Party of Greater New York held its first convention on January 11-12, 1919, a number of prominent members of the Socialist Party were present as delegates. The official attitude of their party had not yet been announced. Those who spoke, however, took pains to state that they did not intend leaving their party, and that they opposed the policy of the Labor Party enrolling individuals as members and not confining itself to the affiliation of unions. On the 20th the national executive committee handed down a statement which clarified the situation. It reminded the members that they could not join, nor endorse or cooperate with the Labor Party. It declared that "the history of all such organizations must be judged by their deeds rather than their promises." It suggested that "we must maintain an open mind and a philosophical attitude towards this new political manifestation in times like these," and it wound up as follows: "It is only by continuing our position and our economic interpretation of events, that we can hope to organize the workers so they will not only declare for industrial democracy but will act through the Socialist Party to gain this goal."

When the Cook County and the Illinois Labor Party were organized, some of the socialist unionists took the floor to oppose their formation. When the Farmer-Labor Party convention of July, 1920, nominated Parley Parker Christensen for president a New York *Call* editorial of August 7 called him a populist, and attacked the platform on which he ran, on the ground that it dealt "entirely with the present ills from which the workers suffer, without attempting to show the people that these ills are the legitimate fruits of the capitalist system." Morris Hillquit at the time published in the *Socialist Review* his opinion of the new party:

The Labor Party would have justified such expectations [of being a class movement on the road to class-consciousness and socialism] and given promise of becoming an active factor in the struggle for the emancipation of labor if it had succeeded in enlisting the support of the bulk of the organized workers in the United States, or failing that, if it had at least established itself as a radical minority within the organized labor movement, determined to wrest the leadership from the hands of the reactionaries. Its whole existence and hope of success lay in the fact that it was frankly a class party—a political organization of labor. Unfortunately the leaders of the new movement seemed to realize this cardinal point only during the formative stages of their party. When they entered upon their first political campaign, they succumbed completely and pitiably to the besetting vice of "practical" American politics, the sacrifice of principle to the desire of momentary political success, the selling of the soul for votes.

The fusion of the Labor Party with the nebulous aggregation of middle-class liberals known as the Committee of Forty-Eight was an irretrievable surrender to the vital working-class character of the new party, and the coupling of its political destinies with the purely imaginary forces of the farming community made confusion worse confounded. It is therefore not to be wondered at that the party has produced a platform which is little more than a heterogeneous assortment of meaningless liberal and radical phrases utterly devoid of the cohesive cement of the modern working class philosophy, nor that it has named for its principal standard-bearer a man whose name and record stand for nothing in the labor movement or in the radical political movement of the country. The Farmer-Labor Party has killed the Labor Party and committed suicide with one blow. It will hardly survive the presidential election for any length of time and will eventually dissolve into the separate incongruous elements which go into its make-up or patch-up.

The socialist leaders resented the intrusion of the labor parties upon the scene. They felt that it had taken many years of work and sacrifice to build up the Socialist Party, they had just come through the white terror of the war period, and above all, they believed that the hour had struck for something more revolutionary than a moderate, reformist labor party. It was natural for them to think that the times called for a revolutionary socialist program in 1919. But they did not know their America and they did not have enough contacts with the labor movement. It was primarily because the Socialist Party was so isolated from the masses in 1918 and 1919 that it was so badly split by the foreign language federations and the left wing elements.

The spokesmen of the party were as wrong in their attitude toward the labor party leadership—they were too close to the eastern border and Europe—as they were in their program of affiliation with the Communist (Third) International, with reservations. The fight of the right, center, and left wings within the Socialist Party prevented hardly any of them from seeing much else than their internal struggle. The determination of the party to try to unite all elements behind Eugene Victor Debs in 1920 and wage a campaign that would keep the comrades busy and secure a vote that would give them new faith, however necessary as a Socialist Party measure, was short-sighted policy so far as the working class movement was concerned. Had the socialist leaders had any real contacts with the militant minority of trade unionists who were carrying on the fight for the labor party and progressive policies all along the line in 1919 and 1920 they could not have so misjudged them. It was, therefore, only in 1921, when the Socialist Party had gotten rid of practically all left wing and communist borers from within, when it turned its gaze from Russia to the United States, and when it had dwindled to the shadow of its former vigorous self, that it faced the problem of re-orienting itself in the light of the developments of the post-war period.

§

When the Socialist Party convention of 1920 was held, in New York City, May 8-14, there was still a group of about one-fourth of the delegates who wanted to tie up the organization with the Communist International and direct it into communist channels. This group was led by J. Louis Engdahl, William Kruse, and Benjamin Glassberg. The majority in the convention also supported affiliation with Moscow but with reservations, that "no formula such as 'the dictatorship of the proletariat in the form of soviets' or any other special formula for the attainment of the socialist commonwealth be imposed," and that "all true socialist forces" be united into one international. The 1920 convention declared that it was "vitally necessary that the workers organize along industrial lines," thus abandoning the old policy of neutrality, and came out for the election of representatives to all legislative bodies by industries as well as by geographic units.

By the time the next gathering took place, June 25-29, 1921, in Detroit, Moscow had handed down the twenty-one points and had rejected the application of the Socialist Party. It was decided accordingly to remain without any international affiliation and a statement was adopted, beginning as follows:

> The Socialist Party of the United States considers that its paramount duty is to build a powerful, revolutionary socialist organization in this country. It is, therefore, resolved to devote all of its energy and resources to this task, believing it to be the most valuable service it can render to the cause of international socialism.

In December, 1920, the largest foreign language federation, that of the Finns, had decided by a two-thirds vote to withdraw. They had turned communist. In the fall of the following year the Jewish Socialist Federation, one of the few active foreign groups left after the 1919 split, also voted in a special convention to leave on left wing grounds. The Bohemian federation seceded at the same time. In the case of the first two, new national federations, loyal to the party, were organized. Shortly after the 1921 convention those English-speaking members who had agitated through the Committee for the Third International and the Workers' Council for communist principles also left the party. As a result of the secessions, with relatively few new members coming in because of the presence of the labor parties, the panic of 1920-1921, and absorption of the party workers in internal controversy, the Socialist Party was down in 1922 to 11,019 dues paying supporters. It had also suffered in the elections.

§

In the November, 1918, elections Meyer London was defeated for Congress but Victor L. Berger was elected by a large plurality. He was not, however, allowed to take his seat in the special session of April, 1919. When the committee of the House made its investigation of his war record and views—on February 20, 1919, he was sentenced to twenty years in prison by Judge Landis—and reported adversely, he was expelled by a practically unanimous vote—only one opposed. On December 19,

1919, he was reelected against a fusion candidate. The following January he was again denied his seat in the House. In the November, 1920, election he failed of being returned by only 6,777 votes in a contest with the republicans and democrats united behind his opponent.

The experience of the congressman from Wisconsin was repeated by the socialist assemblymen from New York City. In November, 1918, only two of the ten socialists running for reelection went to Albany. In most cases the two old parties buried their sham differences and fused in order to accomplish their defeat. The following November, despite fusion and despite the internal warfare in the party, five socialists were elected, Samuel De Witt and Samuel Orr from the Bronx, Charles Solomon from Kings, and August Claessens and Louis Waldman from New York County. After a trial which lasted about ten weeks the committee which had been appointed to investigate their qualifications and eligibility voted seven to six in favor of expulsion and the assembly decided by large majorities to unseat all five.

When Thaddeus C. Sweet, speaker of the assembly, called the five socialists to the bar and lectured them, after which Simon Adler, republican majority leader, moved for the investigation of their eligibility, the New York *Call* ran a headline across its first page in heavy black type: "Died at Albany, January 7, 1920, Representative Government." The labor organizations protested the expulsion of the socialists, as did the Bar Association of New York. The latter appoined a committee composed of Charles Evans Hughes, Ogden Mills, and Joseph Proskauer to plead against the act of the assembly. The case took on national importance. For the socialists Morris Hillquit, Gilbert E. Roe—the former law partner of Senator La Follette—,Seymour Stedman, Walter Nelles, S. John Block, and William Karlin were matched by an equally able array of legal talent hired by the state. The defense by Hillquit and the testimony of Waldman caused some comment among left wing elements still inside the party, to say nothing of those in the underground communist movement.

According to the *American Labor Year Book, 1921-1922*, a responsible socialist writer, David P. Berenberg, contributing the article, "Algernon Lee and Morris Hillquit testified to the purposes of the Socialist Party."

> The St. Louis resolution, which had been a center of attack, was shown to have been an expression of anti-war sentiment, but not an incitement to the destruction of war work. . . . The influence of minors and aliens in the party was shown to be negligible. In an answer to Assemblyman Evans, Morris Hillquit said that he would oppose an attempt on the part of Russia to impose a soviet form of government on the United States against the wishes of the American people.

In defense of his testimony Louis Waldman wrote a series of articles in the New York *Call*. He argued that the government of the state of New York was a people's government, that the government of the United States was not quite a capitalist government, and that he preferred the government of New York to the soviet government of Russia. He declared again that he would fight for this country to repel any invasion and he favored necessary preparation in order to do so. Despite the party rule he claimed he had to vote for appropriations for the militia under the constitution of the state which he swore to uphold when he took his oath of office. The left wingers attacked both Waldman and Hillquit, especially the former, for what they considered their extreme opportunism and made their conduct one more justification for leaving the party.

The five expelled socialists were reelected on September 16, 1920, but were not all permitted to take their seats. Only Orr and De Witt were allowed to enter the assembly, the other three were expelled. The two Bronxites immediately resigned. In November, 1920, three socialists were elected to the assembly, and one to the state senate, Edmund Seidel, the former editor of the *People* when he was a member of the old Socialist Labor

Party. One of the socialists, Henry Jager, was unseated on the ground that he was not a resident of New York state. The rest were not disturbed. In 1921 only August Claessens was elected to the assembly, and he was not given his rightful seat—his "honorable" opponents used time-honored Tammany methods in order to steal the election—until the 1922 session of the legislature was nearly at an end. In November, 1922, no socialist was elected from any district in New York. Meyer London who had been sent to Congress in 1920 was defeated for reelection in 1922 by a gerrymander, whereby nationalities and areas were so shifted about to make it extremely difficult for him to beat a fusion candidate. Outside of Milwaukee which reelected Daniel W. Hoan mayor for his third term in 1922, and which sent Berger back to Congress in the same year, there were no spots in the United States which could claim any socialist elected officials. Judge Jacob Panken held a municipal judgeship in New York City to which he had been elected in 1917.

In the presidential election of 1920 Eugene Victor Debs, still in prison, polled about 900,000 votes, the same figure as he received in 1912, but over 300,000 above that of Benson in 1916. In terms of percentages, the vote showed a considerable decline over 1912, however, although it equalled 1916. In 1912 Debs received 5.9 per cent of the total vote, in 1916 Benson got 3.2, in 1920 Debs raised it to 3.4. La Follette obtained 16.6 per cent of the total vote of 1924, two and one-half times the record poll of the Socialist Party in 1912. And yet the dyed-in-the-wool supporters of nonpartisan political action would not build on that kind of a showing.

§

At its meeting of March 9, 1920, the national executive committee of the Socialist Party informed the World War Veterans who had suggested a coalition of forces for the coming election that "the conditions now prevailing were temporary; that the Socialist Party was based on the socialist movement and that it could not afford to coalesce with any groups and lose its identity on issues, however important, that are only fleeting." In the May, 1920, convention of the party in New York it took but one minute to vote down a resolution calling for cooperation with other groups. At the July, 1920, convention of the Farmer-Labor Party Otto Branstetter took the floor to withdraw the name of Eugene Victor Debs as a possible candidate for president. Nevertheless, by June, 1921, when the Detroit convention was held, the delegates adopted a resolution, with only two dissenting votes, calling for a survey of all radical and labor organizations with a view to securing their cooperation in the political field. Were not the railroad unions ready to launch the Conference for Progressive Political Action, and were not Johnston and some others willing to include the socialists, it is quite probable that nothing would have come of the Detroit resolution.

The Socialist Party was now not able to attract the national unions, apart from the needle trades, under its standard. To its May, 1920, convention it had invited the labor organizations to send delegates. None responded except some radical New York union groups. After the C. P. P. A. was organized in February, 1922, the Socialist Party was glad to unite locally with units of the Farmer-Labor Party, but it refused to send delegates to the conference of July 3, 1923 which the national leaders of the F. L. P. called, on this ground:

A necessary condition to the establishment of a really powerful political party of the working class is the active support of at least a majority of the great trade unions. Unless there is assurance that this support is now obtainable, any attempt at this time to effect the proposed "unity" of the political forces of the entire working class would result in disappointment.

The Socialist Party was pinning its hopes on the C. P. P. A., and especially on the state organizations which had autonomy and could take independent political action if they chose In its reply to the invitation of the Farmer-

Labor Party the socialist national executive committee said that it believed "that by working through state conferences called by that body where the views of local labor organizations in each state will be directly represented, it will at the present juncture best advance the cause of working class unity on the political field." The crash at Albany, when the railroad unionists shut the door first and then after admitting them, expelled the socialists from a conference of the C. P. P. A., was still before them when they wrote their reply to the F. L. P.

In the congressional election of 1922 the Social Democratic Party of Wisconsin did not nominate a candidate against La Follette. In the days when the Socialist Party was more orthodox such action would have called forth, as it once did, tremendous agitation, demands for the expulsion of the state branch and for the recall of Victor L. Berger, and a great hue and cry of "back to the fathers." But in 1922 and 1923 the conventions of the party adopted a set of rules instead, to guide the state organizations in the tortuous path of cooperation with non-socialist groups. When the July, 1924, convention of the C. P. P. A. nominated La Follette, Hillquit took the floor to endorse him. Neither he nor any of the socialist leaders opposed the adoption of the senator's or of the C. P. P. A.'s platforms, which were not socialist documents if measured by the standards set by the Socialist Party prior to 1924. The convention of the Marxians, which immediately followed that of the C. P. P. A., concurred in practically all the actions of the latter by the overwhelming vote of 115 to 17. The newly elected national executive committee, meeting on July 22, 1924, went further. It declared that socialists should cooperate with the C. P. P. A. to nominate independent candidates for Congress.

Where such independent nominations are not made, the socialists should as a rule make their own party nominations. But when a candidate of another party has the official endorsement and approval of the national organization of the C. P. P. A., and the Socialist Party has no chance of election, it may be best, in the campaign of 1924, to abstain from making a rival nomination.

The Socialist Party had in the past refused to make any concessions to those who argued for a less uncompromising policy. I. A. Hourwich, in particular, had written frequently in favor of the party throwing its support to the candidates of the old parties in exchange for concessions, a process which the European socialist parties were and are only too familiar with. But the Socialist Party on the United States refused even to allow its members to leave the fold when the socialist candidate was eliminated in a preliminary election. In the historic 1917 convention at St. Louis, which adopted the anti-war resolution, eliminated the section on sabotage, and united the right, center, and left wings, the Socialist Party also turned down cooperation with the Nonpartisan League. A good deal of water had flowed under the bridge between 1917 and 1924.

§

The socialists worked hard in the La Follette campaign and contributed very generously. They were keenly disappointed with the result of the February, 1925, convention. They proposed unity with the progressives who were anxious for a third party, but on a basis which would have admitted the national, state, and local Socialist Party organizations. They refused to accept a compromise which would allow the state organizations, as autonomous bodies, to organize along such lines as they chose, seeking the cooperation of all groups which had fought together in the 1924 campaign.

The conflict was over an organization such as the C. P. P. A., with directly affiliated unions, farmers' organizations, and political parties, which the socialists advocated, on one hand, and on the other, a body in which economic and political groups did not figure largely but which was organized rather on a geographical basis by individuals, which the third party advocates demanded. By a vote of 93 to 64 the latter defeated the proposition of the Socialist Party. The socialists were glad to have it so. They were not interested in joining hands with the persons who made up the majority, whom they classified as homeless and army-less liberals. They wanted a radical party, with the unions as its backbone. They wanted the Socialist Party to be in it and do for it what the Independent Labor Party had done for the British Labor Party, gradually direct it into socialist paths.

From 1925 until 1928 the Socialist Party put all its resources into the up-hill fight to rebuild its organization. In the congressional elections of 1926 the party's candidates polled 250,000 votes in about twenty states where it was on the ballot. Only in California, New York, Pennsylvania, and Wisconsin did it poll in excess of 10,-000: California, 45,972; New York, 83,482; Pennsylvania, 11,795; and Wisconsin, 40,293. In 1928 the party nominated Norman Thomas for president and James H. Maurer for vice-president. The latter had been elected alderman of Reading, Pa., when this city was captured by the socialists in 1927. Hoan was reelected mayor of Milwaukee in April, 1928, for a four-year term. Berger was again sent to Congress in 1926.

In the New York *Call* of August 18, 1920, a little less than three years after the bolshevik revolution in Russia, Abraham Cahan wrote as follows:

Soviet Russia is not impeccable. But with all its faults, it is the most precious jewel in the possession of civilized humanity. It is far from being above criticism, but as it is, it is the most wonderful thing that has happened since the great French Revolution smashed the bulwarks of Feudalism.

The editor of the *Forward* was expressing the prevailing view of the socialists at that time. But a great change has taken place among them since then. When Bela Low and Dr. and Mrs. Ingerman wrote their first letters to the *Call* against the bolsheviki in Russia and America in 1918 they were *persona non grata,* to put it mildly. Today

the Socialist Party officially demands the recognition of
Soviet Russia by the government of the United States,
but its position is practically that of the European socialists and the Labor and Socialist International toward the
Russian experiment.

At the anniversary dinner to the *New Leader,* the national organ of the Socialist Party, on January 27, 1928,
Morris Hillquit and Algernon Lee represented those
socialists who attacked the soviet government, while Norman Thomas and James H. Maurer spoke for the party
adherents who sympathized with it. Hillquit, who in
1920 wrote *From Marx to Lenin* and who used from time
to time to inspire his followers with his analyses of the
Russian situation, delivered himself as follows in 1928:

> In the first place the soviet government has been the greatest
> disaster and calamity that has occurred in the socialist move-
> ment. Norman Thomas has expressed fears as to what might
> happen if the experiment fails. I say the experiment has al-
> ready failed. . . .
> There is no difference between the soviet government and the
> communist movement here. They are one and the same thing.
> The communist movement was created by the soviet govern-
> ment. If the soviet government ceased in Russia there would not
> be ten communists left in the United States. All the little crazy
> communists, little commissars of the soviet government, as they
> think themselves to be, would go. . . .
> Let us dissociate ourselves from the soviet government and
> thereby make clear that the social democrats have no connection
> with it, bear no relation to it. Demand recognition of Russia
> by all means. . . . It will be a good thing to break down the
> Chinese wall. The masses of Russia will come back to the
> socialist movement.

James Maurer, as reported in the *New Leader,* defended Russia as stoutly as Morris Hillquit opposed it:

> I am the last man to condemn Soviet Russia. If what they
> have over there is communism, I don't care if you call me a
> communist. They are working for a better world to live in.
>
> If I were there, I'd probably be a communist. They asked me
> about the communists in this country and I told them they were
> a bunch of darn fools. . . . I have seen the communists in action
> here. They don't build; they destroy.

The communists there are doing the best under the circumstances. . . . This is a fight of workers, and I don't care what kind of a fight the workers are in, I'm with the workers, first, last and all the time.

§

The railroad unions were the mainstay of the Conference for Progressive Political Action and when they decided to abandon it in 1925 this coalition disappeared. In like manner the Chicago Federation of Labor was the backbone of the National Farmer-Labor Party, and when it decided in May, 1924, to return to the American Federation of Labor nonpartisan political policy this party became only a paper organization.   But while the international union officials had a free hand, the Chicago labor men could no longer fight Samuel Gompers and the ruling group inside the federation, especially when they had been badly crippled by the July, 1923, convention of the Farmer-Labor Party which the communists ran away with.

After the 1920 campaign the National Farmer-Labor Party had sufficient strength to continue the *New Majority,* edited by Robert M. Buck, to which Fred C. Ellis contributed his virile and original cartoons, retain Jay G. Brown as national secretary, and do organizing work in some of the states.   In May, 1922, it called a convention at which some 70 delegates from 17 states were present. In the congressional elections of that year it polled a fair vote in South Dakota (46,033), Washington (35,352), and in a few other states.   But it was already on the wane.   The Minnesota Farmer-Labor Party which elected Hendrik Shipstead to the United States Senate in 1922 was not affiliated.   The leaders of the National Farmer-Labor Party had read themselves out of the Conference for Progressive Political Action, which they condemned as a "scab and dual organization" on the political field, doing what the A. F. of L. already did with its nonpartisan political policy.   They regarded William H. Johnston as being more interested in attracting attention and thereby bolstering up his candidacy for president of the machinists' union than in building up an independent political movement. Moreover, they were in opposition to the conservative international union officials and they wished to appeal to the local unions and the rank and file. The National Farmer-Labor men, therefore, resorted in July, 1923, to the expedient which had built up the party in the first place, a convention of all dissident elements.

They sent invitations broadcast to national, state, and local bodies, unions, farmer organizations, political parties and all sorts of miscellaneous groups—unwittingly thus opening the gates for their own destruction. The Socialist Party declined to send delegates. Only a few national unions such as the Amalgamated Clothing Workers responded. The locals inside the American Federation of Labor did not answer this call as they had the others in 1919 and 1920. Had they done so, there would have been a different outcome to the July 3, 1923, convention. Still, had not the Chicago labor leaders made the fatal mistake of inviting the Workers' Party and the motley group of organizations controlled by them, they would have had a fairly substantial number of delegates from their party branches and sympathetic working class groups, and above all, they would have dictated every step of the proceedings.

It was natural enough for men like Fitzpatrick, Nockels, Brown, and Buck to invite an organization of which William Z. Foster was a general. The first three had closely cooperated with him in the steel strike. Again, the National Farmer-Labor Party men were fighting the international union officers, they were outside the C. P. P. A., they were more or less hostile to the Socialist Party because of its stand in the December, 1922, conference, and they wanted to do something, not merely wait and hope. There stood the Workers' Party, also isolated, with its militant and fearless members who made up in activity what they lacked in numbers. What was easier than for the two to get together? The Farmer-Labor Party leaders did not dream, however, that their guests—so they viewed them—would be other than most thankful for being admitted to their home, admire the fire in the hearth, and say amen. They did not know the representatives of the American communist movement.

§

The Farmer-Labor Party lost the convention and the Workers' Party won it because the latter controlled a majority of the delegates who were there. And the communist organization saw to it that they were in Chicago with credentials. The credentials committee, appointed by the national committee of the Farmer-Labor Party, did not have any policy whatever but merely reported a list of the delegates "whose credentials had been acted upon," to quote from the mimeographed summary of Jay G. Brown. Thereupon the Farmer-Labor Party leaders allowed those who claimed to be delegates to something or other, and who had come in response to the invitation they received, to decide who was and who was not to be seated. The only fight, open or secret, was against the Workers' Party delegates being seated. Many of the delegates who attended were there to see that the communists were seated. And the Chicago Labor Party men had no chance with those delegates not directly under control of the Workers' Party, because they constituted the radical minority who were ready to cooperate or play with the communists and were not concerned whether Moscow dictated or not. The only road left to the Labor Partyites was to bolt. But they did not have enough of a following for that. They had played into the hands of the communists. The latter were not going to unscramble the eggs and produce a *status quo ante*. But this is what the Farmer-Labor Party spokesmen pleaded for in their helplessness.

They wanted the Workers' Party, which had fought so hard to get in, and which at last was in and could report to Moscow that it was "delivering the goods," to withdraw and leave them in complete control. The leaders of the communist party, Foster, Ruthenberg, and others, were anxious to make concessions to Fitzpatrick, Brown, and their group. In fact, they were willing to forego domination of the national executive committee which they easily secured through proper placing of their known and unknown members in the various state delegations. But the Farmer-Labor Party men would make no concessions whatever. They had awakened, if too late. They demanded the unconditional withdrawal of the communist party from the convention and from the old or new organization which might emerge from it. Fitzpatrick said vehemently that they should fold up their tents and scatter with the night. Buck brought in a written statement saying that cooperation was impossible with any organization

. . . which advocates other than lawful means to bring about political changes or is affiliated with or which accepts the leadership of either national or international political organizations whose propaganda and doctrines advocate the overthrow of the government of the United States by other than legal and constitutional methods, such as the Third International.

The Chicago labor leaders found they could not cooperate with the communists because the latter were intent on steering the ship Moscow-way. Instead of letting the trusted and radical Farmer-Labor Party men continue to control and build the minority movement, the disciples of the Third International rushed in and, whether they deliberately wished it or not, so alienated their hosts that they created the bitterest feeling instead of good will. And when they wrecked the convention and set up their "Federated Farmer-Labor Party," they captured themselves. And what was worse, they further isolated themselves.

William Z. Foster wrote in the *Labor Herald* of August, 1923, that "The Federated Farmer-Labor Party will break the chains with which the Gompers bureaucracy keeps the workers of the country bound to the political chariots of their industrial masters." He added: "A sufficient refutation of the yarn about there being no one but communists is had by simply reading the names of its national executive committee, and the organizations they represent." The present secretary of the Workers' Party must have known at the time that the names he gave in his magazine as constituting the committee were largely hand-picked by the communist leaders, including himself, and that they represented in truth practically nothing in the way of economic or political power.

In June, 1924, the communists, again headed by Foster and Ruthenberg, secured control of the St. Paul convention and heralded the news that another hammer had been forged to "break the chains," *etc.* A formidable list of names was again gotten up to represent the numerous states of this vast country. The statement was again made that there were many non-communists upon the national and national executive committees. As a plain matter of fact, the Federated Farmer-Labor Party (the still-born child of the July 3, 1923, convention), and the St. Paul Farmer-Labor Party (the poor unfortunate of June 17, 1924), had no life or soul apart from that which the Workers' Party gave them. They perished the moment the central executive committee of the party here, and of the Comintern (Communist International) in Moscow, decided to throw them into the political limbo. Joseph Manley and C. A. Hathaway, two communists, were not made secretaries of the Chicago and St. Paul organizations in order to allow their hot-house products to grow too far out of the pattern prescribed by their master, the Workers' Party. Naturally enough, when the master withdrew them from their assignments, the Chicago and St. Paul plants withered away and were no more.

The National Farmer-Labor Party had little vitality left after the July convention. Some of its best state branches had withdrawn to play with the communists— until disillusioned—and in Illinois there had been a serious split. The heads of the American Federation of Labor then bore down upon the president and secretary of the Chicago Federation of Labor. The officials of the Illinois State Federation of Labor had abandoned the Farmer-Labor Party, and there was an organized group of labor men in the Windy City ready to step in if Fitzpatrick stepped out of his union office. The outstanding leader of the political movement felt that there was no other way by which he could continue in the trade union field and serve his fellows than by yielding to the nonpartisan political policy. The Chicago Federation of Labor is not today the center of progressivism that it was in 1919-1924, but as long as Fitzpatrick and Nockels run it, it will always retain a degree of militancy which will distinguish it.

The Minnesota Farmer-Labor Party had elected a second United States senator in the person of Magnus Johnson, on July 16, 1923. It had not sent delegates to the ill-fated July convention. It had a prestige and importance which made it the logical party to unite all forces for the presidential campaign of 1924. The Federated Farmer-Labor Party and the old Farmer-Labor Party were eager for it to take the lead. Inside the state were communist and radical elements which were egging it on. The Minnesota leaders, William Mahoney, H. G. Teigan, R. D. Cramer, and others, lent a willing ear. As a result conferences were held and it was decided to hold a national convention. Fitzpatrick, Brown, and Buck strenuously urged the conferees not to invite the communists. But nothing that they could say as a result of their experience affected those of Minnesota, Washington, South Dakota, and Montana in their determination to include the followers of Moscow. It is good pragmatism which declares that there is a world of difference between experience with and knowledge of. The northwesterners had not tasted communist fruit. When they did, they saw the convention of June 17, 1924, go the way of July 3, 1923.

The convention was originally called for May 30, but shortly after the Conference for Progressive Political Action at its February, 1924, meeting decided to call the July 4 nominating convention, a move was made to postpone the St. Paul gathering altogether. The communists who were excluded from the C. P. P. A.—the Minnesota Farmer-Labor Party and the other northwestern independent parties were not—manoeuvred to prevent this, and won Mahoney and Teigan over to their point of view. La Follette and the national committee of the C. P. P. A. issued statements attacking the convention, charging communist domination.

When the delegates assembled in St. Paul the Minnesota hosts found themselves in the same position in which the Chicago men had placed themselves. They were helplessly swimming against a communist current. William Mahoney even failed of election as chairman before a state senator of Montana, Charles E. Taylor, in thorough accord with the communist program. The Minnesota sponsors pleaded for only an organizing committee to lay the groundwork for a real party; the communist-controlled delegates decided as in Chicago for the immediate formation of a new party. A national committee was set up, an executive picked, Duncan McDonald nominated for president and William Bouck, a radical farmers' leader, for vice-president, and a long platform was adopted. The communists went through all the forms.

In less than a month, however, on July 10, five of the seven members of the executive issued a statement announcing the withdrawal of the nominations and pledging support to the Workers' Party. Four communists constituted a majority of the highest body, made up of seven members. The Workers' Party could, therefore, throw the new organization into the discard when it suited its purposes. The statement claimed that the C. P. P. A. by nominating La Follette had "betrayed the farmer-labor masses into the hands of merchants, manufacturers, bankers, and rich farmers, and thus destroyed the only chance for a united front campaign." The truth of the matter was that the new party had melted away in the hands of the communists, the northwestern farmer-labor parties deserted it to support La Follette and the Workers' Party leaders found no advantage whatever in continuing to feed the creature to which they gave birth in St. Paul. Furthermore, they themselves had spoken highly of La Follette and would undoubtedly have accepted him if they were allowed to stay on the inside of the C. P. P. A. Their opportunism and chameleon politics brought on a deep crisis within their own ranks and threatened to split their party.

Foster was arrayed against Ruthenberg. The former wanted to lay most stress on boring from within the unions and practically ignore all substitutes for the Workers' Party. The latter wanted to continue "the slogan of a class farmer-labor party," and have Foster specialize in the industrial field under his direction. Although Foster had two-thirds of the delegates under his wing in the convention of the Workers' Party of August 21-30, 1925, a cablegram arrived a few days before its adjournment, addressed to P. Green, the mediator sent by the Comintern, upholding the contentions of Ruthenberg. Thereupon Foster let his opponent take control of the central executive committee and run the Workers' Party his way, under directions of Moscow. Since Ruthenberg's death Jay Lovestone and Foster have been acting as joint secretaries.

§

After one has patiently studied the history of labor and farmer parties in the United States during the last one hundred years he might decide that it has been a story of one failure after another, of one split after another. He might conclude that whatever the situation elsewhere, these parties somehow do not thrive here. He might list a number of economic, political, racial or other reasons of a fundamental or fleeting character to account for the difference. And so far as action was concerned he would decline to follow a will-o'-the-wisp.

Or, on the other hand, the close student of the problem could declare that the most striking fact about the labor and farmer parties in America over the past century was that they never stopped springing up. They were as inevitable in this country as they were in Europe. Their failure here and their success over there, therefore, depends on the extent to which the conditions on both sides of the Atlantic remain what they are. And nothing is unchangeable except change.

Our interest is in the American scene. Only as we really know it will those of us who favor a labor-farmer-progressive party win our battles. Facts about other lands may be suggestive and even vital, but they cannot be considered decisive. Theories worked out on the basis of conditions in other countries may likewise be very helpful, but they must be considered of secondary importance unless it is shown that they work in the United States. Theories evolved out of older situations, whether abroad or in this country, must also be taken with reserve and skepticism. Because so much is at stake we can afford to bend backward in not overstating the factors in our favor, nor understating the forces against us.

Over fifty years ago, when the Socialist Labor Party was born in 1876, the unity convention adopted a resolution ending with the words: "Let us bide our time. It will come." Only he who has some historical perspective, who realizes how and why the masses move, and how very slowly fundamental social changes can be made, will not give up the fight. Only he who understands that a movement is not for a day, a year, or a man's lifetime, will carry on. We go on and on because we have faith that the future belongs to us. And they who will follow will take up the fight where we left off. Man does not live by knowledge alone. He finds himself only in action. More power to him who dares to do!

INDEX

A

Albany ouster, 421.
Altgeld. John P., 108, 186; reasons for pardoning anarchists, 113.
Amalgamated Clothing Workers, 290, 360, 381.
American Alliance for Labor and Democracy, 382.
American Federation of Labor, and America's entrance into World War, 307; conventions of 1890, 137; 1893, 141; 1894, 144; 1907, 205; 1908, 256; 1913, 295; general strikes, 133; growth of, 163; independent political action, 135; Knights of Labor, 134; La Follette, 363, 411; Sorge's estimate of, 136; see Gompers, Samuel; Foster, Frank K.
American Labor Union, 253, 276.
American Railway Union, 184, 187, 190.
Amnesty and left wing, 340; and Socialist Party, 342.
Anarchists, 110; and Knights of Labor, 147; spies, 114.
Anti-Poverty Society, 49, 50, 51.
Appeal to Reason, 233, 237, 307, 317.

B

Barnes, J. Mahlon, 167, 203, 221, 247, 256.
Bellamy, Edward, 148, 188.
Benson, Allan L., 241, 303, 306.

Berger, Victor L., and A. F. of L., 251; attack by left wing, 337; Debs, 188, 192; first congressman, 221; Gompers, 253; immigration, 269; military preparedness, 305; Milwaukee victories, 231, 423, 427; sentenced to prison, 319; Social Democracy, 194; Socialist Labor Party, 201; socialist unity, 200; unseated, 420.
Boudin, Louis B., 239, 241, 286, 309, 337, 351.
British Labor Party and non-partisan political policy, 254; example for United States, 295; post-war policy, 377.
Bryan, William Jennings, 83, 218.
Buck, Robert M., 384, 391, 429, 432.
Butler, Benjamin F., 66, 71.

C

Cahan, Abraham, 172, 192, 198, 220, 328, 427.
Call, New York, 229, 233, 235, 317.
Cameron, Andrew C., 23, 27, 62, 95, 99.
Carey, James F., 195, 210, 250, 268.
Catholic church, and Henry George campaign, 42, 50; Socialist Party, 227.
Chicago Daily Socialist, 233, 236.
Christensen, Parley Parker, 393.

439

Christian socialists, 242; Haywood's opinion of, 285.
Civic Federation, National, and Debs, 277; miners' union, 259; Socialist Party, 257.
Class struggle, and Gompers, 127, 131; Industrial Workers of the World, 279.
Colonizers, 20, 190.
Committee of Forty-Eight, 363, 389, 392.
Communist International, and left wing, 338; Socialist Party, 347; Twenty-One Points, 332.
Communist Labor Party, 350.
Communist Party, 349, 355; governmental attacks on, 352.
Conference for Progressive Political Action, 363, 398; and British Labor Party, 408; conventions, February, 1922, 401; December, 1922, 402; February, 1924, 407; July, 1924, 408; disappearance of, 416; Farmer-Labor Party, 403; nationalization proposals, 409; New York convention, 406; platform, 410.
Conscientious objectors, 320.
Cooper, Peter, 62.
Courts and independent political action, 16, 39, 388, 410.

D

Danbury hatters' case, 256.
Debs, Eugene V., and A. F. of L., 252, 277, 297; American Railway Union, 184; candidate for president, 218, 268, 418; immigration, 271: I. W. W., 280; left wing, 275, 377; People's Party, 83, 189; Social Democracy, 190; Socialist Labor Party, 191, 282; socialist unity, 199; violence, 286; war, 318.

De Leon, Daniel, 148; and business unionism, 162; Debs, 282; dual unionism, 159; Hayes, Max S., 282; I. W. W., 280; Knights of Labor, 154; Leninism, 360.
Democracy, and industrial freedom, 19; Farmer-Labor Party, 380.
Donnelly, Ignatius, 62, 87.
Dual unionism, and Communist Party, 350; Debs, 277; De Leon, 159; Foster, 360; I. W. W., 281; Socialist Party, 277, 282, 289; Western Federation of Miners, 276; Workers' Party, 360.

E

Eastman, Max, 238, 319, 351.
Eight-hour day, and Knights of Labor, 121; National Labor Union, 23, 26; pure and simple unionists, 133; philosophy, 23, 132.
Engels, Frederick, 299.
Engdahl, J. Louis, 248, 318.
Equal Rights Party, 17.

F

Farmer-Labor Party, and A. F. of L., 385; campaign of 1920, 394; Chicago Federation of Labor, 429; Committee of Forty-Eight, 390; Conference for Progressive Political Action, 403, 429; conventions, 1919, 383; 1920, 390; 1922; 429; 1923, 430; La Follette, 393; nationalization proposals, 379; Socialist Party, 385, 416; Workers' Party, 430.
Farmer-Labor Party of Minnesota, 374, 429, 435.
Farmers' alliances, 75; and middlemen, 367.

Farmers, and Knights of Labor, 124; Nonpartisan League, 363; People's Party, 72; Socialist Labor Party, 155; Socialist Party, 210, 267.
Financial reform, 28, 78, 129, 155.
First International, 92, 127.
Fitzpatrick, John, 53, 360, 381, 387, 389, 430, 432, 434.
Forward, Jewish Daily, 172, 229, 328; see Cahan, Abraham.
Foster, Frank K., 131, 133, 138.
Foster, William Z., 53, 360, 382, 430, 432, 436.
Fraina, Louis C., 338, 351.
Frazier, Lynn J., 371, 408.
Free coinage of silver, 68, 78, 81, 125.
Free land, effect upon labor movement, 22.

G

Gaston, Herbert E., 364.
General strikes, and A. F. of L., 133; war, 307.
George, Henry, 36, 40, 51.
Gerber, Julius, 175, 229, 346.
German socialists and World War, 301.
Germans and socialism in the United States, 90; trade unionism, 90.
Germer, Adolph F., 248, 270, 318.
Ghent, W. J., 221, 241, 305.
Gompers, Samuel, and A. F. of L., 135, 259; Berger, 253; candidate for public office, 140, 158; Civic Federation, 257; Debs, 186, 255; De Leon, 157; Farmer-Labor Party, 386; George campaign, 42; German socialists, 90; industrial unionism, 290; leadership, 219; Marx, 127, 251; nonpartisan political policy, 130, 254; socialists, 126, 259, 295; unemployment, 141; unemployment demonstration, 32; see American Federation of Labor, Debs, De Leon.
Governmental attacks on communists, 352; socialists, 317.
Grangers, 56, 61, 99.
Greenback-Labor Party, and Knights of Labor, 124; convention, 1878, 67; financial program, 25.
Greenback Party, 62.
Greenbaum, Leon, 213, 245, 277, 278.

H

Hanford, Ben, 218, 219, 249.
Hanna, Marcus A., 84, 277.
Hardie, Keir, 184, 296.
Harriman, Job, 197, 203, 210, 274, 300.
Hayes, Max, 197, 201, 203, 206, 238, 250, 252, 259, 282, 294, 380, 394.
Haymarket bomb, 53, 112.
Haywood, William D., 274, 281, 319.
Hillman, Sidney, 290, 381.
Hillquit, Morris, and Albany ouster, 421; A. F. of L., 290; Americanization of socialism, 88; Barnes, 247; Boudin, 337; candidate for public office, 226, 229, 323; Civic Federation, 257; Communist International, 334; Conference for Progressive Political Action, 402, 403; evolutionary socialism, 208, 288; Farmer-Labor Party, 417; farmers, 211; immigration, 271; industrial unionism, 347; I. W. W., 288; Johnston, 408; Keating, 371; labor party, 299; language federations, 269; Russia, 428; Socialist Labor Party, 175, 196; socialist unity, 202; substitute motions, 269; terrorism, 288; World War, 302, 309.

Hoan, Daniel W., 231, 423, 427.
Hoehn, G. A., 136, 173, 203, 208, 210, 276, 277.
Hopkins, J. A. H., 390, 392.
Hourwich, I. A., 191, 194, 241, 426.
Hoxie, Robert F., 219, 221, 223, 275.
Hunter, Robert, 241, 298.

I

Immediate demands, communists, 339; socialists, 205.
Immigration, before 1830, 12; Germans and Irish, 90; communists, 324, 331; Socialist Party attitude toward, 269.
Imperialism, and war, 310.
Impossibilists, 205, 209, 223, 262.
Industrial democracy, 380, 401.
Industrial unionism, and Gompers, 290; Socialist Party, 266; weakness of, 291.
Industrial Workers of the World, 279; Berger, 253; Debs, 275; De Leon, 280; Gompers, 258; Haywood, 284; Hillquit, 288; immigrants, 327; leaders imprisoned during war, 319; opposition to craft unions, 279; Socialist Party, 267, 273; splits, 280.
Injunctions, 186, 254, 410.
International Socialist Review, 204, 233, 238, 284.
International Workingmen's Association, 92.

K

Katterfeld, L. E., 243, 309, 351.
Kearney, Dennis, 66, 109.
Keating, Edward F., 371, 373, 404.
Kennedy, John C., 228, 395, 396.
Kerr, Charles H., 238, 240.

King, Cameron H., 292, 342.
Knights of Labor, 118; and A. F. of L., 134; centralization, 123; conventions, 1878, 122; 1890, 125; 1893, 154; 1894, 156; 1895, 157; District Assembly 49, 38, 154; De Leon, 154; eight-hour day, 121; Greenback-Labor Party, 66, 124; land, 120; platform, 123; populists, 125; Socialist Labor Party, 36; strikes, 121; structure, 123.
Knights of St. Crispin, 22, 28.

L

"Labor faker," and De Leonites, 153, 168.
La Follette, Robert M., 87, 363, 392, 393, 409, 412, 413, 414, 415.
Land monopoly, 59, 66, 78, 129.
Land reformers, 20.
Language federations, 269, 325, 330.
Lassalle, Ferdinand, 94, 98.
Lassallean socialists, 10, 92, 97.
Leadership, A. F. of L., 388; difficulty of changing, 145; free land, 22; Socialist Party, 245.
Lee, Algernon, 229, 241, 274, 302, 320, 428.
Left wing, and Debs, 275; Socialist Party, 337.
Lehr und Wehr Vereine, 106; 109.
Liebknecht, Karl, 301, 309, 338.
London, Meyer, 191, 228, 306, 337, 423.

M

Mahoney, William, 408, 434, 435.
Mailly, Bertha H., 241.
Mailly, William, 246.
Marx, Karl, 88, 92, 94, 127.
Masses, 238, 319.

Maurer, James H., 266, 306, 410, 427, 428.
Mc Bride, John, 140, 145.
Mac Donald, Duncan, 149, 258, 380, 435.
McGlynn, Edward, 42, 44, 50, 52.
McNamara case, and socialists, 287.
Militarism, and Socialist Party, 304, 310.
Milwaukee, labor party, 55, 297; *Leader*, 233, 235; Socialist Party victories, 221, 231, 423, 427.
Mine Workers, United, 258, 360, 387.
Morgan, Thomas J., 106, 139, 142, 181, 207, 238, 269.

N

National Labor Union, 23, 26, 27, 30, 95.
Nationalists, 148.
Nationalization of land, and Socialist Party, 272.
Nationalization proposals of Farmer-Labor Party, 379.
Negro, and Knights of Labor, 47; Farmer-Labor Party, 393; Socialist Party, 213; United Labor Party, 47.
New trade unionism, 150.
Nockels, Edward N., 53, 360, 381.
Nonpartisan League, 363; centralization, 369; dues, 368, 376; independent political action, 375, 376; legislation by farmers, 370; membership, 373.
Nonpartisan political policy of A. F. of L., 36, 132, 254, 255, 371, 387, 388, 396.

O

Old age pensions, and A. F. of L., 251.

Organizing the unorganized, 251, 274, 359.
Owen, Robert, 19.
Owen, Robert Dale, 14, 15, 17.

P

Panics, 1873, 98; 1893, 80; and political action, 400; Republican Party, 85, 413.
Parsons, Albert R., 34, 102, 106, 112.
People, The, 149, 170, 176, 266.
People's Council, 322.
tions, 1896, 83; 1900, 87; Debs, 189; farmers' organizations, 75; Knights of Labor, 125; platform, 1892, 77; Socialist Labor Party, 155; southern states, 79.
People's Party, 72; conven-
Phillips, Wendell, 28, 31.
Pinkerton detectives, 108, 135.
Plumb plan, 399, 401.
Police brutality, 107.
Post, Louis F., 43, 45, 47, 354.
Powderly, Terrence V., 43, 66, 85, 119, 124, 147, 154.
Primary, and Nonpartisan League, 375.
Progressive Labor Party, 48.
Proletarian Party, 356.
Pullman strike, 185.
Pure and simple trade unionism, 127, 128, 219; and De Leon, 150; eight-hour day, 133; Industrial Workers of the World, 279; see Gompers, Samuel.

R

Railroads, control by companies of courts and legislatures, 57; government ownership and Gompers, 130; grangers, 56; populists, 78; strikes, 33, 185; unions, 74, 398.
Rand School of Social Science, 241, 319.

Reed, John, 319, 351.
Reformists, 262.
Religion, and Socialist Party, 327.
Republican Party, in 1870, 29; La Follette, 413; phenomenal rise, 178.
Revolutionists, 262; and war, 317.
Rosenberg, V. L., 115, 116, 137.
Russia, and Socialist Party, 321, 329; Workers' Party, 330, 436.
Ruthenberg, Charles E., 309 318, 325, 351, 354, 380, 404, 432, 436.

S

Sabotage, 286; and Haywood, 285; Socialist Party, 273.
Sacco, Nicola, 113.
St. Louis anti-war resolution of Socialist Party, 307, 310.
St. Paul Farmer-Labor Party, 433, 435.
Sanial, Lucien, 137, 150, 156, 174, 177.
Schevitsch, Sergius E., 45, 47, 116, 140.
Schlueter, Hermann, 91, 199, 328.
Schools, free and labor party of 1828, 13.
Seattle general strike, 395.
Sherman anti-trust law, 254, 256.
Shipstead, Hendrik, 408, 429.
Simons, A. M., 204, 211, 227, 238, 241, 268, 278, 280, 296, 316.
Single tax, 41, 48.
Social Democracy, 190, 193.
Social Democratic Party, 195.
Social Democratic Workingmen's Party, 97, 100.
Socialist Labor Party, and Americanization, 88; A. F. of L. convention of 1890, 137; conventions, 1876, 101; 1879, 109; 1881-1883, 115; 1885-1887, 115; 1889, 117; 1892,
190; 1893, 180; 1896, 181; 1900, 181; elections, 103, 179; George campaign, 38, 44, 46; Gompers, 126, 137; Greenback-Labor Party, 109; immediate demands, 181; "labor fakers," 182; Marx, 201; membership, 180; populists, 155, 181; railroad strikes, 1877, 34; split of 1899, 174; uncompromising policy, 36; unity with Socialist Party, 283.
Socialist Party, Albany ouster, 421; A. F. of L., 250, 252; Communist International, 420; communists, 337; Conference for Progressive Political Action, New York, 406; constitution, 212; conventions, 1901, 204; 1904, 264; 1908, 267; 1910, 268, 325; 1912, 272, 325; 1917, 307; 1919, 346; 1920, 419; 1922 and 1923, 425; cooperation with other groups, 424; economic causes for growth, 217; election results, 216; analyzed, 221; 1914, 306; 1916, 306; 1917, 225, 323; 1920, 423; Farmer-Labor Party, 424; farmer, attitude toward, 269, 271; immediate demands, 205; immigration, 269; I. W. W., 267, 273, 282, 289; labor party, 292, 298; language federations, 344, 420; leadership, 245; left wing, 341; legality, 342; membership, 324, 326; military preparedness, 304; minority report of 1917 convention, 315; political causes for growth, 218; press, 232; progressives, 426; religion, 242, 267; Russia, 427; St. Louis anti-war resolution, 310; the home, 267; trade unions, 211, 274, 424; vote in Massachusetts, 226; Milwaukee, 221, 231, 423, 427; New York, 228; Oklahoma, 232; Workers' Party, 405.

Socialist Trade and Labor Alliance, 151, 161, 165, 258, 282.
Sorge, F. A., 90, 95, 101, 136, 298.
Sovereign, J. R., 148, 154, 156.
Soviet organization in 1877, 34.
Spargo, John, 269, 309, 316.
Stedman, Seymour, 194, 203, 211, 421.
Stephens, Uriah S., 118, 124.
Steward, Ira, 23.
Strasser, Adolph, 90, 97, 101, 126.
Streeter, A. J., 72.
Strikes, and De Leonites, 150; Gompers, 128; Knights of Labor, 122.
Suffrage, manhood, 9, 10.
Swinton, John, 37, 38, 39, 40.
Sylvis, William H., 23, 95.

T

Tammany Hall, and George campaign, 41; Democratic Party, 85; methods of, 229.
Tariff, and A. F. of L., 131; populists, 73.
Teigan, H. G., 365, 434. populists, 73.
Thomas, Norman, 320, 427, 428.
Thompson, Carl D., 248, 268.
Townley, A. C., 87, 264, 367, 371.
Trade union and political action, Conzett, 101; Socialist Labor Party, 105.
Tramps, 108.
Trevellick, Richard F., 23, 30, 62.
Trotsky, Leon, 338, 359.
Twenty-one points of the Communist International, 332.

U

Unemployment, and Gompers, 141; socialists, 142.
Union Labor Party, 52, 72.
United Community Party, 355.
United Labor Party, 39, 51, 54.
United Workers, 100.
Untermann, Ernest, 266, 269, 270, 280.

V

Van Patten, Philip, 34, 102, 115.
Vanzetti, Bartolomeo, 113.
Violence, and Haymarket bomb, 53, 112; Mc Namaras, 287; old parties, 84; pure and simple trade unionists, 287; railroad strikes of 1877, 33; Socialist Party, 273, 286.
Vogt, Hugo, 45, 150, 170, 177.
Volkszeitung, New York, 38, 45, 116, 137, 170, 200.

W

Wagenknecht, Alfred, 318, 348.
War, causes of, 310; Socialist Party, St. Louis resolution against, 310.
Weaver, James B., 66, 71, 77, 79.
Western Federation of Miners, 275; and I. W. W., 279; see Haywood, William D.
Western Labor Union, 276.
Wilson, Woodrow, 256, 306, 378.
Winchevsky, Morris, 172, 192, 194.
Work, John M., 241, 247, 295.
Workers' (Communist) Party, 356; boring from within, 333; Communist International, 357; Conference for Progressive Political Action, 404; cooperation with noncommunists, 357; Farmer-Labor Party, 432; immediate demands, 358; immigrants, 329; labor party, 358; language federations, 330; organizing the unorganized, 359; Russia, 330, 436; Socialist Party, 405; the revolution, 358; trade union versus political action, 351.

Y

Young, Art, 239, 319.